ISLAM AND THE ARABS
IN
SPANISH SCHOLARSHIP

MEDIEVAL IBERIAN PENINSULA
TEXTS AND STUDIES
(M I P)

EDITED BY

C. MARINESCU, JOSÉ MILLÁS-VALLICROSA,
AND HUSSAIN MONÉS

VOLUME III

ISLAM AND THE ARABS IN SPANISH SCHOLARSHIP

LEIDEN
E. J. BRILL
1970

ISLAM AND THE ARABS IN SPANISH SCHOLARSHIP

(SIXTEENTH CENTURY TO THE PRESENT)

BY

JAMES T. MONROE

LEIDEN
E. J. BRILL
1970

The author wishes to thank the University of California for the financial assistance that has made the publication of this book possible

PRINTED IN THE NETHERLANDS

FOR JULIANE

CONTENTS

PREFACE ix
LIST OF ABBREVIATIONS xii

INTRODUCTION 1

Sixteenth century. The origin of modern Arabic studies in Spain: the *Colegios trilingües*.

PART ONE

THE STUDY OF GRAMMAR AND LEXICOGRAPHY

CHAPTER I 23

Peculiar state of Arabic studies in the seventeenth century. Eighteenth-century Arabism: Bernardino González, Miguel Casiri, José de la Torre. Polemic on Arabic culture among the Jesuits exiled in Italy: Juan Andrés, Esteban de Arteaga, Javier Llampillas.

PART TWO

THE STUDY OF POLITICAL HISTORY

CHAPTER II. 49

Early nineteenth-century Arabism. *Afrancesados* and Liberals; the Arabism of the Romantic Age: José Antonio Conde, Pascual de Gayangos.

CHAPTER III 84

Arabism in the second half of the nineteenth century. Krausists and anti-Krausists. Francisco Javier Simonet.

CHAPTER IV 101

Krausists and anti-Krausists (cont.): Eduardo Saavedra, Francisco Fernández y González, Emilio Lafuente Alcántara, Leopoldo Eguilaz y Yanguas, José Moreno Nieto.

CHAPTER V. 128

The precursor of contemporary Spanish Arabic studies: Francisco Codera y Zaidín.

Part Three

THE STUDY OF CULTURAL HISTORY

Chapter VI 151

The Arabism of the Generation of 1898. Julián Ribera y Tarragó, broadening of the horizon of Arabic studies in Spain.

Chapter VII 174

The Arabism of the Generation of 1898 (cont.). Philosophy: Miguel Asín Palacios.

Chapter VIII 196

The school of Asín: his disciples, Emilio García Gómez and Ángel González Palencia.

Chapter IX 220

Twentieth-century Arabic studies in Spain grouped around García Gómez. Maximiliano Alarcón, Jaime Oliver Asín, José Sánchez Pérez, Leopoldo Torres, Balbás, Manuel Ocaña Jiménez, Manuel Alonso Alonso, Darío Cabanelas Rodríguez, Miguel Cruz Hernández, Elías Terés Sádaba, José López Ortiz, Melchor Antuña, Felix M. Pareja, Isidro de las Cagigas, José M. Millás Vallicrosa, Juan Vernet Ginés, Ambrosio Huici Miranda.

Chapter X 246

Attitudes of twentieth-century Spanish intellectuals towards the Arabs in Spain: Miguel de Unamuno, Ángel Ganivet, José Ortega y Gasset, Ramón Menéndez Pidal, Claudio Sánchez Albornoz, Américo Castro.

Conclusion 264

Bibliography 271

Index 292

PREFACE

At present there is no book which deals comprehensively with the history of Oriental studies in the Western world on a satisfactory basis. The work of Gustave Dugat (1868), a compilation of short biographies, and that of Johann Fück (1955) which covers the period from the eleventh century to 1914, are both too broad and sketchy to offer the reader much in the way of the cultural and historical background which influenced European Orientalists. Nor do these books attempt to indicate in what way the work of the Orientalists they discuss succeeded in modifying and influencing the ideas of Western intellectual circles. It has been clear for some time that a history of Western Orientalism cannot be written adequately until prior work is done nation by nation. From such partial surveys a more general study can eventually emerge. By country the history of British and Russian Orientalism is better known to the scholar today, thanks to the writings of Arberry, Lewis, Smirnov and Krachkovskii. Therefore, it is the purpose of this book to fill the lacuna insofar as Spanish Orientalism is concerned. As the following pages will show, Spanish Orientalism in practice was restricted almost exclusively to Arabic studies. Because of the peculiar nature of Spain, occupied, or partly occupied by Muslims from A.D. 711 to 1492, it could rightly be maintained that Spanish Arabism goes as far back as the Middle Ages. However, the Arabism in existence prior to the sixteenth century has been deliberately omitted from this book because it was less the product of intellectual reflection and more the response to an immediate political and cultural challenge. Therefore it was not strictly speaking "Arabism" as an intellectual discipline, but rather an anti-Islamic propagandistic and crusading movement closely related to the Spanish *Reconquista*.

Spanish Arabism has therefore been studied in this book, from the period immediately after the fall of Granada in 1492 until the present. During these four and a half centuries Spaniards have been freed from the immediate political menace of Islam, and have developed a school of thought; an intellectual discipline, which may be termed Arabism in the stricter sense of the word indicated above.

Because Spanish Arabism has until recently been preoccupied

primarily with Spain's own Arab antiquities, the work done by Arabists has in one way or another been influential in helping to shape our understanding of Spanish history and culture. For this reason Spanish intellectuals who are not strictly speaking Arabists, have often used the results of their Orientalist colleagues' investigations to elaborate new theories about the Spanish past. This has led to polemics and to a great deal of scholarly activity outside the strict radius of Arabism which cannot be overlooked in a study of Spanish intellectual ideas.

Thus, because Arabism has enjoyed a more controversial position in Spain than it has in other European nations, this book attempts to show how the scholarship produced by Spanish Arabists was received by Spain's intellectuals, and how the gradual accumulation of information unearthed over several centuries actually modified the prevailing conception of Spanish medieval history. This book therefore outlines the essential cultural references for the Orientalist to understand the intellectual milieu in which the Arabists of Spain were working, and it also discusses Spanish scholars insofar as the latter were indebted to the work done by Arabists.

The purpose of this book is to serve as a guide to those students interested in Spanish Islam. It is hoped that it will be of use to those Orientalists who are unfamiliar with the cultural background which helped to shape the ideas and opinions of the Spanish Arabists whose works they read. Furthermore, it may possibly serve as a useful guide to those Hispanists who desire an introduction to the writings on the subject. The overall history of scholarship in Oriental studies is usually not formally taught at present in our universities, but it is nevertheless essential to the modern scholar's sense of direction in his work. It is necessary if the work of those Orientalists is to be used intelligently, and it is full of human interest, since it illuminates a little known chapter of European intellectual endeavours.

The present study contains a great number of Spanish quotations. These have been cited in translation, for the convenience of readers not knowing Spanish. Their originals are all available in print.

James T. Monroe

University of California, San Diego
La Jolla, California
November 26, 1968

LIST OF ABBREVIATIONS

And.	*Al-Andalus.*
BAE	*Biblioteca de autores españoles.*
BHS	*Bulletin of Hispanic Studies.*
BRAE	*Boletín de la Real Academia Española.*
BRAH	*Boletín de la Real Academia de la Historia.*
Disert. y opúsc.	J. Ribera, *Disertaciones y opúsculos.*
Enciclopedia Espasa	*Enciclopedia universal ilustrada europeoamericana,* ed. by J. Espasa.
Moh. Dyn.	Al-Maqqarī, *History of the Mohammedan Dynasties in Spain,* trans. by P. de Gayangos.
NBAE	*Nueva biblioteca de autores españoles.*
PIHEM	*Publications de l'Institut de Hautes Études Marocaines.*
RABM	*Revista de archivos, bibliotecas y museos.*
REI	*Revue des Études Islamiques.*
RFE	*Revista de filología española.*
ZDMG	*Zeitschrift der Deutschen Morgenländischen Gesellschaft.*

INTRODUCTION

In his book about British Orientalism Professor Arberry shows how as early as the seventeenth century a few visionary scholars began to feel the need for studies of a broader scope than those offered by the traditional European curriculum based on the Latin and Greek classics.[1] In the shrinking world created by Western expansionism these scholars devoted their efforts and at times even their lives to the building of a cultural bridge between East and West. They were furthermore all attracted by what would later come to be called the "Romantic" spell of the East. Yet for an Orientalist such as William Jones (1746-94) who discovered the connexion between Sanscrit, Latin and Greek; published translations of Arabic and Persian poems,[2] and who was a member of the literary group headed by Samuel Johnson, Oriental literature and culture retained in it something exotic and therefore, essentially foreign. This literature was for him a cultural phenomenon worthy of being studied for the strangeness of its appeal but at the same time he and other British scholars who studied the Orient felt no immediate connexion between the latter and their own persons. This aspect of British Orientalism reveals by contrast what is pertinent to Spanish Arabic studies. In Spain, the scholars who devoted their attention to Oriental studies gradually began to unearth a mass of material pertinent to their own national past. Whereas other European Orientalists studied Arabic, Persian, Turkish and Sanscrit, Spanish scholars tended to restrict their scope to Arabic, and particularly to the culture of Spanish Islam. While doing so they recovered many documents shedding a significant light not only on the medieval history of Spain but also on that of Europe in general. Henceforward, from Spain, controversial and sometimes revolutionary ideas about medieval European culture would emanate to the rest of the Continent. In the past three centuries much material has been discovered that has modified the traditional view of the Middle Ages: Arabic chronicles have revealed many aspects of the eight-century-long Spanish crusade known as

[1] A. J. Arberry, *Oriental Essays, Portraits of Seven Scholars*, London, 1960, p. 12.

[2] *Poems, Consisting Chiefly of Translations from the Asiatick Languages*, London, 1772.

the *Reconquista*. But along with the arts of war, it has become evident that those of peace were also cultivated. Today, as a result, we know far more about how the philosophy of Muslim Spain influenced the Scholastics; how the Oriental prose tale affected medieval European narrative art; how Dante reflects the influence of Muslim eschatological literature in the *Divine Comedy*; and how the origins of European lyrical poetry seem to be inextricably connected with the lyrics sung by the Arabs in the courts of Muslim Spain. At times these novel theories have been developed and improved upon by European scholars outside Spain, while at others they have been modified, limited or rejected by them; but they have almost always originated in Spain, thus constituting one of the significant contributions of Spain to contemporary Western scholarship.

The British Orientalists who wrote about the East were both Protestants and the subjects of an empire undergoing its greatest period of expansion. Their Spanish colleagues, on the contrary, were Catholics and lived during the age when the Spanish empire was gradually declining. Thus the latter have all more or less been sentimentally involved in the convulsions Spain has undergone during the course of the past three centuries. This has meant that Spanish scholars have been divided between their admiration for the advances of northern and particularly, Protestant Europe in the fields of science and technology, and between their fear of imitating these advances so freely that science itself should come to conflict with and ultimately destroy the tenets of the Spanish faith. The fact that Spain has failed to modernize politically and economically since around the seventeenth century has meant furthermore that its scholars have devoted much soul-searching attention to the reasons for Spanish "decadence." Many of them have turned to the past; to Spanish history, to comprehend the troubles of the present. But in the study of their past, the conclusions and reactions of Spanish scholars have differed widely: the advocates of modernization among them have seen in the Inquisition and the expulsion of Jews and Muslims, the direct causes of decadence. Golden Age Moriscos, eighteenth-century historians, nineteenth-century liberals, and the polemicists of the twentieth century have tended to look upon the Spanish Muslims as the innocent victims of Catholic intolerance. The conservatives on the contrary, have viewed Spain as a true Christian country, forced to expel from its midst peoples whose presence contributed nothing to Spanish culture and was in fact injurious to the body politic. Between these two extreme positions, many nuances of opinion have existed which have complicated but also enriched the study of Spanish history.

From this it may be observed that while the British Orientalist was surveying the East from the optimistic vantage-point of his own expanding world (Burton, the translator of the *Arabian Nights*, proudly claimed that Queen Victoria was the ruler of the largest Muslim empire in history.), the Spanish Arabist was caught up in a struggle with his own feelings, ideals and national pride which directly coloured his thought and his scholarship.

In a broad sense, it can be asserted that Arabic studies have been cultivated in Spain ever since the Middle Ages beginning with the translators of Toledo, Ramón Martí (thirteenth century) and others. These studies, important though they were, proved to be the result of a need on the part of Spain to confront the spread of Islam in the Iberian Peninsula. Faced with a foe superior in culture, the Spaniards of medieval times were quick to find means to combat an alien and invading civilization by studying its nature and then writing a polemical literature destined at first to halt the Islamic expansion and later to convert the Moriscos of Granada to Christianity. This early Arabism was the product of a living necessity and because of its proselytizing and political nature it was supported to a large extent by Church and State. But Spain began to develop a new type of Arabism in the eighteenth century, devoted mainly to the rediscovery of Spanish medieval history. This second phase was characterized by reflection about the past as the first had been by involvement in the present. It is this second type of Arabism which constitutes the subject of the present work, but first a few words should be said about its origins.

In fact, there was no break in continuity, and one phase gradually blended into the other. If the seventeenth century witnessed the rebirth of Oriental studies in Europe generally, in Spain the second phase begins very hesitantly to appear in the sixteenth. In the seventeenth, Arabic studies disappear almost entirely as a result of isolationism and the general decline of Spanish science, and then in the eighteenth they begin to acquire a strictly modern, scholarly and critical character.

Spanish Arabism during the Renaissance was of a peculiarly unofficial sort. The Council of Vienna had in 1311 decided to recommend the establishment of chairs of Hebrew, Greek and Arabic at the universities of Bologne, Oxford, Rome, Paris and Salamanca, but in spite of the good intentions of the Council, Arabic studies at Salamanca were practically non-existent by the sixteenth century. One chair only was established for Arabic, Hebrew and Chaldean, but throughout most of its existence it remained vacant due to the impossibility of finding one man competent to teach all three of these languages. In 1511 Hernán Núñez de Toledo, later to become famous as *el Comendador Griego*, passed through Salamanca and an effort was made to appoint him to fill the vacant chair. Hernán Núñez, better known as a Greek scholar and humanist, had travelled in Granada, where he learned Arabic as a philologist, in addition to the Hebrew he had already mastered. As a result of internal university politics, he was barred from the trilingual chair and so applied successfully to the rival university of Alcalá in his capacity as a Hellenist. It is curious to note, however, that among those who supported his candidacy at Salamanca there was one Salaya, doctor and astrologer, who argued that "at this university there is a great need for Arabic, especially among doctors of medicine, and since it is said that [Hernán Núñez] is learned in the languages required for the chair, it should be awarded to him, were it only for the sake of his Arabic." [1] In this way the prestige of medieval Arabic medicine lingered on in Spain even when no one could be appointed to teach the language in its universities. In 1542 the university registers mention a salary paid to an unnamed person for teaching Arabic for a short period and on a temporary basis. As it became increasingly obvious that the university policy of combining three languages into one chair was a fiasco, it was finally decided to create a separate chair for each language, and in 1545 the chair of Arabic was given to "the Arabist who is in Barajas," [2] an individual who has not yet been identified, although it appears that there were many Moriscos in Barajas. In spite of the new chair, Arabic studies still did not take a firm foothold in the university, for the Arabist from Barajas did not remain there long. Finally in 1552 Salamanca began toying with the idea of founding a trilingual college patterned after that of Alcalá. The latter became a reality

[1] Marcel Bataillon, "L'Arabe à Salamanque au Temps de la Renaissance." *Hesperis*, 31, 1935, p. 6.

[2] *Op. cit.*, p. 16.

two years later, and in it Hebrew, Rhetoric and Greek constituted a new triad in which there was no longer any place for Arabic, the teaching of which was therefore abandoned at Salamanca. At Alcalá, where a separate chair of Arabic existed, university regulations stipulated that the language should be supported only if students attended the lectures; as a result of this policy Arabic was placed in a popularity contest where it could not compete with other languages of greater interest to Renaissance Humanism. As a result the programme of Arabic studies also failed at Alcalá.

If the position of Arabic at the university level seemed unencouraging, it was more successfully pursued on an extra-official level, particularly since the conquest of Granada, after which many new challenges had to be met and resolved. These non-university studies were directly concerned with the problems of contemporary life, and as such they retained a markedly medieval character. Renaissance Humanism injected a new spirit into their mainly religious and political intent which made them foreshadow the kind of study which would recommence in the eighteenth century.

The treaty of surrender signed by the last Naṣrid monarch of Granada Abū ʿAbd Allāh in favour of Ferdinand and Isabella had stipulated that the Muslims were to retain the right freely to practice their religion. Under the aegis of Hernando de Talavera, first Archbishop of Granada, these terms were at first scrupulously respected by the Castilian Crown. Although a policy of attempting to convert the Muslims was initiated, the campaign was conducted by strictly peaceful means; by resorting to persuasion rather than to compulsion. This policy was relatively more tolerant that the one which would subsequently be adopted, and it was implemented to a large degree by rural priests who could claim Muslim descent on their mother's side, as well as some knowledge of Arabic and of Moorish customs. Many Christian descendants of the *conquistadores* had married Moorish women who gave birth to this race of mixed ancestry. The offspring of such marriages who entered the Church were assigned to the rural parishes of the kingdom, particularly to those of the Alpujarra, where their familiarity with Moorish life made them useful in the campaign of peaceful conversion attempted by the Church.[1]

Other priests did not know Arabic, and it was to these that Fray

[1] *Cf.* Julio Caro Baroja, *Los moriscos del reino de Granada* (*ensayo de historia social*), Madrid, 1957, p. 86.

Pedro de Alcalá addressed his book entitled *Arte para ligeramente saber la lengua arávigo.*[1] As its title indicates, it is a grammar of the Arabic language; the first to be written in Spanish. In its prologue, addressed to Hernando de Talavera, the author establishes the propagandistic intent of his work and repeats the invective commonly pronounced against the name of Muḥammad by medieval Christians:

"When the time of fulfillment, or the fulfillment of the time had arrived, in which it pleased the Sovereign Pity to bring these recently converted peoples out of the darkness and many errors [into which they were induced] by that evil and unmentionable man, vile and accursed, Muḥammad, upon whom the Devil, his teacher had vomited all the errors and heresies which he had sown upon all past heretics . . ." [2]

Since the purpose of the work was a politico-religious one, and the author was unconcerned for the study of literary Arabic per se, he does not write about the classical language of scholars, but rather, about the vernacular tongue which the priests needed to know in order to preach to the common man:

"But for these and for other refinements I care not, because my main purpose is to speak and teach the language of the common people and not the refinements of Arabic grammar." [3]

The book thus deals with the everyday language of Granada, and in it the author included as excercises a group of Christian liturgical texts (the Ave Maria and other passages such as the Creed appear translated into Arabic making it a likely surmise that shortly after the conquest, the Mass was sung in Granada in the language of the conquered rather than in Latin). One of the reasons for teaching the priests Arabic was that Cardinal Jiménez, who aspired to the Spanish conquest of North Africa, wished to have ready an army of priests for the day when they could begin to convert the Moors. Spanish aspirations in North Africa never entirely ceased, but the Spanish impulse was deflected to the conquest of America. The *Arte* further contains a Spanish-Arabic lexicon which is of value today because the Arabic words it contains are recorded in a transcription into the Spanish alphabet. Because of this, their divergence from classical Arabic as well as their

[1] 1st ed. 1505; Photographic reprint by The Hispanic Society of America, New York, 1928, from which the following quotations are made.

[2] *Op. cit.*, p. 1. [3] *Op. cit.*, p. 1.

approximate vocalization can be reconstructed. Hence this book has been of invaluable service in the study of Granadan dialectology and has constituted one of the key sources for the nineteenth-century Dutch scholar R. Dozy's *Supplément aux Dictionnaires Arabes,*[1] at present the best dictionary on Western Arabic, as well as serving as a basis for the Swiss scholar Arnald Steiger's book on Hispano-Arabic phonetics.[2]

Not long after the fall of Granada, however, the relatively tolerant policies of the early friars changed for the worse. In the wake of the sword and the cross came a Castilian rabble intent on securing for itself and its descendants substantial land grants or administrative positions in the city government. As the Moriscos were ousted from their lands the social stability of the kingdom was seriously upset, and soon the Castilian lower classes began to clamour for a harsher policy towards the subjected peoples. The conflict finally exploded in the tragic Muslim revolt of the Alpujarra (1568-71) which was severely repressed. The Granadan Moors were then dispersed throughout Spain and finally all Muslims were expelled from the nation between 1609 and 1614; thus ended the history of Islam on Iberian soil.

The events of this period produced works on Arab affairs both by Moorish converts to Christianity as well as by old Christians. Books were written attacking or defending the government policy with regard to the Moriscos, although, as may be expected, the attacks were published posthumously (as was the case of Diego Hurtado de Mendoza's *De la Guerra de Granada*) or else they thinly disguised their criticism.

Among the Moorish converts the two most outstanding figures were Miguel de Luna and Alonso del Castillo, both from Granada. After their death, when aspersions were cast on the sincerity of their conversion to Catholicism, Don Pedro de Castro, archbishop of Seville wrote the following words in their defense in 1618:

"We had in Granada two honourable men, master Alonso del Castillo and Miguel de Luna, who interpreted these books; they knew the language like Orientals. In the Brief of Granada the interpreter [Gurmendi] says of these two that they belonged to the Morisco people and were of such dubious faith that the one

---

[1] Leiden, 1881.

[2] Arnald Steiger, *Contribución a la fonética del hispano-árabe y de los arabismos en el ibero-románico y el siciliano,* Madrid, 1932.

[Luna] ordered that he be buried outside the cemetery in a hermitage, since it was virgin soil, thereby following the custom of the Moors. He does them injury indeed; it is not so. We all knew that they were esteemed and reputed to be good, Catholic Christians.

Miguel de Luna was an upright man, able and intelligent. He led a Catholic life; he died with all the sacraments in the house of the secretary Alonso de Valdivia, in a place of his. He was in charge of the latter's estate and gave a good account of his administration: *Euge serve bone,* etc. Furthermore His Majesty honoured him by making him his servant and interpreter of the Arabic language, and he has been admitted to the rank of Hidalgo through a suit he made in Granada. As such he enjoyed the rights of Hidalgos and that his person should not be detained." [1]

Luna is usually dismissed by Arabists chiefly because he was the author of *Historia verdadera del rey don Rodrigo, en la cual se trata la causa principal de la pérdida de España.*[2] This book rapidly went through several editions in Spanish and was soon translated into French and English. For a long time it was held to be authentic history although later scholars, particularly in the nineteenth century, were to be unanimous in condemning it as a literary forgery; a falsified account of history.[3] However, Don Faustino de Borbón, of whom mention will be made later, in the eighteenth century wrote an obscure epistle disproving the authenticity of Luna's "History" while recognizing its true fictional character. He concluded as follows:

"Let it therefore be established that this work of Luna's is a

---

[1] *Apud* Darío Cabanelas Rodríguez, *El morisco granadino Alonso del Castillo,* Granada, 1965, p. 15.

[2] 1st ed., 2 parts, Granada, 1592-1600. Translated into English as: *The History of the Conquest of Spain by the Moors. Together with the Life of the Most Illustrious Monarch Almanzor. And of the Several Revolutions of the Mighty Empire of the Caliphs, and of the African Kingdoms. Composed in Arabick by Abulcacim Tariff Abentariq, one of the Generals in that Spanish Expedition, and Translated into Spanish by Michael de Luna, Interpreter to Philip the Second. Now made English,* London, 1687. 2nd ed: 1693 from which the ensuing quotations are made.

[3] Ticknor, echoing Gayangos, says the following about Luna: "How Miguel de Luna, who, though a Christian, was of an old Moorish family in Granada, and an interpreter of Philip II, should have shown a great ignorance of the Arabic language and history of Spain, or, showing it, should yet have succeeded in passing off his miserable stories as authentic, is certainly a singular circumstance." George Ticknor, *History of Spanish Literature,* 3rd ed., Boston, 1866, vol. I, pp. 193-4, n. 56.

mere novel, of which use should not be made in history."[1]

With his eighteenth-century prejudice aganst the novel, Don Faustino de Borbón was not interested in certain aspects of the work which are noteworthy today, but he at least had the merit of pointing out the book's fictional nature.

Julio Caro Baroja has suggested that during the Golden Age of Spanish literature somewhat of the prestige of Arab historiography still lingered on, and he claims that this was what led Cervantes playfully to attribute Arab authorship to *Don Quixote*. In doing so Cervantes was only following the tradition established by certain novels of chivalry, the authors of which pretended to be mere translators from the Arabic. Likewise the historian Ginés Pérez de Hita attributed his *Guerras civiles de Granada*, to a certain "Aben Hamín" who has not been satisfactorily identified with any real Arab writer despite an unconvincing attempt to see in him the person of the Granadan historian Ibn al-Khaṭīb.[2]

Therefore it is plausible to think that in attributing his pseudo-History to an Arab author, Miguel de Luna was following an established literary tradition. When the work is analyzed, it is easily detected that behind the mere conventional use of tradition there lies a most significant ideology and purpose. The work is fictional; it is based on legendary material taken from Spanish balladry and half-remembered traditions which as a Morisco Luna could not have failed to know. Though it is not true history, it contains enough historical facts to be a semblance of the latter. The author takes great pains to give his work the appearance of an authentic translation, even going to the extreme of filling the margins with pseudo-erudite footnotes which make a pretense at discussing the correct translation of Arabic terms purportedly found in the original. But behind all this mish-mash of history and phantasy there lies a purpose which has too often been overlooked. The narrative itself begins as follows:

"In the year 91 of the Hegira, Spain was governed by a King called Rodrigo, of the race of the Goths; a people that came into that country from the farthest parts of the North, and who made profession of the Christian religion. This kingdom did then enjoy a profound peace, and was as much under his subjection, as Arabia

---

[1] Don Faustino de Borbon, *Cartas para ilustrar la historia de la España árabe*, Madrid, 1799, apéndice II, p. 11.

[2] Caro Baroja, *op. cit.*, pp. 131-2, n. 121.

could be formerly to the great Almanzor, our Sovereign lord. Insomuch that this unhappy Prince [*i.e. Rodrigo*] (for we may well term him so) had the freedom to abandon himself to all the vices, whereof idleness is commonly the source." [1]

In this fashion, the opening lines tend to stress the lack of virtue in the Spanish ruler. After a dynastic quarrel over succession the mother of the rightful heir Don Sancho, whose name is Queen Anagilda, writes the following letter to upbraid Rodrigo for having made an attempt upon the life of her son:

"All the laws of knighthood, as well as those of humanity do not suffer the revenging one's self on those that have meant us the most mischiefs, as soon as they can no longer do us any: ay, and generosity requires that we pardon them, tho they have done us hurt; but the least of these virtues is too great for thee: thou wilt not so much as know what these same duties are, and dost not mind the praises that are gained by fine actions; *since that instead of being for the truth, which is the friend of God, thou makest it thy whole business to stifle it,* and to declare thyself against it; *vowing the ruine of him that never had the least thought to offend thee*; *and who, on the contrary, has had so much confidence in thee, that he put himself under thy protection.*" [2]

The Christian king Rodrigo is presented as a profligate who has brought the State to its nadir, and in this outburst against the man who attempts the "ruine of him that never had the least thought to offend thee" but rather "put himself under thy protection" it is easy to detect a veiled diatribe against the similar occurrences in contemporary Spain which Miguel de Luna had witnessed; namely the fate of the unfortunate Moriscos, his kin, for the whole point of Luna's book is to show that whereas the Christians had been cruel and tyrannical in Visigothic Spain, all sorts of supernatural prophecies had conspired to indicate that it was the will of God that Spain should be conquered by a people endowed with greater virtue than the Visigoths, namely the Arabs. Furthermore, Luna tries to show that after the Arab conquest of Spain the Muslims respected the conditions of surrender they granted to the Christians, unlike the policy later adopted by the Christians in Granada:

"He [the Bishop of Granada] was very kindly received by Tariff, who immediately struck up with him in the following conditions:

[1] *The History of the Conquest of Spain, ed. cit.*, p. 1.
[2] *Op. cit.*, pp. 11-12 (underlining mine).

that the Christians should remain in that country if so minded, and should not be molested either in their persons, or estates, or their consciences: that they should not pay any other imposts, than the tribute they were wont to pay to Christian Kings. That if any among them were not willing to stay there, they should be suffered to sell their whole estate, and go into whatsoever country, inhabited by Christians, they should best like." [1]

These were indeed the same terms of surrender granted by their Catholic Majesties to the Moriscos of Granada and violated by the Spanish monarchs. Hence the allusion though covert, remains clear.

Finally, the first part of Luna's work ends in a note of renewed enthusiasm and optimism over Arab rule which stands in obvious contrast to the author's disparagement of Rodrigo, for he describes the prosperous reign of a fictitious caliph he calls Ali Abilhacheck in glowing terms:

". . . He applied himself in good earnest to make regulations upon all abuses that were introduced into the government, and to do justice to all those that required it of him, without making them wait; insomuch that he acquired in a short time not only a great reputation, but also the friendship of all the people; they esteemed themselves very happy in being governed by so good a King. Thus ended the line of the Aboulvalid Almanzors." [2]

From the contrast between Christians and Muslims it is made clear by the author that he was writing a polemical work, the covert intention of which was to reproach Christian Spain for its harsh policy towards the Moriscos. The author achieves this end by creating the image of a rosy historical past in which Muslims had behaved with unparalleled gallantry towards Christians. Thus Luna's book is something more than just a blatant attempt to foist a falsified Arab History on the public; it is a defense of *tolerance*, and as such it belongs in the class of novels of the sort of the *Abencerraje* which also attempts to show how on the level of *virtue* and *tolerance*, both Muslims and Christians could coexist in perfect harmony. It is thus tempting to speculate on the extent to which polemical Morisco literature may have helped shape the image of the "noble Moor" which became so fashionable in Golden Age Spanish literature and lasted till much later as a literary theme in the rest of Europe.

---

[1] *Op. cit.*, p. 90.

[2] *Op. cit.*, pp. 136-137.

The Spanish Arabist Darío Cabanelas Rodríguez has recently written a biography of Luna's close friend Alonso del Castillo.[1] Cabanelas shows that Castillo was probably born between 1520 and 1530, that he was the son of a converted Morisco and a native of Granada who received a degree in medicine at the university of that city. Thus, aside from his knowledge of Arabic, he also read medical treatises written by Greek and Latin authors. In the defense of Luna, previously quoted, Pedro de Castro goes on to say the following about Castillo:

"He was an honourable man, somewhat older, excellent, and in the rebellions of the Moriscos of Granada he always served His Majesty and they allowed him to remain as a faithful inhabitant in the kingdom of Granada, though others, the majority, were expelled from the kingdom. He was the interpreter of His Majesty and of the Inquisition. Nothing was ever discovered about him that was unworthy of a Catholic Christian. He died with the sacraments, and while he was dying in bed, he sang the Creed; he took communion and received the holy sacrament as a viaticum. He said to all those present: 'This thing which I have received is the body of our Lord, Jesus Christ; this is the truth, the rest is false' . . . He made his will and was buried with masses for his soul in the parish of San Miguel." [2]

Castillo died between 1607 and 1610. His work, which was extremely important to the development of Arabic studies in Spain, may be summed up under the following five major headings: a translation of the Arabic inscriptions of the Alhambra (1564), translated letters and documents related to the revolt of the Alpujarra (1568-72), a catalogue of the first Arabic manuscripts collected in the Escorial Library (1573-74), translations of the official correspondence exchanged between the Sultan of Morocco Abū l-ʿAbbās Aḥmad al-Manṣūr and Philip II (1579-87), and a collaboration with Luna in interpretating the *libros plumbeos* or 'leaden books' of the Sacro-Monte (1588-1607).

Castillo's versions of the inscriptions of the Alhambra were the first ever attempted, and have proved to be of great value since they have served as a basis for all subsequent work in the field. Later scholars often corrupted Castillo's versions rather than correcting them so that in one of the most recent works on the subject,

---

[1] *El morisco granadino Alonso del Castillo*, Granada, 1965.
[2] *Op. cit.*, p. 15.

the French Orientalist Lévi-Provençal has often had to uphold the original readings proposed by Castillo.[1] Furthermore, the Morisco scholar, being the earliest to study Alhambra epigraphy, was able to translate the inscriptions on certain tombstones of the Naṣrid kings which have since then been defaced. Thus his work, being the first in time, records inscriptions today irretrievably damaged or lost.

Castillo's documents and letters relating to the war of the Alpujarra were collected and presented to Philip II and consist of five letters translated from Spanish into Arabic, and eighty written in Arabic by the rebel leaders and translated into Spanish by Castillo. They were particularly important to historical writing about the war, because they were used as a first hand source of information by the translator's close friend the historian Luis del Mármol Carvajal (1520?-1600?) who gave a greater measure of authenticity to his own work by following Castillo's versions very closely in his account of the war.[2]

In Golden Age Spain, all roads led to Madrid, and so, in 1573 Castillo went to Court in search of a more stable occupation as official translator to the King. In the Escorial, where he stayed for some time, he made the first attempt at cataloguing the monastery's Arabic manuscripts. The Escorial collection, today one of the richest in Europe, had its origin at this time. The religious and political preoccupations of contemporary Spain had led Spaniards to destroy many Arabic manuscripts that fell into their hands after the taking of Granada. According to Gayangos, Cardinal Jiménez de Cisneros caused eighty thousand Arabic volumes to be burned in the public square of Granada, under the false impression that any book written in Arabic had to be a Koran, and therefore dangerous to the faith.[3] When it is recalled that Cisneros was a scholar and a humanist it becomes apparent why it was so difficult to establish regular Arabic studies at that time. However, it should be remembered that Gayangos was a liberal and as such, he was prone to exaggerate the evils committed by the Church. On the other hand, Simonet, an extreme conservative, considerably

---

[1] *Op. cit.*, pp. 51-55; E. Lévi-Provençal, *Inscriptions arabes d'Espagne*, Paris-Leiden, 1931, pp. 156-158.

[2] *Historia del rebelión y castigo de los moriscos del reino de Granada*, Málaga, 1600.

[3] Pascual de Gayangos, *A History of the Mohammedan Dynasties of Spain*, London, 1840, vol. I, pp. viii-ix.

reduced the number of the books actually burned in Granada.[1] We have no real way of estimating how many books were actually burned, but the work of later Arabists has resulted in the publication of so many important manuscripts, that we may say today that the loss, though unfortunate, was not irreparable. Moreover, years after this public *auto da fe,* Philip II amassed a large quantity of Arabic manuscripts. They were gathered from all the Spanish cities where Muslim culture had flourished, some of them even by Luna and Castillo themselves. These treasures were stored in the Escorial, and to them were added, during the reign of Philip III three thousand volumes belonging to Muley Zidān, Sultan of Morocco, which were taken as booty from three Moorish ships captured by the Spanish navy. Thus in Spain a rich collection of manuscripts was formed. In 1671, however, a fire broke out in the Escorial and Gayangos estimates that it consumed more than three-fourths of its Arabic holdings.[2] Again we must be cautious of Gayangos' estimate, for a great deal has remained and it is difficult to tell how much was actually lost.

The early group of volumes gathered together by Philip II was the one that Alonso del Castillo set about cataloguing for the Escorial Library, and although his work was never published, it served as a basis for the first printed catalogue of the collection, which appeared in 1646 in Latin.[3] It was a list containing little more than author, title and subject, but in spite of its deficiencies it was the only catalogue of the Escorial Arabic holdings in existence until the more complete work done by Casiri in the eighteenth century (of which more will be said in its place), and Derenbourg's catalogue which is in general use today.[4]

In 1579 Castillo was entrusted with translating the correspondence exchanged between the Sultan of Morocco Aḥmad al-Manṣūr and Philip II, so that as in the war of the Alpujarra, his knowledge of Arabic was again made use of by the government. He also had a hand in deciphering the *libros plumbeos* of the Sacro-Monte in Granada. These were a series of documents which began to be

---

[1] Fco. Javier Simonet, *El cardenal Ximénez de Cisneros y los manuscritos arábigo-granadinos,* Granada, 1885.

[2] Gayangos, *ibid.,* p. ix.

[3] Printed by Christian Rav, and reprinted by J. H. Hottinger, Heidelberg, 1658, *cf.* Cabanelas Rorı́guez, *ibid.,* p. 128.

[4] Hartwig Derenbourg, *Les Manuscrits Arabes de l' Escurial,* vol. I, Paris, 1884.

unearthed in 1588 and the gradual discovery of which extended over a period of twelve years. They contained, in Arabic, apocryphal gospels and religious texts outlining a unique syncretism between Christianity and Islam. Throughout the seventeenth century these documents were to arouse a heated controversy over their authenticity. Today it appears clear that, like Miguel de Luna's false History, they were the work of Moriscos, and were planted in the ruins of buildings soon to be demolished for the purpose of creating a compromise with Christianity; a compromise based on dogmatic and ritualistic grounds which would make it easier for the new converts from Islam to accept beliefs and rituals which offended their consciences as ex- or crypto-Muslims. As an example, the *libros plumbeos* recognize the dogma of Papal infallibility but they do so within the framework of a strict monotheistic theology which, after the Islamic tradition, makes Jesus out to be a manifestation of God's Spirit and not His Son. In the realm of liturgy, the documents explain that the chalice used in the Mass contains water—not wine, which is forbidden in Islam—and that it is used by the priest to wash his hands, mouth and face—in other words, to perform the *ġusl* or ritual ablution of Islam. The documents also cast the Arabs in the light of God's chosen people and bearers of His Christian message through the ministry of whom the whole world will eventually be saved. This ideology is basically similar to the one underlying Luna's History, and this leads Cabanelas to suspect that Luna and even Castillo himself may have been involved in the original counterfeiting of these documents, though he does not explain why this ideological purpose could not have been shared by many other Moriscos of the time rather than being restricted exclusively to Luna and Castillo.

In his book, Cabanelas concludes by dwelling on the importance of Castillo as one of those men who were personally involved in the political, ideological and religious struggle which resulted from the conquest of Granada:

"Furthermore, because of what we now know, we can not only affirm that Castillo is one of the most interesting figures among the Granadan Moriscos of the sixteenth century, but we can also judge his peculiar attitude towards the Morisco problem, which for him was no doubt the most serious of his time . . . Since he considered the fusion between Moriscos and old Christians completely impossible to achieve, he attempts to reach a compromise, by trying to bridge the chasm between Christendom and Islam." [1]

A man brought up in the Moorish tradition, Castillo acquired the culture of the Renaissance at the University of Granada. Though his work was largely concerned with political events, his sixteenth-century education lent a new tone to his scholarship so that it was not entirely absorbed by contemporary affairs. This was a significant shift in Spanish Arabism as the latter moved away from the predominantly religious and political sphere and gradually became an independent discipline.

At the same time that Moriscos were interpreting and struggling to save their culture in Granada, Christian writers were also taking an active interest in the affairs of that city. Histories of Granada were written by three major figures: Diego Hurtado de Mendoza (1503-1575) [2] Ginés Pérez de Hita (1544?-1619?) [3] and Luis del Mármol Carvajal (1520?-1600?).[4] Of these authors, the latter is of particular interest since he was a close friend of Castillo, whose translations of original Arabic documents he used freely in his own book.

Luis del Mármol was the bastard son of Pedro del Mármol, scribe of the Audiencia of Granada. It is not entirely clear whether Mármol's family were of Christian or Moorish ancestry though his biographers tend to suspect for several reasons that he descended from Christians though not of noble lineage.[5] In his youth the future historian accompanied Charles V to Tunis in 1535 and for twenty-two years he served the Spanish flag in Africa. Around 1545 he was captured by the Turks and transported as a slave to Tunis, Libia, Tlemcen, Fez, Marrakesh, Tarudent, and even as far as Guinea. He spent seven years and eight months in captivity and during this time he learned Arabic as well as what he called the "African" tongue, by which he presumably meant Berber. Mármol seems to have been ransomed by an unidentified religious Order around 1557, but he stayed on in Africa to explore the vast unknown

[1] *Ibid.*, pp. 235-6.

[2] *De la guerra de Granada*, 1st edition (posthumous) Toledo, 1627. Published in BAE, vol 21, Madrid, 1946, pp. 65-122.

[3] *Guerras civiles de Granada*, 1st part, 1595; 2nd part, 1619. Ed. by Paula Blanchard-Demouge, Madrid, 1915, 2 vols.

[4] *Historia del rebelión y castigo de los moriscos del reino de Granada*, 1st ed., Málaga 1600. Published in BAE, *vol. cit.*, pp. 123-365.

[5] *Cf.* Agustín G. de Amezúa, "Prólogo," in: Luis del Mármol Carvajal, *Descripción general de África*, Madrid, 1953, vol. I, p. 12.

continent as a free man. He therefore belongs to that hardy breed of Spanish explorers who crossed the unknown areas of Africa, Asia and America in the hey-day of Empire. He even seems to have gone as far as Egypt and Ethiopia to gather material for his first work: *Descripción general de África*. Mármol returned to Spain around 1557, then fought in Italy in the army of the Duke of Alba and finally retired to Granada in time to witness the Morisco revolt. When Don Juan of Austria was appointed to quell the rebellion, Mármol was chosen as purveyor of army supplies, and in this way he was enabled to gain a direct experience of the war he wrote about. At its end, he was rewarded for his services with a grant of land, probably confiscated from some unfortunate Morisco, near the city of Vélez Málaga, and in 1571 he settled down there to begin his *Descripción general de África*, of which the first part appeared in 1573. In 1579, Mármol was on the point of being named Spanish Ambassador to Morocco on the strength of his knowledge of Arabic and of the customs of that country, but at the last moment Philip II chose someone of lesser merits than Mármol, but who unlike him, could claim an illustrious birth. He then set about writing the second part of his *Descripción*, which appeared in 1599, published at the author's expense. In the meantime he had finished the *Rebelión* and it was published in 1600, at which time the author informs us he was seventy-six years old.

In his prologue to the *Rebelión*, Mármol speaks of his concept of the role of history, a concept closely influenced by Classicism and the humanistic rebirth of scholarship. After citing his classical models and Spanish sources, he says that he added to these by:

"Borrowing from a few Arabic books which we were able to examine accurately." [1]

If the work itself is checked, it will be found that Arab geographers and historians are occasionally mentioned and quoted with every appearance of authenticity. Thus in describing Spain, Mármol quotes the words of a certain Ibn Rashīd:

" 'This province is encompassed by three strong walls given it by Nature to protect and defend its inhabitants: In the south lie the rugged mountain ranges of Sirgo which were for a long time in the hands of the Christians; to the east lie the Pyrenees; to the north some other mountains wherein the inhabitants of the land

[1] *Rebelión*, ed. BAE, p. 124.

also entrenched themselves against the power of the Romans, the Goths, and the Arabs.' Ibn Rashīd speaks up to here."

The placing of the Pyrenees in the east as well as the generally triangular shape attributed to the Peninsula do in fact accord with the way in which the latter was depicted by medieval Arab cartopraphers,[1] while the Arabic way of ending the quotation with "Hasta aquí dice Abén Raxid," corresponding to the Arabic *intahā kalāmu-hu* 'his words are ended' give an air of authenticity to Mármol's claims to Arabic scholarship.

In this way he was able to contribute a first-hand account of the Morisco rebellion, made all the more valuable because of his knowledge of Arabic, personal friendship with Moriscos, access to their documents and acquaintance with Arab customs. As a result, Mármol's work has occupied a key place in the bibliographies of all those who have written on the Moriscos of Granada after him. This may easily be deduced from the numerous references to his work made by the latest of such writers: Julio Caro Baroja.[2]

Mármol was not the only Spanish traveller in Africa during this period; Diego de Torres, born in 1526 in Amusco, a town in the province of Palencia, went to Morocco in the service of the King of Portugal to ransom Christian captives. For ten years, from 1546 to 1556 he performed this function from his headquarters in Marrakesh, and was permitted to travel extensively throughout the country. He appears therefore to have been in Morocco at the same time as Mármol. While there, he learned Arabic, and upon returning to Spain he composed a history of Morocco during the first half of the sixteenth century [3] drawn largely from his personal experiences and which was borrowed from not only by Mármol but by many subsequent historians.

It may be learned from Torres' book that the cities of Morocco during the sixteenth century contained important communities of free Christian merchants organized around an "alhóndiga de cristianos" or Christian centre for commercial transactions. It was among these groups that Torres found the help and support needed to carry out his mission of ransoming Christian captives. Among

[1] *Cf.* Ibn Khaldūn, *The Muqaddimah, an Introduction to History,* trans. by F. Rosenthal, New York, 1958, vol. I, Plate I, frontispiece.

[2] *Cf. Los moriscos del reino de Granada.*

[3] *Relación del origen y suceso de los xarifes, y del estado de los Reinos de Marruecos, Fez, Tarudante, y de los demás, que tienen usurpados,* 1st (posthumous) ed., Seville, 1586.

these Christians many were Spanish and Portuguese, and the abundance of the former, both free merchants and slaves may be surmised from the following anecdote related by Torres:

"When the *sharīf* was in the mosque [of Marrakesh] on a friday, praying in the company of many judges and officers of his guard, and many of the common people, a man entered the mosque whom I was later to encounter again. He looked like a savage for his hair and beard reached his waist, his face was thin and drawn, his clothes were in tatters, and he was barefoot. He climbed up to the place where the grand judge had preached that day and began saying in Arabic in a loud voice: 'Christ lives, Christ conquers, Christ reigns, Christ will come to judge the quick and the dead and all the rest is a sham.' When the *sharīf* heard this he was amazed and even astonished, and in great wrath he ordered those who formed his guard to kill him. Certain judges and knights begged him to countermand his orders, because the man was a *mahabul*, which in our vernacular means "innocent." Upon this they ejected him from the mosque and he left the city, going to the kingdom of Tarudent where I travelled and met him, and learned from him that he was from Trujillo, and that after he had converted to Islam he had repented and returned to God seeking His forgiveness, and that this was his way of doing penitence for his sins. He was a man of good reason and understanding and wanted to live in Spain. He only spoke to people in sign language. With me, he spoke in secret, and upon my asking him the purpose of his acts in the presence of the king in the mosque, he replied that his purpose was to say the truth publicly to those unbelievers, and that if for declaring it he were to be made a martyr for God's sake, then he would be quite contented. I found the means for him to return to Spain, upon which he took his leave of me, and although I remained for more than two years in that kingdom, I never had news of him, though I tried to get it, and I believe his good intentions must have guided him to Christian territory for his salvation." [1]

Diego de Torres thus left to posterity a portrait of the daily life of that old Morocco under the Saʿdians which lasted undisturbed until the end of the nineteenth century,[2] and the echoes of which

[1] *Cf.* Julio Caro Baroja, *Una visión de Marruecos a mediados del siglo XVI, la del primer historiador de los "xarifes," Diego de Torres*, Instituto de Estudios Africanos, Madrid, 1956, p. 16.

[2] *Cf.* Henri Terrasse, *History of Morocco*, Casablanca, 1952.

may still be heard in the *madīnas* of its imperial cities. Torres' work is particularly valuable. It offers a rich panorama of the socio-political and economic life of the times. From it the reader may learn that relations between Spain and Morocco were rather more frequent than one would suppose. As a result of the migration of Granadan families to North Africa; of the taking of captives by the Barbary pirates and the lucrative business of holding them for ransom; of general commercial interests, and indeed, of geographic proximity and power politics (Morocco courted the favour of Spain to ward off the Turkish menace), relations, even though unwilling and often based on hatred, most certainly existed on a personal level. Such contacts would continue through the eighteenth century and would bring about a renewed interest in Arabic studies among Spaniards. This, plus the stimulus of the war of Granada gave rise to the Arabism of the Renaissance which has been reviewed in the preceding pages. Though that Arabism was largely conditioned by political and religious interests which it in turn served, in the hands of some scholars it began to develop a more detached field of interest which distinguished it from medieval Arabism and presaged what was to come later. Under the impact of Humanism, Arabism became more an independent intellectual discipline and less a product of contemporary circumstances. This tendency, as yet barely outlined, was not to become a full reality until the eighteenth century.

PART ONE

THE STUDY OF GRAMMAR AND LEXICOGRAPHY

CHAPTER ONE

During the seventeenth century Arabic studies in Spain underwent an eclipse. No significant works from that period have survived, while the only one of a general nature whose title has been recorded is a history of Islamic Spain by Marco Obelio Citeroni [1] about which Menéndez y Pelayo briefly remarks that it was similar in scope to Conde's book, and that its author included Spanish translations of a number of poems, among them the elegies of al-Muʿtamid of Seville.

Sebastián de Covarrubias, in his dictionary entitled *Tesoro de la lengua castellana* published in Madrid in 1611, attempts to elucidate the Arabic etymologies of many Spanish words, but he states that in order to do this he was forced to consult Diego de Urrea, the royal interpreter, as well as certain writings of Francisco Guadix, a member of the Order of St. Francis, thus revealing the general lack of information about Arabic then prevailing,[2] for according to Campomanes, the works of these two were never published.[3] Nevertheless the testimony of Covarrubias indicates that knowledge of Arabic was kept alive in certain religious Orders, particularly the Franciscan, a subject which will be touched upon frequently in this chapter.

As earlier, Spain and Morocco had continued to maintain diplomatic contact throughout the seventeenth century. Muley Ismaʿīl had sent his vizier al-Ġassānī al-Andalusī to Spain in 1690-91 to consider various matters with the Spanish Crown, one of them being the return of the Arabic books in the Escorial which were claimed by Morocco.[4] Yet it was not until the eighteenth century that a revival of Arabic studies occurred, and its appearance was motivated by several factors.

One of the main foreign policy problems facing Europe in general

---

[1] *Cf.* M. Menéndez y Pelayo, *La ciencia española*, 3rd ed., Madrid, 1888, vol. 3, p. 254.

[2] Sebastián de Covarrubias Orozco, *Tesoro de la lengua castellana*. Madrid, 1611.

[3] *Cf.* Francisco Cañes, *Diccionario español-latino-arábico*, Madrid, 1787, vol. I, p. xxvii.

[4] *Cf.* Vicente Rodríguez Casado, *Política marroquí de Carlos III*, Madrid, 1946, p. 92, n. 39. The Arabic journal kept by the vizier during his travels in Spain has been published in Larache, 1940, with a Spanish translation; J. Vernet, "La embajada de al-Ghassānī," *And.*, 1953, 1, pp. 109-131.

and Spain in particular during the whole of that century was what to do about the power vacuum which had resulted from the decline of Ottoman hegemony in the Mediterranean. As Turkish might decreased, the European Powers attempted to carve out zones of influence in the Islamic world. The ultimate goal of Spanish diplomacy was to gain possession of the Moroccan coastlands opposite to Spain in order to control the Straits of Gilbraltar, as well as to establish trade relations with the Islamic countries whose markets were a potentially rich field for Spanish commercial expansion. To do this it was necessary to make peace with the Sublime Porte. Charles III and Muḥammad ʻAbd Allāh of Morocco by common agreement put an end to the state of warfare that had existed between their two countries for centuries. A treaty had been signed in 1767 which guaranteed the safety of Spanish shipping from Moroccan piratry. Preliminary negotiations had been conducted between the sovereigns of the two nations through the Spanish missionaries in Fez, particularly friar José Boltas. Another embassy was led by the Franciscan friar Bartolomé Girón who was reputed to be familiar with the ways of Muslim lands. These diplomatic exchanges culminated in 1776 when Sīdī Aḥmad al-Ġazāl visited Madrid and was splendidly entertained by Charles III. In the course of his visit, which turned into a social event for the Spanish aristocracy, the Moroccan ambassador toured the Escorial and again requested the return of its Arabic manuscripts.[1]

The impression left by al-Ġazāl on Spanish society was a lively one indeed, because one of Spain's most distinguished literary figures of that age, José Cadalso, began announcing the preparation of a work entitled *Cartas marruecas* in a letter to Tomás de Iriarte dated 1776, the very year of al-Ġazāl's mission.[2] Furthermore one of the chief characters in the *Cartas* is a Moroccan ambassador named Gazel behind whose name, transmuted by literary art and the inspiration of Montesquieu, it is not hard to discern the figure of the ambassador from Africa.

By 1780 a further agreement was reached between the monarchs of Spain and Morocco, this time directed against England with which Spain was at war. Its immediate result was that Moroccan ports were closed to British shipping.

Finally, the steady policy of courting Muslim nations led to a

[1] *Op. cit.*, p. 86.

[2] José Cadalso, *Cartas marruecas*, Madrid, Espasa-Calpe, 1956, p. xxv.

treaty signed between Spain and the Sublime Porte in 1782 at Istanbul so that the two traditional foes were at last reconciled. The treaty with Turkey was followed by others with its Regencies; Tripoli, Tunisia and Algeria, so that by 1788 the Count of Floridablanca was able to report to the Spanish monarch that:

"The Spanish flag may frequently be seen throughout the Levant, where it had never been known before." [1]

It has already been mentioned that long before these treaties the affairs of Spain and North Africa had become entangled for geographical and historical reasons. Piracy on both sides and the practice of taking captives—a practice going back to the *Reconquista*—had made available numbers of slaves who were used as a source of cheap labor not only by the African States but also by the Spanish.[2]

The taking of captives gave rise to a system of ransom also harking back to the *Reconquista* which, on the Spanish side was chiefly conducted by religious Orders with missions in Africa. Of these Orders, those of the Trinity and of Mercy had been established during the Middle Ages expressly to ransom captives held in Muslim territory, but gradually their work was taken over by missionary orders, particularly that of the Franciscans which by the eighteenth century had established missions throughout North Africa and the Middle East.[3] Paul V in a papal bull dated 1610 had

---

[1] *Cf.* Vicente Palacio Atard, *Los españoles de la ilustración*, Madrid, 1964, p. 326.

[2] Of this unsavoury aspect of history Conrotte says: "In retaliation, slavery subsisted in Spain with respect to Moors and Turks in the eighteenth century . . . as long as a state of war was maintained with Turkey, Barbary, and Morocco, their citizens who fell into the hands of Spaniards were deprived of liberty as were the captives taken by Muslims." Manuel Conrotte, *España y los paises musulmanes durante el ministerio de Floridablanca*, Madrid, 1909, p. 50. Rodríguez Casado gives abundant bibliography on the slaves in Cartagena. Though the Western world is familiar with the captivity of Spaniards in Algeria (Cervantes for example) it should not be forgotten that one of the primary aims of Moroccan diplomacy throughout the eighteenth century was to obtain the return of its subjects held in bondage in Spain. Of Muley Ismaʿīl [r. 1672-1727], the Moroccan champion of Islam who wrote Louis XIV and James II advising them to be converted, Vincent Monteil says: "The privateering at Salé and the capture of 2,000 Christians is attributed to him. But people forget that the Spanish and Portuguese invasions had dislocated the economic administration, and that the Christian 'course' was 'the role of acting as a curb or inhibitor of Mediterranean Islam'." *Cf.* Vincent Monteil, *Morroco*, English trans. by Veronica Hull, London, 1964, p. 50. Also, Henri Terrasse, *History of Morocco, ed. cit.*, p. 135.

[3] Conrotte, *ibid.*, p. 51.

commanded the various religious Orders to teach Oriental languages in their colleges and by 1682 the Franciscans had decided in Toledo to found colleges in Salamanca, Alcalá, Paris and Toulouse for the teaching of Arabic, Greek and Hebrew.[1] To train its missionaries the Order had founded a *Colegio trilingüe* in Seville as early as the sixteenth century. Though the main purpose of the Sevillian college was religious it served as a starting point for a new kind of Arabism, for one of its members, friar Bernardino González composed an Arabic dictionary which was added to and completed by the Franciscans in Jerusalem in 1709. This as yet unpublished work was destined to be the earliest in a series of eighteenth-century Arabic studies. It derived clearly from missionary work and therefore it belonged to a practical type of Arabism involved in contemporary affairs. Yet it is significant because it indicates that throughout the seventeenth century the interest in Arabic never actually died out entirely, but was kept alive by the Franciscan Order. Thus the trajectory of Spanish Arabism during the eighteenth century could be summed up as the gradual secularization of this religion-oriented discipline under the influence of the ideas of the Enlightenment and of the new foreign policy towards Islam developed by its leaders.

Campomanes, the President of the Council of Castile under Charles III and himself an Arabist of some talent, stated the objectives of the Sevillian college, saying that the head of the Franciscan Order, Francisco Albín, had keenly realized the need for the study of Arabic in Spain, for which purpose he had founded the college. In this way the missionaries were destined to collaborate in Spain's expansionist ideals during the eighteenth century when one of them was to declare:

"At present things have changed: the advantage of nations and of trade have shown the need and convenience of re-establishing good harmony with the Eastern and African Powers, while at the same time the interest in preserving the holy places of Jerusalem has served as an incentive to produce the mutual agreement made by the peace treaty signed by Your Majesty and the Ottoman Porte, the African Regencies, and the kingdom of Morocco."[2]

During the seventeenth century the secretary of the Order, José de León, lecturer in Arabic, began to compile a dictionary of the Arabic language, and Bernardino González was sent to the Holy

[1] *Cf.* Francisco Cañes, *ibid.* vol. I, p. ii.

[2] Francisco Cañes, *ibid.*, "dedication to the King," n. p.

Land to perfect and complete it. He arrived in Damascus with the rough draft prepared in Seville and with the help of local Arab Christians he substantially expanded the number of entries in the dictionary. The work was the most complete ever to have been composed in Spanish after that of Pedro de Alcalá. The difficulties surmounted by the authors may easily be imagined, for they had no reference works but the dictionary of Golius for Arabic, while that of the Spanish Academy had not yet been written.[1] The work of González and his collaborators was lost until Asín Palacios came across a copy containing additions up to the year 1727 made by the friars of Damascus. Its chief value lies in the fact that Friar González, in the Spanish-Arabic section of his book includes not only classical words but also colloquial, vulgar and even obscene expressions which are not easily found in contemporary dictionaries. The compiler was sensitive to language and in a very careful and precise way, set about distinguishing many fine shades of meaning in Arabic, for each Spanish word. The Arabic-Latin section deals chiefly with the obscure vocabulary of philosophy, theology and mysticism. Bernardino González, thanks to his education during an age when scholasticism was studied more than it is today, was thoroughly conversant with the technical terminology of the Islamic religion, and since many of these terms are often obscure, he has left a valuable contribution to lexicography in this area.

Friar González was interested primarily in missionary work, but the modernity of his criterion in composing his dictionary shows that Arabic studies were beginning to acquire a more secular nature which would be intensified as the century advanced, until they would attain a certain maturity at its end, when they were integrated into the general current of the humanities. This occurred partly because Humanism, initiated during the Renaissance, though it had relied to a large extent on Arabic works (Pico Della Mirandola quotes a certain "ʿAbd Allāh the Sarracen" in his treatise *De Hominis Dignitate,* to mention only one incident [2]), reacted strongly

---

[1] For a full account of Bernardino González and the *Colegio trilingüe, cf.* Miguel Asín Palacios, "El 'intérprete arábigo' de Fray Bernardino González," *B.R.A.H.*, 1901, vol. 38, fasc. I, pp. 267-279.

[2] Ángel González Palencia has shown that contrary to the commonly held opinion that the Renaissance did away with medieval learning, the inventory of any good sixteenth-century library discloses a profusion of Arab authors in Latin translations printed during that century and even in the fifteenth. *Cf.* A.G.P., *El islam y occidente,* Madrid, 1945, p. 86.

against Islamic learning and consciously limited its scope to the study of classical Antiquity, attempting to discover in Greece and Rome the true origins of European culture.[1]

It was not until the eighteenth century that the knowledge of Arabic hitherto monopolized by religious Orders began to transcend the strictly religious and political fields. This was so because it was stimulated by a new policy towards Islam: the latter had ceased to be a political menace to Europe and particularly to Spain. As a result, religion and politics ceased to be the primary purpose of the Orientalist and he turned to wider interests.

The works of Bernardino González remained unpublished, but the Franciscan tradition was carried forward with the books of Francisco Cañes who settled in Damascus at the Spanish Franciscan College in 1757. He remained in the East for sixteen years and then, back in Spain, he published an Arabic grammar which appeared in 1775.[2] It was intended for the use of missionaries in the Holy Land, and in this respect the book follows in the path laid out by tradition. Yet the influence of the Enlightenment was noticeable because to the purely religious purpose of his work Cañes adds others of a philological nature, claiming that the study of Arabic was indispensable for a clearer knowledge of the origin of many Spanish words.[3] Furthermore he realizes the full significance of Arabic for the study of Semitic philology and the elucidation of obscure Hebrew words of importance in Biblical exegesis,[4] and even admits the validity of Arabic studies in non-religious fields such as poetry.[5]

This recognition was a step forward in the development of Franciscan Arabism, and Cañes was to follow it up twelve years

---

[1] *Cf.* Gustave Dugat, *Histoire des orientalistes de l'Europe du XIIème au XIXème siècle*, Paris, 1868.

[2] *Gramática arábigo-española, vulgar, y literal con un diccionario arábigo-español, en que se ponen las voces más usuales para una conversación familiar, con un Texto de la Doctrina Cristiana en el idioma arábigo*, Madrid, 1775.

[3] "Our Romance borrowed so many words, phrases, and accents from Arabic, that without knowing the Arabic language it is impossible in many cases to understand the meaning of a large number of the very words which we commonly use in speaking . . .," *op. cit.*, Prologue "Al lector", n. p.

[4] "If the Arabic language may be learned without knowing Hebrew, a perfect understanding of Hebrew can never be attained without first or simultaneously knowing the Arabic language . . ." *Op. cit.*, *loc. cit.*, n. p.

[5] "Laymen, who study other subjects in other classrooms, will be able to make use of this grammar also, though in it I have not dealt with Arabic prosody and poetry because this would have lengthened the work . . .," *op. cit.*, *loc. cit.*, n. p.

later by publishing a voluminous Spanish-Latin-Arabic dictionary.[1] But the main purpose of the work remained religious, for in the dedication to Charles III the author establishes a close connection between missionary work in Arab lands and the official foreign policy of Spain, showing how they both worked together with the aim of furthering Spanish interests in Arab lands.

Cañes' dictionary appeared with a long prologue by Campomanes which deals with the history of the Arabs and the importance of the Arabic language to those who desired to study Spanish linguistics. The prologue reveals a more than cursory acquaintance with Arabic on the part of its distinguished author. In it, the latter informs his readers that he had once studied the Spanish section of al-Idrīsī's *Geography* which he had translated and annotated himself.[2] Because of his political activities Campomanes' Arabism was a private pastime, but he translated excerpts from Arab authors on several occasions, and maintained a life-long interest in the field.

The dictionary of Francisco Cañes was luxuriously printed with Arabic type acquired by the Royal Library. Its main purpose remained that of teaching Arabic to missionaries and therefore it was a Spanish-Latin-Arabic dictionary. Because it has no Arabic-Spanish entries it is not directly useful to non-Spanish Orientalists today. Nevertheless, it contains entries in Spanish for each of which many Arabic synonyms are recorded. These delicate shades of meaning are of great value to Spanish Arabists, and because of this, scholars in Madrid are presently engaged in reversing Cañes' work in order to produce a modern Arabic-Spanish dictionary based upon it.

Spain, it has been said, is the only European nation in which the eighteenth century began exactly in 1700 with the installation of the Bourbon dynasty on the throne of Madrid. Its policy, favorable to progress in many areas and aspiring to restore the fortunes of a nation exhausted by religious wars, reached its peak during the

---

[1] *Diccionario español-latino-arábigo en que siguiendo el diccionario abreviado de la Academia se ponen las correspondencias latinas y árabes, para facilitar el estudio de la lengua arábiga a los misioneros, y a los que viajaren o contratan en África y Levante,* Madrid, 1787.

[2] "In Spain one must refer to Arab geographers in order to advance in [the study of] the origin of nations, in which conclusion I have been confirmed by attentively reading Sherif Eldrisi called the Nubiensis, translating him from the Arabic text and annotating his references to Spain." *Op. cit.*, p. xxxix, n. 35.

reign of Charles III (1759-1788) who, while he initiated the revolutionary foreign policy towards Islam which has been outlined, also surrounded himself with able and intelligent leaders such as Campomanes and others who were favorable to Arabic studies.

A little known writer of the age was Don Faustino de Borbón, born in Madrid in 1755 and reputed to be the illegitimate son of Don Gabriel, brother of Charles III. Don Faustino was an Orientalist, and according to Gayangos, "seems to have passed most of his life in the Escurial Library with a view to the illustration of the history of his native country during its occupation by the Moslems, but whose works are little known, and, from circumstances not easily explained, have become exceedingly scarce. His *Cartas para ilustrar la historia de* [*la*] *España* [*árabe*]—the only production of his pen which I have been able to obtain,—were printed at Madrid in 1796, in monthly parts. They relate to a period of Spanish history which is, of all others, the most important, namely, from the insurrection in the mountains of the Asturias to the death of Pelayo in 727. The author has shown vast erudition and learning in the historical antiquities of his country, and occasionally displayed great sagacity in the unravelling of the historical difficulties in which he found himself entangled at every step; but he was evidently no critic, and, while defending with great ardour untenable historical points, he often indulged unnecessarily in the wildest speculations." [1]

Gayangos' estimate is unfortunately all too accurate: for example, Faustino de Borbón, knowing that the original Muslim army that invaded and conquered Spain in A.D. 711 had contained relatively few Arabs, jumped to the erroneous conclusion that the majority of the soldiers in that army were North African Jews who then established a Judæo-Islamic state in Spain. In fact, it is well known today that those forces were composed mainly of Berbers; nevertheless, the author goes to great lengths to prove his thesis. In the process he demonstrates his agility of mind and great ability to reason as well as his little historical sensitivity. Faustino de Borbón's mistakes derive in a large part from his anti-clerical attitude to Spanish history. Since the Jews and Muslims had been the victims of Golden Age Spain, he wanted to show how glorious their achievements had been during the Middle Ages; he exaggerated, twisted

---

[1] Gayangos, *Mohammedan Dynasties*, vol. I, pp. ix-x.

historical truth around to fit his preconceptions and ended up with a version of medieval Spanish history from which the Christians were almost totally excluded—all with the best of intentions. Thus he was a failure as a historian, but deserves to be remembered in the development of Arabic studies as an example of the interest in Spain's Arab past that was increasing as the impulse to proselytize waned.

His book was a series of historical epistles in which he proposed to subject Arab history to a severe *criticism*. In fact, he uses the word *crítica* in the sense that had been made fashionable in Spain by Feyjóo; that is to say, his *Cartas* were *critical* of all accepted tradition and aspired to re-examine the past from an independent point of view, free from the trammels of dogma and superstition. His interest in history was itself a symptom of the age. Richard Herr, in his book on eighteenth-century Spain [1] has shown how historical curiosity had been growing so that as early as 1738 Philip V had founded the Royal Academy of History in order to satisfy the demand for more information about the past. After Feyjóo introduced a new critical spirit into the country, historians had begun to re-evaluate the Spanish past and to distinguish historical fact from legend. The *España sagrada* of the Augustinian friar Enrique Flórez begun in 1747 and the *Historia crítica de España y de la civilización española* (Madrid, 1784-1805) written in Italy by the exiled Catalonian Jesuit Francisco Masdeu were landmarks of Spanish scholarship. They attempted to base their conclusions on a vast array of documentary evidence rather than on legends and fables.

According to Herr, "gradually out of this interest in their country's past, enlightened Spanish thinkers developed an interpretation of their history which was peculiarly their own. According to this interpretation, the Spanish nation had been greatest in the Middle Ages. Its decline began in the sixteenth century after the death of the Catholic Monarchs, Fernando and Isabel. The cause for the fall was also supplied by the new view of history—in the Middle Ages Spain had enjoyed her proper form of government, her 'constitution;' in the sixteenth century this had been destroyed." [2]

This view of history, which determined to a large extent the

[1] *The Eighteenth-Century Revolution in Spain*, Princeton, N. J., 1958, chap. 12.

[2] *Op. cit.*, p. 341.

interest in Arabic studies displayed during the eighteenth century, further proposed that the Catholic Monarchs had made Spain prosper by upholding its medieval freedoms and democratic spirit which were later destroyed by the principle of royal absolutism. The latter tendency reached its zenith with Philip II who repressed the Morisco rebellion of the Alpujarra, and greatly enlarged the authority of the Inquisition (it should not be forgotten that he also founded Spain's greatest Arabic library).[1] It was therefore natural that the progressive historians of the Enlightenment should have looked with sympathy upon the study of the Moriscos, the Arabs, and the Jews; in a word, the victims of sixteenth-century repression,[2] and it was with this motivation that Faustino de Borbón took up the pen to write epistles more polemical than historical in nature.

But if his work was found wanting, the general interest in Spanish medieval history then prevailing made it appear more urgent every day that a more systematic approach was desirable in Arabic studies. In particular, a catalogue of the Arabic manuscripts in the Escorial Library was badly needed, and for the purpose of compiling such a work the Syrian Maronite, Miguel Casiri had already been invited to Spain. With the publication of his catalogue: *Bibliotheca Arabico-Hispana Escurialensis*, which appeared in two volumes between the years 1760-1770 in Madrid, the modern approach to Arabic studies in Spain finally came into its own. Casiri's work was not merely a listing of authors and titles, but also contained numerous excerpts from Hispano-Muslim authors in the original Arabic, accompanied by translations into Latin. This publication immediately opened up the Escorial holdings in the field of Arabic to all of Europe and as such was a long awaited and most valuable contribution to contemporary knowledge about Muslim Spain.

Thanks to the study devoted to Casiri by Michel Breydy [3] many facts are known about his life. He was born in Syria in 1710 and studied theology at the Maronite College in Rome. There he came

---

[1] *Op. cit.*, p. 343.

[2] "According to [Juan Pablo] Forner one must also study the expulsion of the Jews and Moriscos. He asked: Was the exile of four million Spaniards in whose hands lay the nation's commerce and agriculture just and necessary or senseless?" Herr, *op. cit.*, p. 344.

[3] *Michel Gharcieh al-Ghazīrī, orientaliste Libanais du XVIIIème siècle*, Beirut, 1950.

in contact with Don Felipe Ramírez, governor of Jaca who invited Casiri to visit Spain in order to work there as an Orientalist. Once in Spain, Casiri obtained a position at the Royal Library through Francisco Rávago, a Jesuit and former teacher of his who had become Ferdinand VI's confessor. Soon that monarch commissioned Casiri to begin the huge task of cataloguing the Arabic manuscripts of the Escorial. He set to work on this project in 1749, and the final volume of the finished catalogue appeared in 1770. He is also said to have translated several Arabic works; studied the inscriptions of the Alhambra, the Alcazar of Seville and the Mosque of Cordova, and to have done considerable work on linguistics and philology. He was, however, unable to publish these works, though one of them has recently been studied.[1] Casiri was deeply interested in historical and philological problems as may be inferred from the scattered remarks and etymologies to be found in his *Bibliotheca*; this constitutes one more indication of the fact that Arabic studies were beginning to be divorced from their earlier identification with the immediate goals of foreign policy.

Casiri's work gave eighteenth-century scholars, both in Spain and abroad, enough basic information to arouse their curiosity and give them an inkling of the importance of the culture of Muslim Spain. The reaction to it was enthusiastic, and Casiri came to be on familiar terms with Spain's most distinguished intellectuals such as Martín Sarmiento, the Benedictine author of the first history of Spanish literature entitled *Memorias para la historia de la poesía y poetas españoles*, (Madrid, 1775). Sarmiento was interested in, and had written about Arabic poetry using material translated by the English Orientalist Edward Pococke. In an early letter to Casiri he had encouragingly outlined a programme for developing Arabic studies in Spain:

"With half a dozen scholarly Maronites and another half a dozen scholars, either African or Eastern, whom the king could bring to Madrid and assign a decent salary to, and with the good fortune that twenty-four Spanish youths from different provinces should devote their efforts to studying the Arabic language and Eastern literature under the guidance of the abovementioned twelve

[1] *Cf.* P. Massad, "Casiri y uno de sus estudios inéditos," *BRAH*, 5, 144, 1959, pp. 15-47. A manuscript work of his on the etymology of Arabic loan-words in Spanish exists at the Instituto de Valencia de Don Juan in Madrid.

teachers; a most useful academy could be formed at this Court; one which would be the envy of foreigners." [1]

Casiri himself, in a letter to Charles III dated 1783 speaks of the praise showered upon him by scholars all over Europe in gratitude for his having revealed the treasures of the Escorial to them. Nor was this mere self-adulation. In England, Edward Gibbon cautiously had the following words for Casiri's work: "I am happy enough to possess a splendid and interesting work, which has only been distributed in presents by the court of Madrid: Bibliotheca Arabico-Hispana Escurialensis . . . The execution of this work does honor to the Spanish press; the Mss. to the number of MDCCCLI are judiciously classed by the editor, and his copious extracts throw *some* light on the Mahometan literature and history of Spain." [2]

In the section of the *Decline and Fall of the Roman Empire* devoted to the history of Spanish Islam, Gibbon draws extensively from the information made available by Casiri. Thus it was Casiri who became the decisive figure in the process whereby Arabic studies in Spain were secularized. He succeeded in forming a school of disciples such as Ignacio de Asso del Río, Spanish consul in Amsterdam, and José Antonio Banqueri, while the new spirit he infused into his profession soon began to affect the work produced by the religious Orders. This was the case of Cañes, whose dictionary was revised by Casiri to ensure greater accuracy. Other friars were also to work under his direction as will be seen.

With the Aragonese Ignacio de Asso del Río, the studies initiated by Casiri were cultivated by a layman for entirely non-political reasons, for this author evinced an interest in Arabic literature and the history of Muslim Spain. In 1782 he published a little volume in Amsterdam, entitled *Bibliotheca Arabico-Aragonensis*, "ut Aragoniae gloriam diligenter amplificaremus" [3] as he explains to the reader. The book is an anthology of Arabic texts, accompanied by elegant Latin translations, from authors who were of Aragonese extraction. Among the texts included in the collection are two of the *Maqāmāt Qurṭubiyya* or 'Cordovan Séances' of Abū Ṭāhir Muḥammad ibn Yūsuf at-Tamīmī of Saragossa, picaresque tales

---

[1] Letter dated June, 1749. Cf. Ibn al-ʿAwwām, *Libro de agricultura*, trans. by J. A. Banqueri, Madrid, 1802, vol. I, p. 23.

[2] *The Decline and Fall of the Roman Empire*, ed. by J. B. Bury, London, 1911, vol. 5, chap. 51, p. 516, n. 227.

[3] *Bibliotheca Arabico-Aragonensis, ed. cit.*, p. 5.

written in imitation of those of al-Ḥarīrī of Basra; several historical and poetical fragments from the court of al-Muʿtaṣim ibn Ṣumādiḥ of Almería who descended from the Aragonese line of the Banū Tujīb, and some documents referring to the philosopher Avempace who flourished in Saragossa during the age of *Taifas*.

The regional preference shown by the author in his selection is a reflexion of the growing feeling of national—and even regional—pride which developed during the eighteenth century as a defense mechanism against the cultural invasion of France. This theme will appear repeatedly in the works of the Spanish Arabists of that century.

As for José Antonio Banqueri, he was a Franciscan who in 1808 published his major work, an edition and Spanish translation of the *Kitāb al-Filāḥa* or 'Book of Agriculture' written by Abū Zakarīya Yaḥya ibn al-ʿAwwām, a twelfth-century Sevillian botanist.[1] Banqueri was to become a member of the Academy of History.[2] In 1776 he was sent to Madrid by his Order to study Arabic with Casiri, whose competence in the subject had been recognized as unrivalled in Spain. He was appointed to work as a translator at the Royal Library and in a letter to a patron, Don José Antonio de Armona, dated 1781 he discusses this forthcoming edition of Ibn al-ʿAwwām, stressing the importance of this Arab author as a source for learning about new agricultural methods which could be applied in Spain.[3] This idea was firmly fixed in his mind, as it was in that of many progressive Spaniards who were anxious to improve the state of agriculture in their country. Agricultural reform had in fact been one of Charles III's primary targets, and Campomanes was the guiding light of those organizations peculiar to the age known as societies of *Amigos del País*, founded to improve agricultural and industrial production.[4] When

---

[1] Ibn al-ʿAwwām, *Libro de Agricultura*, trans. and ed. by J. A. Banqueri, Madrid, 1802, 2. vols.

[2] Where an unpublished manuscript of his may be consulted: *Discurso sobre la arbitrariedad de la mayor parte de etimologías de nombres arábigos de pueblos*, vol. 10, fol. 2 of Academy Discourses.

[3] "There is no doubt that if [the translation] were to be made, apart from divulging in this way the literary value of this Arab compatriot of ours, farmers would be able to gain from the translated work some special or even unusual enlightenment, unknown in our times, in order to cultivate the soil more effectively." *Cf.* Jerónimo Rubio, "Una carta de Banqueri," *And.*, vol. 18, 1953, pp. 218-223.

[4] *Cf.* Richard Herr, *op. cit.* p. 262.

Banqueri's book finally appeared in 1802, the author, in his dedication to the King, again stressed its significance in the field of agriculture, intimating that Spain had been economically more prosperous in the Arab period because the Arabs had taken great pains to cultivate the soil.[1] From this it appears that eighteenth-century intellectuals looked back on the Arab period of Spain's history as an age of economic prosperity from which the country had later declined. This was part of the general idea that the Spain of the Middle Ages had been superior to that of the Renaissance. At the same time, the French cultural supremacy introduced by the Bourbons came as a shock to many Spaniards, and though they were eager to imitate French and also English culture—often sincerely so—they also strove to rework their own national tradition in order to put it on a level of equality with the rest of Europe. In this sense, though the Spanish eighteenth century nourished itself on foreign ideas, it cannot be claimed that it produced nothing but a servile imitation of Europe, for the reverse side of imitation, in the best cases, was always a true reworking of the national tradition according to the newly imported ideology. Hence a feeling of nationalism prevails in eighteenth-century Spain and it manifests itself in many unsuspected ways. For example, in the sixteenth and seventeenth centuries, bullfighting had been an aristocratic sport restricted to an élite, but in the eighteenth century it was popularized and converted into the mass spectacle we are familiar with today, and which was immortalized by Goya. This was one of the many ways in which Spaniards resisted the French cultural invasion, namely by exaggerating, stressing, and popularizing their own peculiar features, social types, diversions, etc. The Spanish thinker was torn between his desire to emulate a successful foreign culture and his sentimental attachment to his own traditional values. The latter could only be salvaged, in the process of Europeanization, by being infused with a new dignity which would coincide with the ideals of the Enlightenment. Hence the sympathy for the Arab period of Spanish history which is so often encountered during the

[1] "This [agricultural methods] is what Abu Zacaria Ebn el Awam, the Sevillian, declares in the most succinct manner in his *Book of Agriculture* which I am pleased to present to Your Majesty, and the reading of which will divulge much useful enlightenment throughout the kingdom, whereby to improve agriculture in many areas, and to restore the abundance which was enjoyed by the Spanish Arabs, and to which the soil of the Peninsula is so favourable." Ibn al-ʿAwwām, *ibid.*, *Prólogo*, n. p.

age, for the Arabs were felt to be a part of the national heritage; a glorious part which could be compared advantageously with the medieval history of the rest of Europe.

For this reason the Benedictine Martín Sarmiento, who read English authors with ease, had declared:

"I would prefer the Ms. codex in 4° of Ibn al-ʿAwwām of Seville to be translated into Castilian; for it contains a complete course on Spanish agriculture. Furthermore it is very true that Andalusian agriculture is more easily adapted to Castile than English agriculture." [1]

It is natural to expect that Campomanes should have shown interest in this publication, and in fact he wrote a prologue to it, in which he informs his readers that with the supervision of Casiri, he had himself attempted a translation of the *Kitāb al-Filāḥa,* of which he had published two chapters in 1751.[2] Campomanes adds further that one of the main values of the book lay in the fact that it dealt specifically with the agriculture of Andalusia, since its author was a Sevillian, whereas other books written about Spanish agriculture, (such as that of Alonso de Herrera composed during the Renaissance and which relies on Arab authors of al-Andalus, such as Ibn Wāfid [3]), were more concerned with the conditions and problems encountered in northern Spain.[4]

---

[1] *Op. cit.*, p. 14.

[2] "The credit of the present treatise made it desirable in our language during the reign of our lord Fernando VI, of august memory, chapters seventeen and nineteen having been published in the year 1751 translated into Spanish; that is, the first and third chapters of the second part, along with notes and a prologue in which the usefulness of this work is recommended as well as the advantage to be gained by the nation from its total translation and publication.

At that time I composed this prologue, notes, and Spanish version, and since that day it has been my opinion that the treatise of Ebn el Awam is not only useful, but also absolutely necessary to the improvement of agriculture and cattle-raising in Spain." *Op. cit.*, p. [2].

[3] *Cf.* Millás Vallicrosa, "La ciencia geopónica entre los autores hispanoárabes; conferencia pronunciada el dia 5 de marzo de 1953 en el Club Edafos", Madrid, 1954.

[4] "One misses in Herrera the cultivation of certain fruits and plants that abound in the southern provinces of the kingdom and do not prevail in the centre of Spain, such as rice, cotton, *garrofal* cherries and carobs, etc.

From this may be inferred the singular preference for the agriculture of Ebn el Awam, and the advantages that the nation could derive from its publication in our language with the Arabic text and with notes to illustrate and correct it.

". . . In order that the farmers of the Peninsula, especially those of the

Banqueri's edition, although it is not entirely accurate, has been very valuable to modern scholars. Millás Vallicrosa has pursued the subject and published other treatises on agriculture written by Hispano-Arabic authors, while S. M. Imamuddin calls Ibn al-ʿAwwām "the greatest Spanish Muslim botanist . . . the author of the most important encyclopaedic work on agriculture" and relies heavily on him for data about Hispano-Arabic economic conditions in his recent book on that subject.[1] Thus with the work of the Franciscan Banqueri the new, enlightened approach to scholarship won a total victory within the order and superceded the old type of missionary and political activity.

This was also the case of the Hieronymite friar Patricio José de la Torre [2] who carried on the studies begun by Casiri. Born in La Mancha, José de la Torre became a Hieronymite in 1776, and after studying at the Escorial College, he went to Madrid to learn Arabic. In 1797, Jovellanos, then minister, procured a royal scholarship for him to study the Moroccan dialect of Tangier. Then in 1800 he accompanied a Spanish mission to Fez and after returning to Spain three years later, he was admitted to the Academy of History. He was therefore protected by such important intellectuals as Jovellanos and actively engaged in Spain's Moroccan diplomacy. His works, all of which have remained in manuscript, have been studied by Sánchez Pérez and deal with history, philology, folklore and lexicography.[3] The most important is a re-edition of Pedro de Alcalá's dictionary in a 559 page manuscript in the prologue to which the author explains the circumstances under which he was sent to North Africa as well as the purpose, which was to transcribe Alcalá's dictionary into Arabic characters.[4] Dozy later used excerpts from

southern provinces and adjacent islands may [by means of this work] improve their crops and restore them to the flourishing state they were in during the time of the Moors, to which should be attributed, as Don Miguel Casiri thinks, the numerous population of the provinces they occupied in Spain." Ibn al-ʿAwwām, *ibid.*, pp. [3], [4].

[1] *Cf.* S. M. Imamuddin, *Some Aspects of the Socio-Economic and Cultural History of Muslim Spain, 711-1492 A.D.*, Leiden, 1965, p. 161.

[2] For a full account of his work, *cf.* José A. Sánchez Pérez, "Un arabista español del siglo XVIII, Fray Patricio José de la Torre", *And.*, 18, 1953, pp. 450-455.

[3] They are: a) *Noticias históricas de Fez.* b) *Itinerario desde Tánger hasta la corte de Mequínez.* c) *Relación de las puertas de Granada.* d) *Refranes y adagios árabes.* e) *Gramática arábigo-castellana.* f) A re-edition of Pedro de Alcalá's dictionary.

[4] He adds: "To this commission were attached, for the same purpose of

José de la Torre's work in preparing his own *Supplément*, as he himself states in his prologue to that work.[1] The publication of José de la Torre's book was almost finished when all the copies but one were destroyed during Napoleon's invasion of Spain. This was most unfortunate because the chief merit of the work lies in the transcription undertaken by him which, had it been published, would have provided scholars with an excellent dictionary of the spoken Arabic of Granada which differs considerably from classical Arabic. Though Dozy later did exactly that in his *Supplément*, José de la Torre deserves to be remembered as a pioneer in the field.

In order to present a more complete picture of the impact of Casiri's school on the Spanish cultural circles of the age it will be necessary to make a digression to Italy where the next stage of this development occurred.

With the gradual spread of Italian Renaissance poetry throughout Europe, scholars of all nations, and especially those of Italy, began to reflect on the origin of poetry in the Romance languages. As early as 1581, a scholar of Modena named Giammaria Barbieri, had written a treatise entitled *Dell' origine della poesia rimata*.[2] In it the author observed that both Latin and Greek poetry were based upon a *quantitative* system of prosody, while the use of *rhyme* was unknown to classical Antiquity. Therefore, he reasoned, the rhyme and prosodic system based on *stress* which appeared in Provenzal poetry could only derive from a non-classical source. He then pointed to Arabic poetry which according to him possessed both

studying colloquial Arabic, Messrs. Don Manuel Bacas Merino and Don Juan de Arze y Morir, persons of talent and in whom the qualities necessary for this task existed. Of the capability of these two, and of the instruction they acquired thanks to their incessant diligence and work, I have informed one who can be attentive to their merit, encouraging these young men, for the honour and usefulness of the nation, from which it has come about that His Royal Highness has associated them to the Royal Academy of History, under the orders of which they may be of use to the nation in this branch of literature." *Cf.* Sánchez Pérez, *op. cit.*, p. 453.

[1] "D'après M. Simonet, qui l'a examiné, Patricio de la Torre a transcrit l'arabe en caractères arabes; mais il a fait de grands changements au texte d'Alcalá et supprimé beaucoup de mots. À en juger par les extraits que le savant professeur de Grenade a bien voulu me communiquer, la Torre a transcrit correctement quelques mots douteux, pas tous cependant, et je dois avouer que pour le dialecte grenadin de 1500, quand il s'écarte du dialecte marocain moderne, que la Torre connaissait sans doute fort bien, il ne m'inspire pas une confiance bien grande." Dozy, *Supplément*, vol. I, p. xi.

[2] Published by G. Tiraboschi, Modena, 1790.

rhyme and stress. Barbieri further maintained that these two elements had been brought to Provence from Spain, where the Mozarabs had developed a Romance lyrical poetry based upon Arabic prosody. Barbieri was not himself an Arabist, and his information was second-hand. Therefore he made several technical mistakes. (i.e., classical Arabic poetry is based on *quantity*, though *stress* does appear in popular poetry—which he did not know. Furthermore, in late Latin poetry, such as that of St. Augustine, stress does occur, as well as a rudimentary form of rhyme.) His thesis, however, was of extreme importance because for the first time it pointed to the close coexistence and cultural interplay between Muslims and Christians in medieval Spain. Furthermore, the recent discovery of *popular* Arabic poems such as the *muwashshaḥa* and the *zajal*, containing words and even phrases in the Mozarabic dialect has in part confirmed the truth of his suppositions.

Barbieri's treatise remained unpublished until the eighteenth century when the appearance of Casiri's *Bibliotheca* aroused new interest in the Arab antiquites of Spain. During the reign of Charles III, when the Jesuit order was expelled from all the Spanish dominions, many of these exiles left their homeland to settle in Italy, where they came in contact with the Italian intellectual circles of the Enlightenment.

One of the numerous exiled Jesuits was Juan Andrés who became the librarian of the King of Naples [1] and published in Italian and between the years 1782-1799 a monumental work entitled *Dell' origine, de' progressi e dello stato attuale d'ogni letteratura*. Ambitious in its scope, the book was one of the first attempts in Europe to write about comparative literature on a grand scale. It is a broad history of world literature, and in it Andrés devotes much attention to the question of Arabic influences on Spain and indeed, on all of European culture.

In the chapter on Arabic literature he uses the work of the well known Arabists of his time as source material. But when he comes to the subject of Hispano-Arabic literature he relies almost entirely on Casiri, and devotes more attention to Spain than to the Middle East. He claims that it was in al-Andalus that Arab science and literature bore their most splendid fruits, for Andrés, like many of

---

[1] *Cf.* Ángel Valbuena Prat, *Historia de la literatura española*, 6th ed., Barcelona, 1960, vol. 3, pp. 74-75.

the Jesuits in exile was on the defensive with regard to Europe, and was arguing, in Italy, for the cultural greatness of medieval Spain.

Praising the achievements of Arab science in Cordova, Andrés discusses the European scholars from many different nations who travelled to Muslim Spain to learn Arab science. He dwells at length on the importance of Alfonso X and his school of translators; on Roger Bacon and his enthusiasm for Arab philosophy, and on many other glories of medieval Islam. Then, after this long preamble, Juan Andrés asks himself in what measure the Arabs could have contributed to the development of European literature. He proceeds with caution, expressing his bewilderment at finding no record of Europeans who travelled to Cordova to learn Arabic poetry and rhetoric as others did to study mathematics, medicine and astronomy.

And yet, all the other cultural borrowings lead Andrés to suspect that imitation must also have occured in literature. To support his hypothesis he reviews the origins of modern Romance literatures. In the Low Middle Ages, he claims, Latin was used in all forms of writing, but in the areas of Europe more closely connected with the Arabs (Spain, Provence, and Sicily) vernacular poetry made its appearance for the first time. In Spain there were two vernaculars: Arabic and Romance. The Christians in the North, occupied as they were with the *Reconquista,* had little time to compose lyrical poetry, either in Latin or in Romance, but the Mozarabs, living in peace and sharing the rich cultural life of the Arabs, imitated the poetry of the latter which was lyrical as well as being in the vernacular. Juan Andrés concludes that songs in Mozarabic must have existed at such a remote period, and to support his hypothesis he mentions that many Spanish musical instruments bear Arabic names. In matters of music, furthermore, Andrés was well informed, for he was in touch with Casiri's school in Spain, and had used Banqueri's translation of a musical treatise by al-Fārābī.[1] Andrés goes on to claim that rhyme was an invention of the Arabs, basing himself on European Arabists of his age. He knew well that in

[1] "Don Miguel Casiri managed to direct me in the study of the Arabic language, and he trained me in the reading and handling of certain manuscripts, among them, that of Alfarabi dealing with music, a fragment of which, belonging to the Royal Library at the Escorial, he entrusted me with extracting along with composing a Spanish translation requested by Señor Abate Andrés, then resident of Italy . . .," says Banqueri. *Cf.* Ibn al-ʿAwwām, *ibid.*, p. 12.

medieval Latin poetry rhyme had existed long before the Arabs reached Spain, especially in inscriptions and epitaphs, but he humorously declares that it is difficult to imagine that a Provenzal poet such as Guillaume de Poitiers should have studied the clumsy rhyme of Latin epitaphs to compose his more scandalous verses.

It is astonishing to observe how, by sheer intuition, Andrés was able to create a thesis that has occupied scholars ever since. Much of what he claimed has been proven true as more documentation on the origins of Romance poetry has been made available by Ribera, Stern and García Gómez. Though he made a few mistaken assumptions, Juan Andrés showed a keen insight into historical and cultural matters, while the evidence thus far uncovered indicates that he was not entirely wrong in his conclusions.

In spite of this, another Spanish Jesuit, the musicologist Esteban de Arteaga—who apart from his many other accomplishments, also knew Arabic—in his work *Rivoluzioni del Teatro Musicale Italiano* [1] denied the conclusions of Andrés. His opposition to the ideas of the latter touched off a battle of the books in which passion took the lead so that many insulting remarks were exchanged, yet this debate shows the extent to which the work of Casiri had become familiar to Spanish intellectuals.

During this time, the Italian historian Tiraboschi had published between the years 1782-1798 his *Storia della letteratura Italiana.*[2] While he was engaged in its composition he found time in 1790 to publish the manuscript treatise of Barbieri along with an introduction by himself, in which he sided with those in favour of the Arabic thesis, against Arteaga. Nevertheless, the repeated and increasingly violent attacks of Arteaga caused him to moderate his ideas, so that in the later volumes of his *Storia* where he discusses Italian poetry and its origin, Tiraboschi adopts a more cautious attitude towards the problem. He admits that any nation—not necessarily the Arabs—could have invented rhyme, and his new position betrays an insecurity brought about by the insufficiency of his documentary evidence on the subject. Following in his footsteps came another Italian, Saverio Bettinelli, who in 1786 had published the *Risorgimento d' Italia negli Studi, nelle Arti, e ne' Costumi dopo il Mille.*[3] The book is a general history of Italian culture,

[1] Bologna, 2 vols., 1783.
[2] Rome, 10 vols., 1782-1798.
[3] Venice, 1786.

and in the chapter on poetry he discusses the decadence of Latin as a lyrical medium and the appearance of a vernacular love poetry which, he cautiously suggests, could have resulted from the influence of Arabic prosody.

In the same group of Spanish expatriates in Italy was the Catalan Jesuit Javier Llampillas who with others of his Order were refuting the generally adverse opinion of Spanish culture held by precisely such Italian historians as Tiraboschi, Bettinelli, Muratori and others. Between 1778-1781 Llampillas published his curious work in defense of Spanish culture to which he gave the somewhat cumbersome title of *Ensayo histórico-apologético de la literatura española contra las opiniones preocupadas de algunos escritores modernos italianos.*[1] In it he affirms most emphatically that the Arabs in Spain had transmitted their poetry to Castile, from whence it was diffused into Catalonia, Provence and eventually into Italy. To a large extent, he bases his claims on Casiri's *Bibliotheca.*

Eventually, in 1791 Arteaga published a scathing reply to Tiraboschi, Andrés and the partisans of the Arabic thesis, entitled *Della Influenza degli Arabi sull' Origine della Poesia Moderna in Europa.*[2] In it he makes an extensive survey of classical Arabic prosody from an extremely technical viewpoint, and being the only Arabist in the group, he indicates that just as Latin and Greek poetry, that in Arabic is based on *quantity,* not on *stress.* Consequently, he argues, Arabic prosody could not have given rise to the accented verse of Romance poetry. Furthermore he shows that *rhyme* had appeared in medieval Latin poetry before the Arab conquest of Spain. With these arguments, based on his more complete information about classical Arabic prosody he set about demolishing the arguments of his opponents. However, though he knew more classical Arabic than they, his ignorance of *popular* poetry in that language, which not only is based on stress but also contains the same types of rhymes and even rhyme schemes found in Romance poetry, makes his argument today less valid than the less technical though more intuitively historical ideas of Barbieri, Juan Andrés and their Italian partisans.

In this way Spanish Arabism began a polemic about the origins

---

[1] For an account of Llampillas, *cf.* Valbuena, *Historia, vol. cit.,* p. 75. His *Ensayo,* originally written in Italian was translated into Spanish. (2nd ed., Madrid, 1789) by Doña Josefa Amar y Borbón.

[2] Rome, 1791.

of Romance lyrical poetry that has continued down to the present. It was also involved in that other polemic concerning Spanish cultural values which took place in Italy. It crossed the Spanish border and for the first time focused attention on Arab Spain as an essential element in the development of medieval European culture. A discipline that had originated in the work done by Franciscan missions in the Arab world coincided with an expansionist foreign policy that aspired to carve out zones of influence in the Islamic Mediterranean. Because all this occured during the Enlightenment, a gradual shift took place in Arabic studies. Beginning as an ancilla to missionary work they were finally broadened to deal with historical problems of wider significance. These Arabic studies conducted in Spain in turn had an immediate impact on the intellectuals of the country and were ultimately extended to encompass cultural problems of significance to all of Europe, thus arousing the interest of Gibbon and Tiraboschi.

Furthermore, being closely protected by the Bourbon régime, Spanish Arabism found itself in alliance with the progressive forces in the nation which were striving to renovate Spanish life. Because intellectual Spaniards of the Enlightenment were all more or less concerned by the problem of how to assimilate European culture without losing sight of their own heritage, they looked upon Arabism with favour, as a discipline which could help them to recover and even re-activate a part of the nation's medieval history to which they could point with pride. Hence Campomanes and Sarmiento, who had read Quesnai and Adam Smith preferred Ibn al-ʿAwwām's treatise on agriculture to contemporary English and French works in that field, for their ultimate aspiration was to revitalize a forgotten national heritage.

The Arabists, as well as most Spanish thinkers of that age, could be fitted into three main groups: a) those who were motivated by a missionary zeal such as the Franciscans; b) those who were eager to imitate European methods, but did so in such a radical and exaggerated manner that they invalidated their own efforts. This was the case of Don Faustino de Borbón; c) those who sought to adapt European standards to the realities of Spain, while at the same time trying to raise Spanish culture to the level of that in the rest of Europe and thus renew it. This was the case of Casiri's school, which as a group, finally prevailed and exerted its influence on the others, while infusing Arabic studies with a feeling for history which they had lacked before.

Spain now had dictionaries, grammars, and above all, competently trained scholars with whom to confront problems in Arabic studies of a broader scope. The interests of the age had for a long time demanded that a general history of Muslim Spain be written, and this is what Conde was to do in the early years of the following century under a new and different set of circumstances.

PART TWO

THE STUDY OF POLITICAL HISTORY

CHAPTER TWO

The invasion of Spain by the troops of Napoleon at the turn of the century unleashed a war of national resistance. It also caused the loss of the major part of Spain's American colonies. This added economic chaos to the current political problems of the nation and intensified a split between liberals and conservatives that three civil wars have been unable to heal.

The old absolutist state collapsed totally and when in 1813 the army of occupation left Spain and returned to France, about ten thousand of their Spanish collaborators were forced to flee with them, among this group being many outstanding professionals, scientists and men of letters. These men, the cream of the intellectuals of Spain, known as *afrancesados* were followed a year later by a number of patriots and liberals banished by the restored monarch Ferdinand VII who, after returning to Spain had imposed a narrow form of absolutism on his country. He abolished the liberal constitution of Cádiz of 1812, and because of his unenlightened brand of despotism, he soon found himself not only with a nation in ruins, but also deprived of the very men who could have been most capable of undertaking its reconstruction. The country was in dire economic straits as a result of the colonial losses it had sustained. Thus the background of Spain's nineteenth-century problems has been summed up in the following way: "If Spain had recovered rapidly from the ravages of war, the domestic bitterness might have been soothed with time. But Spain's eighteenth-century economic revival had been based on colonial trade: and, abetted by interested persons in England and the United States, the Spanish colonists had been led by the absence of legitimate government in Spain after 1808 to take hesitant but irrevocable steps toward independence. No balm of prosperity came to heal the scission in Spanish society. Instead the scission between progressive-anticlerical and Catholic-conservative Spaniards—the 'two Spains' of recent history—has remained the fundamental problem of Spain." [1]

During the war, the position of the *afrancesados* was that "resistance was not a matter of patriotic feeling but of calculation,

[1] Richard Herr, *The Eighteenth-Century Revolution in Spain*, Princeton, 1958, p. 443.

of patriotic responsibility. No one had a duty to plunge his country into a hopeless struggle which would, moreover, involve a dangerous appeal to the people against the only legal government that existed... The core of the *afrancesado* position was that collaboration, not resistance, was the best way to protect national independence: allegiance to Joseph at least saved Spain from direct military rule from Paris and the division of the kingdom by right of conquest." [1]

In contrast, the position of conservative Spain was that "the 'nerve' of the national defence was constituted by the 'popular masses' and the clergy who hated both *afrancesados* and liberals. Thus patriot liberalism and the treason of the *afrancesados* were involved in a common anathema. This conjunction misses an essential distinction. The liberals were democrats, while the *afrancesados* believed in reform from above. Liberalism meant the sovereignty of the nation, not merely a Spain divided into 'rational' provinces and rid of Inquisition and monks." [2]

Thus the *afrancesado* movement looked to the past; to enlightened despotism of the kind represented by Charles III, and yet it was progressive in the face of reaction, though not sufficiently so to succeed politically. Against this background, the drama of early nineteenth-century Arabism was enacted. One of the *afrancesados* who fled for his life with the Napoleonic troops was the Arabist José Antonio Conde, the importance of whose work was to be incalculable.

Born in 1765, he studied at Salamanca and was associated with the University of Alcalá.[3] While young he devoted himself to Arabic studies, and his position as director of the Escorial library, gave him the chance to become familiar with original sources bearing on Hispano-Arabic history. In this way he was enabled to collect materials for his most important work: *Historia de la dominación de los árabes en España* which appeared posthumously in Madrid during the years 1820-21. The work had the pioneering merit of presenting for the first time a complete version of the history of Islamic Spain and it fired the imagination of its contemporaries.

During the French occupation Conde had been appointed to direct the Royal Library of Madrid, but in 1813 he escaped to

---

[1] Raymond Carr, *Spain* 1808-1939, Oxford, 1966, p. 112.

[2] *Op. cit.*, p. 115.

[3] For a biography of Conde, *cf. Enciclopedia Espasa, s.v. Conde, J. A.*, vol. 14 A., pp. 1050-51.

Paris at the time of the evacuation.[1] There he spent several years arranging the materials for his history. He returned to Madrid in 1819 to put the finishing touches on his work, but was persecuted and oppressed owing to his political position, to the extent that even the consultation of Arabic manuscripts in the Escorial was refused to him. His health was seriously affected and he died in 1820 in official disrepute, though Moratín, Ticknor and others among his friends paid the expenses of his funeral, and Moratín composed an elegy on his death in which he sums up his role as a historian:

Desde que el cielo airado	From the moment that wrathful heaven
Llevó a Jerez su saña,	Took its anger to Jerez,
Y al suelo derribado	And the power of Spain
Cayó el poder de España,	Fell crushed to the ground,
Subiendo al trono gótico	When the children of Ishmael
La prole de Ismael;	Ascended the Gothic throne;
Hasta que rotas fueron	Until the last chains
Las últimas cadenas,	Were broken
Y tremoladas vieron	And the newly conquered Arabs
De Alhambra en las almenas	Saw the crosses of Isabella
Los ya vencidos árabes	Displayed
Las cruces de Isabel,	On the battlements of the Alhambra,
A tí fue concedido	It was granted to you
Eternizar la gloria	To eternalize the glory
De los que ha distinguido	Of those distinguished
La paz o la victoria,	By peace or victory,
En dilatadas épocas	In long ages
Que el mundo vio pasar.	The world has seen go by.
Y a tí, de dos naciones,	And to you was it granted
Ilustres enemigos	To tell of the glories,
Referir los blasones,	Deeds and travails
Hazañas y fatigas,	Of two nations
Y de candor histórico	That were noble enemies,
Dignos ejemplos dar.[2]	And to give worthy examples
	Of historical candour.

Conde's work served as a beginning to the study of a part of history then almost unknown in Europe, if the extracts from Arabic manuscripts made by Casiri are excepted, for though the latter

[1] He had already figured in the list of those who followed Joseph Bonaparte's government when it fled to Vitoria after the battle of Bailén (1808). Cf. Miguel Artola, *Los afrancesados*, Madrid, 1953, p. 110, n. 55, where he is mentioned as "D. José Conde, bibliotecario del rey."

[2] Leandro Fernández de Moratín, *La derrota de los pedantes y poesías*, ed. Louis Machaud, Paris, 19(—), pp. 244-5.

were invaluable in their time, they may hardly be considered to present a coherent and organic picture of Islamic Spain. Conde's history, extending from the Arab invasion of Spain in 711 to the expulsion of the latter in 1492 set up a basic framework which has been accepted by scholars ever since, for the author subdivided the period into historical ages that have remained essentially unchanged down to the present, while at the same time, his ambitious work is the only one which covers the complete period of Arab rule in Spain.

In his prologue to the *Historia*, Conde indicates clearly his sympathy with, and desire to revindicate Spanish Muslim culture before the eyes of his European contemporaries. He was not so generous in his attitude towards the Arabs of his own time, for he says: "after the expulsion of the Arabs from Spain, their literature constantly degenerated; nay, it has continued to do so, until they have at length arrived at the deplorable ignorance into which they are now sunk, not those of Africa only, but of the Orient also."[1] The ideas of eighteenth-century Scottish philosophers had created the belief in North America that the white *farmer* was civilized and superior to the American Indian because the latter was declared to be a *hunter* and therefore a savage.[2] Throughout eighteenth-century Spain the traditional Spanish enmity against Islam had been expressed in similar terms and travellers to Morocco had discussed the "barbarism" of the African Bedouins, and had likewise tried to relate it to economic factors. In this respect Conde was a product of the eighteenth century, as also in the fact that he believed that the Middle Ages in Spain had been superior to the so-called Golden Age. As an Arabist he joined these two ideas to produce his belief that the medieval Arabs had been superior to those of his own time, and in this respect he represents a continuation of the Hispanic "arabophilism" of Juan Andrés. Indeed, Conde is as much a product of the eighteenth century as a forerunner of that later Romantic enthusiasm for the Moors of Granada which his work was destined to nourish to no small extent.

In pleading his cause, he argues that although in history the fate of the vanquished has usually been that their story is told by the winning side, just criticism can be satisfied only after an impartial

---

[1] J. A. Conde, *History of the Dominion of the Arabs in Spain*, English translation by Mrs. Jonathan Foster, London, 1854, p. 4.

[2] Roy Harvey Pearce, *Savagism and Civilization, A Study of the Indian and the American Mind*, Baltimore, 1967.

examination of both accounts, and that only in this way can the historical truth be ascertained.[1] This attitude of balance was the starting point of a long historiographical tradition. Thanks to Conde's followers, particularly Dozy, Codera, Lévi-Provençal and Huici Miranda, it has made possible Luis G. de Valdeavellano's recent book, *Historia de España*, I, *De los orígenes a la baja edad media* (Madrid, 1952) which achieves in a well-documented and scholarly way what Conde had proposed long before: it narrates in parallel fashion the events occurring both in Muslim and in Christian Spain, interrelating the two cultures and illuminating the achievements of the one by means of the other in a systematic way.

The warm sympathy Conde expresses towards the Arab culture of al-Andalus cannot fail to captivate his readers today, as it did his contemporaries. Juan Andrés had attempted a reappraisal of European and Spanish culture, and had emphasized the Muslim contribution to Western civilization, to such a point that he became an ardent enthusiast of things Arabic. The same is true of Conde, who devoted his life to readjusting the distorted picture of Muslim history in its relation to Spanish affairs. He was a member of the Academy of History and had some impact on its work. He observed, for example, that the account given of the Cid Campeador, the Spanish national hero, differed widely in the Arabic writings, from what he had discovered in the Christian chronicles. Whereas Castilian writers depicted the Cid as a brave and generous leader, the Arabs stressed the treachery and cruelty of his nature, and related with pious horror an episode according to which he was alleged to have burned alive the Arab governor of Valencia after the latter had surrendered to his mercy. In all justice to Conde, it should be said that the deflation of the Cid legend, a theme later developed by his arch-critic Dozy was initiated by the Spaniard. Thus with a sense of equilibrium admirable in one living in such a trying period of history, Conde hoped that the truth would be found between the two extremes presented by Arab and Spanish sources. His book was intended to rectify the one-sidedness of Spanish historiography. Hopefully its outcome would be a truly unbiased picture of the medieval situation, since Spain was fortunate in possessing two accounts of its history for that period.

Conscious of the importance of Arabic studies in relation to

[1] *Historia de la dominación de los árabes en España*, 2nd ed., Barcelona, 1844, vol. I, p. vii.

Spanish culture, he paints a deplorable picture of the state of affairs in his day, and regrets that the losses sustained by the Escorial library had never been repaired. He also complains of lack of official interest in promoting the study of Arabic literature which field he considered indispensable in order to understand the Spanish language and the origin of many of its "most flowery and elegant locutions." [1]

In an attempt to rectify the conception Spanish scholars held of the Arab conquest, Conde asserts that what little was known up until then had been taken from totally biased Christian chronicles. This, in his opinion, had distorted and obscured the account of Spanish history to such an extent that the popular conception held in Spain concerning the Moors was that they were ignorant and cruel barbarians who had burned all before them and massacred those who stood in their way.[2] To this prevailing and negative picture of the conquest, Conde opposes that of the newly-subjected peoples of al-Andalus living in a state of ease far greater than any they had ever known under the rule of the Visigoths—the transposition of an *afrancesado* idea onto the history of Spain, quite naturally. He asserts that the Arab historians translated and published up till his time in Europe rarely mentioned the events of al-Andalus with any accuracy, so that his own work claims to fill that gap.

Turning to his direct predecessor Casiri, he indicates the value of the historical fragments published in that author's *Bibliotheca*, but adds that they are insufficient to serve as source material for a comprehensive history of al-Andalus, as had been attempted by Masdeu, the great historian of eighteenth-century Spain. He compiles a long list of errors made by Casiri, though he explains that with all its shortcomings, his predecessor's work had managed to bring a totally unknown side of Spain's past to the attention of learned circles.

As for the sources of his *Historia*, he tells the reader that it was compiled from original Arabic documents, and that they had been translated almost in their own style, so that the work should produce the effect of having been written by an Arab historian. From this it may easily be discerned that the author was attempting to dress his erudition with a certain literary charm by imparting to it the flavour of an archaic style. It was a book directed not only to the

[1] Conde, *Historia*, vol. I, p. ix.
[2] *Op. cit.*, *vol. cit.*, p. x.

scholar, but also to the general reader. Actually, the *Historia* brings together sections translated from the *Qirṭās*, the *Ḥulāl al-Mawshiyya* and other chronicles, generously interlarded with poems, for which he expressed some taste, and which led him, like Juan Andrés before him, to conjecture on the possible transmission of Arabic poetry into Romance. The many poems he inserts in the prose passages of his work, after the manner of the original Arabic texts, are rendered into the octosyllabic *romance* or ballad metre of Spain. He concludes that the Spanish *romance* is an adaptation of Arabic metres, for reasons which are not very clear and which remain unconvincing despite his lengthy explanation,[1] and he promises to publish a translation of Arabic poems with a "preliminary discourse" proving the importance of the Arabic influence on Spanish poetry. Whether or not he ever completed this study has not been determined, it having never been published.[2]

Among the many poems translated by Conde to embellish his history, the following famous one by ʿAbd ar-Raḥmān I to a solitary palm tree growing in his Cordovan palace, may serve as an example of his skill:

Tú también, insigne palma eres aquí forastera,
De Algarbe las dulces auras tu pompa halagan y besan:
En fecundo suelo arraigas y al cielo tu cima elevas,
Tristes lágrimas lloraras, si cual yo sentir pudieras;
Tú no sientes contratiempos como yo de suerte aviesa,
A mí de pena y dolor continuas lluvias me anegan:
Con mis lágrimas regué las palmas que el Forat riega;
Pero las palmas y el río se olvidaron de mis penas,
Cuando mis infaustos hados y de Alabás la fiereza
Me forzaron a dejar del alma las dulces prendas;
A tí de mi patria amada ningún recuerdo te queda;
Pero yo triste no puedo dejar de llorar por ella.[3]

[1] *Op. cit., vol. cit.*, p. xxii.

[2] *Cf.* A. R. Nykl, *Hispano-Arabic Poetry and its Relations with the Old Provençal Troubadours*, Baltimore, 1946, pp. xv-xvi, n. 8.

[3] Conde, *Historia*, ed. Paris, 1840, p. 85. Compare to the more literal version of Nykl:

1 Oh palm, you solitary one, like myself, grow
In a land where you are distant from your kindred:
2 You weep, while your leaves inarticulately whisper,
Not being human in species, not able to speak:
3 Were you endowed with mind, you would weep recalling
Euphrates and the homeland of the palm tree groves!
4 But you cannot return, and I was driven away
By the ʿAbbāsids' hatred, from my kindred.

Nykl, *op. cit.*, p. 18.

Though Conde's claim that the *romance* derives from classical Arabic poetry is dubious, it is important to note the survival of an idea previously defended by Juan Andrés. However, Conde is more accurate when he discusses the Arabic influence on the Spanish language and its early prose style, for he claims that many words, idioms and metaphorical expressions in Spanish derived from Arabic, a fact which is today generally known and accepted. Even more revealing are his comments on Arabic stylistic and syntactic influences on Spanish prose, for he suggests that medieval Spanish prose works were written in Arabic syntax: "Our rich language owes much to the Arabian, not in isolated words only, but even in idioms, terms of expression, metaphoric forms and phrases, all of which serve to justify the remark that the Spanish is in so far but a corrupted dialect of the Arabian. The style and expression of the Chronicon General, compiled by order of Don Alfonso X, and the book of Count Lucanor, with some other works of the Infante Don Manuel, as for example the 'History of Ultramar,' are in fact, written according to the forms of the Arabian Syntax, and nothing but the mere sound of the words distinguishes them from books written wholly in the Arabic tongue." [1]

Though he exaggerated his case somewhat, Conde was essentially correct on this point as has been fully confirmed first by Gayangos, who identified three Arabic tales in the *Conde Lucanor* and recently by Galmés de Fuentes who in his study of the *Calila y Dimna* has shown that the act of translating Arabic into Spanish created medieval Spanish prose while it also marked the latter with a strong Arabic flavour in syntax and style.[2]

In enumerating the sources of his history, Conde mentions many of the principal authors of al-Andalus who will be encountered in future chapters, but the general impression received by the reader is that the *Historia* is a maze of biographies taken from many different writers. The defects of the work are manifold. Apart from the mistakes resulting from the reunion of so many writings of different periods, events are sometimes related twice, and individuals appear under different names, thus confusing the picture. Gayangos lists some of the more concrete defects of the work in his preface to the translation of al-Maqqarī, though it is not difficult for the

---

[1] Conde, ed. London, 1854, p. 22.

[2] *Cf.*, Álvaro Galmés de Fuentes, *Influencias sintácticas y estilísticas del árabe en la prosa medieval castellana*, Madrid, 1956.

present day specialist to find more errors, some of them quite glaring.

It is to be regretted that Conde often used relatively less important sources, and was never able to consult the more complete work of al-Maqqarī. He himself relates how a copy of this work was made for his use at the command of Charles IV, from a manuscript in the Royal Library of Paris, and that this copy had been transmitted to Madrid as early as 1816. However, it was lost, and he was never able to discover its location. It was therefore not until later when Gayangos translated that work, that a clearer version of Andalusian history would emerge. Conde's work then, is full of defects—those of his age—, and yet its importance was such that towards the end of the century Codera would have to carry on a scholarly campaign against it in an effort to create a more accurate kind of Arabism in Spain. The work was rapidly translated into other European languages: first into German by Karl Kutschmann (1821), then into French by De Marles (1825) and finally into English by Mrs. Jonathan Foster (1854) who writes: "On the admirable manner in which the learned and conscientious Author completed his work it is not necessary here to dilate. He frequently allows the Arabian writers to speak for themselves, and with so felicitous an effect, that the reader may almost hear the voices of the speakers, conducting him to the land of the patriarchs. He has by this means imparted infinite life and vigour to his story, many parts of which are more exciting, in the stern realities of their mournful interest, than the most successful inventions of romance; while the manner of their narration is not infrequently invested with great beauty, dignity, and melody of diction." [1]

Other European scholars, however, were quicker to point out the defects of Conde's work. Dozy, in his *Recherches sur l'histoire et la littérature de l'Espagne pendant le moyen âge* (Leiden, 1849) severely censured the author of the book which had launched him out on his own career—a typical case in which the enthusiasm and interest aroused by Conde's work in the youthful Dozy was to become criticism of his mentor during the age of maturity. Dozy went further, for he accused Conde of having intentionally falsified many facts in his work. Spanish Arabists eventually seconded Dozy in this stand; but today when much more is known about the

[1] Conde, *History*, p. vi.

history of Islamic Spain, a more impartial criticism must recognize his good faith. Much of the misunderstanding appears to have arisen from the fact that Conde's book was intended for the general reader, and was therefore devoid of a critical apparatus. He does not mention his sources, and the book was edited posthumously from his manuscript by friends and admirers who knew no Arabic and were therefore incapable of making the corrections that Conde would presumably have made, had he lived. Furthermore, many of the passages which Dozy claimed to be sheer invention or forgery, have been authenticated as new chronicles have been discovered, so that it appears today that Conde used certain texts unknown to Dozy, despite which, because of his lack of critical apparatus his good faith was questioned.

The first edition of Dozy's *Recherches* had a lengthy portion devoted to the controversy against Conde. In his *Spanish Islam* he says: "It is with extreme diffidence that I give this History to the world. In it I traverse ground hitherto untrodden, for—as I have elsewhere tried to demonstrate—existing treatises on the subject are wholly valueless. They are all, in fact, based on the labours of Conde—on the labours, that is to say, of a writer who had but scanty materials at his disposal, who was unable, from the inadequacy of his linguistic attainments, to understand the documents to which he had access, and who lacked the historic sense." [1] In the Spanish translation of the second edition of the *Recherches*, made by Antonio Machado y Álvarez (Madrid, 1878), the Krausist, folklorist and father of the poet Antonio Machado, Dozy suppressed much of the Conde polemic, limiting himself to a reaffirmation of his position, in which he was supported by European Arabists of note, such as De Slane, Défrémery, Renan and William Wright, all of whom had publicly declared that Conde's book did not deserve the confidence which it had been accorded perhaps too easily. Renan speaks of the numerous errors of Conde, of his making two or three individuals out oi one, of his introducing persons who die twice, often before having been born, of his inventing imaginary characters who play imaginary roles, of his having failed to notice that the binder of Ibn al-Abbār's biographical dictionary had confused the page order, so that he played

[1] R. Dozy, *Spanish Islam,* translated by F. G. Stokes, London, 1913, p. xxxv.

havoc with the history of the fourth and fifth centuries of the *Hijra*.[1]

It is true that mistakes of this nature occur in Conde. For example, his geographical confusion of Bobastro (in Málaga), the fortress of Ibn Ḥafṣūn, with Barbastro (in Aragón) led him to garble the whole episode of the revolt of Ibn Ḥafṣūn. But it should be remembered that Conde was a pioneer in his field, working not with edited texts, but with manuscripts which were at times difficult to read. The academic nature of Renan's criticism becomes apparent if we recall that the latter was himself not above phantasy and invention in history.[2]

In spite of everything, the importance of Conde cannot be overlooked. Dozy presents a very good account of the historiography on Muslim Spain after Conde, even if it is only to point up its weaknesses. Historians such as Aschbach, Rousseau Saint Hilaire, Romey and Schaefer made extensive use of Conde's work, so that he came to be the basic author on the subject in Europe up to Dozy's time.

Likewise, fired with enthusiasm by Conde, those Spanish liberals exiled in England such as José Joaquín de Mora (who later went to South America where he wrote the liberal constitution of Chile [1828]), composed works inspired by the Arabist's book. Mora in 1826 published a work entitled *Cuadros de la historia de los árabes, desde Mahoma hasta la conquista de Granada* [3] based on Conde whose general outline he follows, though adding much of his own. The interest in Arabic studies was particularly strong among the literary critics of the emigration in London, for most of them stressed the

---

[1] *Cf.* Dozy, *Investigaciones*, I, p. vi., n. 1.

[2] In the *Life of Jesus*, Renan attributes Jesus' death—with no documentation of course, to the rupture of a heart vessel:

"Everything leads to the belief that the instantaneous rupture of a vessel in the heart brought him, at the end of three hours, to a sudden death." Ernest Renan, *The Life of Jesus*, Doubleday, New York, no date.

Dozy himself was not above romantic wool-gathering, for after telling us that there is little documentation about Visigothic Spain he draws portraits of its inhabitants such as the following: "the nobles sought oblivion of their dangers in revelry, and clouded their brains in the delirium of debauch. . . . the rich, sunk in gluttony and drunkenness, danced and sang; their trembling lips imprinted kisses on the bare shoulders of beautiful slavegirls—while the populace, as though to accustom themselves to the sight of blood or to intoxicate themselves with the odours of carnage, applauded the gladiators who slew one another in the amphitheatre." *Spanish Islam*, p. 219.

[3] Ackermann, London, 1826, 2 vols.

"Oriental" character of Spanish literature. Mora claimed that a knowledge of Arabic history was essential for Spanish speaking peoples because of the profound effects it had on the Spanish language, literature, public and private life.

In this attitude of Mora it is not difficult to discern a prefiguring among the liberals of the emigration, of the question which was later to occupy the thoughts of Unamuno and Ortega, namely whether Spain was European of African. Vicente Llorens believes that Conde contributed not a little to developing an interest in the Arabs of Spain among the liberals; an interest which soon began to take on a Romantic coloring:

"It is enough to recall the *Viajes* of the Catalan *afrancesado*, Domingo Badía which were retranslated into Spanish at a late date. He made the pilgrimage to Mekka after having been circumcised in London, and masqueraded as Prince Alí Bey el-Abassí. His close friend the learned naturalist Don Simón de Rojas Clemente, who also learned the language perfectly, adopted an Arab name, grew a beard, dressed and lived in the Oriental style within Spain." [1]

Rojas Clemente (1777-1827) was a distinguished Valencian Orientalist and botanist who became a close friend of Domingo Badía. He adopted the name Mahomed ben Alí and wore Arab dress in Madrid. Hence he was nicknamed "el Moro sabio." His knowledge of Arabic was of use to him in the study of botany for he appears to have consulted Arab sources in his work and to have been particularly interested in agricultural treatises, for he made additions to that of Herrera which was published in Madrid in 1818-1819.[2] As for his friend Domingo Badía y Leblich (1766-1822 ?) he was born in Barcelona, studied Arabic with Rojas Clemente, and became a famous explorer. He was commissioned by Charles IV's minister Godoy to go to the Arab world disguised as a descendant of the ʿAbbāsid caliphs in order to further Spain's imperialist policies in the Mediterranean. He adopted the name of ʿAlī Bey al-ʿAbbāsī, travelled to England to perfect his Arabic in 1802 where he was circumcised (and suffered a good deal from this operation). Having recovered, he returned to Spain and from thence he disembarked in Tangier in 1803. He visited Fez, travelled through Morocco, Tripoli,

---

[1] Vicente Llorens Castillo, *Liberales y románticos, una emigración española en Inglaterra* (1823-1834), Mexico, 1954, p. 154.

[2] *Cf. Enciclopedia Espasa, s.v.* Rojas Clemente y Rubio (Simón de), pp. 1401-2.

Cyprus, Egypt (where he was received by Muḥammad ʿAlī), and reached Mekka in 1807. Then he advanced to Jerusalem, Damascus, and Constantinople, where he heard of the Napoleonic invasion of Spain. Thus, when Spain's imperialist aims were suddenly cut short, Badía became an *afrancesado* and settled in Paris where he published his memoirs in 1814.[1] He died around 1822, poisoned by order of the Pasha of Damascus, in Aleppo where he had gone in the service of Louis XVIII on his way to spy on British India.

ʿAlī Bey's work enjoyed some vogue and was translated into Catalan (1835) and Spanish (1836). The purpose of his voyage was political and formed part of Godoy's plan to conquer Morocco. He states in his work, for example, that it would be easy to establish a Spanish colony in Oujda (between Fez and Tlemcen) in order to "bring civilization to North Africa." [2] Though this expansion was frustrated by contemporary events, the work of Badía bears witness to the Spanish imperialistic ideals of the turn of the century. It was also of value to later European travellers who visited Mekka in disguise, as was the case of Sir Richard Burton, who cites ʿAlī Bey whose work served him as a guide through the uncharted parts of Arabia he visited in 1853.[3]

Thus Conde and his generation had an impact on liberal thinking. But they were also to be a source ot Romanticism. In her book on the Moors in Spanish literature, María Soledad Carrasco has shown how Conde's work was avidly read by the Romantics, among them Washington Irving and others, both inside Spain and abroad.[4] If Conde's scholarship was later considered weak, at least his impact on his contemporaries was great, as was that of Gaspar María de Nava Álvarez, Conde de Noroña, who flourished at the end of the eighteenth century and whose volume of Oriental poems, re-translated from the English and the French, were published under the title of *Poesías asiáticas puestas en verso castellano*.[5] The work

[1] *Voyages d'Alī-Bey el Abbassí en Afrique et en Asie, pendant les années*, 1803, 1804, 1805, 1806 *et* 1807, Paris, 1814. English ed., London, 1816.

[2] *Cf.* Isidro de las Cagigas, *Los viajes de Alí Bey a través del Marruecos Oriental*, Madrid, 1919, p. 4. For biographical data, *cf. Enciclopedia Espasa*, *s.v.* Badía y Leblich (Domingo), pp. 139-41; Julio Romano, *Viajes de Alí Bey el-Abbasí*, Madrid, 1951.

[3] *Cf.* Sir Richard F. Burton, *Personal Narrative of a Pilgrimage to Al-Madinah and Meccah*, New York, 1964, 2 vols.

[4] *Cf.* María Soledad Carrasco Urgoiti, *El Moro de Granada en la literatura (del siglo XV al XX)*, Madrid, 1956, pp. 244, 246, 250.

[5] Paris, 1833. For a biography, *cf. Enciclopedia Espasa*, *s.v.* Nava Álvarez de Noroña (Gaspar María de), p. 1257.

contains not only translations from Arabic poetry (including Spanish Arabs) but also from Persian and Turkish, and in them the Count of Noroña sees a passion and a fire that presage the Romantic Age:

"I am sure that lovers of true poetry will distinguish these compositions full of fire and picturesque images, from the insipid philosophical rhymed prose that has been reaching us from beyond the Pyrenees and has been sold as sound merchandise. The Spanish genius, which has shone so much for its fertile and gifted imagination, should abandon those Gallic stupidities and not disdain to read the poets of the Orient in whom all is ardour and enthusiasm, and among whom are included a few Hispanic souls whose works lie buried in the Escorial." [1]

The book is valuable because it includes a Spanish translation of Sir William Jones' *Discourse on the Poetry of the Orientals*, thus being an early attempt to familiarize the Spanish public with Arabic poetry and poetics. This line of study, begun by Noroña would be continued by Von Schack,[2] and in our own time by Nykl, Pérès and García Gómez.[3] Noroña's edition contains biographies of some of the more famous *Muʿallaqa* poets of pre-Islamic Arabia, among them Labīd, whose ode he translates as follows:

Ya Mitata no existe; derrocadas
Sus casas, templos y su muro hermoso,
Solo ruinas se ven, piedras gastadas,
Y un desierto estendido y pavoroso.

Los cauces del Riana, ya cegados,
Ningún vestigio de su forma ofrecen;
Como en piedra caracteres grabados
Que al rigor de la edad desaparecen.

¡ Cuántos años corrieron desde el día
Que tus lindas muchachas recatadas

---

[1] *Poesías asiáticas*, Paris, 1833, p. vi.

[2] *Poesie und Kunst der Araber in Spanien und Sicilien*, 2nd ed., Stuttgart, 1877.

[3] For studies of Arabic Poetics, *Cf.* G. E. Von Grunebaum, *A Tenth-Century Document of Arabic Literary Theory and Criticism*, (*The Sections on Poetry of al-Baqillānī's* Iʿjāz al-Qurʾān), Chicago, 1950; Aḥmad Ḍaif, *Essai sur le Lyrisme et la Critique Littéraire chez les Arabes*, Paris, 1917. For Hispano-Arabic documents, *cf.*: ʿAbd ar-Raḥmān Badawī (ed.), *Aristoteles de Poetica, e Graeco transtulit commentis auxit ac critica editione antiqua Arabicae versionis et Alfārābī, Avicennae Averroisque commentariorum*, Cairo, 1953; *idem.*, *Ḥāzim al-Qarṭājannī wa Naẓariyāt Arisṭū fī sh-Shiʿr wa l-Balāgha*, Cairo, 1961.

Admitieron gustosas la fe mía,
Y fueron sus promesas aceptadas!

¡ Cuántas veces rocío regalado
Primavera vertió sobre tu frente!
¡ Y cuántas el tonante cielo el prado
Pulsó con grueso rápido torrente;

Lanzando de las nubes tenebrosas
De la tarde, la noche y la mañana,
Repitiendo en las rocas cavernosas
Su voz el trueno con porfía insana!

Sobre el antes lozano verde suelo
Las ramas de la ortiga agora ondean;
Y en el margen del río sin recelo
El avestruz y la antílope vaguean.

La gazela de grandes ojos mora
Aquí con sus hijuelos, les demuestra
El uso de su planta voladora,
Y en su anchuroso campo los adiestra.

A veces la corriente procelosa
Edificios descubre destruídos;
Como la pluma en mano artificiosa
Escritos restituye ya perdidos;

O cual diestro punzón, que derramando
El glasto por las manos delicadas,
Con finísimas tintas va marcando
En la nieve las venas azuladas.

Me paro a preguntar: ¡ Oh cuán ociosas
Son todas mis palabras y cuestiones!
No hay penas que me escuchen amorosas
Y el viento desvanece mis razones. [1]

---

[1] *Poesías asiáticas*, pp. 83-4. Compare to Nicholson's translation:
"Waste lies the land where once alighted and did wone
The people of Mina: Rijam and Ghawl are lone.
The camp in Rayyan's vale is marked by relics dim
Like weather-beaten script engraved on ancient stone.
Over this ruined scene, since it was desolate,
Whole years with secular and sacred months have flown.
In spring 'twas blest by showers 'neath starry influence shed,
And thunder-clouds bestowed a scant or copious boon.
Pale herbs had shot up, ostriches on either slope
Their chicks had gotten and gazelles their young had thrown;
And large-eyed wild-cows there beside the new born calves
Reclined, while round them formed a troop the calves half-grown.
Torrents of rain had swept the dusty ruins bare,
Until, as writing freshly charactered, they shone,
Or like to curved tattoo-lines on a woman's arm,

Noroña, Badía and especially Conde's work had much impact on the Romantics. However, this was no consolation to Dozy who went so far as to state that Conde hardly knew of Arabic much more than the characters with which it was written, and that he was an impudent and unscrupulous forger.[1] This is simply not true, as any Orientalist can ascertain if he will randomly select a passage from the *Historia* and compare it with the original Arabic text. Generally speaking such an inspection will reveal a degree of accuracy and elegance not usually encountered among translators. The severity of Dozy's harsh judgement was somewhat palliated by Antonio Machado, his Spanish translator, who in his prologue [2] calls Conde the mentor of Spaniards and Frenchmen in Arabic scholarship prior to the appearance of Dozy, and underlines his talent and diligence, reproaching his countrymen for having failed to continue in the line of research initiated by Conde so as "to correct his defects while imitating his zeal." He concludes that Dozy's attack was unjust in its extremism,[3] and he shows that Conde's work, with all its defects was an immense step forward in the knowledge about Muslim Spain. Hence Conde's failure was one of method, not of purpose. Machado also deplores the lack of interest in Arabic studies then prevalent in Spain, yet it is astonishing that living first in a nation in turmoil and then in exile, an individual such as Conde could have achieved as much as he did with none of the modern facilities to aid him in his work.[4]

In any event, until Dozy's reappraisal of Conde's book there is no doubt that the latter had great influence upon European scholarship. Within Spain itself, the repercussions of Conde's book soon made themselves heard among intellectual circles. In a speech delivered by the Duke Evaristo San Miguel [5] a liberal, on the 3rd

---

With soot besprinkled so that every line is shown.
I stopped and asked, but what avails it that we ask
Dumb changeless things that speak a language all unknown?"

R. A. Nicholson, *A Literary History of the Arabs*, Cambridge, 1962, pp. 119-20.

[1] Dozy, *op. cit.*, p. xiii.

[2] *Op. cit.*, p. xviii.

[3] *Op. cit.*, p. xvii.

[4] For a rectification of the Conde polemic, *cf.* L. Barrau-Dihigo, "Contribution à la Critique de Conde," in *Homenaje a D. Francisco Codera*, Saragossa, 1904, pp. 551-569.

[5] Author of the words of the "Himno a Riego," he fought in Aragón against the intervention of the Holy Alliance; a liberal and Secretary of State under the constitutional monarchy of 1820 he was wounded and taken

of April, 1853, on the occasion of his reception into the Royal Academy of History, the Duke discusses the advances made in Spanish historical research, and attributes great importance to Conde's contributions. In his opinion, the popular (and therefore conservative) Spanish conception of the Arabs had been that they were a barbaric and warlike people. No one suspected that their rule over al-Andalus had been no worse than that of the Carthaginians, the Romans or the Visigoths. He quotes Conde as having combatted those who maintained that the Arabs advanced "only to destroy and shed blood." [1]

Conde's book had made it plain to a few, particularly to the liberal element in Spain, that the Arab impact on the Iberian Peninsula had also had certain positive aspects. This point, which Juan Andrés had made long before, is brought home forcefully in the Duke of San Miguel's speech, as he paints a glowing picture of Arab Spain. While the Roman conquerors, he says, had been civilized by the conquered Greeks, the Arabs had the superior distinction of both civilizing and conquering at the same time.[2] In this way a fitting tribute to the lasting values of al-Andalus was publicly expressed in the Academy of History. Behind all the rhetoric it may be discerned that the efforts of the early Arabists were beginning to broaden the basis of humanistic research so that European countries, and especially Spain, would look to Arabic culture as part of their national heritage. At the same time, the Duke dispatches the role of the Visigoths in two words, referring to them as a "barbaric people." With the onset of nationalism throughout Europe, especially in the latter half of the nineteenth century, the positions would be reversed, particularly among conservatives, so that Simonet would conceive of the Arabs as barbarians and the Mozarab descendants of Romans and Visigoths as civilized Spaniards overwhelmed by African savagery.

However, San Miguel's opinion was not shared by the conservatives, for in a reply to the above-mentioned speech, the Barón de la Joyosa asks the Academy how the Arabs could have lived at

prisoner. With the liberal emigration of 1823, he went to England, where he wrote *Los elementos del arte de la guerra* (London, 1826, 2 vols.). Later, in Spain he published a *Revista Militar*. *Cf.* Vicente Llorens Castillo, *op. cit.*, pp. 15, 17, 52, 73, 90, 136, 147.

[1] Real Academia de la Historia, *Discursos*, Madrid, 1858, pp. 210-11.

[2] *Op. cit.*, pp. 215-16.

peace with the vanquished peoples, when the *Koran* preached "intolerance and fanaticism."[1]

There is in this conservative statement an echo of the traditional view of Islam which derived directly from the Middle Ages during which the crusading spirit against Islam became exacerbated in Spain for political reasons. If the statements of the Barón de la Joyosa are compared to those made by the eighteenth-century historian Masdeu in his *Historia crítica de España* (1793): "From the name of their first homeland they are called *Arabs*—from that of their *accursed* Master, *Mohammedans* . . .,"[2] or to those of Pedro de Alcalá, it can be realized that the traditional Spanish conception of the Arabs had not changed radically. Masdeu had based himself almost entirely on medieval Latin and Spanish chronicles for the Arabic section of his work. Though the conservative element was still hostile to Arabism, at least the effects of Conde's history were producing a more sympathetic approach to things Arabic among Spanish liberals such as Mora and Evaristo San Miguel.

In 1814 Fernando VII had overthrown the constitution of Cádiz and imposed upon Spain a despotic régime which lacked the dignity and interest in reform which had characterized his eighteenth-century predecessors. The prestige of the monarchy came to such a low ebb that in 1820 a military revolt spread all over Spain, and the king was forced to swear to uphold the constitution which he had previously abolished. This triumph of Spanish liberalism was the first blow struck against the policy of the Holy Alliance after the defeat of Napoleon. However, that organization, in 1823 sent the Duke of Angoulême to "restore order" in Spain, where another civil war had broken out, this time instigated by the absolutists and with the support of France. Thus in 1823 the absolute government was restored by French intervention, while the liberals were once more forced into exile, many of them for the second time. Most of these liberals went to England, though not a few escaped to France where they were treated with suspicion and closely watched by the French police. Many figures known better as intellectuals than as politicians stayed in Paris.[3]

One of the most distinguished Spanish Arabists of the century,

---

[1] *Contestación, op. cit.*, pp. 233-34.

[2] Juan Francisco de Masdeu, *Historia crítica de España*, Madrid, 1793, vol. 12, p. 1.

[3] *Cf.* Vicente Llorens Castillo, *op. cit.*, p. 19.

Don Pascual de Gayangos y Arce, grew up in this atmoshpere of turmoil, and as a consequence spent a large part of his life outside Spain; if not in actual exile, at least in close contact with the liberal elements abroad. Gayangos was born in Seville in 1809. His father, Don José de Gayangos y Nebot was a brigadier in the artillery corps from 1815 on, and his mother, Doña Francisca Arce de Retz was related to a French family.[1] In 1822, when he was thirteen years old, his family sent him to study in France, and upon his father's death, Doña Francisca, fearful of the persecutions which followed the absolutist reaction of 1823, left Spain and joined her son in Paris.

There Gayangos became proficient in French and learned Arabic with Silvestre de Sacy the professor at the École des Langues Orientales who had put French Arabism on a firm philological basis by emphasizing the study of the classical over the colloquial language.[2] This stage was important in Gayangos' career, for he was destined to bring back to Spain a more philologically-oriented kind of Arabism than that practiced by Conde.

Gayangos made rapid progress in his studies, and after marrying an English girl at the early age of nineteen, he returned to Spain with her in 1828. In the interim it seems that after the death of Conde, Arabic studies in Spain had been cultivated by the Jesuit Juan Artigas who in 1824 had occupied the chair of Arabic at the College of San Isidro in Madrid. His tenure lasted until 1843 when he was killed in a massacre of priests which occurred on Thursday, July 17. Menéndez y Pelayo referred to Artigas as "the best, or rather, the only Arabist there was in Spain at that time," [3] but he was probably not very distinguished, and he was succeeded in his chair by another minor figure, Raimundo Gasset, who occupied the post for the year of 1834-35 and about whose career Gayangos had the following to say: "the only professorship is held by an ignorant Jesuit incapable of making a scholar." [4] After the year 1835 Arabic

---

[1] For a biography of Gayangos, *cf.* Pedro Roca, "Noticia de la vida y obras de D. Pascual de Gayangos," *RABM*, 3a época, 1, 1897; 2, 1898; 3, 1899. Also, *Enciclopedia Espasa, s.v. Gayangos.* For his work as an Arabist, *cf.* M. Manzanares de Cirre, "Don Pascual de Gayangos (1809-1897) y los estudios árabes," *And,* 28, 1963, pp. 445-61.

[2] *Cf.* Johann Fück, *Die Arabischen Studien in Europa bis in den Anfang des* 20. *Jahrhunderts*, Leipzig, 1955, pp. 140-44.

[3] *Cf.* Pedro Roca, *op. cit.*, I, 1897, p. 550, n. 1.

[4] *Cf.* M. Manzanares de Cirre, *op. cit.*, p. 450.

was dropped from the curriculum of San Isidro till the forties of the same century. However, the young Gayangos upon his return to Spain was able to study with Artigas under whom he made rapid progress.

Gayangos' early letters to his friends abroad reveal a nature much impressed by Romanticism. He was familiar with the poetry of Byron and the works of Walter Scott, and also interested in music which he studied with another of the exiled liberals, Don Santiago de Masarnau.[1] Gayangos lived for a time in Málaga where he became a close friend of Estébanez Calderón, a writer and essayist of the Romantic age deeply interested in the Arabian antiquities of Spain. Estébanez Calderón was attracted by the legendary aspects of Hispano-Arabic romance, after the manner of Washington Irving. His influence on Gayangos was considerable, as may be seen in the historical essay the latter wrote for *Plans, Elevations, Sections and Details of the Alhambra*,[2] which is conceived in a literary way and intended for the general reader. The essay could well have been written by some Romantic author, and it is even headed by a verse from Victor Hugo's *Les Orientales*:

> Grenade à l'Alhambra.
> L'Alhambra! L'Alhambra! Palais que les génies
> Ont doré comme un rêve et rempli d'harmonies;
> Forteresse aux créneaux, festonnées et croulants,
> Où l'on entend la nuit de magiques syllabes,
> Quand la lune, à travers les milles arceaux arabes
> Sème les murs de trèfles blancs!

From 1831 to 1836 Gayangos was employed by the Ministry of State in translating the official correspondence with Morocco and the Arab world in general. He also made extracts of the Arabic manuscripts at the Royal Library in order to determine which of them were more worthy of publication. This work made him proficient in Arabic paleography and allowed him to accumulate information he was to use later in his career.

---

[1] (1805-1882), a distinguished musician and musical critic of the Romantic epoch in Spain, who made his debut in London as a pianist. Cf. Vicente Llorens Castillo, *op. cit.*, pp. 55-56.

[2] *From Drawings Taken on the Spot in* 1834 *by the Late M. Jules Goury, and in* 1834 *and* 1837 *by Owen Jones, Archt. With a Complete Translation of the Arabic Inscriptions and a Historical Notice of the Kings of Granada from the Conquest of that City by the Arabs, to the Expulsion of the Moors, by Mr. Pascual de Gayangos*, London, 1842.

Today he is remembered chiefly for his activities as a bibliophile and as an Arabist. It is the latter of these which forms the object of the present study, though it should be remembered that his vast knowledge of Spanish literature was useful in many ways, and that the double nature of his erudition, in the fields of Arabic and Spanish, would draw him particularly to the study of contacts between the two cultures, in which field he was to make several important contributions. By the very nature of his subject, the Spanish Arabist has tended to focus his attention on problems of cultural contacts between East and West perhaps more than his colleagues in the rest of Europe. Spain is a rich laboratory for the scholar interested in this peculiar historical phenomenon. With Gayangos this tendency was first manifested in a more or less rigorously documented way, and it set the mode for later developments. At the same time, Gayangos' multiple activities in two fields, his ease of expression in three languages, his French education and long periods spent in London opened up new perspectives and new methods to him with which he was enabled to renovate Spanish Arabism which had stagnated as a result of the political upheavals of early nineteenth-century Spain. At times he may appear somewhat semi-professional to the modern Arabist; indeed, his approach reminds his twentieth-century readers of a certain gentlemanly dilettantism. In his translation of al-Maqqarī he altered the order of chapters and omitted some important sections, so that he was criticized by professionals for whom he made the translation almost unusable. But the point is that just like Conde, Gayangos was writing for a broad public in Spain—not just for specialists. By rearranging al-Maqqarī he made the book more enjoyable for the general reader whom he had to reach if Arabic studies were to succeed in Spain. At the same time, his semi-foreign upbringing gave him a scholarly training and even more important; a perspective towards Arabic studies which coincided with Spanish liberal ideals and which would later be lost in Spain. Ever since the work of Simonet in the second half of the century, when conservative-Catholic-traditionalist scholarship organized itself to attack liberalism, a nationalistic tendency became more and more pronounced. It claimed that the achievements of Islam in the Iberian Peninsula were due more to the fact that the peninsular Muslims had been ethnically and biologically "Spaniards" than to the cultural importations the Arabs had brought with them from the Orient. This point will be analysed in future chapters, but it should be indicated that in Gayangos' work this tendency was singularly absent. He had lived too long abroad and was too much in contact with foreigners to be bound by a narrow form of nationalism.

Gayangos' period of research enabled him to write an important article on Arabic manuscripts in Spain [1] in which he discusses the establishment of libraries; in the Orient by Hārūn ar-Rashīd, and in al-Andalus by al-Ḥakam II. He included an account of the great libraries of al-Andalus as well as those of Alfonso X of Castile and the Infante Don Juan Manuel, leading up to the Escorial and Philip III. While reviewing the history of the Escorial, he relates an anecdote which is indicative of his anti-clerical opposition to the practices of the Spanish Church of his age. It seems that the friars to whose keeping the Escorial was entrusted had the habit of showing foreigners nothing but bibles for fear they might be heretics. When Gayangos paid a visit to the library, the friars, acting on the supposition that as a Spaniard his orthodoxy was unimpeachable, granted him the favor of showing him a book they claimed had been written by the hand of Saint Augustine. Only after having kissed this dubious relic was he permitted to examine the Arabic manuscripts at will.[2] The mocking irony of the passage in which Gayangos relates this episode is similar in tone to that of the satirical essays of Larra, another French-educated Spaniard of the period.

The establishment of a chair of Arabic studies began to concern the Spanish government, and Gayangos obtained permission in 1835 to go to Paris and London in order to observe foreign methods in teaching that language. There he procured the elementary books

---

[1] *Cf. Westminister Review*, 21, no. 42, October 1st, 1834, pp. 378-94.

[2] "The works they usually show foreigners who visit these two Libraries (the superior and the inferior), are a few ancient, manuscript, richly-adorned, and illuminated Bibles. When the visitors are known to be Spaniards and it is presumed that heresy does not lurk in their breasts, as is the case with me, who am Catholic, Apostolic, Roman, they dare to show what they consider to be of greater value than all the works in the world put together. I remained, therefore, not a little surprised upon noting that one of the Fathers, with an expressive glance, signaled me to follow him, and having led me to a sort of chapel in the same library, where, covered with a curtain and a glass lies a book written, according to him, by the hand of Saint Augustine, he drew it forth, kissed it and handed it to me to do the same, and. . . he told me to take the keys, open the bookcases and look at random for whatever I most desired. In this way, therefore, did I proceed after so benevolent an invitation, to examine the Arabic manuscripts." *RABM*, 1897, I, pp. 556-57.

necessary for beginners and returned to Spain where he occupied the position of professor of Arabic at the Athenaeum of Madrid for the year 1836-37. However, at the end of the academic year he resigned in order to conduct his research at the Escorial. It became necessary to find a supplement to his income, so he returned to London where he published numerous small articles in the *Penny Cyclopaedia, Edinburgh Review, Biographical Dictionary* of the Society for Useful Knowledge, the *Westminster Review,* and *The Athenaeum.* The exiled Spanish liberals in England had contributed many articles to these periodicals, and Gayangos joined in this literary activity so that upon his death the last periodical cited was able to say of him that he "could enter into the wants and aims of English students in a way that no other Spaniard since Blanco White has been able to do." [1]

Among his studies on Arabic themes he established the authenticity of the disputed Arab origin of the early Spanish chronicle known as the *Crónica del Moro Rasis,* a matter of great value, since that work, the Arabic original of which has been lost, is the earliest chronicle on the history of al-Andalus that has come down to us, if only in partial translation.[2] At the same time he pointed out the two-way traffic in culture which had gone on in medieval Spain, for he explains that Arab historians had used translations of Latin chronicles:

"During the reign of al Ḥakam II, and specifically about the time when ar-Rāzī flourished, a translation was made of Paulus Orosius, which is repeatedly mentioned by the geographer al-Bakrī and others. The one written by the French bishop Edelbert also circulated in an Arabic translation, for it is cited by al-Mas'ūdī, a writer from the tenth century, in his *Golden Meadows.* One of the volumes of the chronicle by Ibn Ḥayyān of Cordova deals exclusively with the kingdoms of Asturias and León and was compiled, according to its author's declaration, from original memoirs written by Christian refugees in Cordova." [3]

Earlier, in 1839 he had published an article entitled "Language and Literature of the Moriscos," [4] in which he gave a first account

---

[1] *The Athenaeum,* no. 3651, Saturday, October 16, 1897, p. 529.

[2] *Cf.* "Memoria sobre la autenticidad de la crónica del moro Rasis," in *Memorias de la Real Academia de la Historia,* 8, 1852, p. 4, ff.

[3] *Op. cit.,* p. 24.

[4] *British and Foreign Review,* 8, 1839, pp. 63-95.

of *Aljamía* and *Aljamiado* literature. In the article he sketches a history of the Moriscos, their main literary works, and he explains the *Aljamiado* system of transcription for the first time. His enthusiasm for Morisco poetry allows him to say: "Let any one compare a sonnet of Garcilaso, the Petrarch of Spain, with the true Morisco romances, and he will soon perceive the immense advantage which, in point of simplicity and feeling, these small compositions possess over the best contrivances of the Castilian poets." [1] Gayangos includes extracts from the *Poema de Yuçuf* and the *Discurso de la Luz* of Muhamad Rabadán of Aragón. Unfortunately he did not pursue this line of research, leaving it to his successor Saavedra (who will be discussed later), but to him belongs the merit of having made *Aljamiado* literature known to the world, for in one of his letters he says:

"Upon examining certain manuscripts which are classified in the National Library [in Madrid] under the heading of Arabic documents, I discovered that the majority of them, although written in Arabic characters, merely contained narrations in Castilian or Limousin more or less mixed with Arabic words, according to the education or ability of the writer. I informed my deceased mentor, Baron Silvestre de Sacy of this fact, and he replied that Conde, during his stay in Paris had told him of the matter, and he encouraged me to try to decipher some of them." [2]

In 1841 he was appointed Spanish viceconsul in Tunisia, but did not accept this post, though later he travelled in North Africa and bought the three or four hundred Arabic manuscripts which formed his extraordinary Oriental collection now housed in the National Library of Madrid.

Gayangos' most important work, and the one which has earned him his well deserved fame, is his translation of al-Maqqarī; *The History of the Mohammedan Dynasties in Spain*, published in two volumes in 1840 and 1843 by the Oriental Translation Fund of Great Britain and Ireland. Al-Maqqarī's history of Spain [3] still remains one of the principal comprehensive accounts of the Hispano-Arab period. Its author, a native of Tlemcen (died A.D. 1632) composed a biography of Ibn al-Khaṭīb the famous vizier of Granada,

[1] *Op. cit.*, p. 83.

[2] Pedro Roca, *op. cit.*, 2, 1898, pp. 563-68.

[3] Entitled: *Nafḥu ṭ-Ṭīb min Ġuṣni l-Andalusi r-Ratīb wa Dhikri Wazīrihā Lisāni d-Dīn Ibni l-Khaṭīb* Cairo, 1949, 10 vols.

to which he prefixed a long introduction in eight books,[1] bearing on the historical background of al-Andalus. Since al-Maqqarī's book is one of the most complete and historically accurate on the subject —it is based on a multitude of sources today lost—the choice of this work for translation proved to be particularly intelligent on the part of Gayangos, since it would hopefully rectify the errors of Conde. This the translator attempted to do by applying a stricter methodology as well as the critical apparatus lacking in the work of his predecessor. The notes to Gayangos' translation are in themselves a storehouse of erudition and information not easily obtainable and his work is certainly of far greater reliability than the patchwork history of Conde.

Gayangos believed that the only way to advance in the writing of Spanish history was to make literal translations of Arabic works, even before producing critical editions. This way they could then be compared to Spanish chronicles, and from the comparison of the two versions, a more balanced picture of medieval Spanish history would emerge. In essence this had been the ideal of Conde, but that scholar had had to rely on partial chronicles. Gayangos' choice of the more general work of al-Maqqarī was therefore an intelligent decision.

Gayangos had consulted the President of the Royal Academy of History on the suitability of translating al-Maqqarī, and though he was at first encouraged, the plan was later dropped. Yet he knew that as early as 1816 a copy of the manuscript made under the superintendence of De Sacy in Paris, had been sent to Madrid for the use of Conde by command of Charles IV. Conde was never able to bring this copy to light, and Gayangos also made an attempt, but was denied admission to the Escorial according to him, "from no other motive than my having publicly avowed the intention of making use of my materials in this country [England]." [2] In view of the hostility he encountered in Spain, he obtained the loan of a manuscript copy belonging to William Lembke of Hanover [3] with

[1] 1. Description of al-Andalus, 2. Arab conquest of al-Andalus, 3. History of the Hispano-Arab dynasties, 4. Cordova: Description, 5. Hispano-Arab scholars who travelled to the East, 6. Orientals who visited al-Andalus, 7. Extracts, anecdotes, poetical fragments, etc., bearing on the literary history of al-Andalus, 8. Christian reconquest of al-Andalus and expulsion of the Arabs.

[2] *Cf.* Gayangos, *History of the Mohammedan Dynasties in Spain*, I, p. xviii.

[3] Author of *Geschichte von Spanien*, Hamburg, 1831.

which he began a Spanish translation. During a visit to England the President of the Oriental Translation Fund suggested that he submit a version done into English to the committee of that organization. He accepted, went to London and recommenced his work on al-Maqqarī in English. He rearranged the Arab work by suppressing those parts which he deemed irrelevant to his subject, including almost all of the second part, that is the biography of Ibn al-Khaṭīb. Of the first part he suppressed Book 5 which dealt with the biographies of Andalusians who travelled to the Orient, as well as most of Book 8, a study of Hispano-Arabic literature, which he felt to be of little value in reconstructing the history of al-Andalus.

It would be difficult to give an adequate account of the many treasures stored in Gayangos' translation. There are some which are of great interest in the study of the Arabic sources of early Spanish chronicles. One such example is an amusing legendary version of the history of Spain before the Arab conquest,[1] probably of Eastern origin as Dozy has shown in his *Recherches*, which fantastic though it is, must have been an early legend, since it is quoted word for word in Ibn Khallikān's *Biographical Dictionary*[2] and parts of it made their way into the *Thousand and One Nights*.[3] As Gayangos showed, these stories of a semi-legendary nature, along with accounts of Don Julián and his daughter Florinda of ballad fame reappear almost word for word in the chronicle of Rodrigo de Toledo,[4] and the *Crónica General* of Alfonso X.[5] This is a further indication of the extent to which Christian writers used Arabic documents in compiling their chronicles. By translating such legends, Gayangos was showing the interpenetration of Muslim and Christian culture on Spanish soil, while he was also nourishing the current Romantic interest in medieval Arab Spain. It must be added though, that his critical discernment made him reject these fables as historically unauthentic, for in a note to these legends, Gayangos argues that he would willingly have suppressed them were it not that he wished to show the sources of medieval Spanish

[1] *Cf. Moh. Dyn.*, I, pp. 257-63.

[2] *Kitāb Wafayāt al-Aʿyān*, translated by Baron MacGuckin de Slane, London, 1842, 4 vols. (*cf. s. art.* "Mūsā Ibn Nuṣayr").

[3] *Cf.* Night 316, "Story relating to a certain city of al-Andalus conquered by Ṭāriq Ibn Ziyād."

[4] *De Rebus Hispaniae*, 3, chap. 20.

[5] Ed. Menéndez Pidal, Madrid, 1955, vol. I, chap. 10, pp. 11-12.

chronicles. He says: "The unravelling of the romantic portion of the Spanish annals is not my business at this moment, but it would greatly contribute to illustrate the history of romance in Europe." [1]

Gayangos was one of the first Spanish Arabists to draw attention to the Hispano-Arab strophic poetry known as *mwwashshaḥa* which has become so important today as a probable missing link between Arab and Provenzal poetry.[2] It was not until Ribera and Hartmann, however, that this poetry would be seriously studied. But Gayangos, ever alert and interested in the most varied aspects of Arabic culture, was one of the earliest scholars to point out its existence.

The following is an example of his translation. It is a description of the caliphal palace of al-Zahrā' in Cordova:

> Among the wonders of Az-zahrá, says Ibnu Hayyán, were two fountains, with their basins, so extraordinary in their shape, and so valuable for their exquisite workmanship, that, in the opinion of that writer, they constituted the principal ornament of the palace. The larger of the two, which was of gilt bronze, and most beautifully carved with basso-relievo representing human figures, was brought to the Khalif from Constantinople by Ahmed Al-yunaní (the Greek), and Rabí' the Bishop. As to the small one, which was of green marble, it was brought from Syria by the said Ahmed, although others assert that it came likewise from Constantinople with Rabí'. However, all agree in saying that such were the taste of the designs on these fountains, and the magnificence of the materials, as to make their value almost beyond estimation. The smaller one, above all, appears to have been a real wonder of art. It was brought from place to place until it reached the sea shore, when it was put on board a vessel and conveyed to Andalus. When the Khalif received it he ordered it to be placed on the dormitory of the eastern hall called Al-munis, and he fixed on it twelve figures made of red gold, and set with pearls and other precious stones. The figures, which were all made in the arsenal of Cordova, represented various animals; as for instance one

---

[1] *Moh. Dyn.*, I, p. 515, n. 41.

[2] *Cf. Moh. Dyn.*, I, p. 118, p. 409, n. 14; 2, pp. 526-7. Actually, Casiri had described a manuscript in the Escorial containing *muwashshaḥāt* and *azjāl*, though without attempting to explain what they were:

"Codex nitidis exaratus literis, vocalibusque etiam animatus anno Egirae 863. Christi 1485. in quo ejusdem Auctoris extat opus inscriptum *Series Margaritarum*: ubi plura ingeniosa quidem sed parum pudica de amoribus carmina, quorum alique ad Odarum genus accedunt, vocanturque Arabice *Mauschahat*; alia Versus extemporales dicuntur, quos Arabes *Zagel* appellant. Opus sane rarum, ut pleraque hujus Scriptoris opera, quippe quae a Mahometanis morum, librorumque Censoribus sint proscripta. Is liber ad Regiam Bibliothecam Marochanam olim pertinuit." (Casiri, *Biblio.*, I, no. 432, p. 126-7.)

was the likeness of a lion, having on one side an antelope, and on the other a crocodile; opposite to these stood an eagle and a dragon; and on the two wings of the group a pigeon, a falcon, a peacock, a hen, a cock, a kite, and a vulture. They, moreover, were all ornamented with jewels, and the water poured out of their mouths.

Another of the wonders of Az-zahrá was the hall called *Kasru-l-kholafá* (the hall of the Khalifs), the roof of which was of gold and solid but transparent blocks of marble of various colors, the walls being likewise of the same materials. In the centre of this hall, or, according to some, on the top of the above-described fountain, which is by them placed in this hall, was fixed the unique pearl presented to An-nássir by the Greek emperor Leo, among other valuable objects. The tiles that covered the roof of this magnificent hall were made of pure gold and silver, and, according to Ibnu Bashkuwal, there was in the centre of the room a large basin filled with quicksilver; on each side of it eight doors fixed on arches of ivory and ebony, ornamented with gold and precious stones of various kinds, resting upon pillars of variegated marble and transparent crystal. When the sun penetrated through these doors into the apartment, so strong was the action of its rays upon the roof and walls of this hall that the reflection only was sufficient to deprive the beholders of sight. And when An-nássir wished to frighten any of the courtiers that sat with him, he had only to make a sign to one of his Sclavonians to set the quicksilver in motion, and the whole room would look in an instant as if it were traversed by flashes of lightning; and the company would begin to tremble, thinking that the room was moving away,—this sensation and their fear continuing as long as the quicksilver was in motion. The abundance of quicksilver in Spain made An-nássir conceive the idea of employing it in the manner above described; and it was perhaps the effect produced by that mineral which led to the belief that this hall was perpetually turning round and followed the course of the sun, or, as others have it, that it moved round on the reservoir as on a pivot; and such was An-nássir's care for this building that he would commit the superintendence of it to none other but to his son and successor, Al-hákem. In one thing, however, we find all authors agree, namely, that there never was built a more splended hall than this, either in the times preceding Islam or afterwards. [1]

All these features of Gayangos' work indicate important aspects of his nature: his interest in the Middle Ages, a taste shared fully by his age, as well as his erudition, critical acumen and scholarly

[1] *Cf. Moh. Dyn.*, I, pp. 236-7. For a recent and illuminating study of this kind of architectural *trompe l'oeil* and its development in Islamic art, *cf.* Frederick P. Bargebuhr, *El palacio de La Alhambra en el siglo XI*, The University of Iowa Studies in Spanish Language and Literature, vol. 15, Mexico, 1966, particularly, pp. 116-22.

honesty placed his work on a high rank. In spite of this, it was not well received by Dozy, who, having little knowledge of the kind of Spanish public Gayangos' was aiming to interest in Arabism, was unable to appreciate the value of his research. The latter was accused chiefly of not having written a critical history of the Arab period in al-Andalus, a task far beyond the capabilities of the times, and which even Dozy was unable to complete in its entirely in his own work, *Spanish Islam.* In fact, despite the masterly work of Lévi-Provençal on the caliphal period, that of Codera on the Almoravids, and Huici Miranda on the Almohads a comprehensive history of the period has never been written since Conde, and such a task awaits the pen of a future scholar.

Gayangos' main purpose was not that of writing a critical history, but rather to gather the materials that would be needed in the future, so that such a history could be written with more solid documentation than that of Conde. Furthermore, his translation of al-Maqqarī made it clear that a critical edition of the Arabic text was needed. Later Dozy, Dugat, Krehl and Wright were to collaborate in publishing the complete critical edition of al-Maqqarī under the title of *Analectes sur l'Histoire et la Littérature des Arabes d'Espagne* (Leiden, 1855-61). Thus the significance of Gayangos remained in the fact that his work, with no pretentions to being definitive, challenged European Arabism to continue in this field of research, and made the *Analectes* necessary, as the prologue to that work recognizes: "Enfin M. de Gayangos en publia une traduction à Londres en 1840. Ce savant espagnol a suivi un autre plan que celui de l'auteur arabe; son intention n'était pas de donner une traduction complète, et il appelle lui-même son travail une traduction abrégée. Il a traduit la partie historique des récits et négligé presque en entier celle qui est consacré a la littérature. Remarquable, du reste, par de nombreuses et savantes recherches, l'ouvrage de M. de Gayangos était donc insuffisant pur faire apprécier complètement le véritable caractère du livre d'al-Makkarī. Aussi était-ce un besoin des etudes actuelles de publier le texte de cette bibliothèque arabe-espagnole." [1]

Dozy was bitterly critical of Gayangos, though in fact, the Spanish scholar's work did not deserve the attack it received. It remains today, as perhaps the best and most readable introduction

---

[1] *Analectes,* vol. I, pp. vi-vii.

to Hispano-Arabic studies by an Arab author to have been translated for the use of those who cannot read Arabic.[1]

After 1842 in which he collaborated in *Plans, Elevations, Sections and Details of the Alhambra,* Gayangos turned to Spanish studies and published little about Arabic. In 1853 there appeared a study on law among the Moriscos extracted from *Aljamiado* manuscripts,[2] and accompanied by the edition of two of these. In a note he draws attention to the abundance of *Aljamiado* manuscripts:

"Many other books could be mentioned, all of them written by Spanish Moriscos for the sole purpose of keeping the tradition alive among their people and teaching the precepts of their religion to the uncouth. The treatises of this nature which are preserved in manuscript form in the National Library are more than sixty; there are several in the hands of private individuals, and it can be assumed that many others have been lost. Some, like the *Poema de José el patriarca,* written in Alexandrine verse, the *Historia de Paris y Viana,* translated or imitated from the French; the novel of *Alejandro,* the *Collares de oro,* and others, themselves constitute a novel and elegant literature very deserving of scholarly notice." [3]

The treatises on Muslim religious law he published were valuable in that they revealed the social conditions of the Morisco population of Spain. In this respect Gayangos was a precursor to the type of research done by Pedro Longás in his *Vida religiosa de los moriscos* (Madrid, 1915).

Gayangos' knowledge of Arabic was of invaluable service to him in the publication of medieval Spanish works and initiated a line of research which was to dominate one aspect of Spanish Arabism, that of cultural contacts between Islam and Christian Spain. Thus in a study of the *Conde Lucanor* he established that its author Don

---

[1] Fitzmaurice-Kelly, in an obituary notice sums up the value of the al-Maqqarī translation:

"This is not the fit moment to denote its undeniable defects, nor to revive the polemics scattered up and down the first edition of the late Professor Dozy's *Recherches.* Gayangos steadily ignored the attack and his example may be followed now that he has joined his old-time opponent in the Valley. Whatever his errors of detail, it is beyond all question that Gayangos accomplished an immense mass of necessary and most useful work. . ." *Cf. Revue Hispanique,* 1897, vol. 4, p. 339.

[2] *Tratados de Legislación Musulmana.* 1. *Leyes de moros del siglo XIV*: 2 *Suma de los principales mandamientos y devedamientos, de la ley y Çunna por don Ice de Gebir, Alfaquí mayor y Muftí de la aljama de Segovia, año de* 1462, in *Memorial Histórico Español,* vol. 5, pp. 1-149.

[3] *Op. cit.,* p. 9, n. 2.

Juan Manuel, very probably used Arabic books as sources for some of his stories, and even identified some of these sources themselves.[1]

In his introductory study of the *Libro de Calila y Dimna*[2] he discusses the Oriental origin of this book in the Indian *Fables of Bidpay* and the *Panchatantra*, translated into Pehlevi in the sixth century by the Persian physician Barzuyeh. This version was the one upon which Ibn al-Muqaffaʿ based his Arabic translation. At the close of the eleventh century a physician named Simeon son of Seth translated the work into Greek, after which it became well known in the Byzantine Empire. A Hebrew version existed, which was translated into Latin at the beginning of the fourteenth century and became the parent of all the vernacular European translations. However, Gayangos showed conclusively that the early Arabic edition of Ibn al-Muqaffaʿ had been translated directly into Castilian independently of the other stream of translations deriving from the Latin. This early text was the one he published in the *Biblioteca de autores españoles* for the first time. To support his arguments, he supplies internal evidence: the hitherto known Spanish version repeats many errors made by the translator of the Hebrew text into Latin. Gayangos' text on the other hand, affords clear linguistic evidence of having been made directly from the Arabic, as the end of the book declares explicitly.[3]

In this study, Gayangos was in fact applying the linguistic theories of Conde and achieving marvellous results, for noticing that the translator of his text had kept many names in their original Arabic form, (especially in the case of animals for which there was no Castilian equivalent) and locutions common to Arabic and translated too literally into Castilian,[4] Gayangos rightly con-

---

[1] Three of these stories, those numbered 41, 30, and 47, he respectively traces to a legend about Al-Ḥakam II, a story in al-Maqqarī and another source which he does not mention by name. *Cf. BAE, Escritores en prosa anteriores al siglo XV*, Madrid, 1860, pp. xx-xxi.

[2] *Op. cit.*, pp. 1-10.

[3] "Aquí se acaba el libro de Calina (sic) e dygna, et fue sacado de arábiygo en latyn, e romançado por mandado del infante don alfonso, fijo del muy noble rey don fernando, en la era de mil e dozientos e noventa e nueve anos" i.e. "Here ends the book of Calina and dygna, which was translated from Arabic into Latin, and put into Romance by order of the Crown Prince Don Alfonso, son of the very noble king Don Fernando, in the [Spanish] era of 1299." (*Cf. BAE, op. cit.*, p. 4). The reference is to Alfonso X the "learned," son of Fernando III, conqueror of Cordova and Seville.

[4] For example he noticed that the Arabian wolf-jackal, called "Ibn Awā"

cluded that the Old Spanish version was made directly from the Arabic. In this way he contributed to the understanding of how literary works had been translated in Spain. In doing so he showed the correctness of Conde's assumptions which the latter had never lived to prove. Now that it was established beyond all manner of doubt that important cultural contacts had taken place between Christians and Muslims in the field of the prose tale, a new province was opened up to the European medievalist. Gayangos furthermore illustrated the way in which translation loan words had developed the Old Spanish prose vocabulary.

The long life of Gayangos made him dominate his century, and set the direction which some of his disciples were to follow. After the publication of the *Mohammedan Dynasties* (1843) he occupied the chair of Arabic at the University of Madrid, which he held for many years, and taught that whole generation of Spanish Arabists of the second half of the century: Simonet, Emilio Lafuente Alcántara, Leopoldo Eguilaz, Moreno Nieto, Francisco Fernández y González, and others who will be presented in the following chapters. The unpleasant experiences he underwent because of the political situation of Spain during his early youth made him shy away from politics, though he held important offices. In 1844 he was elected to the Academy of History and in 1881 was named Director of Public Education. Later he became a senator. But he was called to public office more as an eminent national figure than as a member of any particular party.[1] Soon after, he retired to London where he remained to conduct his research in the British Museum on Spanish rather than Arabic themes. He is said to have started learning Persian at the age of eighty, but he died in London in 1897 as the result of a street accident.

Gayangos' last contribution to Arabic scholarship was made when in 1851 he translated Ticknor's *History of Spanish Literature.* He had helped Ticknor earlier, by sending him fragments of *Aljamiado* literature which Ticknor included in the appendix to his work.

---

appeared in the Castilian version as "Abnue" and not as the "vulpes" of Giovanni di Capua. Likewise he says: "Whenever the word *nafs,* which means both 'soul,' 'spirit,' and also 'body,' 'person,' appears in the Arabic original, our translator renders it by *soul,* as in the passage on page 30. 'I offer you my *soul* (*i.e.* my 'person,' 'body'), for you to eat from it and satisfy your hunger,' " (*BAE*; *ed. cit.*, p. 7).

[1] *Cf.* Eduardo Saavedra, "Pascual de Gayangos," in *Ilustración española y americana,* Madrid, n. 38, Oct. 15, 1897, vol. 41, p. 227.

Among these were extracts from the *Poema de Yuçuf,* Mohamad Rabadán's *Discurso de la luz y descendencia y linaje claro de nuestro caudillo y bienaventurado Anaví Muhamed,* and an anonymous poem in praise of Muḥammad. Ticknor calls Gayangos "among the most eminent scholars now living, and one to whose familiarity with whatever regards the literature of his own country the frequent references in my notes bear a testimony not to be mistaken." [1]

In attempting to place Gayangos' work as an Arabist in its historical perspective, it is clear that he dominates the first half of the nineteenth century, the latter part of which is filled with the names of his disciples. Gayangos therefore continued that tradition which in the eighteenth century had flourished under the protection of the Enlightenment, and of which the last exponent was the *afrancesado* Conde. Now Arabism had become a subject of interest to the liberal intellectuals of Spain, and as a liberal, Gayangos was to prepare the groundwork for the scholarship of the second half of the nineteenth century. Indeed, the liberals of this later age, particularly the *Krausist* founders of the Institución Libre de Enseñanza were to be interested in Arabic studies to a significant extent. Gayangos' daughter Emilia de Gayangos was married to Juan Facundo Riaño, a Granadan and close friend of the *Krausist* Don Francisco Giner, so that even by family connections the liberal circles of the Romantic Age were closely related to the *Krausists* of the latter half of the century.[2]

Gayangos' life thus coincides with Liberalism, and this should be taken into account to understand the function that Arabic studies had in Spain during his period. It is on the literature of Romanticism that Gayangos and Conde left the most profound mark. Yet whereas the rest of Europe would manifest great enthusiasm for the Arabic element in Spanish life,[3] Spanish intellectuals themselves

[1] George Ticknor, *History of Spanish Literature,* 3rd ed., Boston, 1866, vol. I, p. xiv.

[2] *Cf.* Vicente Cacho Viu, *La Institución Libre de Enseñanza,* Madrid, 1962, pp. 234-5.

[3] Washington Irving says to a friend: "You may remember that, in the course of the rambles we once took together about some of the old cities of Spain, particularly Toledo and Seville, we frequently remarked the mixture of the Saracenic with the Gothic, remaining from the time of the Moors, and were more than once struck with incidents and scenes in the streets, that brought to mind passages in the "Arabian Nights." You then urged me to write "something in the Haroun Alraschid style," that should have a dash of that Arabian spice which pervades every thing in Spain." *The Alhambra:*

would, if liberal, recognize this influence with regret, as constituting the main factor which had prevented Spain from becoming a modern nation like the rest of Europe. If conservative, they would deny this influence or seek to disguise it. This is why a liberal such as Larra viewed the peculiar customs of Spain (such as bullfighting, which he thought to be of Arab origin) as a manifestation of barbarism which it would be well to suppress if Spain were to join the congress of European nations.[1] This attitude became important in the writing of liberal historical works such as that of José Joaquín de Mora. It was a prolongation of the eighteenth-century feelings of insecurity and it was to persist so long that in 1845 and in far-away Argentina, when Sarmiento was attempting to explain the inner structure of Argentine history as that of a continuous struggle between the barbaric *gaucho* of the plains and the civilized man of the city, (after the fashion of Ibn Khaldūn's opposition of nomadic to sedentary life) Sarmiento constantly compares the *gauchos* to Bedouins. Sarmiento had travelled in Algeria, and so knew Arab life. He compares the customs of the Argentine pampa to those of the deserts of Arabia; he speaks of the strength of character needed to lead caravans, and concludes that this need had led to the establishment of brute force over law and order. Carried away by his analogy he even speaks of "American Bedouins."[2]

In this way the Arabic studies conducted in Spain were incorporated into the wider problem of the reasons for so-called Spanish "decadence." This resulted in a pessimistic attitude among liberals for they began to feel that their country carried an almost "hereditary" Arab "stigma" which had corrupted its institutions and way of life, as a result of eight centuries of coexistence with Islam, and from which it was impossible to escape.

As a result, the conservative-traditionalist line of scholarship was to become more militant in the second half of the nineteenth century. It was to organize itself and attempt to deny the influence of the Arabs on Spain as will be seen in the ensuing chapters. At the same time, the liberals, following in the path of Gayangos would initiate a lively debate in which they attempted to show that the

a Series of Tales and Sketches of the Moors and Spaniards, Philadelphia, 1832, "Dedication."

[1] *Cf.* Larra, *Artículos de costumbres*, ed. *clásicos castellanos*, vol. 45, Madrid, 1959, pp. 25-33.

[2] *Cf.* Domingo Faustino Sarmiento, *Facundo, civilización y barbarie*, New York, 1961, pp. 32-33.

Arab influence had been overwhelming. This explains the enormous enthusiasm which Asín produced in the present century among liberal elements when he tried to show that if Spain was "Arabized," so were Dante, Thomas Aquinas, and a great part of medieval European thought.

CHAPTER THREE

Arabism during the second half of the nineteenth century developed under the aegis of the German philosopher Krause. This period in Spain proved to be one of instability resulting from the Peninsular version of the European revolutionary movements of 1848. Abortive attempts were made to liberalize the regime of Isabel II, such as the Revolution of 1854 during which a liberal petition was submitted to the Queen, to which she responded by declaring a state of siege. Madrid answered by open revolt and this state of affairs continued until in 1868 a military "pronunciamiento" ousted the Queen. She was replaced in 1871 by the Italian Amadeo I, who, having upheld the Constitution, had to pay for this by losing his throne in 1873. Then Spain entered the turbulent era of its first Republic which in 1874 was overthrown and the monarchy restored under Alfonso XII. In Cánovas del Castillo the new king found a strong conservative minister, and under Sagasta, a liberal opposition. For twenty years these two leaders, by common agreement, alternated peacefully in power, and the Constitution of 1876, though satisfying neither liberals nor conservatives, was a workable arrangement which lasted till 1917.

Underneath the kaleidoscopic succession of governments and constitutions the true sense of the age lay in the struggle between liberals and conservatives. The mid-nineteenth century Spaniard suffered from a vague sense of inferiority with regard to Europe, and this feeling in the decades before and after the Restoration was to be expressed by three attitudes: 1. the Spanish genius, outstanding in its capacity to understand the nature of God and man, was considered incapable of conducting abstract reasoning in the field of philosophical or scientific thinking. 2. To this psychological interpretation of Spain's backwardness the historical school answered by granting the present inadequacy of Spanish life, but turning to historical factors (Inquisition, Arabs, etc.) to explain the reasons for Spanish decay. 3. The school of historical-determinism was opposed by that of the traditionalists who maintained that it was not Spain, but rather Protestant Europe, which had broken the spiritual and cultural unity of the Continent. This school identified Spanish culture with Catholicism and considered as un-Spanish any innovating tendency.

Into this atmosphere of dissatisfaction and self-criticism "Krausism" was introduced by Julián Sanz del Río in 1857. Sanz del Río spent many years studying and teaching the doctrines of Krause, and after gaining numerous converts to his ideas he became the target of the conservative wrath of Isabel's government in 1867, at which time he was deprived of his professorship at the University of Madrid. The Neo-Kantian doctrines of Krause do not concern us directly,[1] except insofar as they dominated the intellectual life of that period and led to their most effective results not in abstract theorization, but in the creation of the Institución Libre de Enseñanza in 1876 by Francisco Giner de los Ríos, a devoted Krausist. The Institución was one of the most original educational centres in Spain in that it was independent both of Church and State, and produced the most important intellectuals of contemporary Spain.

It is very necessary to keep these developments in mind, because Arabic studies during this period will tend to be drawn more and more into the overall problem of Spanish "decadence," and the Spanish Arabists will express varying attitudes toward their subject related in some way, either for or against, to the ideas initiated by Krausism. Most of these Arabists were disciples of Gayangos who, having reached maturity during the mid-nineteenth century, began to make themselves known to the reading public at that time. With rare exceptions, their Arabism was peripheral to other more pressing duties. This, added to the anti-Arab feeling of Simonet, and the premature deaths of others, prevented the emergence of a vigorous tradition and the appearance of outstanding figures. However, their publications as well as their various attitudes towards their subject make the work of these Arabists a preview to that of our own century.

One of the most controversial figures of this age was Francisco Javier Simonet, born in Málaga in 1829, where he studied three years of philosophy and three of theology.[2] In 1845 he went to Madrid to study law, where he met the future minister Cánovas,

---

[1] For a full account *cf.* Juan López Morillas, *El krausismo español, perfil de una aventura intelectual*, Mexico, 1956.

[2] *Cf.* Gómez Moreno, "Unas cartas de El Solitario," in *BRAE*, Madrid, 1953, vol. 33, p. 213.

then a student himself, who, being a nephew of Estébanez Calderón, introduced the young Simonet to his uncle. Estébanez Calderón had learned Arabic first from the Jesuit Artigas,[1] and later from his friend Gayangos whose better preparation in France had permitted the latter to be of help in clarifying Calderón's difficulties. Because Calderón's Arabism had turned more toward literature than scholarship [2] he has not been awarded the place he otherwise deserves in this study. Suffice it to say that Calderón had been closely connected with the liberal movements of the early eighteen hundreds.[3] At his house the young Simonet was to study Arabic along with Eduardo Saavedra, Enrique Alix and even Cánovas himself, who though life's circumstances forced him to abandon this line of endeavour, maintained a lifelong interest in Arabic studies. In 1859 Simonet finished his career in law, and in 1862 he received the chair of Arabic at the University of Granada. Hardly had he taken possession of his chair when Estébanez Calderón wrote him the following words from which all of Simonet's endeavours were to stem:

> We Malagans are the children of that literary cycle, and in particular we have an interest in Arab things. If you are able to establish this subject in that University on a sound basis *and with the purpose of* [elucidating] *what is Castilian and of good Spanish race*, you will be deserving of much gratitude. [4]

The views of Calderón found a ready sympathizer in his disciple, for Simonet was to dedicate his life to elaborating his theory that if anything worth mentioning had come from the Muslims in al-Andalus, that was because they were first and foremost Spaniards. This idea was the transposition onto the field of Arabism of the traditionalist view of Spanish history. Simonet, a pious Catholic, educated in a religious environment first, and then in Estébanez Calderón's school, ended up by affirming the conservative attitude toward Spanish cultural problems. Becoming well known for his scholarly works, he was on friendly terms with the anti-clerical

---

[1] In whose honour he composed an ode. *Cf.* A. Cánovas del Castillo, *"El Solitario" y su tiempo*, Madrid, 1883, vol. I, pp. 74-77.

[2] On this activity as well as his correspondence with Gayangos, *Cf. op. cit.*, vol. I, pp. 249-253, vol. 2, p. 317-392.

[3] A. Cánovas del Castillo, *"El Solitario" y su tiempo, biografia de D. Serafín Estébanez Calderón y crítica de sus obras*, 2 vols., Madrid, 1883.

[4] Gómez Moreno, *op. cit.*, p. 217, Letter dated Madrid, Feb. 12, 1862, (underlining mine.)

Dozy with whom he corresponded, though ideologically there was much to separate the two scholars. In 1867 he received the degree of Doctor in Philosophy and Letters, and was a corresponding member of the Academy of History. He wrote many books,[1] and if we judge from their titles it becomes plain that in them he attributes great importance to the role in Spain's history of Mozarabs and the Catholic Church. Simonet, in short, opposed Gayangos' vision of al-Andalus and brought to light the role of the Romanic peoples in the Muslim empire. Inspired by this goal, he collected from Arabic and Christian sources the materials for his major work, the *Historia de los mozárabes de España,* the purpose of which was to magnify the role played by the Christians in al-Andalus.

The controversial nature of this work, even in his own time is revealed to us in a letter to Simonet, written by Estébanez Calderón in 1866 in which he informs the author that among others Gayangos had opposed the publication of the book by the Academy of History.[2] Indeed, the work remained unpublished till 1897 at which time, the author having died, Saavedra prepared it for the press.

In order to present linguistic evidence for his position Simonet prepared a *Glosario de voces ibéricas y latinas usadas entre los mozárabes,*[3] which attempted to demonstrate the extent to which Romance had been spoken in al-Andalus. His vehemently anti-Muslim and pro-Christian attitude finds eloquent expression in the

---

[1] *Leyendas históricas árabes,* Madrid, 1858; *Descripción del reino de Granada sacado de los autores arábigos,* Madrid, 1860; *Historia de los mozárabes españoles*; *Catálogo de voces ibéricas y latinas usadas entre los mozárabes,* (1880-89); *Discurso sobre la utilidad de los estudios de los autores arábigos para ilustrar la historia de España,* Granada, 1866; *Discurso sobre la edad de oro de la literatura arábigoespanola* Granada, 1865; *Omar ben Hafsón. Estudio biografico*; *El Concilio III de Toledo,* Madrid, 1891; *Elogio del doctor Francisco Suárez y de la Compañía de Jesús* 1875; *Mision civilizadora de la Iglesia Católica y de la nación española en el descubrimiento del Nuevo Mundo,* Granada, 1884; *Influencia del elemento indígena en la cultura de los moros del reino de Granada,* Málaga, 1896; *Crestomatía arábigoespanola* written in collaboration with Lerchundi, Granada, 1882; *Los santos mártires Ciriaco y Paula,* Málaga, 1865. *Cf. Enciclopedia Espasa, s.v. Simonet.*

[2] "Insofar as the monograph on the Mozarabs is concerned, when it was put to vote, I expressed the opinion that it should be accepted, but I was left alone, while those who opposed it were all the Aljamiados [*i.e.* Arabists] of the Academy without excluding Pilate [*i.e.* Gayangos], who voted on their side despite being the sponsor of the book." (Gómez Moreno, *op. cit.*, p. 235, Madrid, April 29, 1866.).

[3] Madrid, 1888.

Descripción del reino de Granada (1860), an extract from Ibn al-Khaṭīb, where, in the Arabic title page he calls himself *'Abd al-Masīḥ Francisco Javier Simonet al-Malaqī,* that is to say, "The servant of the Messiah F.J.S., from Malaga." Thus the Catholic Simonet, by means of an Arabist's joke identified himself with the Christians of al-Andalus, the importance of whom it was to be his duty to make clear. It is necessary to add that Simonet greatly exaggerated the importance of the Mozarabs,[1] so that the day has come when non-Arabists should beware of using his theories, and Arabists should consult his works only when fully aware of their author's motives. Though in this respect Simonet's work has been superseded, he remains the starting point for a whole current of Spanish Arabism, and as such he is very worthy of attention.

In his prologue to the *Historia de los mozárabes de España* he expresses his intention of writing the history of those "Spaniards" as he calls them, who were conquered by the Arabs though managing to maintain their religion and national spirit as well as the Christian culture of ancient Spain. These heroes, in Simonet's eyes, underwent persecution and martyrdom, yet they contributed to the "restoration" of a new Spain.[2] This expression of the belief in an unbroken Spanish history going back to pre-Roman times is an understandable reaction to the vague sense of inferiority experienced by the nineteenth-century Spaniard who observed the achievements of his European contemporaries. The extremism of Simonet's reaction is, however, violent and he uses harsh terms to describe both Muslims [3] as well as Jews.[4]

When he enumerates his historical sources, Simonet speaks highly of Cardinal Cisneros, whom he praises for having restored the archaic Mozarabic ritual in Toledo at the end of the fifteenth

---

[1] An attitude accepted by some historians such as J. Vicens Vives who says: "Millás Vallicrosa's criticism of the theories of C. Sánchez Albornoz has persuaded me that the truth is to be found in the understanding of this twofold phenomenon: conversion of the peasantry to Islam and diminishing of the role attributed to the Mozarabs as a dissident element in the South and as a nationalist one in the North." *Cf. Aproximación a la historia de España,* 2nd ed., Barcelona, 1960, p. 228.

[2] *Cf. Hist.,* p. vii.

[3] *Hist*: "Mahometan superstition" (p. xv), "Arab arrogance" (p. xvi), "Muslim fanaticism" (p. xli), "the insatiable Sarracen greed" (p. 43).

[4] *Hist*: "Banished race" (p. 43), "the Hebrew nation. . . everywhere mercenary and rancorous" (p. 42).

century. He also praises the classical historian Mariana, who had not consulted Arabic sources, Flórez, Casiri, Masdeu, and others. Indeed, Flórez's *España sagrada,* drawn almost entirely from Christian documents is one of the principal sources of Simonet who found in that author the traditional orientation with which he himself sympathized.

Insofar as his Arabic sources are concerned, Simonet states that most of the authors such as Ibn al-Qūṭiyya, Ibn Ḥayyān, Ibn Ḥazm, and Ibn Bashkuwāl were racially "Spaniards" though Islamized, while he adds that the "fanaticism" of their new religion did not permit them to attribute much importance to their "racial" brothers the Mozarabs.[1] Thus he ends up rejecting the Arabic historiographic tradition almost in its entirety. He opposes the more serene scholarly tradition initiated by Conde only to fall into the worst kind of onesidedness in his conclusions. Simonet attacked all the Arabists before him, stating that recent historiography had falsified the account of Spanish history by ascribing too much importance to the Arab conquest. He assures us that contrary to commonly held opinion, Muslim rule in Spain as opposed to other regions, was precarious and subsisted only at the price of constant border warfare against Christianity.[2] Thus the conquerors were neither strong enough to destroy the native population nor numerous enough to repopulate the Peninsula.[3] However, though the truth of this statement cannot be doubted, this by no means contradicts the fact that the Muslims of al-Andalus, be they Arabs, Berbers, Slavs or native Peninsulars were the essential factor in shaping the destiny of al-Andalus for several centuries, and in their role as Muslims were to have an enormous impact upon Spanish history. This Simonet was unable to understand very clearly. However, one of the most interesting points he brings up in his work, and which today has once more been aired in recent historical investigations, is his refutation of the opinion that the Mozarabs gradually lost their racial and national feeling of solidarity as they intermarried with the Muslims. He claims that these Mozarabs, upon being freed from the Muslim yoke, obtained from the Christian monarchs several privileges based almost exclusively on their not having sullied the purity of their lineage by marriages

---

1 *Cf. Hist.*, p. xxiv-xxv.
2 *Op. cit.*, p. xxxii.
3 *Op. cit.*, p. xxxiii.

with Muslims.[1] Although in his day Simonet was not able to give a balanced interpretation of this fact, it remains to some degree exact and was to have enormous consequences on Spanish history. In effect, the Koranic doctrine regarding marriages between Muslims and non-Muslims expresses that it is better for a Muslim to marry within his own religion, though marriage to Christian and Jewish women is regarded legal and honorable.[2] That is to say that a Muslim man may marry a Christian or Jewish woman who would be expected eventually to accept Islam and bring up her children as Muslims. On the other hand, a Muslim woman may not marry a non-Muslim man, because her Muslim status would be affected, since the wife ordinarily takes the nationality and status given by her husband's law.[3] As it applied to al-Andalus, this aspect of Islamic doctrine meant that Mozarabic women could marry Muslim men, though their children were brought up as Muslims. On the other hand, it was rare, at least in theory (though a few exceptions did occur to confirm the rule) for a Muslim woman to marry a Mozarab. In this social situation, a large part of the Christian population was gradually being absorbed into Islam. As a reaction to this general tendency, the Mozarabs developed their religious fervour along new and unsuspected lines as Simonet showed in sketching the history of the Mozarabic martyrs. But more important in its results on their mentality was the fact that as a consequence of Muslim legislation every Christian was assured that his religious belief was a perfect guarantee of his not having any Muslim ancestry. Thus in the Mozarabic mind, religion in its function as a guarantee of lineage, eventually became identified with it, so that it became

---

[1] "They obtained from the restoring monarchs most unusual privileges for their candour and nobility, based mainly on their *not having stained their lineage or corrupted their Spanish or Visigothic blood, by uniting themselves to and mingling with the Moors. . .*" (*op. cit.*, p. xxvi).

[2] "Do not marry unbelieving women (idolaters), until they believe: a slave woman who believes is better than an unbelieving woman, even though she allure you. Nor marry (your girls) to unbelievers until they believe: a man slave who believes is better than an unbeliever, even though he allure you. Unbelievers do but beckon you to the Fire." (*Koran*, S. 2, v. 221).

"(Lawful unto you in marriage) are (not only) chaste women who are believers, but chaste women among the People of the Book (i.e. Christians and Jews) revealed before your time,—when ye give them their due dowers, and desire chastity, not lewdness, nor secret intrigues." (*Koran*, S 5., v. 6).

[3] *Cf. The Holy Qur-an*, ed. by ʿAbd Allāh Yūsuf ʿAlī, Cambridge, Massachusetts, 1946, vol. I, p. 241, n. 700.

important to discover for oneself Visigothic ancestors to prove the purity of one's faith and lineage. This social phenomenon was aggravated within al-Andalus by the conversion of large numbers of the native population which in turn led to large scale discrimination. In al-Andalus, the new converts suffered social ostracism to an extent unknown in the Orient, where adoption into the Arab tribes brought some measure of social status to the convert or *mawla*. In al-Andalus, however, the Arab tribes did not adopt *mawlas* at all.[1] The friction between Arab and non-Arab throughout the empire led to a wide-spread discontent which found its literary expression in the *Shuʿūbite* or "nationalist" movement which had its origin among certain Persian Muslims who ridiculed the Arabs by claiming for Persia the glory of having developed the benefits of civilization. This movement, studied by Goldziher,[2] was not unknown in al-Andalus. In 1889 Goldziher published an article on the Andalusian *Shuʿūbite* movement [3] in which he studied the figure of Ibn García. Simonet was of course unable to consult this study by Goldziher, written after his time, but he does mention Ibn García, whom he describes as a "Christian" who wrote against the Islamic faith.[4] This in fact is not true, for Ibn García was a Muslim. His literary epistle or *risāla* was directed not against Islam, but against Arab nationalism within the Muslim world. The polemical literature of the *Shuʿūbiyya* in al-Andalus is not too well known, though in most cases it takes the form of the earlier controversy in Persia, making frequent references to Persian themes rather than to specifically Andalusian ones, thus indicating the extent to which the polemic had become a literary exercise. This is owing in part to

---

[1] *Cf.* Armand Abel, *Spain: Internal division*, in *Unity and Variety in Muslim Civilization*, ed. by Gustave E. von Grunebaum, Chicago, 1955, pp. 213-214.

[2] Ignaz Goldziher, *Muhammedanische Studien I*, Halle, 1888-90, p. 143 ff.

[3] *Cf. Die Šuʿūbijja unter den Muhammedanern in Spanien*, in *Zeitschrift der Deutschen Morgenlandischen Gesellschaft*, vol. 53, 1889, pp. 601-620.

[4] "There is also a record of the fact that at the end of the twelfth century a Christian named Ibn García flourished in this country and wrote against the Mahometan religion. He was refuted by two theologians and scholars of Islam, namely the Granadan Abdelmonim ben Alfaras, who died in the same city in 597 (1200) and the Malagan Mohammed ben Ali, known as Ibn Abdirrabbihi, who died in 602 (1205). Ibn Aljatib in his *Iḥāṭa*." (*Hist.*, p. 791, n. 2). See my monograph: *The Shuʿūbiyya in al-Andalus: The Risāla of Ibn García and Five Refutations: Introduction, Translation and Notes*, University of California Publications: Near Eastern Studies, 13 (Berkeley-Los Angeles, 1969).

the remarkable traditionalism of Arabic literature; once the theme had been established, it was modified in style and presentation rather than in content.

According to Goldziher, Ibn García was a descendent of a family which had converted to Islam who, according to al-Balāwī, used the *nisba* or genealogical name *al-Bashkunsī* "the Basque."[1] He wrote his *risāla* to Abū ʿAbd Allāh ibn al-Ḥaddād, court poet of Muʿtaṣim ibn Ṣumādiḥ, lord of Almería, and in it he says many notable things in defense of the non-Arabs over the Arabs. In his arguments, as in those of Orientals before him [2] the significance of lineage plays an important role.[3] The extracts from Ibn García's *risāla* (included in Derenbourg, *Les Manuscrits Arabes de l'Escurial* I, num. 538 (10) fol. 26r-29r) published by Goldziher in his study are notable in many respects, and deserving of more attention than has been accorded them. The *Shuʿūbite* movement had as a matter of fact been known much earlier in al-Andalus, for Ibn ʿAbd Rabbihi of Cordova (died AD 940), descended from an enfranchised slave of the Umayyad caliph Hishām ibn ʿAbd ar-Raḥmān (788-796) has left us a miscellaneous anthology of extracts dealing with literary education, entitled *Al-ʿIqd al-Farīd*, or "The Unique Necklace," which is divided into twenty-five books, each bearing the name of a different gem, and "contains something on every subject,"[4] and in which he discusses the *Shuʿūbite* movement.[5]

---

[1] A poem in al-Balāwī (*Alif-Bā*, I, p 350, b. 19) says about Ibn García: "And so, who is this man who sought to depreciate (the Arabs) in what he wrote of foolishness, contained in pages ?

"When one is asked: "Who?" They answer: "Ibn García. It sufficed him in respect of nobility that the Christians were his tribesmen,

"From whom he learned hardness of heart and crudeness; though he himself is crude and his speech is rude." (*Cf.* Goldziher, *op. cit.*, p. 606, n. 2.—My translation).

[2] Such as al-Jāḥiẓ and Ibn Qutayba. Cf. *Kitāb al-ʿArab*, by Ibn Qutayba for example.

[3] In this respect Goldziher says:

"Die Muwalladūn stehen entweder im regelmässigen Verhältnis von Mawali innerhalb des Organismus der grossen arabischen Familie, oder sie lassen auch diese Formalität vollends fallen, indem haben sie sich einen regelrechten arabischen Stammbaum beilegen. Wir haben bereits anderswo ein Beispiel dafur angefuhrt, was man unter dem Ausdruck *saḥḥaḥa nasabahu, tasḥiḥ al-nasab,* die Anpassung oder Richtigstellung der Genealogie, zu verstehen habe." *Cf.* "Die Šuʿūbiyya," p. 603.

For a translation *cf.* my monograph.

[4] *Cf.* Nicholson, *A Literary History of the Arabs*, p. 347.

[5] Book 12 of this work, entitled *Ansāb al-ʿArab* "The lineages of the Arabs"

These facts indicate the importance on a social level of what Simonet had pointed to; that is to say, that as in other lands, in al-Andalus the Arab conquest introduced a theoretical religious equality accompanied by an actual social friction which grew worse as time went on. These social pressures based on lineage made books on genealogy extremely popular so that many distinguished Andalusians of native origin (i.e. Ibn Ḥazm) tried to relate their family trees to Arabian tribes.

This on the one hand, and the Koranic laws on marriage on the other, created a situation unique in European history, in which the Mozarabs identified their religion with their lineage. These feelings, which were alive in al-Andalus at the end of the twelfth century, swerved the course of later Spanish history. What Simonet could not see from his traditionalist point of view, was that this situation which left a deeply rooted identification of lineage with religion, was to flare up into a tragic conflagration later on with the "estatutos de limpieza de sangre" and the inquisitory practices of Golden Age Spain. Simonet, who saw the Iberian Peninsula as the eternal repository of an Orthodox, Spanish, Catholic civilization, could not sense that it was in reality the presence of the Arabs and the conditions they imposed which were to change the course of Spanish history, making Spain diverge from the predominantly secularized development history took in the rest of Europe. This had been sensed by earlier Arabists, as we have observed in the case of Gayangos. Outside Spain, scholars of the importance of Dozy felt the same way about Spanish history. The latter had indeed written that the Arabs had imposed upon the conquered natives not only their language, but also to a certain extent their religion,[1] a statement which Simonet would not allow to pass unchallenged. His orientation is such that he tries to minimize the importance of Arabic studies, complaining of the excessive

---

presents the arguments for and against the problem. The importance of lineage in the Arab society will be realized from the chapter headings of this book: *On the lineage and nobility of the Arabs, The origin of lineage, The nobility of the Banī Hāshim and Banī Umayya, The nobility of Quraysh, The status of the Arabs of Quraysh, The nobility of the Arabs, The genealogists, The noble houses, The names of the sons of Nizār, The lineages of Muḍar, The words of the Shuʿūbiyya who are the partisans of equality, The refutation of the Shuʿūbiyya by Ibn Qutayba, The refutation of Ibn Qutayba by the Shuʿūbiyya.*

[1] *Cf.* Simonet, *Hist.*, p. xxxviii.

zeal with which Spanish Arabists had turned to the study of Islam.[1]

Attacking the problem of the language spoken by the Mozarabs, he considers that the Arabs failed to learn Romance out of haughtiness or lack of interest so that the subjected peoples were forced to learn Arabic to communicate with their new masters. However, the Mozarabs never forgot, but rather preserved the use of the Romance dialect within the radius of the home. As commonly occurs in Simonet, he contradicts himself further on while discussing Álvaro of Cordova and his complaints over the Arabization of Christian youth.[2] The trouble with Simonet's theories is that the facts he adduces are subject to divergent interpretations. Although the question of the relationship of the Mozarabic dialect to Arabic must be re-evaluated before any definite conclusions can be reached, it is important to indicate that in the Arab world a linguistic dichotomy has always existed between the literary language and the vernacular tongues, a dichotomy present even in pre-Islamic Arabia. The fact that in al-Andalus Romance served the function of a vernacular speech by no means modifies this general trait, the difference between al-Andalus and other Islamic countries being in this case one of kind though not of degree. This by no means affected the literary style of the official language which remained essentially Eastern in its inspiration. In the case of Ibn García, for example, we find that though he attacks the Arabs, he does so *as a Muslim, in Arabic, and entirely from within the tradition of Arabic literature*. In this respect, Simonet's disquisitions on language may today be seriously questioned.

Simonet, in his *Historia*, embarked upon a long lamentation on the injustices committed by the Arabs against the Mozarabs whom he describes as shining examples of selfless martyrdom, a glorious page in the annals of Spain, and an episode in the "continuous

[1] "In imitation of the Mahometans themselves, who as a rule know no other world than the Islamic, these eulogizers of Arabic culture, forgetting, or being ignorant of the great literary, scientific, and social progress achieved by our nation under Visigothic rule, have come to imagine that the Saracen conquest introduced all sorts of arts and knowledge into Spain, ranging from agriculture to philosophy, and that it deprived the subjected population of its national Hispano-Latin language, replacing it with Arabic. And what is even more serious, if we judge the quarrels and discord between conquerors and conquered from the tribunal of their criticism, is that they have judged the case in favour of the former, praising the tolerance of the Muslims and deploring the fanaticism of the Christians." (*Op. cit.*, pp. xli-xlii).

[2] *Cf.* pp. xlii-xlviii.

crusade" of Spanish Catholicism against the infidel.[1] The fact that this was a nineteenth-century reaction to European values can be seen in that Simonet compares the Arab conquest of 711 to the French invasion of 1808. He praises the Spanish war of Independence against Joseph Bonaparte, and severely condemns the *afrancesados* whom he compares to the Visigothic magnates who had collaborated with the Arabs.[2]

The weakest point in Simonet's arguments in favour of Mozarabic culture lies in the fact that he himself was forced to admit that as time went on and absorption into Islam continued, the Mozarabic population gradually diminished and ceased to play a significant role in the community.[3] At the same time that he indicates the gradual disintegration of all but a remnant of the Christian population of al-Andalus, Simonet distorts the truth by attributing excessive importance to Mozarabic "influences" on Andalusian culture. Even his own facts speak out eloquently against his conclusions: he shows how all cultural forces favoured conversion to Islam; how the Mozarabic Church, which far from descending from a Visigothic *Catholic orthodoxy* as he claims,[4] continued to be torn by heresies of all sorts and to show signs of evident decay by the second half of the eighth century.[5] Insofar as literature is concerned we observe a gradual turning toward usage of the Arabic language on the part of the Mozarabs.[6] The degree to which the Mozarabic Church was controlled by the Muslim authorities is exemplified by the fact that the emirs of Cordova intervened in the naming of bishops and

---

[1] *Op. cit.*, p. liv.

[2] *Op. cit.*, pp. 35, 39.

[3] *Op. cit.*, pp. 140-141.

[4] The Visigoths were largely Arians before the conversion of Recaredo in A.D. 589.

[5] Cixila had governed the Diocese of Toledo from 744 to 753 and had adopted the heresy of Sabelius, an African heresiarch who denied the real distinction of the three persons of the Trinity. Bishop Egilanus governed the Diocese of Elvira from 777-784 and became a heretic. Elipandus, Metropolitan of Toledo (b. 717, d. 808) fell into the heresy of *adoptionism* which according to Alquin, originated in Cordova and maintained that Jesus was not a real and natural son of God, but only an adoptive and nominal son. (*op. cit.*, pp. 266-267). These heresies are all obvious attempts to make the doctrine of the Trinity palatable to Islam. They therefore represent a state of intermediary religions.

[6] Said, Metropolitan of Bætica wrote a commentary to the scriptures which he left in Arabic. A certain Juan de Sevilla, possibly the same Said, translated the Gospel into Arabic. *Op. cit.*, pp. 321-322.

authorized the celebration of ecclesiastical councils.[1] Heresy invaded the Mozarabic community to such an extent and its defections were so numerous that the staunch Christian lower classes became more agressively militant, thus preparing the way for the numerous voluntary martyrdoms which followed. The resulting repression of the Mozarabic zealots clearly indicates that al-Andalus was governed essentially by Islamic and not by Christian law, a fact which Simonet did not care to recall. Tolerance on the part of the conquerors was dependant upon respect for the Islamic institutions on the part of the conquered, and it was only when this balance was broken that retaliations were carried out. Simonet mentions a Christian named Perfecto [2] who in a discussion with some Muslim theologians committed the unpardonable offence (in the view of Islamic jurisprudence) of slandering their religion. They retaliated by inciting a riot against him and accused him of having insulted their Prophet. This pattern of voluntary violation of the established law continued, and a number of zealots presented themselves before the judges of Cordova to declare their anti-Muslim convictions. Though the retaliation was usually prompt, it is significant to note that one judge remonstrated with a Christian youth, and tried to explain to him the gravity of his offence before convicting him.[3]

Though these martyrs may form a glorious page in the annals of the Church, it should be understood that socially, they were in a subservient position and were more influenced than influencing. Furthermore, all these martyrs spoke, read, and wrote Arabic with great ease, and we may judge that it became their mother tongue from the fact (mentioned but unstressed by Simonet) that in the Mozarabic manuscripts written in Latin, numerous marginal annotations are to be found explaining *in Arabic* the meaning of unfamiliar Latin terms.[4] A Christian who has recourse to Arabic to translate Latin terminology must surely be considered to be highly Arabized, as was the case in al-Andalus, where some of these Mozarabs

---

[1] *Op. cit.*, pp. 337-338.
[2] *Op. cit.*, p. 386.
[3] *Op. cit.*, p. 393: "Perhaps being in a state of drunkenness or of frenzy, you do not realize what you are saying; you have forgotten that it is an unbreakable law of the very Prophet you have so daringly insulted, that whoever dares commit so serious an offense should be awarded the maximum penalty."
[4] *Op. cit.*, p. 639, also, *Glosario*, plate facing p. xxxii.

adopted Arabic names.[1] The suppression of their movement against Islam led to mass emigrations to Christian Spain where in 852 Ordoño I granted the monastery of Samos in Galicia to some Cordovan monks. It may be supposed that these expatriates in northern Spain brought with them their system of values and were thus influential in the development of Spanish history.

Once the problem of Christians versus Muslims had quieted down in al-Andalus, the social problem of Arabs versus non-Arabs; the *Shuʿūbiyya* movement, began to develop. Simonet agrees that these struggles were based on race rather than religion,[2] and he goes into an analysis of local rebels such as ʿUmar ibn Ḥafṣūn, who exemplified the profound social disharmony *within Islam*. However, Simonet wastes no time in making true "Spaniards" of these rebels. Thus he mentions that in 887 what he calls "los españoles de Elvira" [3] captured an Arab warlord named Yaḥya, whom they killed along with his followers. Aroused by their success these "Spaniards" found a mouthpiece in the words of their poet ʿAbd ar-Raḥmān ibn Aḥmad of Abla. However, the poem their author wrote in honour of the occasion [4] was composed entirely in the traditional terms of Arabic poetry, and expressing *Shuʿūbite* sentiments. These "Spaniards" of Elvira threw into the Alhambra a paper containing more Arabic verses by the same poet,[5] which challenge, functioning entirely within the conventionalisms of Arabic poetry is indicative of the degree to which these peoples had become Arabized.[6] Simonet's

---

1 Simonet notes the case of a certain *Servio Dei* (*cf.* p. 437) and obvious translation of *ʿAbd Allāh.*

2 *Op. cit.*, p. 503: "The character of these struggles and wars was, it would seem, based more on race than on religion."

3 *Op. cit.*, p. 542-43.

4 "The lances of our enemies have been broken, and we have destroyed their arrogance. The *vile rabble*, as they call us, have undermined the bases of their power. For how long have the dead bodies of their kin, cast by us into this well, waited in vain for an avenger." (*Op. cit.*, p. 545).

5 "Their mansions have become deserted, converted into wastelands through which hurricanes violently blow whirlwinds of dust.

"In vain do they, sheltered in the fortress of Alhambra, hatch their wicked plots, for therein are they surrounded by dangers and defeats." (*Op. cit.*, p. 545).

6 Note the theme of the deserted encampment as it is employed by al-Asadī in reply to the above:

"Our mansions are not deserted, nor are our fields converted into wastelands. . .

"Our castle protects us against all offense; in it will we encounter glory, in it do triumphs await us, while for you there will be defeats." (*Op. cit.*, p. 545).

"Spaniards" were not guerrillas fighting for Christian supremacy, but for social equality with the Arabs, *within Islam.* After the creation of the Caliphate by ʿAbd ar-Raḥmān III, Simonet declares that these social equalitarians, good Muslims all, lost their identity within Islam, whereas the few remaining Mozarabs retained their religion as the only remaining feature of their "national character."[1] With the Reconquest, their status improved due to the favour with which the Christian monarchs looked upon the purity of their lineage, all of which indicates the extent to which social conditions in al-Andalus had helped to shape that identification of religion with lineage which was to bring Spain to greatness and tragedy.[2]

Simonet's other works reveal the same attitude which prevails in his *Historia.* Thus in the *Glosario de voces ibéricas y latinas usadas entre los mozárabes* he carries the problem to the field of language. In a preliminary study of the Mozarabic dialect he affirms his traditionalist standing by again attacking his predecessors, especially Juan Andrés whom he challenges for having stated that the Andalusians were instrumental in restoring to Europe both science and belles lettres, as well as in creating and developing the vernacular tongues and inventing the prosodic system of the Romance languages.[3] Against this idea Simonet brings to bear the authority of the great historian Ibn Khaldūn whom he quotes as saying that the Arabs were incapable of founding or governing an empire and that they had ruined every country they conquered.[4] Actually, though Ibn Khaldūn did make this statement, Simonet forgets that the genius of that historian is in itself proof of the vitality of Islamic culture. However, intent on playing down the role of the Arabs in history, Simonet mentions that most of the learned men of al-

---

[1] *Op. cit.*, p. 602.

[2] Alfonso X conceded to the Mozarabs of Toledo in 1259 the privilege of not paying the tax known as *almoneda* for the following reasons:

"Otrosí: por fazer bien e merced a los nobles caballeros mozárabes de Toledo que *vienen directamente del linaje de los mozárabes a quienes ciñeron espada los de mi linage o sus ricos homes . . . o Nos . . .* otorgamos que hayan este mismo quitamiento de moneda." *I.e.* "Furthermore: in order to perform an act of beneficence and of honour to the noble Mozarabic gentlemen whose swords were girded on them by those of my lineage or their lords. . . or by Us. . . we grant that they be exempted from this same *almoneda.*" (*Op. cit.*, p. 687).

[3] *Glosario,* p. xxxix, n. 1.

[4] *Op. cit.*, p. xlii.

Andalus were of native origin [1] and as linguistic proof of the importance of the Mozarabs he states that the number of Romance words which appeared in Arabic manuscripts was almost as great as the number of Arabic words in Spanish. However, these words appear above all in works on botany, and are usually in the form of explanatory notes which by no means displace the Arabic word. Thus, for example, in mentioning the wealth of Romance words to be found in the *Dīwān* of Ibn Quzmān, Simonet overlooks the popularizing nature of that poet's muse. The words found in the work of Ibn Quzmān are colloquial expressions which represent little borrowing in the fields of science, philosophy or political institutions. Unlike the influx of technical terms from Greek into Eastern Arabic, the foreign words which appeared in al-Andalus were used in literature for their picturesque or literary effect. Furthermore, many of these foreign terms are explanations or translations which do not really replace the Arabic term but simply gloss it.[2] After discussing the vast number of words in Spanish which have an Arabic etymology; and important words at that, which reflect the adoption of Islamic institutions, Simonet is reluctantly forced to admit that the Mozarabic words in Arabic, by contrast, exerted an influence which hardly went beyond that of the dictionary.[3] He concludes by once more contradicting himself in stating that his research has had the double purpose of vindicating for the "Hispano-Latin" nation the honour of having preserved its language and literature during the centuries of "foreign domination" and also of investigating the origins of the Spanish language.[4]

One of the important contributions made by Simonet to the history of Spanish linguistics was that of indicating the link between Vulgar Latin and the Romance dialects of the Peninsula. By showing that these dialects did not arise spontaneously in the North, but rather, had existed all over the Peninsula, especially in the South, before the Arab invasion, he made a significant advance in the study of Romance linguistics.

Simonet likewise published a work entitled *Santoral Hispano-*

---

[1] *Op. cit.*, pp. xliii-lix.

[2] Simonet mentions that Ibn Buclarix of Saragossa, in his *Dictionary of Medicine* writes: "Man in Persian is *mardom* and in Latin *vir*." (*Op. cit.*, p. xcvi). In this case, as in others, neither *mardom* nor *vir* replace the Arabic word *insān*.

[3] *Op. cit.*, p. cxxxi.

[4] *Op. cit.*, p. cxciv.

mozárabe escrito en 961 *por Rabi Ben Zaid, Obispo de Ilíberis* (Madrid, 1871) which is of great interest because of the highly Arabized state of its Latin, as well as for the number of saints it lists who, though unknown to Western Christendom, were familiar to Coptic Egypt and the East.[1] This indicates the close connection between the Mozarabic Church and that of North Africa and the Middle East.

In sum, carried away by his traditionalist view of a Spain opposed to innovation, Simonet transposed his traditional attitude on the problem of Spanish "decadence" to the field of Arabic studies. Though his theories were exaggerated, they had the merit of pointing to the inner problems of Andalusian culture and the relationship of the conquered peoples to their conquerors in the fields of politics and linguistics. This work on the part of Simonet was to open the way for the future studies of Ribera on the *azjāl* of Ibn Quzmān, as well as for the present day studies on the *muwashshaḥāt.* [2]

Simonet, in spite of his anti-Arab attitude, was to be of very great significance in the development of Spanish Arabism, because he was the starting point of a nationalistic trend in these studies which for the first time began to speak of *Spanish* Muslims, instead of the *Arabs in Spain,* thus suggesting that Islamic culture in al-Andalus had been primarily a Spanish phenomenon which owed little to Eastern importations. This idea of an unbroken continuity in Spanish culture from the most remote ages, including Roman, Visigothic and Arab rule, was to become the main battle-cry of traditionalism.

---

[1] For example, the entry corresponding to March 9 reads: "In ipso est Egyptus festum *almagre,* qui liniunt cum ea portas eorum et cornua vaccarum suarum. Et nominatur festum cere, et est introitus Christi ad altare." (*Santoral* p. 20) Likewise, the entry corresponding to April 22 states: "In ipso est christianis festum Filippi apostoli in domo almégdis (id est Jerusalem)". (*Op. cit.*, p. 21). *Domo almegdis* is the Arabic Bait al-Maqdis or "the holy house", the common Muslim denomination for Jerusalem.

[2] Actually, Simonet's correspondence with Dozy indicates that he had studied Ibn Quzmān's *Dīwān,* though he never incorporated his material into a work on that poet. *Cf.* Gómez Moreno, *op. cit., BRAE,* Mádrid, vol. 33, 1953, p. 216.

CHAPTER FOUR

If Simonet represented the traditionalist approach to history, others were to be more closely in touch with the progressive movement represented by Krausism and the Institución Libre de Enseñanza. This organization looked upon Arabic studies with a favourable eye. Thus we learn of a professor of Arabic, Fernández y Ferraz, a close friend of Giner de los Ríos who taught at the Institución and later went to Costa Rica where he organized educational programmes and conducted research in American Indian languages.[1] Since his research in the field of Arabic was insubstantial, his main importance lies in the fact that he exemplifies the interest of the Institución in Arabic studies; an interest which led it in 1880 to name Dozy honorary professor,[2] as well as to encourage the publication of articles on Oriental subjects. A regular collaborator in the periodical of the Institución was José Ramón Mélida, an Orientalist of minor significance, but who seemed to be equally familiar with Arabic, Sanscrit, and other Eastern languages. In an article dated 1883, he presents a defense of Arabic studies in which he complains of the excessive attention paid by Spanish scholars to Latin studies while neglecting Arabic, which he identifies with what is more natively Spanish.[3] His words reflect the liberal tendency of the age to bring Arabic studies to the forefront, and are in direct opposition to the ideas of Simonet, for whom Spain was substantially Latin, and for whom the Arabs had acted as a mere external accident.

One of the more important Arabists of this age, also connected with the Institución was Eduardo Saavedra y Moragas to whom

---

[1] For an account of Fernández y Ferraz's life, *cf. Enciclopedia Espasa, s.v.* Fernández y Ferraz.

[2] *Cf. Boletín de la Institución Libre de Enseñanza*, vol. 8, Madrid, 1884, p. 145.

[3] "The excessive attention paid to the Latin language and to its valuable monuments by Spanish men of letters, ever since the age of the Renaissance; the excessive desire to find out *about foreign matters, while viewing native ones with disdain*; and finally, the scant popularity it has enjoyed and enjoys today, have contributed to make the study of Arabic epigraphy merely the minor concern of a rare scholar." *Cf.* José Ramón Mélida, "Memoria acerca de algunas inscripciones arábigas de España y Portugal," in *op. cit.*, vol. 7 Madrid, 1883, pp. 366-67.

considerable attention should be paid in order to follow the development of Arabic studies in Spain.

Saavedra had been a disciple of Gayangos, with whom he always maintained the closest friendship. He also studied with Estébanez Calderón. Born in Tarragona in 1829, he came to Madrid where in 1847 he was licensed to teach Arabic. Arabism, however, was only one of his many activities. Thus in 1851 he finished his studies in engineering, and in 1870 he received a degree in architecture. From these facts it will be observed that the sciences occupied a large part of his activities so that he may be considered to represent the constructive and progressive element in Spanish society, intent on creating a better future for the nation, after the model represented by Europe. From the point of view of scholarship, this would mean that if Simonet had defended the Mozarabs and the values of the Church, Saavedra would defend the Moriscos and their valiant stand against the excesses of the Inquisition.

Saavedra worked as an engineer for the province of Soria, as also for the Northeastern railways, and taught for the Ministry of Public Works, as inspector of highways, canals and ports, counsellor in Public Education, Senator, member of the Academy of History of which he became director, as well as taking part in many other public activities too numerous to list.[1] As a historian, Arabist, geographer, engineer, architect and man of letters he wrote more than two hundred works. Among those on Arabic themes the most noteworthy are: *Escritos de los musulmanes sometidos al dominio cristiano*,[2] *La geografía de España del Edrisi*, (1881); *Estudio sobre la invasión de los árabes en España* (1892). He also left unfinished an *Historia arábiga* which is said to be of some value. The importance of Saavedra may be observed from the many references to him made by his friends and contemporaries in official speeches. Arabists such as Ribera speak of his vast erudition, and the number and style of these panegyrics indicates that they are something more than the commonplaces usually found in necrological literature.

Ribera speaks particularly of the interest he took in Arabic studies and the assistance he offered to his friends in spite of the many duties which called him away from his scholarly activities.

---

1 For an account of Saavedra's life, *cf.*: *Enciclopedia Espasa, s.v. Saavedra y Moragas, E.*

2 His entrance speech into the Academy of Spanish. 1878, in *Memorias de la Real Academia Española*, vol. 6, 1889, 141-328.

He mentions Saavedra's integrity and moral rectitude which kept him above the petty rivalries common in all professions.[1] In this almost puritanical severity it is possible to discern some of the traits peculiar to the Krausist group and which the latter had popularized in Spain. Saavedra's generosity was such that he collaborated in the publication of Simonet's *Historia de los mozárabes* in spite of the fact that he disagreed with the defunct author's opinions. Indeed, the tables at the end of the book were composed entirely by Saavedra, who otherwise supervised the publication of the disorderly and illegible manuscript. Comparing him to his close friend Codera, Ribera says that the two coincided in their severe and pure moral and religious tendencies, and that they both shared the same ideals and beliefs, of a broad and liberal nature in social and political matters. At the same time they were united in their "ambiciones científicas,"[2] a statement made all the more interesting because it was precisely at this time that the rationalist doctrines of Krause had led, in Spain, to much talk about "scientific" history, and naturally, "scientific" Arabic studies. As Juan López Morillas has explained in his work on Krausism,[3] the Spanish word *ciencia* was at this time extended to include areas of meaning implicit in the German word *Wissenschaft.*

Saavedra, being more practical than the scholarly and retiring Codera, helped the latter to consolidate Arabic studies in Spain and to organize them into a united effort; a "school" if one will, which drank deeply in the "scientific" tradition of historical interpretation. He also did his utmost to assist and encourage young and aspiring Arabists to complete their studes.

Codera also had much to say in memory of his lifelong friend. He stressed the fact that Saavedra's multiple occupations had made Arabism, of necessity, a secondary activity for him, though he adds that in this field he produced works of true merit.[4] Codera mentions that his work as an engineer of public works allowed Saavedra to acquire a direct knowledge of Spanish topography which he was able to use fruitfully in clarifying many problems of Hispano-

[1] *Cf.* Julián Ribera, *Huellas, que aparecen en los primitivos historiadores musulmanes de la Península, de una poesía épica romanceada que debió florecer en Andalucía en los siglos IX y X*, Madrid, 1915, pp. 6-9.

[2] *Cf. op. cit., loc. cit.*

[3] *Cf. El krausismo español*, Mexico, 1956, pp. 90-94.

[4] Francisco Codera, *Contestación*, in *Discursos leídos ante la Real Academia de la Historia*, Madrid, 1915, pp. 67-71.

Arabic geography.[1] Saavedra collected an enormous quantity of data on topographical matters, but he was never able to publish his material which still awaits the appearance of a geographically inclined Arabist.

One of the more important aspects of Saavedra's work was his attempt to broaden the scope of Arabic studies by establishing cultural contacts with Islamic countries. Indeed, the most salient feature of Spanish Arabism before Ribera was its somewhat provincial narrowing down of scope to include only the activities which had taken place in al-Andalus. But Saavedra had attended the opening of the Suez Canal in his capacity as an engineer, and had taken advantage of this opportunity to tour Egypt and make contacts with the people of that country. Realizing the importance of such cultural trips he used his influence to have Ribera sent as attaché on a diplomatic mission to Morocco, with the specific order of buying as many books as possible. The vicissitudes undergone by Ribera do not concern us here,[2] though it is important to note that he brought back some important Arabic manuscripts, and thus initiated a series of cultural exchanges which have never ceased to illuminate the field of Spanish Arabic studies.

It has been mentioned that Cánovas del Castillo was interested in Arabic studies. In his reply to Saavedra's inaugural speech to the Royal Spanish Academy, Cánovas fondly recalls his friendship, begun early in youth, for the distinguished Arabist. He relates how the two met at the home of his uncle, Estébanez Calderón, where it seems that Cánovas took no small part in the literary discussions on Arabic themes,[3] while Estébanez Calderón took a singular interest in assisting Saavedra in his work.

---

[1] However, Lévi-Provençal has questioned some of Saavedra's work on topography in our own times, and the whole problem is under revision by Jaime Oliver Asín.

[2] Of this mission Codera says: "The official character of his mission was of no use to him in such circumstances; so much so, that to the repeated pleas made to the ministry of state of the Sultan by the [Spanish] ambassador, the former turned a deaf ear, until it finally replied that if Señor Ribera wished to visit the library of the Sultan he should first embrace Islam. In spite of this, Señor Ribera was able to acquire some books, through the mediation of certain Jews, as well as works of greater significance, when he entered by surprise into a Moorish bookstore, to which he was thereafter unable to return, because the bookseller would block his way whenever he saw him coming." *Cf. op. cit.*, p. 71.

[3] "It was there, that by lending an attentive ear to the frequent literary discussions about the speech, writing and literature of the Semitic peoples

Saavedra was on good terms with the Institución Libre de Enseñanza. In 1878 he delivered a lecture there on the Koran,[1] which is revealing of the tempo of the times.

López Morillas has explained that Krausism brought with it an interest in history, to the point that historiography pervaded almost all fields of intellectual endeavour in Spain. This, according to López Morillas was a symptom of dissatisfaction with the present. Spanish thinkers scorned contemporary Spain in the name of a past grandeur or a hoped-for renaissance. At the same time these historically-minded thinkers, being devotees of reason, did not look upon history as a temporal projection of human life, but rather as the incarnation of an abstract idea in time. History thus becomes a sort of measurement of the distance which separates real life from the ideal; what *is* from what *ought to be*.[2] This in a sense makes for bad history, because it presupposes an absolute standard and encourages dangerous value judgements. This, in effect is exactly what Saavedra comes to in his lecture at the Krausist stronghold. The lecture itself presents in simple terms the fundamental facts about the Koran, and the basic tenets of Islam. Saavedra was an enlightened Catholic, and his rationalism prevented him from falling into the bigotry of Simonet. However, in his analysis of the Koranic doctrine he is inevitably led into a comparison with Christianity, and at this point his sense of judgement is lost, for he argues that although the Koran preaches the knowledge of an only God, eternal, omnipotent, creator of heaven and earth, this conception of a God full of majesty and awe, lacks the main features of the God of the Gospels, that of being God the Father, dispenser of grace, not only out of mercy, but also out of love for His creation. From this Saavedra concludes that the Muslim admires and fears God, but that the Christian is united to God by a feeling of pure love which transfigures the soul and elevates it beyond the horizon of earthly

---

in general, and of the Spanish Moors in particular, for the first time I heard the news, which is still not commonly known, that a certain portion of our own literature lay hidden behind the characters, legible to very few, of that conquered, exiled, extinct people; and not an indifferent portion, but rather a most interesting one."

Cánovas del Castillo, *Contestación*, in *Memorias de la Real Academia Española*, vol. 6, Madrid, 1889, pp. 194-7.

[1] *El Alcorán, 8a Conferencia* (25 *de Febrero de* 1878). Institución Libre de Enseñanza, Madrid, 1878.

[2] *Cf.* Juan López Morillas, *op. cit.*, pp. 191-194.

things.[1] It is clear that this idealist tendency to emit value judgements mars the conclusion of Saavedra's work. However, it must be stated that when dealing with non-religious subjects he was far more clear-sighted.

Saavedra was very insistent upon the importance of Arabic studies to Spain, and he even claimed that no Christian nation had such a basic need to study Muslim history as did Spain. He was aware that other European countries were developing Arabic studies as a necessary instrument for political influence and colonial relations, but he felt that Spain in particular had a record of Arabic civilization which should be considered part of its national heritage. This is not to say that Saavedra thought that Spain was an African nation; on the contrary, he realized that many of its institutions were of Roman origin. However, he saw clearly that this Roman world had been profoundly modified by its contact with Islam.[2] Hence he distinguishes between the work of European and Spanish Arabists. The former tended to study works of a broader, more general nature, whereas the Spaniards had restricted their scope to the affairs of the Peninsula.

In *La geografía de España del Edrisi*, (Madrid, 1881), Saavedra presents the main aspects of the great Arab geographer's work dealing with al-Andalus, thus clarifying many problems of toponymy. Actually Conde had worked on Idrīsī, as had Gayangos, Simonet and others, but Saavedra brought to his work a *de visu* knowledge of Spanish topography which he had acquired on his many field trips. In this work, among other things, he observed that there was a close correlation between the *climes* of Idrīsī and the ecclesiastical divisions set up by the Visigoths in the Peninsula, which fact served as an illustration of the way in which the Arabs had adopted many forms of local administration.[3]

This detailed knowlege of Spanish topography was of great service to Saavedra in the writing of his *Estudio sobre la invasión de los árabes en España* (Madrid 1892), for he was enabled, with few texts at hand, to reconstruct the scene of battlefields, and give added dimensions to his study. In this book a definite tendency

---

[1] *Cf.* Saavedra, *op. cit.*, p. 137

[2] *Cf.* Mariano de Pano y Ruata, *Las coplas del peregrino de Puey Monçón, viaje a la Meca en el siglo XVI*, in *Colección de estudios árabes*, I, *Introducción* by Saavedra, Saragossa, 1897, pp. ix-xi.

[3] *Cf. Edrisi*, pp. 8-9.

toward a rational interpretation of history may be observed. Krausism had definitely made faith the handmaiden of reason and not its mistress. Thus when Saavedra attempts to find an explanation for the legend of the House of Wisdom in Toledo,[1] he concludes that since Rodrigo needed funds in order to combat against his rebellious lords, he laid his hand on the treasure of royal crowns which his predecessors had deposited in the basilica of St. Peter and St. Paul next to the palace of king Wamba. This act according to Saavedra must have seemed a terrible sacrilege to the people of Toledo. The story was exaggerated as it passed from mouth to mouth, so that when the Arabs invaded the Peninsula, popular opinion held the conquest to be an act of divine justice.[2] Of course, it is impossible to determine to what extent what Saavedra proposed may have been factual, the important thing being to note the rational and positivistic approach he takes toward a problem of historical authenticity.

At the same time, in his reconstruction of battle scenes, Saavedra made good use of his geography. According to him, the battle between Rodrigo and the invaders which took place on July 19, 711, was of such a nature that the Goths realized the danger of having unfavourable terrain behind their backs, and so they changed their position and drew the fighting towards the plains of Barbate, near Casas Viejas, where, according to Saavedra, "the heat almost dries the river during summer." There the Gothic knights could maneouver with greater ease. The historian adds that the Arab riders, in contrast, were poorly horsed as a result of having crossed over from Africa under adverse circumstances. From this he concludes that the "clouds" of Arab horsemen described by romantic authors were entirely fantastic.[3]

It is true that Saavedra had fewer sources for his history than those of which we dispose today, but in spite of this he was able to create a vision of al-Andalus based mainly on factual material, yet not lacking in a certain life-like quality despite its being largely an external history which hardly took into account the cultural expressions of the Andalusian population (poetry, art, etc.). Yet this kind of work had to be initiated before attempting the other, more

---

[1] For a complete version of this legend, *cf.* Gayangos, *The Mohammedan Dynasties*, I, pp. 257-263.

[2] *Cf. Invasión*, pp. 40-41.

[3] *Cf. Invasión*, pp. 71-72.

delicate and complicated analysis, and in all justice Saavedra deserves credit for his laudable attempt which in a large part helped to take Spanish Arabism out of the realm of vagueness.

The most interesting of Saavedra's works is his inaugural address to the Spanish Academy in which he outlined the importance of *Aljamiado* literature.[1] Gayangos had worked on this subject before, and had provided the American Hispanist Ticknor with a few *Aljamiado* texts for his *History of Spanish Literature*. However, Saavedra's work, because of its completeness and the mass of important documents it listed and discussed, opened new horizons in the study of an important portion of Spanish literature, in which, unfortunately, little has yet been accomplished.[2]

It has been mentioned that Saavedra was to take up the defense of the Moriscos just as Simonet had done in the case of the Mozarabs. From the very beginning, Saavedra expresses a warm spirit of tolerance for these people. He establishes that their Muslim faith which they preserved in the face of adversity and persecution made it possible for them, like the Jews, to form a closed society; a distinct nation within Spain, in spite of the fact that they belonged to the same race as the Christians. This observation indicates that Saavedra, unlike Simonet attributed greater importance to cultural phenomena than to those which result from mere biological factors.

Since the Moriscos spoke the Romance dialects of the Peninsula, the books intended for popular consumption were written in these dialects, whereas the only people who knew Arabic were the learned: theologians, scholars, etc. However, the uneasy awareness of the fact that Spanish was not the cultural language of Islam, as well as a feeling of protest against Christian domination led the Muslims to call Spanish *ʿAjamiyya*, that is to say the "foreign language." This became the Spanish *Aljamía*.[3] However, the Arabic alphabet persisted in use long after the actual language had disappeared, possibly in order to keep these books out of the reach of the ever watchful enemies of Islam. The Muslims were thus put in the uncomfortable position of having to use the Christian language

[1] *Escritos de los musulmanes sometidos al dominio cristiano*, in *Memorias de la Real Acad. Esp.*, vol. 6, Madrid, 1889, pp. 14-328.

[2] For a more recent and complete account of *Aljamiado* literature, *cf.* L.P. Harvey, in *The Encyclopaedia of Islam, s.v. Aljamía*, new ed., vol. I, London, 1960, pp. 404-405.

[3] *Cf. op. cit.*, pp. 141-142.

in spite of themselves. In this respect Saavedra transcribes the bitter lament of a *faqīh* who complained that he had been forced to write in the language of the Christians because his correligionaries had lost all contact with Arabic culture.[1]

According to Saavedra, the religious characteristics which divided the Muslims from Christianity, predominate in Morisco literature, based largely on books of piety. Just as the Mozarabs had earlier tried to adapt Christianity to Islam, Saavedra discusses the Muslim heresies which, as a result of Christian intolerance, arose as attempts were made to adapt Islam to Christianity. He refers especially to the famous "*libros plumbeos*" of Granada, the result of an abortive attempt at the end of the sixteenth century, to fuse Islam and Christianity. Between the years 1595 and 1597, excavations at the Sacro-Monte in Granada brought to light some falsified Gospels written in Latin and Arabic, stating that "there is no God but God and Jesus, the Spirit of God." These were attempts to make it easier for Muslims to accept a diluted version of the Trinity. However, the Moriscos, as Saavedra explains, did not sympathize so much with Catholicism as they did with Lutheranism. This was partly due to political reasons, and partly to coincidences in dogma. In any case, Saavedra had the merit of bringing to light the work of the eighteenth-century Englishman J. Morgan who in North Africa had met the descendants of Spanish Moriscos. These assured him that their elders would have converted more readily to Protestantism than to Catholicism. In Africa, Morgan acquired an *Aljamiado* manuscript written in 1603 by the Aragonese Morisco Mahomet Rabadán. This work, in verse, is a lengthy exposition of Islamic doctrine for popular consumption, and which Morgan claims to have heard chanted in Spanish by the exiled Moriscos. Morgan translated a large part of this work into English,[2] while Latin and French translations soon appeared. The book is remarkable in that it gives an account of the mystical or *Ṣūfī* activities

[1] "Not even one of the members of our religion knows Arabic, in which our Holy Koran was revealed, nor does he understand the truths of the faith, nor grasp their pure excellence, unless they are conveniently declared in a foreign language, such as that of these Christian dogs, our tyrants and opressors—may God confound them ! Thus, may I be pardoned by Him who reads what lies written in men's hearts, and who knows that my intention is none other than to open the path of salvation to believing Muslims, even if it is through so vile and despicable a means." *Disc.*, pp. 144-145.

[2] *Mahometism Fully Explained*, Mahomet Rabadán, 1603, translated by J. Morgan, London, 1723, 2 vols.

in seventeenth-century Spain among the Muslims, it contains bitter passages against the Inquisition,[1] and finally, a complete account of the famous journey of Muḥammad to heaven around which so much of the Asín polemic on Dante has hinged. Since it is clear that the *mi'rāj* or "ascent to heaven" was alive in *romance* verse in the early sixteen-hundreds in Spain, there is no reason to doubt a somewhat wider diffusion of the medieval versions than has been generally supposed.

Saavedra indicates that much of this *aljamiado* literature reveals familiarity on the part of its authors, with that of Castile. He mentions for example, the case of one refugee in Tunis who in his works reveals much knowledge of the poetry of Lope de Vega.[2] Indeed, if these compositions were to be collected, an important anthology of Morisco poetry could be created. Another poet, a certain "Ybraim de Bolfad" of Algiers, "ciego de la vista corporal, y alumbrado de la del corazón y entendimiento" [3] expounds all of Islamic doctrine, and in a commentary on this treatise we are told how the Inquisition interrupted the performance of a play about the miracles of Muḥammad, with no little danger to the author and the actors.[4] Another Morisco exiled in Africa, Juan Alfonso, exclaims against Christian Spain:

> Accursed Spanish raven
> Pestiferous Cerberus
> Who with your three heads
> Stand at the the gate of Hell. [5]

It will be noted that the author is perfectly familiar with Greek mythology, though the *"Cerberus"* with its three heads is a bitter condemnation of the Trinity.

Saavedra believed that such a mastery of Spanish versification implied a long acquaintance with that poetry on the part of the Moriscos. This leads him to a study of earlier *Aljamiado* poetry of the fourteenth century, and he quotes examples which resemble the

---

[1] Morgan's work, published in France, Holland, and England, yet unknown in Spain, was brought to light as part of the anti-Spanish campaign conducted by Northern Europe and known as the "leyenda negra." *Cf.* Saavedra, *op. cit.*

[2] *Disc.*, p. 165.

[3] *Op. cit.*, p. 168.

[4] *Op. cit.*, p. 169; also, Fco. Fernández y González, *Estado social y político de los mudéjares de Castilla*, Madrid, 1866, p. 237, n. 1.

[5] *Op. cit.*, p. 170-171.

zajal type poems of the Archpriest of Hita.[1] Saavedra was the first Spanish Arabist to notice the metrical similarities between this *Aljamiado* poetry and that of Medieval Spain. Later Ribera was to carry this conclusion further in his study of Ibn Quzmān and his poetry, thus drawing astonishing consequences. It is interesting to note that in his investigations of Mudéjar poetry, Saavedra came upon what may be termed *muwashshaḥāt* "in reverse," that is to say, compositions mainly in Spanish, but retaining a refrain in Arabic.[2]

---

[1] If the following *zajal* was actually written in the fourteenth century, as Saavedra suggests, and as the archaism of its language implies, then it is of some importance as a possible source for the theme of the "dark night of the soul," and may help to support Asín's ideas with regard to St. John of the Cross.

Señor, fes tu aççala sobr'él	Lord, bless him
y fesnos amar con él	And make us be loved with him,
sácanos en su tropel	Bring us forth with his followers
jus la seña de Mohammad	To the sign of Mohammad
Fazed aççala de conciencia	Bless with awareness
sobre la luz de la creyencia	The light of the faith;
e sillaldo con rreberencia	Seal it with reverence
y dad aççalem sobre Mohammad	And give peace to Mohammad
Tu palabra llegará luego	Your word will arrive then,
e será rrecibido tu ruego,	And your prayer will be heard,
e y abrás aççalem entrego:	And you will have total peace.
esos son los fechos de Mohammad.	Such are the acts of Mohammad.
Quien quiere buena ventura	Whoever desires good fortune
alcançar grada de altura	*And an ascent to a lofty station,*
porponga en la noche escura	*Let him utter in the dark night,*
l'aççala sobre Mohammad.	Blessings upon Mohammad.

Cf. op. cit., p. 186.

[2] *E.g.*

Señor, por Ibrahim el del fuego,	Lord, by Ibrāhīm, he of the fire,
Que sobre él fue frío y salvo luego;	Who was cool on it, and then was saved,
Señor, apiada nos por su ruego	Lord, pity us for the sake of his prayer,
E danos tu gracia y perdón entrego	And give us total grace and pardon.
Ye arham errahimiyina !	Oh most Merciful of the Mercifull!
Pon tu salvación sobre Mohammad tu mensajero,	Place your salvation in Mohammad, you Prophet
Y sobre los annabíes [prophets] desde Edam el primero,	And in the prophets, from the first of them, Adam,
Y de los arraçules [apostles] fasta el postrimero;	And in the apostles, up to the last one;
Gual hamdu lillahi almalico adday-imo algafero	And praise be to God, the Lord, the Eternal, the Forgiving;
Ye arham errahimiyina !	Oh most Merciful of the merciful !
Ye rrabbo alalamiyina !	Oh Lord of the worlds !

Cf. op. cit., p. 187.

Finally after making an extensive survey of *Aljamiado* literature as it was known in his day, Saavedra ends up by expressing his sympathy for the cause of the Moriscos, arguing that it was the result of blind passions and hatreds that destroyed that important member of the nation which would otherwise have had much to contribute to the wellbeing of Spain.[1] From this it can be concluded that whereas Simonet had represented the traditionalist attitude towards the problem of Spanish decadence, Saavedra saw it more from the liberal, historical angle. For him, fanaticism and intolerance had destroyed the Moriscos, and undermined the vitality of Spain. However, Saavedra dreamed of a modernized Spain which he placed in the future, but which he also worked incessantly to help create.

The Spanish professor and scholar Francisco Fernández y González, known more commonly as a literary critic, was a firm adherent to the doctrine of Krausism [2] as well as an Arabist and historian of note. Born in Albacete in 1833, he was the son of a veteran of the Spanish war of Independence. A man of rare talent and prodigious learning, his life was completely immersed in study. He won the chair of General and Spanish Literature at the University of Granada, where he taught from 1856 to 1864, after which he was promoted to the chair of aesthetics in Madrid. In 1867 an anti-Krausist purge of the University resulted in his loss of this chair, though he was restored to it one year later and continued his activities there for the rest of his life, that is to say, for half a century.

Fernández y González was a member of the Academies of History (1869), of Moral and Political Sciences (1867), of San Fernando (1881) and of the Spanish Language (1889). His record of attendance at these institutions was outstanding, so that it is stated that he attended 1,887 sessions of the Academy of History, a record in his time. Of few writers may it be said more fittingly than of Fernández y González that he lived a totally intellectual life. His erudition was extremely broad, and his skill in classical and Oriental languages unusual.[3] Though engaged to some extent in politics, he avoided

[1] *Op. cit.*, p. 194.

[2] *Cf.* López Morillas, *ibid.*, p. 139. In Granada he taught German philosophy to Fco. Giner de los Ríos. *Cf.* Vicente Cacho Viu, *La Institución Libre de Enseñanza*, Madrid, 1962, p. 104.

[3] *Cf. Enciclopedia Espasa*, *s.v. Fernández y González.*

the temptations and distractions afforded by that field, and was able to pursue the course of study he had set as his goal.[1]

Among his works, those dealing with Arabic and Hebrew studies are both numerous and of great interest, in that they helped to illuminate problems which had not been touched upon previously,[2] while as a journalist he collaborated in the progressive journals of the age, such as *Revista de España*, *La España Moderna* and others.

His adaptation of the *Historia de al-Andalus por Aben Adhari de Marruecos* (Granada, 1860) is of importance for it increased the number of Arabic chronicles known up to his time. The work is not a complete translation, in that he only included some of the more important passages. The first volume begins with the conquest in 711 and leads up to the dynasty of the Umayyads and the civil wars prior to the establishment of the caliphate by ʿAbd ar-Raḥmān III. At the end of the work, the author includes a list of subscribers which offers a good indication of the extent to which works on Arabic erudition were being read in Spain by different circles of society. It begins with no less than Queen Isabel II, and includes Sanz del Río, the patriarch of Spanish Krausism, as well as important intellectuals such as Manuel Tamayo y Baus, Gaspar Núñez de Arce and Emilio Castelar. Among the Arabists it lists Gayangos,

---

[1] *Cf.* Antonio Maura, *Don Fco. Fernández y González*, in *BRAE*, vol. 4. fasc. 19, October, Madrid, 1917, pl. 407.

[2] He translated and commented upon the *Ordenamiento de las aljamas judías*, the *Crónica de los reyes francos*, the *Historia de al-Andalus* by Ibn Adhārī al-Marrakušī, the Arabic book of chivalry *Ben Zeyyād ben Amīr, el de Quimera*, he corrected and amplified the work of Casiri, he published studies such as *La escultura y la pintura en los pueblos de origen semítico*, *Los moros que quedaron en España después de la expulsión de los moriscos*, *Los establicimientos españoles y portugueses en Africa*; *Plan de una biblioteca de autores árabes españoles*; *Berceo o el poeta sagrado de la España cristiana del siglo XIII*, *Instituciones jurídicas del pueblo de Israel en los diferentes Estados de la península Ibérica*, *Primeros pobladores históricos de la península Ibérica*, *Estudio numismático-histórico sobre las medallas llamadas de Agila II*, *Los hijos de Witiza según los textos árabes*, *Estudios clásicos en las Universidados españolas durante la época del Renacimiento*, *Influencia de las lenguas y letras orientales en la cultura de los pueblos de la península Ibérica*, *El mesianismo en la península Ibérica durante la primera mitad del siglo XVI*, *Estado social y político de los mudéjares de Castilla*, *Las doctrinas del doctor iluminado R. Lulio*, *Historia de la critíca literaria*. His philosophical works, in which he gives proof of his Krausist leanings are: *Estética* which only includes the *Metafísica de lo bello*, (Granada, 1862), *La idea de lo bello* (Madrid, 1873), *Naturaleza, fantasía y arte* (1873), *Lo ideal y sus formes* (1876) and *Lo sublime y lo cómico*.

Simonet, Estébanez Calderón, Eguilaz, Moreno Nieto, and Lafuente y Alcántara.

It is important to note that in his vision of history Fernández y González was typical of his age, in that he combined the traditionalist viewpoint with the progressiveness and desire for renovation which characterized the Krausist school. Thus in his inaugural address to the Spanish Academy: *Influencia de las lenguas y letras orientales en la cultura de los pueblos de la península Ibérica,*[1] he adopts the traditionalist attitude of considering Spain as an eternal entity unmodified by the external accidents of history. However, unlike Simonet, he considers Spain's "substance" as being basically African and Oriental, whereas the "accidents" were Roman or Visigothic. Starting from this premise he pushes back the influence of Oriental cultures on Spain to pre-historic times, long before the Arab conquest. He argues that long before this time, the peoples of the Peninsula manifested a very marked Oriental character.[2] Incorporating the linguistic theories of the time into his analysis, he claims that the primitive Stone Age inhabitants of the Peninsula spoke a language connected to modern Basque, which he attempts to relate to Mongolian dialects, more especially to Turkish, while making peripheral disquisitions on the connections between Basque and Ancient Egyptian and Chaldean. He supports this theory with copious linguistic evidence, and aside from the great difficulties involved in proving such a relationship, a modified form of that theory has today begun to win favour once more.[3]

Having thus established what he claims to be the "Oriental" nature of Spanish culture, Fernández y González comes to the Arabs whose invasion he considers conclusive in having reaffirmed this deeply rooted Orientalism.[4] In all justice it should be mentioned that this version of history is just as arbitrary as that of Simonet in that it is based on the idea that man is the passive recipient of influences rather than the active incorporator of his living circum-

---

[1] In *Discursos leídos ante la Real Academia española,* Madrid, 1894.

[2] *Op. cit.,* p. 2.

[3] *Cf.* Rafael Lapesa, *Historia de la lengua española,* 4th ed., Madrid, 1959, pp. 20-21 for abundant bibliography.

[4] "In spite of the slight nuances due to the Celts, Greeks, Romans, Suevi, and Visigoths, who were all in greater or lesser degree representatives of Latin superiority, the Muslim invasion extended and brought into sharper relief the highly Oriental character of the civilization of the Iberian Peninsula during the Middle Ages." (*Cf. op. cit.,* p. 12).

stances, which he re-elaborates in accordance with his goals, aspirations and external possibilities.

Thus from the point of view of Fernández y González it was important to show the way in which these influences were transmitted, which he proceeds to do at length in the remainder of his work. Though today we may tend to disagree with his notion of history, his importance lies in the many areas of cultural transmission between Muslims and Christians which he studied, thus expanding the work of Gayangos. He therefore mentions the many Arab customs which entered Spain through the Mozarabs.[1] Other more literary influences can be observed in the Arabic sources of the *Grande e general estoria* of Alfonso X, and in the field of law, he observes that Muslim legislation appears in the *Fueros municipales españoles,* and the *Siete partidas* in which many maxims and principles of law are attributed to Aristotle, according to formulae borrowed from the Arabic book *Dichos y hechos de los filósofos.*[2]

One of the most controversial cases of cultural transmission studied by Fernández y González was that of the influence of the *maqāmāt* on Juan Ruiz, Archpriest of Hita. He describes the Arabic literary genre known as *maqāma,* invented by al-Hamadhānī (d. A.D. 1007) and developed by Ḥarīrī of Baṣra (A.D. 1054-1123). Arguing that the Spanish clergy were well versed in Arabic literature during the Middle Ages he explains that the Archpriest of Hita had given his *Book of Good Love* the form of a *maqāma,* as well as testifying that he had composed songs for Moorish girls, that he knew Arabic and was familiar with Arabic musical instruments. Several of the stories included in the *Book of Good Love,* according to Fernández y González were also to be found in the *Libro de los huertos* written by his contemporary, the Granadan writer Ibn ʿĀṣim who dedicated his book to Yūsuf II of Granada.[3] This aspect of Juan Ruiz's work, hitherto unknown, presents a good example of the way in which much of the information amassed by nineteenth-century Arabists passed almost unnoticed till fairly recently. The ideas of Fernández y González, expressed in 1894 fell on deaf ears.

[1] *Op. cit.,* p. 39.

[2] *Op. cit.,* p. 52. This information had been mentioned with some reservations, by no less than Joaquín Costa. *Cf. Estudios jurídicos y políticos,* chap. III, *Influencias de la ciencia política mudéjar en la de Castilla,* Madrid, 1884, pp. 97-99.

[3] *Op. cit.,* p. 55.

It was not until 1948 when Américo Castro, perplexed by the strange elements and literary structure of the *Book of Good Love,* pointed to Arabic sources as a possible solution for problems which other critics had been unable to explain, that Fernández y González's theory began to be reconsidered.[1] In 1961, María Rosa Lida de Malkiel, in a study of the *Book of Good Love* [2] returned to what had been said by Fernández y González,[3] amplifying her study by showing that the Jews of Catalonia from the twelfth to the fourteenth centuries had assiduously cultivated the *maqāmāt* and introduced innovations which were steps in the direction of the *Book of Good Love.* Thus she concludes that:

> The Book of Good Love belongs to the literary genre of the Semitic *maqāmāt,* an essentially didactic genre. The teaching of the *maqāmāt* is, above all, moralizing; they also display the author's literary virtuosity and diversified knowledge, that is to say, those very same categories of teaching which the *Book of Good Love* offers. [4]

Returning to Fernández y González's work, he goes even further in attributing other unsuspected Spanish achievements to Arabic cultural inspiration. Thus he claims that the translation of Arabic science into Spanish and Latin favoured the study of navigation, so that a figure as important as Christopher Columbus, in a letter to their Catholic Majesties states that his readings of Averroes moved and stimulated him to undertake the discovery of the Indies.[5] If, as some scholars have tried to prove, Columbus was actually a converted Jew, in close contact with the school of navigation in Mallorca in the hands of Jewish scholars, the possible influence of Arabic science on the discovery of America may be

---

[1] *Cf.* Américo Castro, *España en su historia: cristianos, moros y judíos,* Buenos Aires, 1948, pp. 396, etc. For a criticism of the theory expounded by Américo Castro, *cf.* Emilio García Gómez, *El collar de la paloma, tratado sobre el amor y los amantes de Ibn Ḥazm de Córdoba, Introducción,* Madrid, 1952, pp. 50-59.

[2] *Two Spanish Masterpieces, The "Book of Good Love" and "The Celestina," Illinois Studies in Language and Literature,* vol. 49, Urbana, 1961.

[3] *Op. cit.,* p. 20.

[4] *Op cit.,* p. 25.

[5] *Op. cit.,* p. 56. He quotes Columbus: "Aristotle says that this world is small, that its water is scant, and that it is easy to cross from Spain to the Indies, while this is confirmed by Averroes and discussed by Cardinal Pedro de Aliaco," n. 54, p. 63.

very plausible,[1] though the Judaism of Columbus has not yet been proven conclusively.

From all this, Fernández y González concludes that Spain must look to Greece and Rome as the common cultural heritage linking it to Europe, but that as inhabitants of the Iberian peninsula, Spaniards should be proud of the days when Englishmen, Germans, Frenchmen and Italians came to seek knowledge in Toledo and al-Andalus.[2]

As an example of the constant struggle the Arabists of this period had to maintain to have their ideas accepted, it should be noted that the reaction to Fernández y González's speech was unfavourable. In his reply, Francisco A. Commerelán y Gómez points out that the Orientalist had hardly mentioned the Roman and Visigothic elements in Peninsular culture, which he then proceeds to do himself at great length.[3] Applying the racist ideas of the time he stresses the importance of Aryan as opposed to Semitic culture, arguing that works such as the *Calila y Dimna* were made popular in Spain because their Aryo-Indian origin made them acceptable to the "Aryo-Spaniards,"[4] thus entirely overlooking the fact that the Arabic version of the *Calila y Dimna*, translated by Ibn al-Muqaffaʿ had been entirely reworked and adapted to suit Muslim taste. Turning from this to Jewish culture he affirms that it had hardly any influence on Spain because the Spanish people looked upon the Jew (as also the Muslim) as an enemy of their religion, country and race. Dismissing the Semitic world from any part in the formation of Spanish culture, he concludes that the doctrines of Islam were "doctrines to which the Muslim peoples contributed not the slightest originality, and which were deformed and perverted by them with the materialistic and gross influence of the Koran." [5]

Fernández y González's principal work with regard to Arabic studies is undoubtedly his *Estado social y político de los mudéjares de Castilla*, (Madrid, 1866), in which he studies the political vicissitudes of the Reconquest, the legislation applied to the Mudéjares, as well as devoting important chapters to the literary and cultural achievements of these people, and their transmission to Spanish

[1] *Cf.* Millás Vallicrosa, in *Tesoro de los judíos sefardíes*, vol. 6, Jerusalem, 1963, pp. vii-xvi.

[2] *Op. cit.*, p. 58.

[3] *Cf. Contestación*, in *op. cit.*, p. 100.

[4] *Op. cit.*, p. 100.

[5] *Op. cit.*, p. 104.

culture. It has been stated that he was opposed in his ideas to Simonet, and in this respect, he claims that if the Mozarabs had preserved Latin culture within Islam, they also lost no time in assimilating Arabic works received from the conquerors,[1] adapting Arabic poetry and rhymed prose to their own needs, so that they were rewarded with high positions by the caliphs. To illustrate the extent to which the Christians in the north later adapted Islamic forms of life Fernández y González cites an Arabic epistle written by Alfonso VI to the Almoravid leader Yūsuf ibn Tāshufīn in which the Christian king styles himself the "Emir of the Christian religion," a title obviously copied from Islam.[2] In chapter 10 of this work, the author discusses at length and in detail the influence of Arabic culture on Spain through the mediation of the Mudéjares, and mentions that in spite of the Reconquest, the subjected Muslims continued their literary and scientific activities and were influential in the development of Spanish literature. This cultural contact reached a high peak during the reign of Ferdinand III at which time the Mudéjares of Murcia, Cordova, Seville and Toledo experienced a renaissance in letters which had an enormous repercussion in Spanish works on history and the sciences.[3]

Fernández y González points to the numerous Arabic words which entered the Spanish vocabulary, and mentions grammatical and syntactic borrowings from Arabic which illustrate the cultural superiority of Islam over medieval Christendom.

Though Fernández y González was misled by the historical ideas of his age, he was not as closed to a sympathy for Spain's Arab past as was Simonet. Having a sincere appreciation of the cultural importance of al-Andalus, he speaks of the intolerance of Christendom with regard to the Mudéjares and Moriscos, but adds that this attitude was the inevitable result of the historical realities of medieval Spain. Neither passing judgement on the past, nor diminishing the importance of the role played by the Mudéjares in Spanish culture, he joins the traditionalist vision of history to the spirit of renovation derived from his Krausist leanings by concluding that it is better to base a worthy future upon an understanding of history,

---

[1] *Op. cit.*, p. 18.

[2] "From the *emīr* Adhefonx (Alfonso) to the *emīr* Yusuf-ben-Texufin. After the customary good wishes, etc. You know well that I am the *emīr* of the Christian religion, as you are that of Islam." (*Op. cit.*, p. 40.)

[3] *Cf. op. cit.*, p. 153.

than to waste time in fruitlessly regretting the past.[1] In this sense it will be seen that Fernández y González gave to his Arabism a twist which projected his thinking toward a better future for Spain.

Among certain other Arabists a tone of greater severity and condemnation of medieval Christian intolerance is to be observed. Such is the case, for example, of Emilio Lafuente y Alcántara, born in Archidona (Málaga) in 1825 in which town he was to die in 1868. Lafuente y Alcántara, another of Gayangos' disciples, was a member of the Academy of History as well as director of the library of San Isidro. Gifted with great erudition and love of scholarship, he spent a part of his life writing on Arabic topics. Some of his works were: the *Inscripciones árabes de Granada,* (Madrid, 1860), the *Ajbar machmua,* (Madrid, 1867) an anonymous eleventh-century chronicle which he published in Arabic with an accompanying translation into Spanish, *Relaciones de algunos succsos de los últimos tiempos del reino de Granada* (1868), and his *Catálogo de los códices adquiridos en Tetuán* (1869).[2]

In the introduction to his *Inscripciones árabes de Granada,* Lafuente y Alcántara stresses the abandonment in which Arabic monuments were left in Spain, attributing such a state of affairs to a scorn for the Arabs which had developed among the Spanish people because of the long war of expulsion which they had waged against Islam during the Middle Ages. This had led to the utter ruin of Arab monuments and to the destruction of libraries. Like Gayangos, his disciple had bitter words to say against Cardinal Cisneros, who, he claims, while being worthy of eternal memory for his knowledge and interest in Humanism, had consigned thousands of Arabic manuscripts to the flames under the intolerant influence of his age. As if that were not enough, Lafuente y Alcántara complains that Charles V, by building his massive stone palace in the middle of the Alhambra had destroyed a large part of the Moorish structure, as if to overshadow and humiliate the home of the Banī l-Aḥmar.[3]

In spite of this general spirit of intolerance, Lafuente y Alcántara

[1] "Above the sterile vainglory of judging the errors of the men of the past with inflexible severity, we should entertain the noble ambition of basing the improvement of the present on the experience of what has passed." *Op. cit.*, p. 245.

[2] For an account of his life and work, cf. *Enciclopedia Espasa, s.v., Lafuente y Alcántara.*

[3] *Cf. Inscripciones árabes de Granada,* Madrid, 1860, pp. v-vi.

is surprised at the zeal displayed by Philip II in collecting Arabic manuscripts. He is astonished to see that "austere" and "fanatical" monarch, as he describes him, making continuous efforts to amass these books,[1] after which he comes directly to his subject by discussing the urgent need to publish the Arabic inscriptions of Spain before they are effaced by unskilled restorations. Pointing out the value of the Arabic poems of the Alhambra written by Ibn Zamraq, he is led to write an early account of the nature of Hispano-Arabic poetry which may be considered of some importance, since nothing serious has been done in this field until our own times in which García Gómez has made a profound study of Hispano-Arabic poetry.

Lafuente y Alcántara discusses the difficulties encountered by any translator of Arabic poetry; difficulties which he attributes to its unfamiliar metaphors, subtle conceits and frequent ambiguity of meaning. He claims that its play on words and sacrifice of content to form constitute its main feature, and gives a description of its development from the pre-Islamic *qaṣīda* or "ode" which was closely connected to Bedouin life, to the later courtly panegyric. Then he outlines the history of attempts made in Spain to translate Arabic poetry. Alonso del Castillo, the converted Morisco interpreter of Philip II and secretary in charge of official correspondence with Morocco was the first to copy the poems of the Alhambra, of which a translation existed in the possession of Estébanez Calderón. Later translations were made by Echevarría, who published his work in 1764, though his Arabic was hardly sufficient for such a task. Afterwards came Pablo Lozano, a contemporary of Conde who merely republished the work of Castillo along with some ill-advised "corrections."[2] This state of affairs inspired Lafuente y Alcántara to publish his complete edition of the inscriptions, containing many of the poems of Ibn Zamraq in fairly trustworthy and elegant translations. His work was to awaken an interest in Hispano-Arabic poetry so that when Von Schack published a book on this subject,[3] the Spanish writer and diplomat Don Juan Valera was to follow by translating it from the German, rendering the numerous Arabic poems into elegant Neoclassical verse.[4]

[1] *Cf. op. cit.*, p. vi.

[2] *Cf. op. cit.*, p. x.

[3] A. F. von Schack, *Poesie und Kunst der Araber in Spanien und Sicilien* (2nd ed., Stuttgart, 1877).

[4] *Poesía y arte de los árabes de España y Sicilia*, Von Schack, trans. by Don Juan Valera, Madrid, 1881.

The frequency of historical allusions to the kings of Granada contained in the poems translated by Lafuente y Alcántara moved the latter to add an historical summary of the events of the Naṣrid dynasty, a period which up until his time had been obscure owing to the lack of sources and the political complications of the last days of Granada. However, the author discovered new documents which he published in an appendix, along with the genealogical table of the Naṣrid dynasty,[1] thus greatly enhancing the documentary value of his work.

In his work entitled *Relación de algunos sucesos de los últimos tiempos del reino de Granada* (Madrid, 1868) Lafuente y Alcántara publishes further documents of interest for the study of the Granadan period. He speaks of the misinformation of medieval Spanish chroniclers, in spite of the fact that Isabella the Catholic had commissioned Hernando del Pulgar to write a brief compendium on Granadan history, which he never completed. [2] Our author therefore publishes an incomplete but valuable account of the last days of Granada written by Hernando de Baeza, an interpreter to Abū ʿAbd Allāh, last king of Granada. The chronicler Baeza seems to have made use of Arabic sources, and his personal relationship to the Naṣrid court made it possible for him to give a direct account of some of the palace intrigues. Among the many episodes illustrative of Spanish literature we may single out Hernando de Baeza' account of the historical events which form the background of the famous Spanish ballad of *Abenámar*. It seems that a certain "Muley Çad" had fled to Archidona, from where he sent his son Abū l-Ḥasan to the Castilian king Juan II. Abū l-Ḥasan entered the presence of Juan II accompanied by one hundred and fifty knights, among them a distinguished figure called "Abenámar, aquél a quien dice el Romance que preguntó el rrey don Juan: ? *Qué castillos son aquéllos* ? [3]" The meeting took place in Olmedo, and the Spaniards at that time composed the ballad, using Arabic themes in its elaboration.

As an appendix, Lafuente y Alcantara adds a series of epistles, some in Arabic, others in Spanish, relating to a novelesque duel between D. Alonso de Aguilar and D. Diego Fernández de Cordova, Marshal of Castile and later Count of Cabra. The Arabic letters of

---

[1] *Op. cit.*, p. xiii.
[2] *Cf. Relación*, p. vi-vii.
[3] *Op. cit.*, p. 3.

the king of Granada to D. Diego grant him permission to enter his territory bearing arms in order to hold this duel. The last letter indicates that D. Diego waited for a whole day, though his opponent never showed up.

Undoubtedly one of the most important tasks undertaken by Lafuente y Alcántara was the publication of the *Ajbar Machmua,* a brief chronicle, yet interesting owing to its relative earliness. It begins with the Arabic conquest of al-Andalus and leads up to the reign of ʿAbd ar-Raḥmān III and the founding of the caliphate of Cordova. The chronicle existed in a unique anonymous manuscript in Paris, which had been studied by Gayangos. From a copy made by the latter, Lafuente y Alcántara prepared his edition which was accompanied by a translation into Spanish. The chronicle is relatively valuable in that it avoids the phantasy commonly found in medieval historiography; the narration is precise and taken from authentic sources. Thus for example the flight of ʿAbd ar-Raḥmān I from Syria after the destruction of the Umayyads in the East, seems to be narrated in the very words used by that monarch. The value of the *Ajbar Machmua* edition is enhanced by the addition of an appendix containing some medieval Latin versions of the Arab conquest, as viewed by Christendom, as well as a geographic index which attempts to clarify the derivation of the place names mentioned in the anonymous Arabic chronicle.

An Arabist of the traditionalist school and close friend and collaborator of Simonet was Leopoldo Eguilaz y Yanguas, who devoted his main efforts to philological and especially linguistic studies.

Eguilaz was born in Mazarrón (Murcia) in 1829 and later became a corresponding member of the Spanish Academy. At the University of Granada he acted as dean of the School of Philosophy and Letters. There he worked with Simonet whom he helped in preparing his linguistic study of the language of the Mozarabs. The Romantic discovery of Sanscrit, and Bopp's theory of the Indo-European languages had awakened some response in Spain and Eguilaz was one of those who worked on translations into Spanish of Indian literature, producing books such as: *Ensayo de una traducción literal de los episodios indios, la muerte de Yachnadatta y la elección de esposo, de Drampadi* (1861), accompanied by critical notes and the original text in Sanscrit. He wrote an important *Glosario etimológico de las palabras españolas de origen oriental* (1886) as well as *Estudio sobre el valor de las letras arábigas en el alfabeto castellano* (Madrid, 1874), and *Reseña histórica de la conquista del reino de Granada por los reyes católicos, según los cronistas árabes,* (Granada, 1894).

His *Estudio* is an important contribution to the knowledge of medieval Spanish. In it he claims that the advances made by Bopp, Grimm, and others, in linguistics had paved the way for the writing of an historical grammar of the Spanish language. However, he rightly indicates that first the phonetic value of the Old Spanish alphabet must be established insofar as many sounds common to Vulgar Latin had been radically modified in the Peninsula. Fortunately, the Arabic, Mudéjar and Morisco transcriptions of Romance words made it possible to reconstruct the phonetic value of the Old Spanish alphabet. As a derivation from this work, Eguilaz discusses the possibility of elaborating a uniform system of transcription for Arabic and which would be based on the medieval system found in *Aljamiado* literature, only with the process being inverted. This system, which he outlined, was in fact the one used by Spanish Arabists until recent times when the journal *Al-Andalus* adopted a more precise system of transcription which offers more similarity to the one in international usage.

In basing his method of transcription on the usage of medieval Spain, Eguilaz was in a sense making the utmost of the Spanish national tradition; a tendency common at this time as we have seen when it was applied by Simonet to historical interpretation.

He further points out the possibility of gaining information about the pronounciation of colloquial Andalusian Arabic from the medieval *Aljamiado* and colloquial Arabic texts. Of the latter he gives as an example an elegy of the last king of Granada written in Latin characters, from which he attempted to derive the original Arabic spelling. Eguilaz also published a reconstruction of the Catholic *Creed* in Arabic which Pedro de Alcalá had included in his grammar in Latin characters.

In the *Glosario etimológico*, Eguilaz amplified his linguistic studies and attempted to refute the theories of W. H. Engelmann [1] and Dozy, who had spoken of the superiority of Peninsular Arabic civilization to that of the Spaniards, a superiority based on the large number of Arabic words which entered Castilian and other

[1] Co-author along with Dozy of *Glossaire des mots espagnols et portuguais derivés de l'arabe*, 1869.

Peninsular Romance dialects. Though he recognizes this fact, Eguilaz, as Simonet, attributes far greater importance to the Romance and even Christian influences on Arabic culture, basing himself on the authority of Ibn Khaldūn who had spoken of the imitation of Christian customs on the part of the "Mudejarized" Arabs of Granada.[1] Eguilaz overlooks the fact that this was a very late development which took place long after the mass of Arabic words had entered the Peninsular dialects. The fact that Simonet had also made use of this passage by Ibn Khaldūn indicates the familiarity which existed between the two Arabists and which was based on the sharing of ideas in common.[2]

Eguilaz also conducted historical research, and in his *Reseña histórica de la conquista del reino de Granada* (Granada, 1894) he outlines the history of this period after having consulted the original Arabic sources (al-Maqqarī and others), claiming his work to be a supplement to that of Conde, where that period is not included since none of the Arab historians which Conde was able to study had dealt with the Granadan period. It is curious to note that at so late a date Conde's work was still so highly regarded. Eguilaz, however, compiled a much more careful period study than his predecessor, and was able to study some unusual and interesting documents such as the autograph letter of surrender written in Arabic by Abū ʿAbd Allāh to the Catholic Majesties [3] a photocopy of which he includes in his book.

Another Arabist of traditionalist tendencies, more important for his political and intellectual position than for the few works on

---

1 "Every people living on the frontier of another, the superiority of which it acknowledges, acquires these habits of imitation. This occurs *in our days* [fourteenth century] with the Andalusian Arabs, who because of their relations with the Galicians [the Christians of Castile and León], have adopted not only the costumes of the latter, their manners and habits, but also the fashion of decorating the walls of their houses and palaces with images or pictures." *Cf. Glosario*, p. vii. I have followed Equilaz's translation. The passage may also be consulted in F. Rosenthal'a English translation, *The Muqaddimah*, New York, 1958, vol. I, p. 300. The words I have underlined indicate that Ibn Khaldūn knew well that this was not the case in the heyday of the caliphate of Cordova.

2 Equilaz himself tells us so: "I express my most sincere thanks to my excellent friends. . . and particularly to the distinguished Orientalist Don Francisco Javier Simonet, whose profound knowledge of the subject I have always consulted usefully and profitably." *Glosario*, p. xvi.

3 Dated at Andarax, July 8, 1493 (Ramaḍān 23, 898 AH). *Cf. Reseña histórica*, pp. 78-79.

Arabic studies which he left behind him, was José Moreno Nieto. Born in Siruela (Badajoz) in 1825 he died in Madrid in 1882. He began his studies in Toledo where his interest in Arabic was aroused, though he devoted most of his energies to the study of philosophy and law. He received his degree in Madrid in 1846, and soon after occupied the chair of Arabic in Granada. Active in politics, he joined the progressive party and in 1854 was elected to represent Granada as a deputy to the constitutional Cortes, where he began to tend towards the political right wing by speaking against universal suffrage and defending religious unity. The unfavourable reception of his ideas made him retire from politics, and he spent his time lecturing on Arabic philosophy at the Athenæum of Madrid. After returning for a time to Granada, he established his permanent residence in Madrid and once more became involved in politics. Breaking with his party, he joined the Liberal Union. In 1864 he joined the Academy of History where he read an address on Hispano-Arabic historians in which he included in the form of an appendix, a catalogue of these historians.[1] From 1859 he taught history at the University of Madrid, and soon after he prepared an Arabic grammar. He took an active part in the constitutional Cortes of 1869 and during the reign of Amadeo I he was named Rector of the University of Madrid. He continued in office during the Republic, and in 1874 he was named Director of Public Education. But after the Restoration, under the conservative régime of Cánovas he resigned. However, he soon recognized the monarchy of Alfonso XII, and joined the conservative party led by Cánovas.

Moreno Nieto's consistent shift toward conservatism was determined by his strict adhesion to traditionalism. It is important to indicate that between the years 1865-1867 a certain hostility toward Krausism came to the forefront in Spanish intellectual circles. Articles appeared demanding the destitution of those professors at the University who spoke out against Catholicism and the monarchy. Sanz del Río, Castelar and others were considered subversive, so that a campaign began against them which reached maximum proportions in 1867 when many professors were dispossessed of their chairs. Among these anti-Krausists we may include Moreno

[1] *Cf.* Moreno Nieto, *Estudio crítico sobre los historiadores arábigo-españoles, Discurso leído ante la Real Academia de la Historia, 29 de Mayo de* 1864, in *Colección de discursos académicos*, published by the Ateneo de Madrid, Madrid, 1882.

Nieto [1] who since 1858 had studied idealist German philosophy and came to adhere to Hegelian thought.[2] Later he attended discussions in which he sided against the Krausist group, with whose logic he was unable to agree. He felt that the "spontaneity of life" [3] which he claimed for his own thought would be stifled by rigorous logic.

His opposition to the positivistic philosophical renaissance which Krausism initiated in Spain accentuated by contrast his conservative leanings. Moreno Nieto was an outstanding orator, and it is a pity that he did not leave a larger number of written works. In 1868 he wrote: *Estado actual del pensamiento en Europa,* and in *El problema filosófico* he expresses the feeling that Christian society is incompatible with rationalism. As for his works on Arabic, they are of minimum importance. Apart from the study of Hispano-Arabic historiography and his Arabic grammar, he had planned to write a history of the Arabs in al-Andalus in collaboration with his close friend Lafuente y Alcántara, though the death of the latter put an end to this plan.[4]

In reviewing the state of Arabic studies in Spain during the second half of the nineteenth century it becomes clear that on the one hand, the gradual intensification of nationalistic feelings throughout Europe, and on the other, the inner feeling of insecurity common to Spanish intellectuals vis-à-vis Europe was not favourable to the development of Arabism. In Spain these studies inevitably became connected to the overall problem of Spanish "decadence," and the historical views which led scholars to envisage Spain as an eternal and unmodified essence upon which external influences fell haphazardly only to be Hispanized, led to a nationalistic view of the Arab invasion. Thus these Arabists (most of whom were historians) either considered Spain as being essentially Latin and Visigothic—as was the case of Simonet—or they envisioned an Oriental Spain which had been superficially Romanized—as in the case of Fernández y González. Between these two extreme positions there were varying degrees of compromise.

Consequently, this Arabism, though it was either unsympathetic

---

[1] *Cf.* López Morillas, *op. cit.,* pp. 184-185.

[2] *Cf.* U. González Serrano, "Bocetos filosóficos VIII Moreno Nieto," in *Revista Contemporánea,* vol. 124, 1902, p. 667.

[3] "Hervor de vida"—his favourite phrase. *Cf. op. cit.,* p. 667.

[4] *Cf.* U. González Serrano, *op. cit.,* p. 676.

or overly concerned with the problem of the Arabs and their relation to Spain, was important mainly for the immense amount of factual information which it uncovered and handed on to the next generation.

CHAPTER FIVE

There is no doubt that the most outstanding of Gayangos' disciples, in whom Spanish Arabism acquired a new vigour, was Francisco Codera y Zaidín, whose skepticism in matters of scholarship prepared the positivistic groundwork for modern Arabism. Up to Codera, it seems that with rare exceptions, the most important Spanish Arabists had been Andalusians. Now the focus of Arabic studies was to gravitate towards Aragon, the homeland of Codera. It has also been noted that up till this time, Spanish Arabism had been the target of repeated attacks from extra-Peninsular European scholars; notably Dozy. However, with Codera, Spanish Arabism won international fame and became in a sense respectable.

Codera was a man of modest, unassuming manners, who did not become a public figure as was deserving of his work.[1] The son of well-to-do farmers, he was born in Fonz in the province of Huesca in 1836. After finishing his primary education, he spent four years studying Latin and rhetoric with the Aesculapian priests at Barbastro; after which, an early inclination to join the clerical ranks made him study philosophy at the Seminary of Lérida, where he distinguished himself for his knowledge of metaphysics.

In 1855 he went to Saragossa where he continued his studies in theology for four years, only to make a sudden and radical change in his career; neither the first nor the last in his life, and which seems to have been the result of his great flexibility of temperament and adaptability to the advances of the age he lived in. It seems that during his years as a student in Barbastro, he had lodged at the home of a carpenter whose trade he learned during his free moments. This introduction to practical skills opened new horizons in his life, for it attracted him towards the exact sciences, so that as a young seminarist he taught himself algebra, geometry and draftsmanship without the help of a teacher. Procuring a modern text on physics he applied himself to the mastery of that science, and even fashioned several physical instruments for use in his experiments. This scientific interest attracted him to Saragossa

---

[1] For an account of Codera's life and works *cf.*: the *Introducción* by Eduardo Saavedra to *Homenaje a Don Francisco Codera*, Saragossa, 1904, pp. ix-xxvii. This work contains a complete bibliography of Codera's writings.

where more opportunities existed for the pursuit of his field of study. There he studied natural history along with his regular theological courses. Entering the faculty of Science, he studied physics, chemistry, geography and Greek. His brilliance was such that he was offered an assistantship in Science, but the suppression of the department of Science at the University of Saragossa, decreed in 1858, put an end to his plans for a scientific career. Undismayed by this incident he enrolled in the first year of letters, and after his second year, a difficulty caused by conflicting course hours decided his career in favour of literary studies and law rather than theology.

In the summer of 1860 he was driven by poor health to seek rest at Barcelona, where he occupied himself in learning French, later followed by English, German and even Basque. He returned to Saragossa to receive his bachelor's degree in philosophy and literature, but his thirst for knowledge, having exhausted the possibilities of Saragossa, led him to the nation's capital, where he continued his studies in the same field. Soon he won the chair of Latin and Greek at the secondary level for Lérida and took possession of it in 1863.

From that moment on, his career gravitated definitely towards the study of classical languages. He finished his doctorate in Lérida and won a chair in Greek, Hebrew and Arabic at the University of Granada, and in 1868 he occupied the same chair at the University of Saragossa. In 1874 he won the chair of Arabic at the University of Madrid, where he remained until his retirement in 1902.

Codera had learned Hebrew at the faculty of theology in Saragossa, after which he took up the study of Arabic with the old grammar written by the Dutch Arabist Erpennius (1584-1624). These two languages he perfected in Madrid, studying under the Hebraist Severo Catalina, and Gayangos, who always considered him to be his most outstanding student and favorite disciple. In Granada he had taught Arabic as well as Greek, and had done the same in Saragossa.

His Arabic, learned late in his career, was therefore never as proficient as he would have hoped, though this, instead of hindering his progress, had the beneficial effect of inspiring him with a constant wariness and critical skepticism which in its long range effects was to take Spanish Arabism out of the realm of facile conjecturing and place it on more solid ground.

Once in Madrid, the new Arabist became convinced that the publication of an inexpensive and simple text on the rudiments of Arabic grammar was a first necessary step towards the establishment of modern Arabic studies. In this his practical training came to his aid, for he composed and himself lithographed a simple and concise series of notes on grammar for use in his own classes.

Realizing that knowledge about the history of al-Andalus was no luxury, but rather an essential part of Spanish historical research, he devoted his efforts to the formation of a group of young Arabists to carry on the work of Gayangos, Lafuente Alcántara and Simonet. For this purpose, and at the invitation of Gayangos, he would take to his teacher's home the students who showed more promise in Arabic studies. With these young men he worked on a personal basis, training them in the interpretation of texts and manuscripts, in the classification of coins, and at the same time rendering them every possible means of assistance.

In this way he began to study numismatics in its relation to Hispano-Arabic history, and found in this apparently arid discipline an exact means to determine problems of Andalusian chronology. He had begun this study quite early, and had published several articles on the subject; these he put into the form of a book: *Tratado de numismática arábigo-española* (1879) which was printed only after immense difficulties which he surmounted with what his friend and biographer Saavedra termed "Aragonese tenacity."[1] In order to publish this work he had to acquire Arabic type and to design by himself the plates and inscriptions on the coins. His practical training served him to the extent that he even invented and constructed a special printing press suited to his purpose and needs. As will be shown further on, his studies in numismatics allowed him to rectify several important points in Andalusian history. According to Saavedra [2] the teacher never tired of insisting to his disciples on the need to abstain from suggesting possible readings of inscriptions when not in possession of absolute certainty with regard to their interpretation. He tried to impress on their minds the value of the difficult art of not knowing and showed them constantly that ignorance was less shameful than wilfully deceiving others.

---

[1] *Cf. Homenaje a Don Francisco Codera, Introducción* by E. Saavedra, Saragossa, 1904, p. xv.

[2] *Op. cit.*, p. xvii.

This passion for truth, at times so extreme that it bordered on skepticism, resulted in an endless effort to clarify and correct historical details and to combat previous errors by denouncing in no uncertain terms the mistakes of his predecessors and contemporaries. The desire to illustrate the hitherto obscure part of the Arabic history of Aragón had been the stimulus which first led him to the field of Arabic studies. To this subject he dedicated his inaugural lecture for the course of 1870-71 at the University of Sarragossa, outlining the main events of the Muslim conquest of Aragón and Navarre. This study he later broadened in his inaugural address to the Academy of History, which he read in 1879. His Arabic studies, born out of his interest in Aragonese history, were in no wise bound by any provincial or regional narrowness, for he also published many articles to illustrate the Muslim history of other regions of al-Andalus. He was, for example, the first to combat the unfounded opinion that ʿAbd ar-Raḥmān I had intended to make Cordova and its Mosque a rival to the holy shrines of Mekka.

In spite of the vast extent of Codera's factual knowledge on the subject of Peninsular Islam, he was ever the first to admit and reiterate that he was incapable of writing a general history of the Arabic period in al-Andalus, and he stressed the opinion that a long series of monographs on special subjects had first to be written, so that in the course of fifteen or twenty years enough sound material would be available for future generations to attempt more general works on the subject. In this sense, though that work was eventually conducted outside Spain, it can be observed in retrospect that Codera founded the modern school of Arabic investigation which in a large part made possible the work of Levi-Provençal. Meanwhile in order to achieve this ultimate objective, Codera saw clearly that many books and basic bibliographic material were needed, and so he set about to increase the existing resources of the Arabists of his time. As a critic he encouraged all useful work he came across, defending Casiri against the extremism of Dozy's attacks, while he began a campaign of relentless condemnation of all those works derived from the unfortunately premature book by Conde. To Conde, he opposed the more sound works of Gayangos and Dozy.

In order to acquire more works relevant to the history of al-Andalus he made an official trip in 1888 at government expense, to Tunis, Constantine, Algiers and Oran, where he visited public and private libraries, made extracts from valuable works, coming home laden with manuscripts and copies which he bought with his government travel allowance and then selflessly donated to the Academy of History.

Recognizing the value of the Arabic collection of the Escorial he set about repairing the manuscripts which had been thrown into a courtyard to save them from the fire of 1671. In the process, many of them had come apart because of this rough handling. Codera attempted to replace loose pages in their appropriate bindings, and he succeeded in restoring the collection to some extent.

Feeling that it was necessary to do for Arabic literature what had been done with Latin and Greek, that is to say, to publish original works in Arabic so that they could circulate and be consulted by specialists, Codera proposed that one hundred basic works on Peninsular Islam should be edited and published. Being a practical man as well as a thinker, he himself began the task by founding the *Bibliotheca Arabico-Hispana*, a true momument to scholarship, the object of which was to make easily accessible the basic works of Andalusian culture. Since Arabic printing was extremely expensive and inaccurate in Madrid at that time, he himself decided to undertake the task in his own home, with his own type, and with the aid of his students. Acquiring permission to take rare manuscripts home from the Escorial, an incredible episode began, in which a small group of amateur printers carried on their work in Codera's cellar, with the original manuscripts at hand for consultation. Later, the publication was continued in Saragossa for reasons of economy, and with the aid of Codera's brilliant disciple Ribera. In this way, from 1882 to 1895, ten volumes appeared including important biographical dictionaries on Andalusian cultural achievements,[1] all indispensable works for the writing of Andalusian cultural history, as well as being basic works of reference for general historical problems of the Arab period. Codera managed to sell about one hundred copies of each volume, almost all outside Spain, while at home he was seriously criticized by many colleagues who saw little value in the publication of Arabic books which few could read. However, Cánovas del

[1] They include: the *Aṣ-ṣila* by Ibn Bashkuwāl, the Dictionary of aḍ-Ḍabbī, the *Almocham* of Ibn al-Abbār, the *Complementum libri Aṣṣilah* by the same, the *Ta'rīkh 'Ulamā' al-Andalus* of Ibn al-Faraḍī and the *Fahrasa* of Abū Bakr ibn Khair.

Castillo, the protector of Spanish Arabism, made the State subscribe to two hundred copies. By this means, with the three hundred copies which were sold, the expenses of publication were covered, with no profit to the editors. However the protracted Spanish involvement in Cuba led the government of Sagasta to cancel the State subscription to Codera's publications, and the Arabist was informed that the order had been suspended because of the need to use that money in buying war equipment.[1] In this way, the *Bibliotheca* planned for a hundred volumes, was discontinued after the publication of ten.

Codera's intense activity in the field of Arabic studies never led him to neglect the practical side of his personality. Ever since childhood he had been familiar with farming, and his scientific knowledge was of aid to him in his attempts to improve the state of Spanish agriculture, to which goal he devoted numerous publications, as well as inventing better equipment and indulging in experimental farming, and the use of mineral fertilizers which he introduced into his farms and by so doing, convinced others of their effectiveness.

Codera was a frugal man, simple in his customs, and so austere that it seemed as if he had not given up his priestly vocation. His religious feeling was directed constantly towards helping others, and both his speech and literary style were plain and straightforward, avoiding the empty rhetoric common in his age. A patient scholar, he never accepted conclusions without thorough proof, and was ever the first to admit his own ignorance of any problem that might arise. According to his friend Saavedra, his motto was to "feed the hungry and teach the ignorant."[2] After retiring from the University in 1902, Codera spent his last years in Aragón, where he devoted his time to his agricultural pursuits and died in 1917 in the province of Huesca.

As the founder of modern Spanish Arabism, his importance is enormous. Apart from the *Bibliotheca,* he facilitated the task of historical reconstruction for his successors by extracting more than fifty thousand notes of all kinds on the Arabic antiquities of Spain, which he classified and left in the hands of his students. They may still be consulted today in the Instituto Miguel Asín, and have

---

[1] *Cf. Enciclopedia Espasa, s.v. Codera.*

[2] "Dar de comer al hambriento y enseñar al que no sabe," *cf. Homenaje,* pp. xxvi-xxvii.

served as the groundwork for more than one important study. The reputation of this work of unparallelled generosity (since he realized he would never be able to use these notes himself) went beyond the frontiers of Spain, for the Italian prince Leone Caetani di Teano translated these fifty thousand notes into Italian for the benefit of scholars in his own country.[1] The importance of these handwritten notes in Spain itself is amply attested by García Gómez [2] who mentions that they continue to be used along with his personal books, and that the Instituto Miguel Asín is pervaded by an atmosphere which he created, and which has become a tradition.

In reviewing the tradition of Spanish Arabism which Codera so profoundly modified, García Gómez states that Conde having fallen into disrepute, the Romantic pseudo-Orientalism which expressed itself through literary means had also become extinct with Estébanez Calderón (d. 1867). Gayangos, Codera's most direct precursor, was, as has been noted, a distinguished amateur Arabist equally at ease in Arabic and Spanish literature, but maintaining an essentially non-professional attitude. As for the remainder, though some were outstanding as was the case of Lafuente y Alcántara who unfortunately died prematurely in 1868, they did not succeed in creating a solid tradition of Arabic studies, some because other, more pressing occupations drew them away from Arabic; others because they died young. The only Arabist by profession was Simonet, but his anti-Semitic spirit resulted in a negative picture of the history of al-Andalus.

In the face of this, Codera's significance stands out clearly. With his precise and unadorned prose, he set himself apart from the literary bombast and pseudo-science of his age. Thus his writings possessed a quality of cold objectivity most unusual at the time, and though his Arabic career was begun late in life, the change was a total one; therefore, since he did not combine his professional activities with any other, Spanish Arabism with Codera, lost its amateurish qualities so that he set the mode for a more professional attitude to these studies.

At the same time, it is stressed by García Gómez [3] that the relative

[1] *Cf.* Isaac Cattan, *L'orientaliste espagnol Francisco Codera y Zaidín, Revue Tunisienne,* Tunis, 1918, vol. 25, num. 126, pp. 128-129.

[2] *Cf.* García Gómez, *Homenaje a Don Francisco Codera* 1836-1917, in *And.* 15, 1950, pp. 263-274.

[3] *Op. cit.,* p. 270.

lateness of Codera's change towards Arabic studies kept him from mastering the Arabic language, a fact which he knew and was always ready to admit. Because of this his philological preparation was inferior to that of many of his contemporaries outside Spain. Nevertheless the research methods initiated in Spain by Codera were nothing less than revolutionary if we compare the thousands of written notes he left to his followers, with the work of a scholar such as Menéndez y Pelayo, whose vast erudition remained unwritten, and as such was fated to disappear as a method of investigation. These notes of Codera's, along with the ten volumes of his *Bibliotheca* established the basis for future scholarship. In this sense it may be said that he planned a history of Islamic culture in al-Andalus, within the general framework of which Spanish Arabic studies are still functioning.

Though profoundly Catholic, Codera, unlike Simonet, had a deep admiration for Arabic culture, and was able to instill this feeling into his disciples. This attitude was to make possible the admiration for Islamic culture expressed in the works of Asín, himself a member of the clergy.

Perhaps in another aspect Codera was even more influential, for since his time, Spanish Arabists have existed as a well defined school with its own tradition, a rare phenomenon in Spain, where great achievements have often tended to result from the efforts of isolated individuals, and as such, too often disappear with their creator. In this respect Codera, by establishing a warm and personal relationship with his most promising disciples, succeeded in creating a group feeling which insured the continuity of the Arabist tradition in Spain. Codera was fortunate in finding disciples such as Ribera and Asín whose efforts established a vigorous tradition of Arabic studies. For this reason, García Gómez fondly recalls the nickname which these two disciples were given by their friends, and which he extends to the whole school, himself included: the "Beni Codera."[1]

A study of some of Codera's works will help in clarifying his position with respect to Arabic studies, and will point up some of his more important contributions.

In his inaugural address to the Academy of History, Codera explains that his interest in Arabic was first aroused because he

---

[1] *Op. cit.*, p. 274.

thought that in the Arabic chronicles he might find many facts pertinent to the history of Aragón. Since there was no professor of Arabic in Saragossa, he first attempted to learn that language by himself, but finally had to give up the attempt till later.[1] In the same speech, Codera gives vent to his anti-Conde compaign which he relentlessly pursued all his life in an attempt to create a more sound scholarly method. He expresses the feeling that Conde's critics had been exaggerated only in their violence, though he feels that their criticism was otherwise well founded. He indicates that outside Spain Conde had ceased to be an authority, whereas Spanish scholars continued to quote him without knowing that his competence and good faith had long since been questioned.[2] He lists specific instances in which Conde had been misled, and adds that those who wish to devote their attention to Arabic studies should first learn how to doubt and be prepared to admit their ignorance. For Codera it was not humiliating not to know something, whereas it was dishonourable to be accused, for lack of humility, of having falsified history as was the case of Conde. However, it should be understood that Codera's implacable severity towards Conde was the result of his attempt to stamp out once and for ever the influence of that writer on Spanish historiography, a necessary step to a more accurate version of history. As we have shown, Conde's faults probably resulted from the adverse circumstances in which he was forced to work, as well as the intervention of the inexperienced hands of his editors. This for Codera was no excuse, since he himself was faced with the task of reconstructing Arab history, to which effort he dedicated the final pages of his speech, by making a plea that the Spanish government aid in extending the study of Arabic by requiring knowledge of that language from those who were to work in libraries and archives. He argues that since the Arabic domination of al-Andalus occupied more than half the extent of Spanish history, it would be impossible to study medieval history without a profound and complete analysis of all the Arabic documents existing in Spain.[3]

In his work on numismatics, Codera explains the importance of his subject as an aid in historical research, since, as he says, the

---

[1] *Cf. Discursos leídos ante la Real Academia de la Historia en la recepción pública de Don Francisco Codera y Zaidín*, Madrid, 1879, p. 2.

[2] *Op. cit.*, pp. 3-4.

[3] *Op. cit.*, p. 52.

Arabic coins of al-Andalus almost always mention the place and year in which they were minted,[1] while beginning with the reign of ʿAbd ar-Raḥmān III, they always add the name and titles of the caliph.[2] When the caliphate collapsed in the first third of the fifth century of the *Hijra,* the history of al-Andalus became hopelessly complicated by the large number of independent kingdoms of Taifas. However, the governors of these petty kingdoms all produced coinage of their own, and this made it possible to clarify certain points in chronology. For example, the information found on coins made it possible to determine the exact year in which al-Muʿtamid of Seville conquered Cordova.[3]

The Naṣrid coins of Granada, like those of the Almohads include the genealogy of the reigning sovereign in such detail that it is often carried to the seventh generation, thus affording a mine of information in constructing genealogical tables and establishing their chronology.[4]

In showing the development of Arabic coinage in al-Andalus, Codera accumulates inscriptions from which striking conclusions may be derived. For example, he indicates that shortly after the conquest of North Africa, the Arabs had introduced coins which still bore Latin inscriptions, but which contained the new Muslim propaganda. By stressing the monotheism of God without mentioning the prophethood of Muḥammad these coins were inoffensive to the newly subjected peoples.[5] Other such coins, bearing the name of the general Mūsā ibn Nuṣayr, likewise avoiding mention of Muḥammad are also extant.[6] After the conquest of al-Andalus, and beginning in the year 712, this same practice was introduced in the new province, and coins bearing inscriptions of a similar character are common.[7] Gradually, as the Peninsula became more and more Arabized, the reference to Muḥammad crept into the inscriptions, and eventually the coinage was struck entirely in

[1] *Cf.* Codera, *Tratado de numismática arábigo-española,* Madrid, 1879, p. v.

[2] *Op. cit.,* p. vi.

[3] *Op. cit.,* p. viii.

[4] *Op. cit.,* p. ix.

[5] Here is an example of such a coin, struck in Africa with its Latin inscription as follows: "In nomine Domini misericordis solidus feritus in Africa. Non est Deus nisi unus cui nullus alius similis." *Cf. Numismática,* p. 41.

[6] "In n(omine) Domini unus D(eus). Muse F(ilius) Nusir Amira." *Cf. op. cit.,* p. 55.

[7] *E.g.,* "In nomine Dei. Non Deus nisi Deus solus. Novus numus solidus feritus in Spania anno. . ." (*Cf. op. cit.,* pp. 47-48).

Arabic.[1] What is even more significant is that Alfonso VIII of Castile struck coins in Toledo with their inscriptions entirely in Arabic though containing the Christian counter-propaganda. These coins are an eloquent testimony to the intense Arabization of Toledo at the end of the thirteenth century,[2] since the Christian monarch would not otherwise have had to issue coinage in Arabic.

Ever preoccupied by the history of al-Andalus which demanded being written with ever greater urgency, Codera turned his attention to this question in his study entitled *Decadencia y desaparición de los almorávides en España*.[3] There he claims that such a history remains to be written, for in spite of Dozy's work published forty years previous to the time when Codera was working, much was left to be done, since the Dutch scholar had carried his investigations through the period of Taifas without touching the age of the Almoravids, the Almohads, the Marīnids and the Naṣrids of Granada.[4] This leads him once more to an attack on Conde whom he this time absolves from the imputations made concerning his lack of knowledge of the Arabic language, only to reproach him even more severely for his bad faith and lack of humility in not recognizing difficulties, as well as for his tendency to cut the Gordian knot rather than untying it or confessing his ignorance in scholarly points which he could not solve for lack of data. Thus he cautions Spanish scholars against relying on Conde, and warns non-Arabists never to consult his work. He is less harsh with Gayangos, though he indicates clearly that the *Mohammedan Dynasties* is not in itself a critical history of al-Andalus and that this desired goal could not yet be achieved in Spain, because Arabic studies were not sufficiently advanced.

---

[1] Thus a dirham of Hishām II (366-399):

"There is no God but one God who has no partners—well said !— The Imām Hishām, prince of the faithful, fortified by God.—ʿĀmir [the Ḥājib Almanṣūr]—In God's name this *dirham* was struck in al-Andalus in the year... Muḥammad is the prophet of God who sent him with the message." (*Cf.* pp. 91-106).

[2] One such coin bears the following inscription:

"The Imām of the Church of the Messiah and its Pope. In the name of the Father, the Son and the Holy Ghost, one God. He who believes and is baptized will be saved (*cf.* St. Mark, chap. 16, v. 15). The prince of the Catholics Alfonso ibn Sancho, may God fortify him and aid him to victory. This *dinār* was struck in Toledo during the course of the year 1251 of the Spanish Era (= AD 1289)."

[3] *Cf. Colección de Estudios Arabes*, vol. 3, Saragossa, 1899.

[4] *Op. cit.*, p. vii-viii.

Therefore, he advises that the only course open to serious scholarship is that of writing monographs on particular problems, so that at some later period a history could be synthetized.[1]

As far as his own limitations are concerned, in his work on the Almoravids, he modestly states that he had only attempted to write what he calls an "external history" based on political events and chronology, while entirely avoiding an "internal history" of the institutions, customs, commerce, industry and ideas of the Muslims of this period, not because he felt that these aspects were irrelevant to history, but because he did not know them and felt that nobody else was in a more favourable position than he. However, he points to the many manuscripts on such subjects which were extant, and incites others to study them. It is precisely in this plea of his, that the cultural studies of Ribera seem to have found their point of departure, for Ribera was to answer the challenge by publishing al-Khushānī's book on the *Judges of Cordova* as will be seen in due course.

In a volume of collected monographs entitled *Estudios críticos de historia árabe española* [2] Codera reiterates his condemnation of Conde's work in even stronger terms and devotes some pages to regretting the inadequate condition of Arabic studies in Spain. He again expresses the opinion that no one was capable of writing a history of al-Andalus in his days, he least of all, for as he says:

"Although for a quarter of a century I have been the person under the greatest obligation to know Arabic and even to work in the latter; yet it is not my duty to know more Arabic than everybody." [3]

Here he speaks of his plan for publishing Arabic texts, saying that in the course of twenty years some hundred volumes could be published so that the new generation could re-write the history of medieval Spain. Unfortunately, he adds, the scarce demand for such books makes State protectionism necessary; and he regrets the failure of the Spanish government to continue supporting the *Bibliotheca* which had had to be discontinued after the publication of the tenth volume,[4] and he pleads for more interest in Arabic studies with the zeal of a missionary.

---

[1] *Op. cit.*, pp. xiv-xv.
[2] *Cf. Colección de estudios árabes*, vol. 7, Saragossa, 1903.
[3] *Op. cit.*, p. xiii.
[4] *Op. cit.*, pp. xiv-xv.

In a volume entitled *Estudios críticos de historia árabe española* (*segunda serie*) [1] Codera included four studies reprinted after years had elapsed since their first appearance. These monographs refer particularly to the history of Catalonia, Aragón and Navarre, and in the introduction he explains that his personal interest in the history of these regions was what had inspired him to study Arabic, adding that this interest otherwise had no connection with his early theological career.[2]

The first article, entitled: *Importancia general que tiene para España el estudio de la lengua árabe, y especial para los que han nacido en el antiguo reino de Aragón* is a reprint of his inaugural lecture at the University of Saragossa originally published in 1870. The regionalism expressed in the title is by no means an expression of his true feelings for he states clearly that his intention is to clarify the importance of Arabic studies for all of Spain.[3] For Codera, this importance may be summed up under two main headings: first, for its bearing on medieval history, and second, for its significance in the study of comparative philology. He shows how the literary culture of medieval Islam was far greater than that of Europe during the same period, for, as he explains, from the eighth to the thirteenth centuries the Muslim world bore aloft the sceptre of knowledge in all fields. This expressed itself in a bibliographic wealth unparalleled by Christendom. As an example, he mentions ʿAbd al-Mālik ibn Ḥabīb as-Sālimī of Huétor (near Granada), of whom it was said that he wrote one thousand and fifty books of all kinds, according to Ibn al-Khaṭīb.[4]

Thus Codera concluded that it was possible to know more about the culture and history of Islam than about the intimate life of European nations in the Middle Ages, since European chroniclers, following the Graeco-Latin tradition wrote histories of the leaders and sovereigns of their nations, of the principal wars, etc., without concerning themselves with the personal life of lesser individuals

[1] In *Colección de estudios árabes*, vol. 8, Madrid, 1917;

[2] *Op. cit.*, p. 94, n. 1.

[3] *Cf. op. cit.*, p. 2-3.

[4] *Cf.* Casiri, *Bibliotheca Arabico-Hispana*, vol. 2, p. 107. This idea has been accepted today. R. W. Southern says: "A comparison of the literary catalogues of the West with the lists of books available to Moslem scholars makes a painful impression on a Western mind, and the contrast came as a bombshell to the Latin scholars of the twelfth century, who first had their eyes opened to the difference." *Western Views of Islam in the Middle Ages*, Cambridge, Massachusetts, 1962, p. 9.

as did the Arabs in their numerous and voluminous biographical dictionaries which are stocked with anecdotes revealing the social conditions of the times. In this respect Codera was perfectly justified, for Asín was to show later that we have more records about Islamic mysticism in al-Andalus than we have about the Spanish mystics of the Golden Age. Likewise García Gómez, Henri Pérès and Nykl have shown how much more biographical material there is on the poets of the period of Taifas than on the fifteenth-century Spanish poets of the *Cancioneros*.

Speaking of the philosophy of history, Codera recalls that Ibn Khaldūn was a worthy predecessor of Vico and Montesquieu,[1] and in this respect, he attacks Simonet for having quoted Ibn Khaldūn as having censured Arabic historiography for not taking into account the different changes and circumstances undergone by nations with the passage of time, so that the Arab historians had tended to judge the past by the present state of affairs. Simonet had concluded from this that Islam constituted a culture in which nothing changed, and which confused the past with the present and the future. For Simonet, the Arabs had never grasped the nineteenth-century idea of progress nor that of man's gradual perfection in history. But to this, Codera replies that at the time in which Arabic culture flourished, that is to say, the Middle Ages, no nation be it European or Asian had attained this critical attitude toward history. Claiming that such a tendency to judge the past by the standards of the present had existed until fairly recently in Europe, Codera delivers his *coup de grâce* to Simonet by observing that as far as we know it was Ibn Khaldūn, in the fourteenth century, who first drew attention to this new historical approach.[2]

In this sense, we see clearly the open minded sympathy for his subject which Codera always maintained in his Arabism, and which distinguished him to such an extent from Simonet.

Turning to the importance of Arabic studies in comparative philology he points to the work of the brothers Grimm and to Bopp, and adds that of the great linguistic groups studied in his time, the Semitic languages constituted a rich field for linguistic analysis. Of the Semitic languages, Hebrew and Arabic were then the best known ones, while Assyro-Babylonian was at that time being rediscovered. However, of these, Arabic is the richest in vocabulary

[1] Codera, *ibid.*, p. 15.
[2] *Op. cit.*, pp. 18-20.

and grammatical forms, as Codera points out, and therefore indispensable for any comparative study of these languages.[1]

As for Arabic culture in al-Andalus, Codera gives a glowing account of Andalusian literature and stresses the importance of Arabic historiography which had confirmed and added much factual material to the knowledge of medieval Spain, all of which had discredited the critical history of Masdeu who in the eighteenth century had declared that almost all Christian documents in Spanish archives had been forged.[2] From all this, Codera concludes in the following manner:

> The subject I recommend to you has, it is true, few inducements, and above all it demands somewhat greater perseverance than others, and perhaps that is the reason why Spain, though it is the country that should cultivate this subject more than any other, is such that in no other is it less esteemed. You, my dear youths, born in the classical soil of perseverance in study, are in a position to begin to acquire knowledge of the Arabic language so that when you shall have completed your literary careers and some of you are in your homes, while others are in possession of the positions which you have earned by your efforts, you may be enabled, by way of amusement and diversion, to devote yourselves to reading Arabic texts; and in this way perhaps it will be possible to cleanse our beloved nation of the stain that lies upon it for having neglected these studies. [3]

Codera's propagandist attitude and apologetics in favour of Arabic studies put him in the midst of the battle between traditionalists and liberals which was being waged in Spain during the second half of the nineteenth century. Since the reactions to Codera's work are a good way of determining the extent to which Arabic studies were penetrating into the general milieu of Spanish scholarship it is necessary to offer an illustration of these reactions.

The reply to Codera's inaugural address to the Royal Academy of History [4] was read by the traditionalist Vicente Lafuente, a fact which in itself boded no good for the acceptance of Codera's ideas. This speech, written in a sarcastic tone, is an example of the subtleties of the anti-Arabist reaction cloaked in a tone of apparent sympathy for the cause of Codera. Vicente Lafuente begins by indicating that this small but energetic group of Arabists had

---

[1] *Cf. op. cit.*, p. 30.
[2] *Cf. op. cit.*, p. 45.
[3] *Op. cit.*, pp. 95-96.
[4] *Cf. Discursos*, Madrid, 1879.

entered the lists of Spanish historiography and had begun to overthrow and destroy all its enemies; to give the lie to Christian chronicles, annals and legends, even going to the extreme of substituting the clerical (and therefore official) history of Spain with the works of the believers in the *Koran*. Having thus aroused his audience by such a beginning, the author explains that the traditionalist school looked with some suspicion upon these Arabists, and not without good cause, for Lafuente argues that for over a century, whenever any scientific or historical discovery had been made, it had at once been used to the dishonour of God. Thus, he adds, all the enemies of God, of the Catholic Church, of tradition, of antiquity and of the principles of authority have come to the defense of the Arabists; have spurred them on, as it were defending the Moors against the monuments of antiquity as represented by Catholicism. Because of this, the author feels that Arabism has come to be as disreputable as was the study of Hebrew at the end of the sixteenth century, when Fray Luis de León, Arias Montano and others were denounced to the Inquisition by the Spanish Hellenists as Judaizers.[1]

Turning to Arabic chronicles, Lafuente points out their general unreliability, by claiming that when a Christian chronicler; be he a monk or a bishop, such as the Pacense, Silense, Sampiro, Sebastián de Salamanca or Jiménez de Rada, tells us that a given battle was won by Christendom, whereas Ibn Khaldūn, Ibn al-Qūṭiyya, al-Maqqarī or another Muslim writer claims that it was won by the Moors, we are left in a quandary as to whom to believe. In this event, he adds that the modern and rationalist school is always on the side of the Arab chronicler; for the Arab, who in his homeland and in Algeria is "lazy, deceitful, thieving," is now presented in Spain, according to the new fashion, as "chivalrous, gallant, truthful; a troubadour, musician, poet, artist, agriculturalist and even a theologian after his own fashion."[2]

From this point, Vicente Lafuente turns to an attack on the general reliability of the Spanish Arabists themselves. He claims that apart from the forgeries committed by the Arabs, scholars should beware of even more serious forgeries which in their name certain Spaniards had perpetrated. In this point, Lafuente refers to Conde whom Codera had demolished in his own speech, but he

[1] *Cf. Discursos*, p. 84.
[2] *Op. cit.*, pp. 87-88.

phrases this in such a way as to imply that Conde was only the first of a long line of potential forgers which probably included Codera himself.[1] Having thus insinuated the general untrustworthiness of Arabists, he asks himself once more which side, Muslim or Christian was to be believed in its account of history. He states that he cannot give credit to the fables of Pelayo de Oviedo, the product of senile delirium, when compared to the narrations of al-Maqqarī, Ibn Khaldūn and the anonymous writer of the *Ajbar Machmua.* However, in spite of this, he expresses a preference for the reliability of the Christian chronicles, as long as their authors display a certain guarantee of honesty and scholarly veracity. The Christian writer for Lafuente, is acceptable "when he gives evidence of being what Quintillian called a *vir bonus,*" a quality which in his opinion is difficult to expect of the Muslim historian, "in whose religion it is not required to be an honest man,[2] which would be asking a great deal in view of Muslim morality."

These unbelievably prejudiced ideas about Islam betray clearly the apologetic nature of the traditionalist reaction, which found itself constantly on the defensive and retaliated by means of the most virulent and unfair arguments. At the same time the speech of Lafuente betrays a faint tone of acceptance of Arabic studies in that he after all does attribute some value, though not much, to Arabic scholarship. If Lafuente could have found a way of reconciling Arabic studies with the Catholic tradition as he conceived it, he would no doubt have been more ready to accept and grant them their due place in Spanish historiography. This was what some of the more intelligent traditionalist scholars would do, as is the case of the nineteenth-century critic Menéndez y Pelayo, who in his history of the origin of the novelesque genre had incorporated the findings of Gayangos on the transmission in Spain of the *Calila y Dimna.* Menéndez y Pelayo granted the importance of the Arabic tales as a necessary precursor to the development of the novelistic technique, though as shall be seen in studying Ribera, he gave little credit to the theories of poetic transmission, basing himself in this instance on Dozy. Menéndez y Pelayo at first did

---

[1] "And this gives rise to an even worse idea, namely that of investigating the origin of the forgeries that were committed not by the Arabs, but rather, were passed off in their name by certain abovementioned Spaniards, *as well as others soon to be mentioned.* (*Op. cit.*, p. 89). My underlining.

[2] "Hombre de bien", *op. cit.*, p. 91.

not grant much importance to the role of Muslim philosophy in the European Middle Ages, but it must be said that his ideas changed as more evidence was brought to light by Asín, while at the same time he was ever the first to encourage studies and research on Arabic themes. Thus, Menéndez y Pelayo, who had had a low opinion of Muslim philosophy wrote the introduction to Pons Boigues'[1] translation of Ibn Ṭufayl, and in these pages he expressed genuine interest in the new areas of knowledge which were being discovered. He himself later encouraged Asín's early work on al-Ġazālī and thus came to modify his early opinion.

A far more significant example of the way in which the gradual publication of Arabic texts was slowly exerting an influence on Spanish scholarship is seen in the fact that Spanish critics who knew little or no Arabic were beginning to search Arabic literature for the sources of many Spanish works. This may be observed in the *Homenaje* prepared for Codera, in which articles on Arabic themes written by thinkers such as Menéndez y Pelayo and Menéndez Pidal are included. Thus Menéndez y Pelayo contributed a study entitled *La doncella Teodor* [2] in which he relates Lope de Vega's play by that name to a tale from the *Arabian Nights* which had been translated into Spanish in the Middle Ages.[3] Gayangos possessed a manuscript of this Old Spanish recension which was consulted by Menéndez y Pelayo who, aided by Asín in the Arabic part of his research, was able to prove the Arabic origin of the fable which Lope had utilized in the elaboration of his play. At the same time, Menéndez y Pelayo shows little sympathy for Arabic literature, since he begins his study by claiming that the Semitic peoples had never given evidence of inventive phantasy, and that in the background of all the Arabic collections of fables an Indo-European origin was to be detected, be it Sanscrit, Persian or Greek. At the beginning of the nineteenth century, Silvestre de Sacy had stressed

[1] A brilliant young Arabist disciple of Ribera whose early death cut short a promising career. He left an *Ensayo bio-bibliográfico sobre los historiadores y geógrafos arábigo-españoles* as well as a work entitled *Apuntes sobre las escrituras mozárabes toledanas*. For his bio-bibliography, *cf.* "Vida y obras de D. Francisco Pons y Boigues," *R.A.B.M.* 2, 1900, pp. 496-512; 609-624; 714-723, by Pedro Roca.

[2] *Homenaje*, pp. 483-511.

[3] *The story of the slave girl Tawaddud*, night 454 ff., *Arabian Nights*. The text of the medieval Spanish translation may be consulted in Hermann Knust, *Mittheilungen aus dem Eskurial*, Tubingen, 1879, pp. 506-517 (*Capítulo que fabla de los enxemplos e castigos de Teodor, la donsella.*).

the Islamic affiliation of the Arabic collection known as the *Thousand and One Nights*, but Menéndez y Pelayo is pleased to recall his refutation by William von Schlegel who had pointed out the Indian origin of many of these fables in 1833.[1] The fact is that according to a text by al-Masʿūdī which Menéndez y Pelayo quotes, the Persian and Sanscrit origin of many of these stories is clearly established, and there is no reason at present to question such an assertion.[2] However, for us it is more interesting to point out that Menéndez y Pelayo's attitude is revealing of his age and the position of the traditionalist school in Spain with regard to Arabic culture. In Germany the nationalist feeling which found its expression in an anti-Semitism which was to lead to such tragic results in our own century already at a very early age was inclining scholarship towards the aggrandizement of Aryan as opposed to Semitic culture. This explains the attitude of Schlegel in stressing the Aryan sources of the *Arabian Nights* while giving little thought to the intense process of Islamization which these tales underwent when they were translated and adapted to the Arabic language. In Spain, for similar nationalistic reasons Menéndez y Pelayo was to give welcome to such ideas. We have already seen that the phenomenon of nationalism in Spain was further complicated during the second half of the nineteenth century by the historical insecurity of Spanish intellectuals vis-à-vis the rest of Europe. López Morillas in his book on Krausism explains that during this period Spain looked to Germany for cultural inspiration in contrast to the respect for France which predominated during the eighteenth century. In this sense, while Spanish scholarship was being forced to pay some attention to its Arab past, it is often influenced by racist ideas which tend to exalt the "eternal," "Aryan" Spaniard. This is the case with Menéndez y Pelayo and in general with the traditionalist school. Arabists like Codera, on the other hand, represent an outgrowth of early nineteenth-century Spanish liberalism, and as such make a constant defense of Spain's Semitic past. Though the conflict has never actually been resolved, as we shall observe in further

---

[1] *Cf. op. cit.*, p. 486.

[2] G. E. Von Grunebaum has today stressed this though making a particular study of Greek elements in the *Arabian Nights*. *Cf Medieval Islam*, Chicago, 1961, chap. 9 *Creative Borrowing*: *Greece in the "Arabian Nights,"* pp. 294-319. Though that scholar adds: "Islamic civilization is thoroughly syncretistic, and it proves its vitality by coating each and every borrowing with its own inimitable patina." *Op. cit.*, p. 319.

chapters, it becomes clear that at this time the work of Spanish Arabists was beginning to be seriously considered by the opposite camp, and that the latter was slowly beginning to adapt its own views to the new information acquired, though without radically changing its basic attitudes.

PART THREE

THE STUDY OF CULTURAL HISTORY

CHAPTER SIX

The end of the nineteenth century marked a crisis in Spanish history, for during the deceptively calm period which followed the Restoration and the end of the last Carlist war, from the years 1880 to 1895, Spaniards were deluded by the superficial calm which had been attained, and acted as if the profound social problems present since 1812 at least, were non-existent.

In this intellectual and socio-political climate a group of writers such as Unamuno, Azorín, Baroja, Valle-Inclán and others, were to grow up. They all felt a certain emptiness and lack of purpose and meaning in Spanish history. The Spain of Cánovas to them was sadly inconsistent and lacking in historical perspectives worthy of being admired. Of course, no one listened to these brilliant young thinkers, until the Spanish-American war, and the loss of Cuba and the Philippines in 1898 brought Spain to its senses and made it turn toward a radical questioning of its inner strength and system of values. It was thus in 1898 that the loss of the remnants of empire resulted in a period of self-questioning which was to bring to the forefront a group of brilliant intellectuals all bent upon creating— on a metaphysical rather than social basis— an inner equilibrium for their country. Most of these men followed two directions. On the one hand they reacted profoundly to orthodox Catholicism; and on the other, disillusioned by the faith in reason and history which had motivated the Krausists and all the later schools of thought in the second half of the nineteenth century, they tended to affirm and stress *life* as the more total medium of which reason is only a part, and within which it functioned, while the *life* they speak of is in no way to be explained rationally. This led to an anti-historicism in which all the generation of 1898 began to despise the superficial attempts to assimilate Spain to Europe made in the nineteenth century, while at the same time it envisioned the day when Spain could play a new role worthy of its past grandeur while also remaining faithful to its old traditions. This attitude represents a difficult and unstable compromise between the progressive and traditional forces, and precisely because it was a compromise on the level of idealism rather than on that of social and economic realities, it was doomed to failure politically, though it produced exquisite works of art and an authentic literary renaissance.[1]

Feeling that Spain's destiny was ill-starred, from all over the country thinkers began to produce programmes of reform. Most of them proposed that Spain deal with problems such as land reform, education, industrialization, social reorganization, etc. At the same time, a tendency toward introspection became more and more noticeable, which preached the reordering of Spanish affairs on a spiritual level in accordance with Spain's ancient traditions. This was to make men like Unamuno, disillusioned with the advocates of the "Europeanization" of Spain, preach the "Africanization" of Europe, that is, making Europe less "materialistic" and more spiritually inclined.

The ideas current at this time were to leave a mark on the new generation of Arabists in Spain, first represented by Julián Ribera y Tarragó, of whom it may be stated that though slightly older than the generation of 1898 proper he devoted his life to the "Africanization" of Europe by bombarding the scholarly world of his time with publications in which he revealed the many instances in which Europe had adapted important cultural institutions from the Arab world. Some of his theories were to be accepted and later expanded; others have gradually been refuted or have shrunk in significance, but it is important to point out the direction taken by his work, since it is inseparable from the intellectual milieu within which he grew up and conducted his research.

Born in Carcagente, in the province of Valencia, in 1858, Ribera began to study Arabic with Codera in 1882, at the age of twenty-four. He held the chair of Arabic at the University of Saragossa from 1887 until in 1905 he was transferred to the Central University in Madrid to teach the history of Jewish and Islamic civilization. From 1913 he occupied the chair of Hispano-Arabic literature at the same University, where he taught until his retirement in 1927, at which time he established himself in his home province of Valencia where he died in 1934. A member of the Spanish Academy from 1912 and of the Academy of History from 1915, he carried the tradition of Spanish Arabism to new depths of maturity by following the ideas which Codera had initiated. He was an Arabist of remarkable philological preparation, and unlike many of his predecessors who had tended to venerate Arabic studies more as a

[1] For a full account of the Generation of 1898, *cf.* Pedro Laín Entralgo, *La generación del noventa y ocho*, 4th ed., Madrid, *Austral*, 1959.

grammatical exercise than as a manifestation of the humanities, he delved deeply into cultural problems. According to Asín, reverence for the Arabic language in itself had been a constant plague among certain Spanish linguists, though this attitude had been combatted by Gayangos and Codera. Ribera was to banish this tendency from the new school which Codera had organized.[1]

For Ribera, the grammatical study of the Arabic language was no more than an instrument and a means to a more complex study; a key to the past, and not an end in itself. However, the history of the past has two facets. Up to Ribera, Spanish Arabists had fixed their attention almost exclusively upon the political or external history of al-Andalus; a tendency which we have seen reach its climax with Codera. This was actually a common feature of almost all historians up to the second half of the nineteenth century. In the case of al-Andalus it was furthermore essential and almost unavoidable to begin by outlining the external history of the Arab period, whose political phenomena, being more evident, were more widely documented in the Arab chronicles. In this sense the attempts of Conde had been rash beyond measure, whereas those of Codera were modest and almost over-cautious. In order to envision the background of the Andalusian political society and to explore the inner structure of its organisms, the undercurrent of its ideas, institutions and customs, it was first necessary to end the task of clarifying the apparent, external history. This having been attempted to some extent by Codera and his generation, Ribera turned toward the inner history of cultural manifestations, initiating in Spain the study of Islamic history and culture on a broad and deep basis. In order to do this, he had to extend the scope of Spanish Arabism into fields hitherto neglected, namely those dealing with Arab culture in the Middle East. In this respect he represents a vital turning point, for up till his time Spanish Arabists had devoted their attention almost exclusively to Peninsular affairs, and as a result had been severely criticized by European scholars such as Dozy who saw in their limitation of scope an inevitable sign of weakness and scholarly provincialism. Thus Ribera, with his studies on the Niẓāmī college of Baghdad and his work on Arabic music opened up wider horizons for Spanish Arabism which his

[1] *Cf.* Asín Palacios, *Introducción,* in Julián Ribera, *Disertaciones y opúsculos,* vol. I, p. xvii, for this point, as well as for a complete biography of Ribera.

disciples such as Asín and García Gómez were quick to follow. With hardly any precursors in his field of activities he opened up almost unexplored areas of knowledge such as the history of educational institutions in the Arab world, that of libraries, bibliophilia, legal institutions, philosophy, poetry and music. At the same time it should be pointed out that all of Ribera's explorations of Eastern culture were motivated by his interest in their relevance for understanding al-Andalus and its impact on Spain and Europe. Thus, as we shall see, he studied the Niẓāmī school of Baghdad in order to explain the functioning of educational institutions in al-Andalus, and also because as a reformer of modern Spain he wished to eliminate State control over education and establish a free system such as had existed in al-Andalus. In this sense, Ribera's Arabism coincided with the reforming spirit which as a precursor of the generation of 1898 was one of his main features.

In the matter of cultural phenomena, continuity of tradition was to be Ribera's fundamental axiom, so that his study of the educational system of al-Andalus was expanded to show the links and parallels between the medieval European university system with its degrees, diplomas and exams, and the similar system of State controlled education invented by the Chinese, adapted by the Sassanids, and continued by the Arabs in the Niẓāmī school of Baghdad.

In the same way, his study of the Aragonese official known as the *Justicia* made it likely in his day that this was another of the many legal institutions Christian Spain had copied from Islam. His analysis of the main features of the thought of the medieval mystic Raymond Lull led him to find precursors to this figure in the life, theosophic and mystical doctrines of Andalusian *Ṣūfis* such as Ibn al-ʿArabī of Murcia. Likewise his study of the poetry of Ibn Quzmān led him to the discovery that the strophic system, the prosody and themes of that poet's works were remarkably similar to those of the Provenzal troubadours. The history of music was also enriched by his investigations, since being a rare combination of Arabist and musician, he was able to outline the history of the origin, development, schools and methods of Arabic music, both in the Orient and in al-Andalus. At the same time his careful analysis of literary and musical documents opened up suggestive fields in the study of European music for he claimed that the main features of Andalusian music were strikingly similar to those of the *Cantigas* of

Alfonso X, the songs of the troubadours and the minnesingers. Spain thus appeared to be the connecting link between the Arabic musical tradition (itself inherited from Byzantium and Persia) and that of medieval Christendom.

According to Asín, Ribera's thought was based on philosophical and sociological grounds, since independently of the French sociologist Tarde, and years before the German ethnologists Graebner and Ankermann, Ribera conceived and developed his theory of *imitation* to explain the transmission of human culture, outlining its laws and the rules of method necessary to its application in historical research. This he did to argue for the Arabic origins of the Aragonese *Justicia,* while at the same time taking part in a heated debate over the "scientific" character of history in which he defined the limits of science and history and concluded that science was a necessary prerequisite to history though not its ultimate goal. In matters of education, he wrote extensive studies in which he came to the refreshing conclusion that the true method of education was to outline the best way in which to *learn* rather than the best method of *teaching,* a point of view which was typical of the inner regeneration in cultural matters proposed by his generation. Thus Ribera distinguished between the *maestro* who worked with his disciples and taught them by letting them collaborate in his research, and the *pedagogo* who lectured from his dais while maintaining no personal contact with his students. His own education he claimed to have been a total waste of time spent in the verbalist and bookish atmosphere of the Spanish centres of learning of his time, and where he was unable to discover his true vocation throughout the boring years spent in the Faculty of Law. He finally chose his career in Arabism at the University of Madrid upon coming into contact with Codera. Both teacher and pupil have mentioned the different stages of this life of intimate collaboration which lasted from 1882 to 1885,[1] during which time Ribera acquired the linguistic, philological and paleographic skills necessary for his future research, while helping his teacher to prepare the edition of the first three volumes of the *Bibliotheca Arabico-Hispana.*

Ribera's first essays on Arabic themes were the outcome of information gleaned from the texts of the *Bibliotheca* relating particularly to the history of his home province of Valencia. He studied

[1] *Cf. Discursos leídos ante la Real Academia de la Historia en la recepción pública del Sr. D. Julián Ribera y Tarragó,* Madrid, 1915.

regional toponymy, compared the chronicles of the Cid with Arabic sources, and identified the author of the Arabic elegy on the fall of Valencia.[1] This identification made it possible for Menéndez Pidal to clarify certain doubtful points about the elegy,[2] as also about the history of the Cid. Although in his later works Ribera ceased to deal with his native Valencia as much as he had done at first, he yet managed throughout his life to publish short essays in the *Almanaque de las provincias* dealing with Valencian topics. Many of these essays were republished in his collected works, entitled *Disertaciones y opúsculos*, while some of his final works were collected posthumously in 1952 under the title of *Opúsculos dispersos* most of which deal with Valencian toponymy and history.

In 1887 Ribera occupied the chair of Arabic language at the University of Saragossa, and this period of his life spent in the Aragonese capital was to be that of his greatest activity. The chair of Arabic was of recent creation, and he lacked the means necessary for his work. However, a rich collection of Arabic and Aljamiado manuscripts had been discovered some few years earlier in Almonacid de la Sierra (Aragón), and it served as a source of material with which to conduct his research.[3] Ribera reorganized the publication of Arabic manuscripts on a more economic basis, transported the Arabic printing press made by Codera to Saragossa, and thus was able to publish the final volumes of the *Bibliotheca* between 1893 and 1895.

However, discovering that this publication of original texts without translation limited their use to specialists, and realizing that this enterprise, laudable in itself, was in the Spain of his day exposed to mockery on the part of even the learned who did not realize that these editions were indispensable for the writing of future monographs, Ribera planned and initiated the publication of the *Colección de estudios árabes*, a series of small volumes destined to popularize Arabic research without an excess of critical apparatus. From 1897 in which the first volume appeared, until 1903 when the *Colección* was discontinued, seven volumes were published bearing the result of the labours of Ribera, Codera and their disciples; Pano,

[1] Al-Wakkashī.

[2] *Cf. Homenaje a Codera.*

[3] A catalogue of this collection was published: J. Ribera y M. Asín, *Manuscritos árabes y aljamiados de la biblioteca de la junta*; *noticia y extractos por los alumnos de la seccion árabe*, Madrid, 1912. The mss. are now housed in the Instituto Miguel Asín in Madrid.

Gaspar Remiro, Pons Boïgues and Asín. Two later volumes written by Codera appeared in 1917.

In order to give wider diffusion to his investigations and those of his colleagues and students, in 1900 Ribera, along with his friend Eduardo Ibarra, professor of history at the University of Saragossa, founded the journal known as the *Revista de Aragón*. This journal steadily increased its output during its six years of existence in Saragossa. Though plagued by insufficient financial backing, its quality was outstanding,[1] so that Joaquín Costa wrote warm words of praise to Ribera for this achievement, claiming that it was a journal far superior to the intellectual environment of Aragón.[2]

The first of Ribera's works on cultural and historical matters, entitled *La Enseñanza entre los musulmanes españoles*, was published in Saragossa in 1893. A work of great erudition, it proved to be entirely novel in its conception, since that subject had not been treated either by European Arabists, or by Arab scholars themselves.

As a reformer prior to the generation of 1898, Ribera was interested primarily in the problem of State intervention in education, and his conclusion was that in al-Andalus the Islamic State had not as a rule intervened directly in education, contrary to common practice in the Middle East. Thus he characterized the organization of Andalusian education as being the result of individual or social efforts on the part of private citizens, with no pressure from the State. True to his age, Ribera sees in this freedom of the individual, the origin of all the exceptional progress made in cultural and scientific fields in al-Andalus, in contrast with the East where he claims that State interference had disrupted the normal development of scientific learning .From this point Ribera was to launch out in a series of liberally oriented articles criticizing State intervention in the educational system of the Spain of his day.

---

[1] . *Cf. Disert. y Opúsc., Introducción*, p. xxxi.

[2] "The service you perform with your journal cannot even be appreciated enough by Aragón for the latter to express its gratitude: according to a common expression, in good, inexact, moral philosophy, *it does not deserve it*, it does not deserve your journal. Is Aragón to blame, or is the rest of Spain to blame for not being in the proper condition to digest strong, European dishes such as this one ? As long as the social situation remains unchanged, either there should be no journal, or the case should be handled as one of guardianship (of the State over an immature country), by making publication official, or by subsidizing it wherever a serious intellectual circle is being formed; one which is altruistic, progressive, European, such as the one you are shaping." *Cf. Disert. y Opúsc., Introd.*, pp. xxxi-xxxii.

Goldziher in his *Muhammedanische Studien* (1890) had written about the methods of transmitting *ḥadīths* though with little stress on the educational aspects involved. Later the Syrian Jurjī Zaydān in his *History of Islamic Civilization* (1904) devoted two chapters to the study of schools and libraries in Islam,[1] but he only wrote a brief and insufficient outline of the subject. Basing himself on European sources, he entirely overlooked Ribera's work eleven years after its publication, thus falling into the errors of Schack, Dozy and others who had spoken of State intervention in the Andalusian educational system. Ribera had refuted these ideas, but the little attention paid to Spanish books resulted in Jurjī Zaydān's ignorance of a monograph which would have been most useful to him.

Ribera planned to continue this work by making a general study of educational institutions in Islam. An article entitled *Origen del colegio nidamí de Bagdad* [2] published in 1904 was to constitute the first chapter of a book which he never completed, though he collected a great amount of material for it and made frequent references to it in his later works. In this article he studied the early *madrasas* founded by Persian sovereigns, and found in these institutions of learning an Oriental and especially Chinese origin, though he claimed that a Christian and Byzantine tradition was not absent, thus indicating another link between Islam and classical culture. According to Asín, who had access to Ribera's notes for the unfinished book, the educational institutions of the Middle East, because of State intervention, were inevitably used as instruments of political manipulation. This system was an imitation of Chinese education, and was, according to Ribera, adopted by the Sassanids who transmitted it to the Arabs. On the other hand, neither Greece nor Rome had practiced this type of intervention in educational matters, and such a free system maintained itself in Europe till the thirteenth century when official initiative on the part of the monarchs of various countries in the West resulted in the creation of universities which coincided in many respects with the Oriental *madrasas*.[3]

Another challenging theme was that treated by Ribera in his article entitled *Bibliófilos y bibliotecas en la España musulmana*,

---

[1] III, 199-214.
[2] In *Homenaje a Codera*. Also included in *Disertaciones y opúsculos*.
[3] *Cf. Disert. y opúsc.* pp. xxxvi-xxxvii.

which explored and illuminated the organization of libraries among the scholars of al-Andalus. The author surveys the vast field of Islam in the Peninsula and tries to determine the reasons for the enormous diffusion of books among the Arabs. He claims that this was due to the abbreviated nature of the Arabic script; so similar to shorthand, and to the use of paper rather than parchment. Unfortunately these seem to be only incidental factors rather than motivating forces, since if it is true that the nature of Arabic script made it possible to compress more into each page, that in itself does not explain the vast amount of bibliographic material available to Muslim scholars. He then reviews the principal libraries of Cordova and other cities, and paints a vivid portrait of the typical Andalusian bibliophile.

Between 1900 and 1903 Ribera wrote another series of studies on the nature of exams: *La supresión de los exámenes, Los exámenes en China,* etc. The first of these consists of a series of lectures delivered at the University of Saragossa, whereas the second is a collection of articles published in various journals. In them Ribera puts aside his scholarly apparatus, and sketches his conclusions in a humorously ironic vein, suggesting that the official type of university exam should be substituted by popular judgement on the merits of the candidate, an idea which is closely connected to the faith in popular wisdom which would be espoused by the generation of 1898. Just as Unamuno speaks of *intrahistoria*; the history of the popular residue left after important events, dates, names, have been abstracted from history, so Ribera has visions of an "intra-university." Recognizing, however, the impossibility of suppressing exams as long as an official monopoly of degrees is maintained, he announces his intention of further studying the problem of university degrees. This study he completed ten years later with *La superstición pedagógica.*

At the same time he was conducting his research on education, derived from his Arabic studies, and oriented towards social reform, Ribera had begun to prepare a historical work on the legal institutions of Islam, possibly influenced by the juridical studies of the University of Saragossa where he had worked since 1887. Among the medievalists and jurists of Aragón, the uniqueness of the *Justicia* as a Christian institution had been considered a basic fact, but Ribera's familiarity with Arabic sources convinced him of its Islamic origin. In his work on the subject: *Orígenes del Justicia de*

Aragón, a masterpece of dialectics, he begins by making a detailed study of the historical facts which pointed to coexistence between Muslims and Christians in medieval Spain. He studied many cases of cultural contact particularly when they represented an instance of direct borrowing from Islam in Aragón. He deals at length with judicial problems, and shows that almost all the Christian legal authorities were adaptations of Islamic institutions. Having claimed that the *Justicia* had no precedents in the Christian world, and applying his theory of imitation, he gave a high degree of plausibility to his hypothesis that the *Justicia* was imitated from Islam. Ribera discovers furthermore that the same institution had existed in Valencia and Murcia during the age of the *Reconquista.* Leaving aside his theoretical arguments in favour of his thesis, he goes on to show that in the *Kitāb al-Aḥkām as-Sulṭāniyya,* or "Book of the Principles of Government" "the extensive manual on Muslim jurisprudence written by the Shāfʿite lawyer al-Mawardī (d. A.D. 1058) of Baghdad, the functions of this magistrature are defined and catalogued under the title of *Ṣāḥib al-Maẓālim* or 'lord of injustices,' and that they furthermore coincide with those of the *Justicia.* Both the Muslim and Christian functionaries were in fact judges named at will by the sovereign, endowed with ample powers directly derived from the sovereign, and which are not only judicial but also executive insofar as the judges have power of action against delinquent officials whose crimes they may punish.

Ribera further claimed that this institution derived from pre-Islamic Persia and had been adopted by the Umayyad and ʿAbbāsid caliphs of the Orient, as well as by the African and Andalusian dynasties—among them the kings of *Taifas* whose territories were contiguous to Aragón. More recently, however, historians such as Luis de Valdeavellano have rejected Ribera's thesis, showing that the institution of the Justicia derived from Visigothic law. It is probable that as more is learned about the connexion between Roman and Islamic law, certain coincidences will be attributed to a common source rather than to imitation.

Ribera's theory is argued on two levels; the theoretical and the factual. Insofar as the first is concerned, his theory of imitation was of capital importance for it was to serve as a basis for all of his later investigations. As summed up by Asín, this theory states that imitation is "directly proportional to the possibilities of access to the model, to the latter's desirability, to the desire for it on the part of the imitator, to the model's intelligibility, to the intelligence of the imitator and to the abundance of means to implement the imitation."[1]

As we have seen, Ribera applied this law to the case of the *Justicia* of Aragón. It seems that several ethnologists for whom this problem of methodology was of primary importance had begun to study it in the nineteenth century, such being the case of Quatrefage (1810-1892) in France and Sumner Maine (1822-1888) in England. In the twentieth century this theory gained wider favour, for Pinard de la Boullaye outlined it and examined the gradual stages of its development from its origins to its final organization in the work of Graebner, Ankermann and Schmidt (1911).[2] Fifteen years earlier in 1897 Ribera had established a similar criterion in order to distinguish those cultural analogies resulting from imitation, from those due to coincidence or the original innovation or inventiveness of the agent. Thus he argues that not all analogies proceed from direct imitation, for some cultural coincidences depend upon analogous racial, geographic, environmental, or psychological features common to different civilizations. Ribera therefore warns that not all analogies in cultural matters can be explained by direct imitations. Thus a distinction between analogies resulting from imitation and others resulting from similarity of media or tendencies is often difficult to make. However, Ribera argues that though two savages; one in Africa and another in America may well slake their thirst by applying their mouths to the surface of a mass of water, by cupping their hands to catch that water, or even by using a shell or some other primitive instrument, they will not coincide in drinking from earthen vessels like those of Sagunto which bear inscriptions in Latin or Greek. In the same way, two savage peoples may dwell in rude huts similarly constructed, but no matter how much their civilization may advance, without imitation they will not develop Gothic cathedrals. Though an obscure zone will always remain, in which it is impossible to speak of imitation with any degree of certainty, yet a large number of complex cultural phenomena show clear signs of having resulted from direct or indirect imitation.[3]

---

[1] *Disert. y opúsc., Introduc.*, p. xlvii.

[2] *Cf. Le mouvement historique en ethnologie*, in *Semaine internationale d'ethnologie religieuse*, Milan, 1925.

[3] *Disert. y opúsc., Introducc.*, pp. xlix-li

Pinard de la Boullaye did justice to Ribera by awarding him a place of honour in his study of the scholars who had developed this theory, for without being a professional ethnologist, Ribera had managed to outline the general laws which governed the technical aspects of the theory of imitation, which derived from and was directed towards the peculiar problems of cultural transmission in Spain. In this sense Ribera finally gave theoretical structure to a problem which had occupied scholars concerned with al-Andalus ever since Juan Andrés.

In 1893 Spain had become involved in Moroccan affairs, and a minor conflict at Melilla, the Spanish enclave in the African coast had cost the life of general Margallo. This conflict was to bring down the government of Sagasta and restore Cánovas to his last tenure of office in 1895. The difficulties between the Spanish and Moroccan governments were temporarily settled by the embassy of Martínez Campos who signed a treaty of peace. Ribera was attached to this embassy upon recommendation from Saavedra and Codera, and his stay in Marrakesh gave him much first hand information about the problem of Morocco and Spanish intervention. In view of the policies of European governments at that time, he felt that Spain would do well to intervene in Morocco in order to keep the area out of French hands, and so he wrote a number of articles on the subject, which were published in the *Revista de Aragón* between 1901-1905. Observing the lack of technical preparation in Spain for dealing with North African affairs he inferred total failure for this policy unless certain necessary steps were taken. He pointed to the general ignorance of Arabic, of Islamic affairs and of Muslim psychology which prevailed in Spanish diplomatic circles, and suggested a joint effort of cooperation on the part of the ministries of State, War and Public Education to prepare the necessary trained personnel for the Moroccan venture. Ribera advocated the founding of a Centre for Arabic studies to implement his plan, and he outlined the details of its organization with some care and precision. His project was favourably received in official circles, for Maura, the conservative leader, adopted it without modifications, though the political instability of Spain upset the plan on the eve of its implementation. A cabinet crisis developed, the government fell, and the new minister of education did not implement the decree. In later years, the constant defeat of Spanish foreign policy in Morocco showed how far-sighted Ribera's judgement had been; and France in the meantime, having learned wisdom from its first fiascos in Algeria, prepared itself carefully to intervene in Morocco, for which purpose it created a school in Tangier, organized along the lines of the Centre for Arabic studies which Ribera had suggested Spain should found.

In view of the failure of his plan for a Centre of Arabic studies, he composed a book entitled *La superstición pedagógica* in which he affirmed that the only way to create scholars was to associate students to the work of their professors, and expressed the hope that sooner or later these ideas would crystallize in the creation of new institutions of learning.

In 1910, the *Gaceta* gave legal birth to the *Centro de Estudios Históricos,* whose goals had remarkable coincidence with Ribera's ideas, since the *Centro* proposed to initiate a select number of students in research methods by permitting them to share with their instructors in the early stages of historical investigation. Ribera's cooperation was requested, and so he and his small school of Arabists joined the *Centro.* The results of their labour, added to their new-found official protection, were so fertile that within five years the catalogue of publications of the *Centro* was listing twelve works on Arabism which had been recently published.

After being named professor of Arabic literature at the Central University, and chosen member of the Academy of Spanish, Ribera decided to conduct research on themes which would be of interest in illuminating the history and literature of Spain. This opened a new phase in his career, during which a number of discoveries were made, namely that of the pre-history of the Spanish Romance language, the origins of Provenzal lyrical poetry, of European epic poetry, the nature of Arabic music and its influence on that of medieval Christendom.

He began by studying the language in al-Andalus, and came to conclusions even more startling than those of Simonet who, deceived by his anti-Arab prejudices had claimed that the Romance words he found in Arabic texts were used exclusively by the Mozarabs. Ribera claimed further that this vocabulary formed part of the linguistic patrimony of all Andalusians, both Muslims and Mozarabs. According to him, the close co-existence of the two groups resulted in the preservation of the Romance language which was soon learned by the conquerors in spite of their constituting a directing minority. He indicates as proof of this the fact that al-Khushānī in his *Kitāb Quḍāt Qurṭuba* (which Ribera published and translated as *Historia de los jueces de Córdoba*) mentions that the Romance dialect was familiar to all strata of society in Cordova; even in the courts of law and the royal palace. Today we may question Ribera's conclusions to some extent, for though it is true that one judge of Cordova mentioned by Ribera is described as having spoken only Mozarabic (*'Ajamiyya*), the whole tone of that passage suggests that he was an exception to the rule. Ribera cites Ibn Quzmān who used Mozarabic in his poems, though it should be noted that in Ibn Quzmān the relatively few Romance words are inserted in Arabic poems to add a certain local colour to what are otherwise essentially Arabic compositions insofar as their poetic inspiration is concerned. In this sense it may be said that Ribera united and fused the approach of the traditionalists as represented by Simonet, with the progressive school of historians who showed more sympathy for Arabic culture. This phenomenon was to be a peculiar feature of the intellectual approach of the generation of 1898 which sought to find a reconciliation between the opposing groups.

One of Ribera's most important studies is that of the *Dīwān* of Ibn Quzmān,[1] in which he opens up vast new perspectives in the study of the origin of Romance poetry. In the first pages of this work he goes back to quote directly from the early opinions of Juan Andrés, and contradicts the ideas of the most authorized Orientalists and Romanists, who since Dozy, had denied any possible influence of Arabic poetry, on that of medieval Europe. He points to the *Dīwān* of Ibn Quzmān as an example of an elaborate poetic system which illuminates that of Europe with which it is closely connected:

"This affirmation, which may seem daring to you, nonetheless offers no novelty. Father Andrés defended a far more resolute opinion: '*this custom of the Spaniards of versifying in the language, measure and rhyme of the Arabs, may justly be called the first origin of modern poetry.*' "[2]

The strophic form which Ribera found in these poems is remarkable for its close similarity with that of European poetry and in this he was right in pointing to an important relationship between two thematically divergent lyrical systems.

It is well known that classical Arabic poetry, both pre- and post-

[1] *Cf. Disert. y opúsc.*, pp. 3-92.
[2] *Disert. y opúsc.*, pp. 5-6.

Islamic is written in monorhyme, that its lines are subject to certain invariable rules of quantity, to measure by feet, as is the case of Latin and Greek poetry, and that all the lines in one poem have the same regular number of feet. The songs of Ibn Quzmān on the other hand, are of a syllabic, stress measure and do not always have verses of equal length. Another original innovation is the strophic combination of rhymes. Whereas Graeco-Latin poetry is unrhymed, and classical Arabic poetry is monorhymed; that of Ibn Quzmān possesses consonant rhyme, but with varying rhymes in its strophes, each one of which has an equal number of lines, varying from four to fifteen, rhyming according to a large possibility of combinations which may all be reduced, however, to the basic type aaa*b*ccc*b*ddd*b*, etc.

Insofar as the themes of this poetry are concerned, Ribera indicated that those of pre-Islamic poetry were not to be found in Ibn Quzmān, thus suggesting that their origin was to be found in Romance poetry. Today, however, the development of Arabic poetry is better known, and it seems clear that most of the themes of Ibn Quzmān's *azjāl* derive from ribald versions of the courtly love poetry known in Arabic as *ġazal* and cultivated in the East very soon after Islam by ʿUmar ibn Abī Rabīʿa, then later by Ibn al-Aḥnaf, Ibn al-Muʿtazz, Abū Nuwās and others.

Ribera claimed a twofold influence. On the one hand, Galaico-Portuguese poetry, upon coming into contact with that of the Arabs, acquired rhyme which had been unknown within the Western tradition derived from Greece and Rome. On the other hand, Arabic popular poetry as exemplified by the *azjāl* of Ibn Quzmān acquired certain themes such as the *aubade* from Europe. We must at present suspend judgement concerning the second of these influences for lack of sufficient certainty in our information,[1] however, the formal strophic similarity of the *zajal* to early Peninsular poetry in Romance is undeniable, and it allowed Ribera

[1] Though Abū Nuwās in the East had earlier experimented with the theme of the morning, as in one of his panegyrics beginning: "The crying cock did sing, so give me to drink ! The morning draught was sweet."

غَرَّدَ الديكُ الصَدُوحُ   فاسقِنى ! طابَ الصَّبُوحُ

The *ṣabūḥ* or "morning drink", derived from the root *ṣabaḥa* "to visit early in the morning" has been translated literally in the Andalusian expression still heard today "tomar la *mañana*" "to drink the morning drink."

to explain the origin of the troubadour poetry in a way diametrically opposed to that of the Romanists. Applying his law of imitation he concludes that Andalusian poetry, itself influenced by Spanish poetry, served as a model for that of Provence, and therefore inspired all the later European lyrical schools. This theory, although it was opposed by Menéndez y Pelayo, Amador de los Ríos, Renan and Dozy, gained recognition from Burdach in Germany, Massignon in France, Carolina Michaelis in Portugal and Menéndez Pidal in Spain. Although further discoveries such as that of the early *muwashshaḥāt* with *kharjāt* in Romance have shed more light on the problem, the relative lack of knowledge about the earliest lyrical compositions of this genre both in Romance and Arabic makes it at present impossible to tell in which direction the otherwise evident influence went. It is undeniable that there is a definite formal or structural similarity between these two poetic systems, though the thematic parallels are not always so clearly convincing. Thus Sir Hamilton Gibb has summed up the problem with caution in the following way:

> The causes which led to the development of the strophe in Spain and not in the East are obscure; the influence of popular songs in Romance has long been suspected, and is reinforced by the recent discovery that in the earliest *muwashshaḥs* the envoi was actually in Romance. Some part may be due also to the special developments in the West of Arabic music (in Arabic *ṭarab*, the probable connexion of which with 'Trobador' is too tempting not to note in passing). [1]

---

[1] H.A.R. Gibb, *Arabic Literature, An Introduction*, 2nd ed., Oxford, 1963, pp. 109-110. To what Ribera has already said on the possible connexion *ṭarab-trobar*, I should like to add that in the medieval Spanish version of *La Doncella Teodor* translated from the Arabic, that learned damsel says to the king: "e aprendí tanner *laud* e *canón* e las treynta e tres trobas,. . ." i.e. "And I learned to play the lute and *qanūn*, as well as the thirty-three melodies." (*Cf.* Menéndez y Pelayo, *La Doncella Teodor*, in *Homenaje a D. Fco. Codera*, p. 500. The two instruments mentioned are Arabic: *al-ʿūd* (lute) and *qanūn* (a trapezoidal psaltery). Though we do not know the exact version from which the Spanish recension was translated it is possible that the Arabic text had a *ṭarab* which was rendered as *troba*. Indeed, one version in the *Arabian nights* says: "She played upon it (the *ʿūd*) twelve melodies to the point that the assembly was overcome by reason of the *ṭarab* . . . and the Prince of the Faithful *ṭariba* ('was overcome by a quivering emotion'). (Night 454, the *Tale of the slave girl Tawaddud*).

That this connexion is no mere supposition is indicated by the fact that in the fifteenth century *Cancionero de Hernando del Castillo* (vol. 2, section:

In his later study on the origins of European epic poetry Ribera mentions that he had suspected the prior existence of a purely Romance poetry in al-Andalus which was to be the precursor of what he terms the "hybrid" poetry of the *Cancionero de Abencuzmán.* In this study he quotes a passage by now quite famous, from the *Dhakhīra* of Ibn Bassām, the difficulties of which led him to a misinterpretation from which he found what he considered to be positive proof of the existence, at the end of the ninth century, of a popular literature, entirely in Romance, in al-Andalus, invented by the blind poet Muqaddam of Cabra. The passage is to be found in the *Dhakhīra* in the account given of the life of 'Ubāda ibn Mā' as-Samā'. It states that Muqaddam of Cabra invented the original *muwashshaḥa* which he composed out of hemistichs of poetry. These poems are totally lost, but Ibn Bassām relates that Ibn 'Abd Rabbihi was the first to adopt this kind of *muwashshaḥa.* He traces the development of the *muwashshaḥa* in the hands of various poets up to 'Ubāda, all of which would tend to indicate that the strophic forms of al-Andalus were developed gradually by the experimentation of individual poets (whose names are well known, though not their *muwashshaḥāt*) and that the finished structure was later adopted by Europe. In this sense, though Ribera saw the evident connexion between strophic Andalusian poetry and primitive Spanish and Provenzal lyrics, he was misled

---

Obras de burlas, No. 1032, p. 283) there is to be found the following: "*Otra copla a Juan Poeta* fecha por un cavallero que, estando jugando, le demandó que le diesse algo, y él dióle una doble quebrada, y una copla que dezía:

Por me aver importunado	For having importuned me
os dó esta dobla quebrada,	I give you this broken doubloon,
qu' es razón que al retajado	For it is fitting that the circumcised
que gela den retajada:	Should be given something circumcised:
y no 's espantés, grossero	Do not be amazed, you rude fellow,
poeta, Juan Taraví,	*You poet, Juan Taraví,*
pues que le hizo el platero	For to it the silversmith did
lo que a vos hizo el Rabí.	What was done to you by the Rabbi.

It is not known whether Juan Poeta was this famous character's real name, or whether "poeta" simply meant "John the poet" which is more likely. In any case, "poeta" is identified as late as the XVth century with *ṭarabī,* the Arabian "troubadour."

For a recent modification of Ribera's etymology which still considers it to be derived from the Arabic, *cf.* Richard Lemay, "A propos de l'origine arabe de l'art des troubadours" in *Annales, Économies, Sociétés, Civilisations,* 21ème année, no 5, Sept.-Oct., 1966. 990-1011. Lemay derives *trobar* from the root *ḍaraba* 'to strike.'

by his ideas on the "Spanishness" of the Andalusian Muslims, which made him identify nationality and cultural features with racial characteristics, for he claimed that the racial Semitism of what he called "los musulmanes españoles" was almost infinitesimal, and at any rate not sufficiently pronounced to warrant for them the name of Semites or Orientals after the third or fourth generation from the conquest of 711.[1] To exemplify this he shows that the custom practiced by the Umayyads in Cordova, of marrying native wives gradually diluted their "Arab blood" to the point that Hishām II whose genealogy is filled with Arab names was racially less than one thousandth per cent Arab.[2] This theory does not take into account the fact that cultural phenomena are not always explicable on racial grounds, and this Ribera must have sensed, for later on in the same work he tries to rectify his judgement by claiming that the Arab element, though scanty, imposed its tongue and customs, its political and religious organization and coloured Andalusian society in such a way that everyone was Arabized, "just as a small amount of red dye is enough to redden the waters of a pond," though, he adds—"this does not mean that the chemical composition either of the water or the dye is sensibly altered by combination."[3]

This comparison of human life with inert substances, and his appeal to chemical analogies once again betrays the idea of the eternal, substantial Spaniard which was prevalent among Spanish scholars. Though this idea had been expressed by Simonet as a traditionalist, Ribera being closer to the generation of 1898 was trying to integrate two opposing tendencies and so fell into contradiction in identifying cultural with racial phenomena.

Following his line of reasoning, Ribera claimed that he could infer the existence of a popular Romance epic poetry which had existed in al-Andalus and derived from a hypothetical Arabic epic poetry written in colloquial metres. Here he ran into certain difficulties which have subsequently made his theory fall into discredit. However, he showed that two poets from ninth century al-Andalus named al-Ġazzāl and Tamīm ibn ʿAlqama had written poems on essentially epic themes relating to the conquest of Spain, in *rajaz* metre (the most prosaic in Arabic).

To this he adds that the primitive Muslim chronicles of al-Andalus had made use of indigenous Latin chronicles and popular

[1] *Cf. Disert. y opúsc.*, p. 10.
[2] *Op. cit.*, p. 16. [3] *Cf. Disert. y opúsc.*, p. 26.

tales in Romance, and studies three legends retold by Ibn al-Qūṭiyya, all of which bear the imprint of phantasy and a popular taste. Unfortunately neither the early *rajaz* compositions nor any poetic versions of the tales in Ibn al-Qūṭiyya have come down to us, so that Ribera deduced a Romance epic poetry from Arab chronicles on slender evidence and his theory will remain unconvincing until further, more concrete facts are provided.[1]

Ribera concludes that centuries after his hypothetical Andalusian epic poetry, the French and Castilian epic tradition could not have arisen from spontaneous generation. Gaston Paris, Léon Gauthier and Joseph Bédier affirmed that the French epic was autochtonous and that other traditions such as the Castilian were born by imitation of French models. Ribera inverted the terms and decided that French epic poetry as well as that of Spain, the main subject of which is the Crusade against Islam, were born upon contact with the now lost Andalusian epic tradition.

Between 1912 and 1924 Ribera spent twelve years of almost total incommunication with the public, during which time he carried his research on the *Dīwān* of Ibn Quzmān into the realm of music, and finally in 1922 he offered a solution to the enigma of medieval music and its origins. Beginning with a study of the *Dīwān* and the *Cancionero de Palacio* he discovered that the songs of the former, like those of all Arabic music, lacked musical notation, though he found that the architectural structure of the music of the fifteenth-century Spanish songs was identical in its nature to the architectural structure of the words of Ibn Quzmān's lyrics in eighty-five per cent of the cases. Furthermore he found similar rhyme schemes and coincidences in the *Cantigas* of Alfonso X. From this point, Ribera undertook to study the history and nature of Arabic music, a task which had not yet been undertaken. Fortunately there was no dearth of textual material, for although no annotated melodies existed, the *Kitāb al-Aġānī* or 'Book of Songs,' a monumental poetic and musical anthology composed by

---

[1] Two late Hispano-Arab *rajaz* poems have been discovered since Ribera wrote, and his theory has been expanded and reworked by Lutfi Abdel Badi, *La épica árabe y su influencia en la épica castellana*, Santiago de Chile, 1964. Alvaro Galmés de Fuentes is at present working on the subject and has found new insights to the theory. See also, James T. Monroe, "The Historical Arjūza of Ibn ʿAbd Rabbihi of Cordova: A Tenth-Century Hispano-Arabic Epic Poem," *Journal of the American Oriental Society*, 90, III. 1970.

Abū l-Faraj al-Iṣfahānī on the basis of an earlier work by Ibrāhīm of Mosul (ninth cent.) was extant. Ribera saw in that work evidence to infer that Arabic music, vocal and instrumental like that of the West, had made use of the diatonic scale and had known harmony and rhythm.

After outlining the history of Arabic music in the Orient and ascertaining its nature, he showed how it had been transplanted to al-Andalus in Umayyad times by Ziryāb, the famous singer of the age of Hārūn ar-Rashīd. The musicians and singers of al-Andalus, whose history Ribera outlined up to the fourteenth century, adopted and popularized this Oriental music, converting it from monodic to choral and adapting the structure of the melodies to the strophic character of the *zajal*. From this point the music penetrated into Christian Spain, where poets wrote their strophes according to a 'zajalesque' structure to facilitate their adaptation to the new music [1] which remained popular in Spain until the middle of the seventeenth century.

It is impossible to go into the details of Ribera's analysis here but let it at least be said that he tried to show that in music, as in the other arts and sciences, the Andalusian had been instrumental in the Africanization of Europe. However, in recent times his musical theory has lost favour.[2]

From the works we have been able to examine and the rich variety of subjects which captured Ribera's attention it can be observed that a current of logical continuity existed in his thought. The similarity of his method can be detected in all his historical studies for at each step in his argumentation he systematically applies the laws of imitation discovered by himself. His one concern was to revindicate the cultural worth of al-Andalus; a task which had been attempted in the eighteenth century by Juan Andrés but which, despite the contributions of specialists in the field, had not been taken too seriously by late nineteenth-century Spanish

---

[1] If so, it is clear that the Christians imitated the Arabic *zajal* and not vice-versa.

[2] The slowness with which these studies progress is evidenced by a recent publication which collects Ribera's theories, quotes his books in its bibliography, and has little that is new to add on the subject. I refer to: *The Pelican History of Music*, ed. by Alec Robertson and Denis Stevens, Baltimore, 1960, vol. I, pp. 118-131, also, p. 325. A more recent opinion is that of Juan Vernet, who rejects the connexions between the *Cantigas* and Arab music. cf. *Literatura árabe*, Barcelona, 1968, p. 219.

scholars, including Arabists such as Simonet. Even though some of his ideas have had to be rectified today, it cannot be doubted that to Ribera is owed the serious consideration of Peninsular Islam and its role in the development of European culture, now accorded to it by historians. He tried to base his demonstrations on more solid grounds and above all, brought a unified concept of philosophy to bear on his research. Thus it may be stated that with Ribera, Spanish Arabism for the first time left a definite mark on European scholarship. It has been noted that many of Conde's ideas, as well as some of Gayangos', were poorly received by Dozy. The work of Ribera, deriving as it did from the methodological precision of Codera's school, acquired a reliability which made Spanish Arabic studies internationally respectable. In spite of this Ribera had to spend most of his life fighting against the traditional Spanish prejudices against Islam. This can be detected in Alejandro Pidal's reply [1] to Ribera's inaugural address on Ibn Quzmān, at the Spanish Academy, in which that scholar delivers a long diatribe on the virtues of Christianity and the evils of Islam claiming glory for Spanish Catholicism and the heroes of the *Reconquista* who increased the dominion of the Cross and planted the Christian flag in Granada thus making it triumph over "all that orb of fatalistic barbarism that threatened to turn it all [*i.e.*, Spanish Catholicism] into a world of listeners to Ibn Quzmān's *Dīwān*." Forgetting that the listeners to Ibn Quzmān's lyrics were also contemporaries of Averroes and of the elevated doctrines of Ibn al-ʿArabī, Alejandro Pidal paints a sombre picture of what would have been Spain's fate, had Islam prevailed in the Peninsula.[2]

Likewise the attitudes of nineteenth century scholars with regard to Arabic influences in the formation of Romance poetry were

---

[1] Alejandro Pidal, *Discurso*, in *Discursos leídos ante la Real Academia Española en la recepción pública del señor D. Julián Ribera y Tarragó*, Madrid, 1915, pp. 90-91.

[2] "Then, with the Koran instead and in place of the Gospels, With Averroes and Ġazālī in place of Saint Thomas; with Ibn Ḥazm or Ibn Quzmān in place of Dante and the epic songs of *The Cid*, we, the Spanish people, would not have been the knight-errant of European civilization against the Arab, Protestant and Turk. We would be instead the vile slaves and like the mournful eunuchs of the *seraglio* of a Sultan protected by some French Republican, and instead of the glory of having been the saviours of the civilized world in the critical days of the Modern Age, we would be vegetating in the ignominy of marketplaces and harems, like the sons of the Galician slavegirls, the sons of the Moorish quarters of Cordova and Toledo." *Op. cit.*, *loc. cit.*

anything but favourable to Ribera who quotes several adverse judgements to his ideas. Thus for example, Milá y Fontanals had stated: "Fewer facts than speculative arguments have always been adduced." [1] Amador de los Ríos likewise was skeptical in saying that: "This influence has been sensed rather than analysed."[2] Renan and Dozy had predisposed Romanists against this theory by their unfavourable judgements. The first had said:

> Provenzal poetry . . . owes nothing to the Muslims. An abyss separates the form and spirit of Romance poetry from the form and spirit of Arabic poetry . . . Christian poets . . . would have been unable to understand the language and spirit of Arabic poetry. [3]

The second had added:

> Knowing whether Arabic poetry has had an influence on Spanish poetry . . . is an *idle* matter; we would rather it were not discussed, although we are convinced that it will continue to be discussed for a long time yet: everyone has his own mania. [4]

With such precedents Menéndez y Pelayo the traditionalist authority of nineteenth-century Spain was able to say rather bluntly: "Of lyrical poetry nothing was transmitted, nor could it have been transmitted in the Middle Ages,"[5] though it must be said in all fairness that he leaves the question undecided and after the discovery of the *zajal* and *muwashshaḥa* he displays a greater sympathy for the theory of poetic imitation.[6]

From such adverse judgements as these we may appreciate the significance of Ribera's titanic efforts to illuminate one important aspect of Spain's past; a task in which he initiated a fruitful line of research, as the work of recent scholars on the *muwashshaḥāt* has proven amply.

---

[1] *Obras completas*, vol. 4, 392, *apud* Ribera.

[2] *Historia crítica*. 2, 429, *apud* Ribera.

[3] *Histoire des langues sémitiques*, 387, *apud* Ribera.

[4] *Recherches*, 3rd ed., vol. 2, appendix, p. lxiv, n. 2, *apud* Ribera.

[5] *Antología*, vol. I, pp. 75-77.

[6] ". . . Later research seems to have proved the existence of certain genres of popular or popularizing poetry, such as the *zajal* (sonorous hymn) or the *muwashshaḥa* (song of the girdle), as well as the existence of travelling singers and female *jongleurs* who entered the Christian kingdoms, and since, as is notoriously clear, they influenced music and dance, it can also be supposed that they transmitted a song or two to us. The Archpriest of Hita is a reliable authority for this." *Cf. Antología de poetas líricos castellanos*, I, Madrid, 1914, p. lxvi.

During his last years Ribera retired to his native province of Valencia, where he devoted himself to writing a series of articles on regional toponymy [1] until his death in 1934.

García Gómez writes of him that the first appearance of his theories on poetry shocked the scholarly world, and had the merit of opening up new horizons in the study of Romance and Hispano-Arabic philology, unleashing debates on a subject which will continue to be a bone of contention among scholars for some time to come.[2] Placed between two men of genius: Codera and Asín, Ribera with his energy and vitality strengthened the other two, so that García Gómez calls him the trunk of the Spanish Arabist school, of which Codera was the root and Asín the "delicate flower."[3] For García Gómez, Ribera's ideas on the prior existence of an Andalusian Romance lyrical poetry which served as a basis for Hispano-Arabic poetry was the background from which the ideas resulting from the discovery of the Mozarabic *kharjāt* were to take shape, and he insists on the great importance of Ribera as an initiator in Spain of a serious school of Arabic studies [4] which maintained a living tradition and perfect continuity.

---

[1] *Cf.* Ribera, *Opúsculos dispersos,* Tetuán, 1952.

[2] García Gómez, "Don Julián Ribera y Tarragó," in *And.*, vol. 2, 1934 pp. iv-v.

[3] García Gómez, "Primer centenario del nacimiento de Don Julián Ribera Tarragó." *And.*, 23, 1958, p. 208.

[4] *Op. cit.*, p. 209.

CHAPTER SEVEN

If Ribera was a direct precursor of the generation of 1898, and as such already displayed many of the traits common to these writers, his disciple Miguel Asín Palacios was a full-fledged member of that generation, who devoted his life to investigations of Islamic spirituality in its most varied aspects. The anti-historicism of the generation manifested itself in Asín, in his attempt to trace forms of spiritual life through the most varied cultures in order to discover an underlying and deeply rooted source of religious feeling in mankind. Thus his work led him to claim Christian origins for Eastern Islamic *Ṣūfism* and as a corollary to this thesis, Islamic origins for medieval European scholasticism, illuminism, and eventually for the work of Dante. Asín, because of his daring ideas is today a highly controversial figure in the world of Arabic studies. His claim of Christian origins for Islamic spirituality illustrates the anti-historicism of the generation of 1898 for whether his thesis be right or wrong—and this is at present difficult to decide—his method of sketching the history of inner spirituality; one might well say, the history of religious ideas, without considering the social, political and economic milieu in which they functioned and were developed, is dangerous insofar as it creates a one-sided picture and denies the possibility of there being a Muslim spirituality independant of that of other religions. These facts should be carefully kept in mind, as we review the works and thought of Asín.

Born in Saragossa in 1871, he was one of three children in a family of modest means. His father having died while Asín was still a child, his mother took on the burden of providing for her children. As a child, Miguel Asín was clever, nervous, and gifted with a talent rare in one of his years. He began his secondary education with the Aesculapians and concluded it with the Jesuits of Saragossa, among whom he acquired an interest in classical studies and mathematics. Upon leaving school he considered becoming an engineer, but his family's financial situation did not allow him to leave Saragossa, and so he enrolled at the faculty of Philosophy and Letters at the university, while at the same time he studied at the "*Seminario Conciliar*" with the object of joining the clerical ranks. This he achieved by singing his first Mass in 1895 in Saragossa.

His Arabic studies were to stem from his meeting with Ribera, who, it will be recalled, had come to Saragossa in 1887 at the age of twenty-nine, to teach Arabic. After four years at the university, Asín was attending his classes, attracted no doubt by the enthusiastic professor who had managed to revive Oriental studies in Saragossa. The university was at that time seething with activity and Ribera was one of its most distinguished members.[1] Soon there was a close bond of friendship between Ribera and the young priest, who together formed what García Gómez has termed "the Dioscuroi of Spanish Arabism." Indeed, there were only thirteen years of age difference between them, so that they may almost be considered as belonging to the same generation.

Ribera was at that time working hard to publish his books. Asín had studied dogmatic theology at the seminary with Juan Cruz Aránaz, and this decided his choice of scope in Arabism, for with the aid of Ribera he now began to study Arabic books on theology in editions recently arrived from Cairo; books never opened in Spain since the days of the Arabs: the works of Ġazālī, Averroes, Ibn Ḥazm and Ibn al-ʿArabī. After a year of studies in Madrid, Asín received his doctorate in Letters with highest honours in 1896, and defended a thesis on Ġazālī before a committee of which Menéndez y Pelayo and Codera were members. This was important for Asín, because it was the beginning of a friendship with Menéndez y Pelayo which led him to his future research on the philosophical ideas of al-Andalus, toward which goal he was constantly encouraged by the Spanish scholar who was ever intent upon proclaiming the past glories of his Spain. By 1898 the fateful events leading up to the catastrophe of Spanish colonialism had taken place. The fact that Spain was now reduced to its Peninsular limits polarized Spanish intellectual activities in two directions. On the one hand we encounter the soul-searching criticism of Spanish life and culture common to the age, and in which Ribera participated in his articles entitled *La clínica del Doctor Brayer* (an anagramme of his own name) or in his ironic attacks on Spanish education. Asín, however, did not choose this path, but rather that of hard work and serious research which was to originate a new type of Spanish

[1] For an account of Asín, *cf.* E. García Gómez, "Don Miguel Asín, 1871-1944 (Esquema de una biografía)," *And.*, 9, 1944, p. 270.

scholarship and science, just as the critical attitude of other writers was to create a new kind of literature.

Asín continued his research, amplifying his doctoral thesis with the aid and encouragement of Menéndez y Pelayo. Thanks to a series of letters exchanged between the two at this time, we are able to observe the nature of his studies, as well as to appreciate Menéndez y Pelayo's constant encouragement of the young Arabist.[1] These letters all relate to the development of Asin's doctoral thesis on Ġazālī which Menéndez y Pelayo insisted he should rework into the form of a book, attributing particular importance to the influence of Ġazālī on Raimundo Martí and Raymond Lull. Asín in turn asks for help in obtaining one of the few copies in Spain of Martí's *Pugio Fidei* in order to continue his research. These letters show that Menéndez y Pelayo was able to appreciate the value of Arabic studies for Spain. Thus it may be said that though he was a staunch traditionalist, he had accepted Gayangos' studies on medieval prose translations into Spanish, had modified his ideas on the origin of Romance poetry after the work of Ribera, and was actively supporting the research of Asín. In this respect he is of first rate importance in showing how the development of Arabic studies was gradually beginning to leave a mark on Spanish thought.

At this time the general trend of Arabic studies in Europe had begun to change [2] so that in almost every nation new men appeared who became interested in the study of the inner recesses of Islamic spiritual creativity (Nicholson, Macdonald, Nallino, Horten, Nyberg, Massignon, etc.). In Spain, the intellectual revolution of the generation of 1898 coincided with this tendency. It was represented mainly by Asín, who was to be one of the main figures of the new school, not only because of his capacity for research, but also because his religious training gave him a very good background in scholasticism which facilitated his dealing with the technicalities of other religions. His own deeply religious convictions gave him as well a certain sympathy for the mystics of Islam. Arberry had said that the "student of Ṣūfism ought himself to be something of a *Ṣūfī*,"[3] a condition which Asín met rather well.

---

[1] *Cf.* Angel González Palencia, "Correspondencia entre Menéndez y Pelayo y Asín," *And.*, vol. 12, 1947, pp. 391-414.

[2] *Cf.* García Gómez, *op. cit.*, p. 272.

[3] A. J. Arberry, *An Introduction to the History of Sufism* (*The Sir Abdullah Suhrawardy Lectures for* 1942), Oxford, 1942, p. 61.

Finally his doctoral thesis of 1896 appeared in 1901 as a book entitled *Algazel: Dogmática, moral y ascética* with a prologue by Menéndez y Pelayo. The work was of capital importance for the Spain of its day, and Menéndez y Pelayo expresses great admiration for the author's courage and determination in tackling so difficult a subject, and expresses pride in the fact that a young Spaniard had undertaken these studies with hardly any precursors.[1] Indeed, this was the turning point in Spanish Arabism, for up to Ribera, Spanish Arabists had dealt almost exclusively with problems directly related to al-Andalus. Ribera was the first to carry his investigations eastwards, but to Asín belonged the glory of first conducting serious research on Oriental themes in order to illuminate the medieval phenomenon. However, it must be understood that Asín's interest in the philosophy of the Middle East was in a sense directed towards his illumination of Hispano-Arabic intellectual currents, as Menéndez y Pelayo states in his prologue [2] in which he stresses the enormous significance for European thought of the work of Raimundo Martí who read Ġazālī's works and incorporated his ideas into the *Pugio Fidei* which was in turn directed against the Latin Averroists.This Latin work was soon to be influential on Thomas Aquinas' *Summa Contra Gentes* destined to the refutation and conversion of Muslims and Jews.

At this time Asín was living from a meagre stipend in Saragossa, and was almost sent by the archbishop of that city to a rural parish where his Arabic studies would have come to an end. The intervention of some influential friends saved him from this fate, and his two generous friends Codera and Ribera helped finance his studies in Madrid. Seeing that no chairs in Arabic were vacant in Spain at that time, Codera retired voluntarily in order to vacate his chair in Madrid. Ribera then allowed Asín to occupy this chair while he chose to remain in Saragossa. After a brilliant competitive

[1] García-Gómez, *op. cit.*, p. 273.

[2] "I urged its author to give greater breadth to his subject and so turn the dissertation into a book, incorporating into it a complete study of Ġazālī's works, and also dealing with the capital issue of his influence on the philosophy of the Spanish Arabs who revered this Persian doctor as a master, as well as his influence on medieval Christian philosophy, to which, likewise via Spain, and at times via quite unexpected routes, the greater part of his thought arrived." *Cf.* Asín, *Algazel: Dogmática, moral, y ascética*, Saragossa, 1901, pp. xv-xvi.

exam Asín took possession of his professorship in 1903 in succession to Gayangos and Codera.

Once in Madrid, Asín lived with Codera, in whose house and at the University he soon made many friends. He attended the literary gatherings held by Menéndez y Pelayo, and frequented the home of Guillermo J. de Osma, the collector who later was to found the museum of Arab antiquities in Madrid known as the Instituto de Valencia de Don Juan (1916), which published a number of works on Arabic erudition, and in general favoured Arabic studies. Asín became closely associated not only with scholars, but also with politicians such as Alejandro Pidal and Antonio Maura, and aristocrats such as the Duke of Alba, all of whom were to be influential in his life. Soon after, Asín was named *Sumiller de Cortina del Palacio Real* and was to be seen engaging in conversation with Alfonso XIII, so that there began between the scholar and the monarch a cordial friendship which only the death in exile of the latter would bring to a close.

From the Saragossan period, the printing of the *Homenaje* to Codera remained pending, and it appeared in 1904, bearing Asín's much discussed article entitled *El averroísmo teológico de Santo Tomás de Aquino* in which he develops the study on Raimundo Martí to show how Islamic doctrines penetrated the intellectual milieu of European scholasticism. Asín first outlines the main streams of theological thought in Islam, Judaism and Christianity, and he finds that the clash between reason and faith produced by the study of Aristotle led in the three religions, firstly to a theological reaction against Aristotle; secondly to a definite antinomy between the Peripathetics and revealed law, and finally to a synthesis of the two. The first stage is represented in Islam by Ġazālī, in Judaism by Yehuda ha-Levi, and in Christianity by the Augustinian school of William of Auvergne and Alexander of Hales. The second stage is represented by the Muslim *philosophers*, by Avicebron among the Jews and by the so-called *Averroism* of Siger of Brabant, among the Christians. Finally those who attempt to harmonize the conflict in each religion between dogma and philosophy were Averroes, Maimonides and Thomas Aquinas.[1] After studying the coincidence between Averroes and Thomas Aquinas on several points, Asín asks himself whether it is really a matter of coincidence or rather

[1] *Cf.* Asín, "El Averroísmo teológico de Santo Tomás de Aquino." in *Huellas del Islam*, Madrid, 1941, p. 14.

a case of imitation. Following in the footsteps of Ribera with whose theory of imitation he was very familiar he rejects the solution of coincidence as being too easy. He claims that in the history of ideas, as in biology, spontaneous generation is an unacceptable explanation. Asín therefore outlines the probable paths of contact between East and West, and brings to the forefront the figure of Raimundo Martí, proving beyond the shadow of a doubt that the latter had translated a small treatise by Averroes (an appendix to the *Kitāb Falsafa*) and incorporated it into his *Pugio* under the title of *Epistola ad Amicum*. Thus it resulted that Martí used the *Kitāb Falsafa* to undo the theological knot of divine knowledge of individuals according to the doctrines of Averroes, this being the same method later used by Thomas Aquinas.[1]

From this Asín concludes that the Dominican Order had entrusted to its Arabists and Hebraists such as Martí the translation of philosophical texts for the use of Christian thinkers. The excellent organization of the Order made it possible for Thomas Aquinas to have within reach many priceless documents and works of Arabic theology which he used against Islam as well as in developing Christian theology. At the same time, this Arabic erudition, in Asín's view, was an adaptation of Christian dogma taken from the Eastern Church and elaborated by Ġazālī, Avempace, Ibn Ṭufayl and Averroes.[2] In this way Asín bares to us a whole world of ideas which streamed from East to West.

During this period, Ribera had remained in Saragossa, where his chair was suddenly supressed by a reform in the university system. In 1905 he took possession of the chair of the history of Jewish and Muslim civilization in Madrid, so that the master and disciple were united once more, and the fruit of their collaboration was the short lived though important journal *Cultura española* (1906-1909). Meanwhile Asín was writing reviews and articles. In the midst of his work, a brief trip to Granada resulted in his cataloguing of the Arabic manuscripts of the Abbey of Sacro-Monte, a small but choice collection of uncertain origin, which seems to have been presented to the Colegiata del Sacro-Monte by Philip II at the time when that monarch had brought together the Escorial collection. Simonet had made an earlier catalogue of the manuscripts, of little value since he had committed numerous errors and seems not to

[1] *Op. cit.*, p. 67.
[2] *Op. cit.*, pp. 68-69.

have understood their content too well, and so Asín described them to specialists stating that their value resided not in their number (20) but in the variety of subjects represented, in the importance of the authors of some of these works, in their bibliographic rarity and in their paleographic interest, since they make it possible to study the development of handwriting in al-Andalus from the eleventh to the seventeenth centuries.[1]

In 1912 the Academy of Moral and Political Sciences elected him to occupy the place left vacant by the death of Menéndez y Pelayo, and he occupied his seat in 1914 presenting as an inaugural address his capital study *Abenmasarra y su escuela: Orígenes de la filosofía hispano-musulmana.* In a copy of Goldziher's work *Le livre de Mohammed ibn Toumert, Mahdi des Almohades* [2] existing in Asín's library, García Gómez has discovered a passage underlined by Asín [3] which suggests the desirability of compiling the doctrines of Ibn Masarra from the polemical material directed against him and his school.[4] From this note Asín's monograph seems to have begun, for in it he studies the obscure background of early Andalusian Islam in order to bring to light the singular innovation of Ibn Masarra: his fusion of the Plotinian system of the pseudo-Empedocles and its most salient feature, the hierarchy of five substances presided over by a spiritual primary matter, with *Muʿtazilite, Shīʿite* and *Ṣūfī* elements. He traces the thought of the Masarrite school through its diverse ramifications both among Andalusians such as Ibn al-ʿArīf and Ibn al-ʿArabī who gave back to the Orient the legacy they had received from it, as well as among the Jews (Avicebron) and Christians of the Franciscan or pre-Thomist school which led up to Bacon and Raymond Lull.

Asín begins by outlining the origins of Muslim thought in the East during the first three centuries of Islam. Then he devotes a chapter to Hispano-Arabic thought during the same period. Coming finally to Ibn Masarra, he gives a detailed summary of his life as he found it in the biographical dictionaries published by Codera, and attempts the difficult task of reconstructing Ibn Masarra's philosophy with no extant texts by that author upon which to

[1] Asín, "Noticia de los manuscritos árabes del Sacro-Monte de Granada," in *Obras escogidas,* vols. 2, 3 of *Historia y Filologia árabe,* Madrid, 1948, pp. 78-79.

[2] Algiers, 1903.

[3] P. 69, n. 2.

[4] *Cf.* García Gómez, "Esquema de una biografía," p. 277.

base his arguments. Thus it was at that time only possible to reconstruct Ibn Masarra's system through indirect means; by studying the works of his disciples and those who refuted or attacked him.[1] He groups these scattered references to Ibn Masarra around the doctrine of Empedocles as it was understood by Oriental mystics and sums up Ibn Masarra's philosophy saying that it coincided remarkably with the doctrines of the pseudo-Empedocles since 1) its point of departure was the Plotinian conception of the *One* which explains the universe as the result of an emanation through five substances, 2) it conceived the divine throne as a symbol of primary matter, 3) it denied to the *One* the knowledge of emanated essences since this knowledge was the particular attribute of the *Intellect*, 4) it propounded an ascetic doctrine based on the purification of corporeal matter in order to arrive at a totally spiritual eschatology which denied physical reward or punishment in the afterlife.

Added to this Plotinian structure certain purely Islamic elements are to be found, such as the *Muʿtazilite* belief in the absolute freedom of man and the created divine knowledge, the *Shīʿite* belief in the possibility of acquiring prophethood, or the *Ṣūfī* methods to obtain purity of soul. From this it resulted that Ibn Masarra, under the guise of Muslim *Bāṭinism* propagated the Plotinian system of the pseudo-Empedocles in al-Andalus.[2]

Asín then studies the school of Ibn Masarra, its vicissitudes, development and influence on later thought, concluding that this spectacle of cultural transmission is in reality a rebirth of Greek philosophy under the surface of the Islamic civilization, and later, in our own Renaissance. Thus Asín's favourite theory, that of Greek thought modified by Christian mysticism and after being adopted by Islam, later transmitted to the West, is restated to indicate, as he says, that: "There is no break in continuity in the life of collective thought." [3]

Ibn Masarra's works are influential in the ideas of Ibn al-ʿArabī whose books were avidly read in the East. The neo-Platonic current of Ibn al-ʿArabī as well as the Aristotelian ideas of Averroes entered Europe where they provoked the thirteenth century polemics in the world of Scholasticism, for Duns Scotus was the legitimate heir of

[1] *Cf. Obras escogidas*, I, p. 53.
[2] *Op. cit., vol. cit.*, p. 113.
[3] *Op. cit., vol. cit.*, pp. 166-167.

Ibn Masarra while Thomas Aquinas followed the teachings of Averroes.

By indicating this influx of Arabic philosophy into European thought, Asín was in a sense "Africanizing" Europe, so that the last vestiges of the early nineteenth-century liberal pessimism with regard to Spain's Arabic "character" would disappear. If Spain were Arabized and as a result unadaptable to the ways of life in the rest of Europe, Asín was showing that all of Western Europe had been Arabized in its day. Thus the reason for Spain's ills had to be looked for elsewhere.

This study led Asín to Dante, for a passage of his *Abenmasarra* speaks of the European Scholastics who harmonized in an all inclusive *wisdom* the realms of faith and reason, the latter of which was only possible through divine illumination. These thinkers coincide with the Muslim illuminists or Ishrāqī school. Asín adds: "To the same group belongs, in my opinion, Dante Alighieri, though historians of scholasticism include him among Thomists or Aristotelians," [1] and he explains that the frequent light symbols in Dante led him to this conclusion. Furthermore, the allegorical ascension of the mystic as expressed by Ibn al-ʿArabī in the *Futuḥāt* coincided with the ascension of Dante and Beatrice in the *Paradiso.*

This brief and sketchy note written in 1914, was to turn into his now famous work five years later: *La escatología musulmana en la Divina Comedia* which he presented as an inaugural address to the Academy of Spanish. At first an astonished silence surrounded Asín's thesis, after which a multilingual clamour arose in many fields. The surprise of this unexpected interpretation of the figure of Dante and the immense accumulation of Islamic eschatological texts as well as the well ordered logic of Asín's argumentation make this work a momument in Arabic studies which is still the object of controversy today. It rapidly went through several editions in Spanish and opened a new era in Dante studies, while even those who deny the truth of its central thesis must admit its importance as the best existing study of Islamic eschatology.

Asín argues that when he studied the allegorical ascent to heaven of Ibn al-ʿArabī he noticed that it was a mystical adaptation of the *miʿrāj* of Muḥammad, a well known legend constantly mention-

[1] *Abenmasarra,* Madrid, 1914, pp. 120-121, n. 2.

ed in Islamic theological literature in which the Prophet travels from Jerusalem to the throne of God. This *mi'rāj* was preceded by a night journey or *isrā'* to the mansions of the underworld. From this he concluded that the Islamic legend must be a precursor to the *Divine Comedy*.[1] New surprises awaited Asín's investigation, for he found that many of the Christian legends which Dante knew and used, also had Islamic precursors. Dante had possessed a universal erudition and his thirst for knowledge led him to read everything he came across. Since his century was saturated by Islamic art and knowledge, the possibilities of influence were very great. Asín traces the origin of Islamic eschatological literature from the Koran to the *isrā'* cycle developed by popular imagination, and follows up with a study of the *mi'rāj* cycle, tracing the later development of the tradition as it is eleborated by Ibn al-'Arabī and on a different level by Abū l-'Alā al-Ma'arrī. He compares all these sources with analogous passages in the *Divine Comedy*, studies the topography of Hell according to Ibn al-'Arabī and Dante [2] as well as the Christian and Muslim versions of Purgatory. Then he turns to the Latin sources of Dante, and shows that many of them contain Islamic elements to the point that some versions even retain the original Arabic names of the characters, and he concludes that the transmission of these models to Italy was entirely possible. So he invokes Ribera's theory of imitation which he had made his own saying:

> The *resemblance* between the model and the copy is clear; so are the *priority in time* of the first to the second and the *communication* between the two. We do not believe that the place of honour belonging rightfully to Islamic literature in the most solemn cortège of the precursors of the Dantesque poem can henceforward be denied to it. [3]

The book was rapidly sold and appeared in an abridged version in 1927. A second edition, accompanied by what Asín called *Historia y crítica de una polémica* appeared in 1943. In it Asín sums up the major imputations of his adversaries and attempts to rectify them one by one. The original book was not well received in Italy

---

[1] *Cf. Dante y el Islam*, vol. I, serie B, Madrid, 1927, p. 17-18. Asín was preceded in this daring thesis by E. Blochet, *Les sources orientales de la Divine Comédie*, Paris, 1901.

[2] *Cf.* Asín, *op. cit.*, pp. 106-107.

[3] *Op. cit.*, p. 318.

in 1919, though it was soon published in English at the expense of the Duke of Alba. The main thesis of Asín's book, as has been indicated by Moscati, has recently been given added weight by the discovery of the *Libro de la Escala,* published simultaneously by the Italian Cerulli and the Spaniard Muñoz Sendino in 1949.[1] This *Libro de la Escala* turned out to be a complete version of the *mi'raj* translated into Spanish, French and Latin at the order of Alfonso X, and its recent discovery and publication in a sense confirmed though it limited Asín's thesis—unfortunately, five years after his death.

According to Muñoz Sendino, the legend of the *mi'rāj* was translated in Seville in 1264, first into a rough draft in Castilian (today lost) made by a learned Jew, and from this copy, into Latin and French by Buonaventura of Siena, an Italian at the Castilian court. In his work, the Italian gives us the first French translation of an Arabic work made in Spain, as well as the probable source of Dante, since French and Latin were the cultural languages of Europe, and the translation was made almost at the time Dante was born in Florence.[2]

Muñoz Sendino places the composition of the *Divine Comedy* in the year 1307, in its early and incomplete form. By that time—fifty years after the translation of the *mi'rāj* made in 1264—manuscripts of that legend circulated throughout Europe and it was highly probable that one of them could have reached Dante.[3] The discovery of this manuscript was important, because it was precisely the means of transmission of the *mi'rāj* legend to Dante which had constituted the weakest point in Asín's argument. The appearance of a trilingual translation at the time of Dante's birth increased the probability of his having had some information and knowledge of the Islamic legend.

In the same year in which Muñoz Sendino published the *Libro de la Escala,* the Italian scholar Enrico Cerulli published a study of the manuscripts entitled *Il "Libro Della Scala" e la questione delle fonti arabo-spagnole della Divina Commedia,*[4] in which he gathered a large number of medieval European versions of the

[1] *Cf.* Francisco Cantera Burgos, *Los estudios orientales en la España actual, Oriente Moderno,* 1955, p. 237.

[2] *Cf. La Escala de Mahoma, traducción del árabe al castelleno, latín y francés, ordenada por Alfonso X el sabio,* José Muñoz Sendino, Madrid, 1949, pp. xi-xii.

[3] *Op. cit.,* p. 197.

[4] Vatican, 1949.

mi'rāj based on the Arabic texts studied by Asín. He discovered the *Libro de la Escala* independently of Muñoz Sendino, and his work brings together a number of other texts written by Western medieval authors between the ninth and fourteenth centuries and dealing with Muslim eschatology, most of them proceeding from the pen of Castilian and Catalan writers unknown up until then. He sums up the problem of the Islamic sources of the *Divine Comedy* by saying that these sources are principally contained in the *Libro de la Escala*, the *Collectio Toletana* and other Western versions of Islamic eschatology, all of them popular works which became part of the cultural patrimony of Europe in the twelfth and thirteenth centuries by way of Spain. In this sense, he argues that Asín's theory can no longer be taken to suggest direct relationships between Italian and Arabic literature, but rather an indirect relationship with Spain as the connecting link.[1] Thus he has the following to say of Asín:

> And even so,—and may it be said to the honour of Miguel Asín Palacios who posed this problem—what a value that testimony in the *Commedia* assumes! It is clarified by the name of the Arab people who were then providentially fulfilling the great historical role of transmitting the heritage of Greek thought to Europe, and by the name of noble Spain, the first among nations in defending Christian Europe during the seven centuries of the *Reconquista*, and the first also in receiving and transmitting to Western Europe everything that, in the daily contacts of peace and war, she could receive in abundance, in the cultural and artistic fields, from that same Oriental world against which she opposed her sword in the battlefield. [2]

At this time Asín's life was occupied by close contact with Ribera, by his discussions at the home of the Duke of Osma, now converted into the "Instituto de Valencia de Don Juan," and by yearly trips in June to the Escorial where he consulted the Arabic collection and taught a group of young Augustinians of whom the fathers Morata and Antuña were to be the most promising Arabists. His work between 1920 and 1930 was considerable, and among many other monographs he wrote *Los precedentes musulmanes del "pari" de Pascal*, in which he compares the thought of the French philosopher to that of Ġazālī.[3] Previously in 1914 Asín had discovered the

[1] Cerulli, *op. cit.*, p. 545.

[2] *Op. cit.*, p. 549-550.

[3] *Cf. Huellas del Islam*, Madrid, 1941, pp. 232-233 for a resumé of his conclusions on this subject.

plagiarism of the Ikhwān as-Ṣafā' perpetrated by Anselmo Turmeda and he stated that Menéndez y Pelayo had noticed in his *Orígenes de la novela* [1] that Turmeda was full of enigmas and contradictions, though he had thought that Turmeda's sources were mainly those of the Italian *novelle*. However, Asín showed that the Mallorcan friar's *Disputa* was no less than a direct translation of an Arabic work on the dignity of man over animal life written by the Brothers of Purity. According to Asín, Turmeda led a double life, deceiving both Christians and Muslims, for he called himself Friar Anselmo Turmeda when he wrote his plagiarism in Catalan, and signed himself 'Abd Allāh when he divulged his *Polemic against Christianity* in Arabic among Muslims. In the *Disputa* he passed off as his own what he had translated from Arabic authors whereas in his *Polemic* he made extensive use of the anti-Christian arguments of Ibn Ḥazm's *Fiṣal,* and described Christian rites in an absurd way, falsifying ecclesiastical texts in order to gratify his Muslim readers.[2]

However, the central focus of Asín's studies at this time was occupied by two of the most important figures in Andalusian thought; Ibn Ḥazm of Cordova and Ibn al-'Arabī of Murcia. He had studied Ibn Ḥazm earlier in 1907, and later he had worked on the only manuscript of the *Ṭawq* or "Dove's Neck Ring" in Leiden before Petrof prepared his edition of that work. In 1916 he had translated the *Akhlāq* under the title of *Los caracteres y la conducta* (Madrid, 1916). Now his interest turned toward the *Fiṣal,* the monumental history of religions of the Cordovan scholar. A study of this work served Asín as an inaugural address to the Academy of History in 1924, and in it he sums up the importance of Ibn Ḥazm by indicating his enormous influence on Islamic thought. According to Asín, the Cordovan had solved many theological problems at the same time as Ġazālī, and before Averroes. He had created a school of theology in al-Andalus which preserved his name up to the sixteenth century in North Africa. All the later Muslim writers of anti-Christian polemical treatises were Ḥazmites who based their work on the first part of the *Fiṣal.*[3] In the books published by the Academy there appeared between 1927 and 1932 five volumes of

[1] Vol. I., introd., pp. cv ff.

[2] *Cf. El original árabe de "La disputa del asno contra Fr. Anselmo Turmeda,"* in *Huellas del Islam,* Madrid, 1941, pp. 159-160.

[3] *Cf. Discursos leídos ante la Real Academia de la Historia en la recepción publica del señor D. Miguel Asín Palacios el día* 18 *de mayo de* 1924, Madrid, 1924, p. 57.

which the first was a biography of Ibn Ḥazm and the other four were a translation of large portions of the *Fiṣal.* In this work, after speaking of Ibn Ḥazm's significance, Asín adds that in spite of this, he was hardly known to historians of philosophy. It was thus the duty of Spain to make known to the world his most important works until the time when they could be analysed more carefully. For this reason, considering Ibn Ḥazm as part of the patrimony of Spanish culture, Asín offered his work to the public as a provisional study.[1]

He pays particular attention to Ibn Ḥazm's work as a theologian and historian of religion and philosophy, excluding from his plan the literary and poetic qualities of the Cordovan scholar revealed in his *Ṭawq,* his nature as a jurist which Goldziher had outlined in his *Ẓāhiriten,* his work on political history studied by Dozy, and his main features as a practical moralist which Asín himself had outlined when he translated the *Akhlāq.*[2] Asín thus limits himself to a detailed exposition of Ibn Ḥazm's biography, and a total analysis of the *Fiṣal* accompanied by a translation into Spanish of the more important chapters.

Between 1925 and 1928 Asín published in the *Boletín de la Real Academia de la Historia* four monographs on Ibn al-ʿArabī, in an attempt to follow up his Masarrite studies. In 1933 he published the *Maḥāsin al-Majālis* or "Virtues of the *Ṣūfī* Gatherings" written by Ibn al-ʿArīf of Almería. The work appeared in Paris with a translation into French, and was of considerable importance since Ibn al-ʿArīf stands in the chain of *Ṣūfism* between Ibn Masarra and Ibn al-ʿArabī, and represents the attitude of renouncing everything that is not God, including mystical states, favours and charismata received from God, an attitude which is fundamental in Ibn al-ʿArabī. It seems that this mystical system had certain precedents in the East, but it was organized and rigorously applied to each state of spiritual life, in al-Andalus. That system was maintained in the Peninsula and later adopted by the *Shādhilī* school, one of whose last members was Ibn ʿAbbād of Ronda (fourteenth century) who made of it the basis of *Ṣūfism.*[3]

During the same year Asín published his *Vidas de santones*

[1] *Cf.* Asín, *Abenházam de Córdoba y su Historia crítica de las ideas religiosas,* I., pp. 5-9.

[2] *Op. cit.,* p. 9.

[3] Ibn al-ʿArīf, *Maḥāsin al-Majālis, texte arabe, traduction et commentaire par M. Asín Palacios,* Paris, 1933, p. 16.

Andaluces [1] extracted from the "Epistle of Sanctity" by Ibn al-'Arabī of which it constitutes the third part. This treatise is one of the most complete documents on Andalusian *Ṣūfism* and as Asín points out, its importance can be guessed if the reader will imagine the value of a work by Teresa of Avila or John of the Cross in which these authors had consigned all kinds of data about their spiritual guides and colleagues. In this sense the work by Ibn al-'Arabī gives us a better picture of the Islamic mysticism of his time than we possess with regard to the Spanish mystics of the Golden Age. According to Asín the work is also important in that it gives us an anticipated vision of the Spanish sect of *alumbrados* or "illuminati" who spread their teachings throughout Christain Andalusia and Castile during the sixteenth century. Asín at this point already suspected that the *alumbrados* possessed many peculiarities which related them more closely to the Islamic *Ṣūfīs* than to the German and Flemish mystics with whom they were usually compared, and this idea was to be expanded into his posthumous work in which he relates the *Shādhilī* school to the *alumbrados*.[2]

As a culmination of his studies on Ibn al-'Arabī, Asín had published in 1931 one of his principal works: *El islam cristianizado*, a careful study of *Ṣūfī* activities mainly as seen through the complicated writings of Ibn al-'Arabī. He compares his doctrines to those of Eastern Christian monasticism, so that just as he had found Islamic sources for Christian cultural phenomena in the case of Dante and the Scholastics, he sets out to reverse his ideas and finds Christian sources for Islam as he had done with Ġazālī. In doing this his goal was to re-establish the unity of history and human culture and combat the spectres of the "proles sine matre creatas." From this point on, Asín sees new Islamic influences on Spanish Renaissance mysticism. As for his ideas about Ibn al-'Arabī, he asks himself as a Catholic whether it is possible to speak of an authentic mystical movement within Islam which is as valid as that of Christianity. His attitude of tolerance leads him to an affirmative answer, though his Catholic training makes him attempt to show the Christian background of Islamic mysticism.[3] Asín claims therefore, that the analogies between Christian and Islamic

[1] Madrid, 1933.
[2] *Cf.* Asín, *Vidas de santones andaluces*, Madrid-Granada, 1933, pp. 13-14.
[3] *Cf. El islam cristianizado*, p. 5.

mysticism are the result of imitation, and so he sets out to show what contact the Arabs had with Christianity in the East, pointing out that Christian monasteries had existed in the Arabian peninsula and the *rāḥib* or "monk" had appeared in pre-Islamic poetry (in the *Mu'allaqa* of Imrū' al-Qays for example). In this way, the value of Asín's book on Ibn al-'Arabī resided mainly in his commentaries and explanations of the Murcian *Ṣūfī's* writings.

Codera had died in 1917, and Ribera had retired in 1927 and had vacated his chair at the University in favour of González Palencia In the meantime, a new generation of Arabists appeared: Vila, Lator and García Gómez. The monarchy of Alfonso XIII was followed by the Second Republic during which occasional outbreaks of anti-clerical violence made Asín liable to personal danger. As a priest, Asín had no sympathy for the reformist ideals of the Republic, and this conservative side of his nature may be observed in a later article entitled *Por qué lucharon a nuestro lado los musulmanes marroquíes* [1] published in 1940 after the Civil War. In this article he refers to the Loyalist side as "la España sovietizada" [2] and uses other terms to indicate what he considered to be its ungodliness. He asks himself why the Moroccan forces supported the Nationalist cause and goes into a long dissertation in which he concludes that the Muslims as well as the Spanish Nationalists (whom he equates with the authentic spirit of Spain) both enjoyed a long tradition of religious manifestations which were at times the common heritage of both religions. Thus he quotes Ibn Ḥazm as having said that one should trust a religious man even though he be of a different religion from one's own, but that one should on no account trust a man with with no religion, and adds:

> And that precisely was what the Marxists were to the Moroccans who fought on our side: irreligious men, or as they themselves call them in their language: *kilāb bi-lā dīn* 'dogs without religion.' [3]

The years 1932 and 1933 marked an epoch in Spanish Arabism, because in the first the Schools of Arabic Studies in Madrid and Granada were created, and in the second, the founding of the journal *Al-Andalus* gave Spanish Arabists for the first time an important means of expression which unlike the *Colección de*

[1] *Cf.* Asín, *Obras escogidas*, vols. 2 & 3, Madrid, 1948, pp. 127-152.
[2] *Op. cit.*, p. 129.
[3] *Op. cit.*, p. 146.

estudios árabes founded by Ribera, was equipped to publish techniclaly complex articles directed to specialists in the field of Hispano-Arabic studies. *Al-Andalus* began to appear under the direction of Asín who wrote many articles to ensure its continuation. At this time he studied a hitherto unknown description of the ancient Pharus of Alexandria written by Ibn ash-Shaykh of Málaga (1933), and translated the *Libro de los cercos* by Ibn as-Sīd of Badajoz (1940). However, the most important of these monographs was the one entitled *Un precursor hispanomusulmán de San Juan de la Cruz* (1933) in which he outlined the methods of the *Shādhilī* Ibn ʿAbbād of Ronda in the light of their possible relationship to the mysticism of John of the Cross. Previously, in *El islam cristianizado* Asín had discussed the importance in the history of mysticism, of the attitude of renouncing charismata, a method adopted by the *Shādhilī* school. Asín had pointed out the similarity between this attitude and that of the Carmelite school of John of the Cross. Now he expanded this theme which he considered to derive from Pauline doctrines spread in Islam by the Persian *Ṣūfī* Hallāj in the Orient, and expanded in the West by Ibn al-ʿArīf in the eleventh century. This doctrine was inherited by Ibn al-ʿArabī of Murcia in the twelfth century and was spread through al-Andalus and North Africa. In the Rīf, ʿAbd as-Sallām ibn Mashīsh transmitted it to Abū l-Ḥasan ash-Shādhilī, founder of the sect which still exists today, but whose major exponent was Ibn ʿAbbād of Ronda (d. A.D. 1394).[1]

Asín gives a biographical account of Ibn ʿAbbād whom he defines as an ascetic writer, an expounder of homilies and a spiritual director of consciences. Going into the doctrine of the renunciation of charismata he states that Ibn ʿAbbād's belief, like that of the Carmelites was that it is more meritorious to renounce charismata and to avoid asking God for them since this attitude of renunciation destroys selfishness and vanity.[2] In comparing the technical vocabulary of the *Shādhilī* school with that of John of the Cross he explains that the Muslim mystics use the terms *qabḍ* "straitness" and *basṭ* "ampleness" in a way which corresponds to the Spanish Christian mystic's usage of *aprieto* end *anchura,* while each term is identified in either language with the symbols of "night" and "day." From this Asín cautiously puts forward his theory of imitation

[1] *Cf. Un precursor hispanomusulmán de San Juan de la Cruz,* in *Obras escogidas,* vol. I, Madrid, 1946, pp. 245-246.

[2] *Op. cit.,* p. 268.

though the lack of documents of an intermediary nature to prove the transmission keeps him from formulating any decisive judgement. It is probable that such documents may some day be found, particularly in *Aljamiado* literature which is extremely rich in devotional treatises.

In the midst of these interesting though minor works, Asín undertook what was to be another of his major books; that of his old age. Once again he turned his gaze to Ġazālī whom he had studied in his youth. In 1929 he had translated the *Iqtiṣād* in the series published by the Instituto de Valencia de Don Juan, under the title of *El justo medio en la creencia, compendio de teología dogmática de Algazel,*[1] and in its prologue he had again stressed the importance of Ġazālī's dogmatics insofar as they were related to scholastic doctrines. Since Ġazālī's work had become the syllabus of orthodox or *Sunnī* Islam, Asín saw the value of translating this compendium into Spanish for the benefit of non-Arabists.

Now Asín turned to the *Iḥyā'*, the *opus magnum* of the Eastern thinker, and he analysed it in three heavy tomes (the fourth is a crestomathy of Ġazālī) entitled *La espiritualidad de Algazel y su sentido cristiano.*[2] The method employed is his usual one for he makes an excellent translation of the greater part of the work as well as including summaries of the less important passages. At the bottom of each page he includes a concordance with analogous Christian texts taken from the Scriptures and the ecclesiastical doctors. This work, which once more attempts to attribute Christian sources to Ġazālī's thought, is of a controversial nature, and whether one agrees or not with his interpretation it must be admitted that his commentaries and exposition of Ġazālī should constitute one of the essential components of any serious bibliography on that thinker.

Stating in its prologue that his intention is to study the Christian significance of Ġazālī's works he adds that he has deliberately excluded from his study the Islamic sources which were influential in shaping Ġazālī's thought, firstly because that work had been partly carried out by Goldziher, Macdonald, Massignon and Nicholson, and secondly because his main purpose was to stress the Christian background of Islamic thought; a subject which

[1] Madrid, 1929.
[2] Madrid, 1934-41.

he claims had been deliberately neglected by previous scholars.[1] The thesis of Asín is in a sense one-sided, because to explain away all of Islamic spiritual life as the result of Christian influences implies that there is no such thing as an authentic religious spirit among the Arabic speaking peoples. From this point of view Islam, rather than constituting an independent, active culture with its own peculiar forms of life becomes a mere passive recipient of influences. For these reasons Asín's thesis was not well received by A. J. Arberry who, though he granted the importance of the book [2] reviewed the various works written by Asín, and concluded that

> to argue tendentiously, as I fear not a few non-Muslims have done, that all that in their view is good in Islam is of foreign origin, and must be traced to one or another non-Islamic source, is not so much honest scholarship as the worst form of sectarian bigotry. [3]

The publication of *Algazel* which took place between 1934 and 1941 coincided with the Spanish Civil War, and Asín spent this period at his summer residence in San Sebastián which city was one of the safest of the Nationalist zone. During this time he was isolated from his books and friends, but he engaged in teaching Latin to secondary school students, and worked on manuscripts from Oxford and Berlin of which the Duke of Alba was sending him photocopies in which he studied the works of Avempace.

At the end of the war, he returned to Madrid in 1939 and recommenced his activities by continuing the publication of *Al-Andalus* and reorganizing the Schools of Arabic Studies since they had been integrated into the *Consejo Superior de Investigaciones Científicas* of which he was named first vice-president. He began once more to teach in the University (which he had abandoned in

---

[1] *Op. cit.*, pp. 9-10.

[2] "It is by any standard an impressive achievement, and constitutes by far the most important monograph on Ghazālī so for written."

Cf. A. J. Arberry, *An Introduction to the History of Sufism, The Sir Abdullah Suhrawardy Lectures for* 1942, Oxford, 1942, p. 53.

[3] *Op. cit.*, pp. 54-55. He adds: "On the basis of these examples, the merest fragment but perhaps a representative fragment of Palacios's methods of reasoning, it is impossible to feel a very secure faith in his judgement and the result of his researches. In saying this, it is by no means my wish to detract from the very high merit of this great scholar's contribution to Ṣūfī studies; but I feel it my duty to record my opinion that, in using his books, the researcher should make due allowance for the sectarian bias which has unfortunately to some extent affected the outlook of a brilliant and most industrious worker."

1934) where he continued until his retirement in 1941. In that same year he republished his four studies on Thomas Aquinas, Turmeda, Pascal and John of the Cross in a book entitled *Huellas del Islam*. The prologue of this work summarizes his previous studies and characterizes his methods and objectives. In it he claims that in the history of culture there is never a definite break in continuity, and that ideas, the most delicate product of human culture are subjected to this law thanks to which progress is possible. He explains that the illustration of this principle had inspired all his works over the years, since he had tried to show the influence of Eastern Christian thought on Islam and also that of Islam on Western Christianity. He adds that this general orientation of his work was the result of the heritage he had received from Ribera.[1]

During his last years Asín published works such as his *Contribución a la toponimia árabe de España* (1944) and a *Glosario de voces romances registradas por un botánico anónimo hispano-musulmán* (*siglos XI-XII*) (1943), in which he speaks of the oral quality of the information collected by an anonymous Muslim botanist who often explains the colloquial Mozarabic names of plants as well as recording popular superstitions about them.[2] This work, because of the quantity of Mozarabic words in it is useful for the study of the Romance dialect of al-Andalus, since it is the oldest document extant apart from the *Glosas emilianenses* and *silenses* published by Menéndez Pidal.[3]

Finally Asín continued his research on *Ṣūfism* in an effort to link the post-Ibn al-ʿArabī movements to Spanish mysticism. The outlines of this study were already present in *El islam cristianizado*[4] and in his study on the analogies between Ibn ʿAbbād of Ronda and John of the Cross. Now Asín showed that the *Shādhilī* ideas in al-Andalus branched out into two main currents: that of orthodox mystics such as Ibn ʿAbbād and that of miracle-mongering holy men who attracted audiences with their debased spiritual practices. Likewise at the beginning of the Golden Age in Spain, we find a mystical current equally divergent into two main streams: that of

[1] *Cf. Huellas del Islam*, pp. 7-8.

[2] *Glosario* pp. xvii-xviii.

[3] *Cf. op. cit.*, pp. xxxix-xl. Here is a sample of these entries: "*Kattān* (flax), known as *al-abertal*. Thus called because its capsules when dried, open and drop their seed. That is why it is called *abertal* which means "open"... In Greek it is called *linosh* and in Latin, *lino*." *Op. cit.*, p. 1.

[4] *Cf.* pp. 273-274.

the austere orthodox mystics which culminates in the Carmelite school of Teresa of Avila and John of the Cross, and that of the heretical *alumbrados* and *dejados*, whose origin had never been satisfactorily explained. Asín suspected a zone of contact; he collected material and wrote a cautious prologue and the first part of a future book devoted to the study of the *Shādhili* masters. It is regretted that death interrupted his labours so that the first part of his work, published in *Al-Andalus* was never concluded. He died in San Sebastián in 1944 and was buried in that same city.[1]

It would be a severe injustice to Asín not to mention the lengthy series of informative articles he wrote on the most diverse subjects, many of which were reprinted in his *Obras escogidas*. Some of them were written to provide material for *Al-Andalus* and are of a delightful nature for he was a master of prose style and was able to cover a wide range of topics.[2]

His influence, and the heated debate over his ideas have been of great importance throughout Europe, and in Spain, one of his biographers says of him:

> Asín Palacios, with the abovementioned works, with *Huellas del Islam*, with *Algacel* turns into a gigantic figure of the research world, almost as important for the understanding of our culture and history as Menéndez y Pelayo and Menéndez Pidal. [3]

As may be expected from the character of his work, Asín's ideas have found less sympathy among Islamic scholars. In his recent book entitled *Three Muslim Sages, Avicenna-Suhrawardi-Ibn ʿArabī*, professor Ḥossein Naṣr quotes Asín and refers to him at length in his study of Ibn al-ʿArabī, but he has the following to add:

> It is the refusal of the vast majority of Orientalists to accept this fundamental aspect of Islam [he speaks of *Ṣūfism*] as a part of the Islamic tradition and an intrinsic element of its orthodoxy that has made the picture of Islam in most Western eyes such a dry and sterile

---

[1] *Cf.* García Gómez, "Esquema de una biografía," *And.*, 9, 1944, pp. 267-291.

[2] *E.g.*, *Origen y carácter de la religión almohade*; *El "Libro de los animales" de Yāḥiẓ*; *Bosquejo de un diccionario técnico de filosofía y teología musulmanas*; *Sens du mot Tahafut dans les oeuvres d' al-Ġazālī et d'Averroes*; *Un tratado morisco de polémica contra los judíos*; *El baño de Zarieb*; *La polémica anticristiana de Muḥammad al-Qaysī*, to mention only a few of these articles.

[3] G. Torrente Ballester, *Panorama de la literatura española contemporánea*, I, 2nd ed., Madrid, 1961, pp. 230-231.

> one, devoid of any spirituality or beauty. Among the few well-known Western scholars who have conceded the Quranic origin of Ṣūfism one can name Margoliouth and especially Massignon and Corbin, whereas most of the other famous scholars, like Horten, Nicholson, Asín Palacios, and more recently Zaehner and Arberry, have posited a Hindu, Neoplatonic, Christian, or even Zoroastrian origin for Ṣūfism, mistaking too often the borrowed formulations of the Ṣūfīs with the inner experience and realization which is based absolutely on the grace, or *barakah* issuing from the Prophet. [1]

Nonetheless, Asín's role in reviving the intellectual life of Spanish universities can hardly be sufficiently stressed, since he in Arabic studies, Menéndez Pidal in Romance literature and Manuel Gómez Moreno in art history formed a most impressive triad which trained Spain's foremost twentieth-century scholars. Asín, with his exhaustive and methodical scholarship gave a greater reliability to Arabic studies than had his mentor Ribera, many of whose theories seem not to have withstood the test of time as well as those of his disciple.

---

[1] Ḥossein Naṣr, *Three Muslim Sages*, Cambridge, Massachusetts, 1964, p. 156., n. 1.

CHAPTER EIGHT

Of the disciples of Asín and Ribera who have continued the tradition of Arabic studies in the University of Madrid, the two most important are Ángel González Palencia and Emilio García Gómez.

González Palencia was born in 1889 in Horcajo de Santiago, province of Cuenca. After studying Latin, philosophy and theology he enrolled in the faculty of Philosophy and Letters at the University of Madrid where he received his *licencia* in 1910 after which he worked as an archivist in Toledo. He had studied with Asín in 1909-10, and the latter used his influence to have his former student transferred from Toledo to Madrid in 1913, where he began working in the National Historical Archive. At this time the Spanish Arabists were incorporated into the new Centro de Estudios Históricos and González Palencia began at once to show evidence of his talent by collaborating in the publication of the *Catálogo de los manuscritos árabes y aljamiados de la Biblioteca de la Junta para Ampliación de Estudios* (1915), as well as by contributing to the volume *Miscelanea de estudios y textos árabes* (1915) together with M. Alarcón, the important *Apéndice a la edición Codera de la "Takmīla" de Ibn al-Abbār*. In the same year he presented as his doctoral thesis a study on the *Kitāb Taqwīm adh-Dhihn*, under the title of *Rectificación de la mente. Tratado de lógica de Abusalt de Denia*. The previous year he had obtained a scholarship to study in Rabat, though the First World War interrupted his labours, so that in 1916 he began to teach in Madrid.

When Ribera and Asín withdrew from the Centro de Estudios Históricos, González Palencia began to devote himself more exclusively to his work as an archivist, though without entirely giving up Arabism. In 1921 he published, together with Juan Hurtado y Jiménez de la Serna, late professor in Madrid, a manual entitled *Historia de la literatura española* which in 1949 went through its sixth edition, having become the standard textbook on the subject. Out of his work as an archivist came *Los mozárabes de Toledo en los siglos XII y XIII* [1] a valuable mine of priceless and

[1] 4 vols. in folio, 1926-1930, published by the Instituto de Valencia de Don Juan.

difficult documents. González Palencia wrote a number of books of a popularizing nature among which may be counted his *Historia de la España musulmana* [1] a brief resumé of the work done up to his time, and the *Historia de la literatura arábigo-española,*[2] a very useful manual since it presented a general panorama of Hispano-Arabic literature and included the recent findings of the Spanish Arabists, thus presenting a more up to date picture of the subject than was to be found in Von Schack's book which had dealt only with poetry and art.

When Ribera retired from the University in 1927, the archivist competed for and won his professor's chair, and his new duties made him turn more towards Arabic studies in which he published folklore works and children's books of Arabic tales to which he made additions from 1930-39. He also published an edition of the *Iḥṣā' al-'Ulūm* or 'Catalogue of sciences' by al-Fārābī in 1932, and a new Spanish translation of *Ḥayy ibn Yaqẓān* by Ibn Ṭufayl which was far superior to that of Pons Boïgues and which was edited in 1934 and reprinted in 1948 by the Escuelas de Estudios Árabes of Madrid and Granada.

In 1931 González Palencia joined the Academy of History and delivered an inaugural address entitled *Influencia de la civilización árabe* which constitutes a resumé of Arabic influences on Spanish and European culture and outlines the comparatist theories towards which the Spanish Arabist school has always tended. González Palencia in 1943 visited the United States where he lectured at Stanford University, Harvard, Cornell, Columbia and other American centres of learning. During the Spanish Civil War he stayed in Aragón and continued his research, as well as directing the School of Arabic Studies in Granada, thus assuring its continuity. He returned to the United States in 1938 and after the war resumed his functions in Madrid where he joined the Spanish Academy in 1940, and in 1945 he sponsored the entry of García Gómez into the same institution, making a plea for the continuity of Spanish Arabism after the death of Asín.[3]

After the Civil War, his attention was taken up more by Spanish

---

[1] *Editorial Labor,* 1925. 2nd ed., 1929, 3rd ed., 1932.

[2] *Labor,* 1928, 2nd. ed., revised, 1945.

[3] Referring to himself and García Gómez he declared: "Together will we carry upright the lighted torch of Arabic studies in Spain, as long as God is served." *Cf.* García-Gómez, "Don Ángel González Palencia (1889-1949)," in *And.*, 14, 1949, pp. i-xi.

than Arabic studies, though he became director of the Instituto Miguel Asín in 1944 and wrote articles for *Al-Andalus* while at the same time he supervised the edition of Asín's *Obras escogidas* and published books such as *El arzobispo don Raimundo y la Escuela de traductores de Toledo* (1942), *Versiones castellanas del Sendebar* (1946) and the *Disciplina Clericalis* (1948). He died in an automobile accident in 1949, leaving behind him the memory of a life entirely devoted to scholarship. Though many of his books on Arabic are in the form of general studies of a popularizing nature, they represent the summing up of the material uncovered by Ribera and Asín, and as such they have a useful place in the world of scholarly synthesis. His work on Spanish literature and history is perhaps more voluminous than that on Arabic, though such books as that on the Mozarabs of Toledo are indispensable to the contemporary Hispanist as well as being important in that they represent a new attitude towards the Mozarabs quite different from that of Simonet.

If we examine some of González Palencia's works we will be able to detect a new spirit creeping into Spanish scholarship as a result of the labours of the Arabist group. In this sense many of his manuals and textbooks are important in the acceptance of Arabic cultural influences which they reveal. Thus for example, in his *Historia de la literatura española* we find that Hispano-Arabic literature is included in the general area of what he terms "Spanish" literature. All the great Arabic writers of al-Andalus are found consorting with such strange bedfellows as Seneca, Lucan, Quintillian, according to the general programme for Spanish literature outlined by Menéndez y Pelayo.[1] Though this inclusion of Hispano-Arabic literature within the general framework of Spanish literature is peculiar, since the Arabic character of the writings of al-Andalus cannot be denied, it represents a step in favour of accepting the impact of Arabic culture on Spain. It also reflects the ideas of Ribera, and ultimately, Simonet.

In González Palencia's *Antología de la literatura española*, a companion volume to the previous work, the reader will be surprised to find several authors of al-Andalus represented in translation. Thus for example the famous elegy on the decadence of Peninsular

---

[1] *Cf.* Menéndez y Pelayo, *Introducción y programa de literatura española*, published by Miguel Artigas, Madrid, 1934.

Islam written by Abū l-Baqā' Ṣāliḥ ibn al-Baqā' of Ronda [1] is included in this work according to the rendering into Spanish verse by Juan Valera, translator of Von Schack. According to González Palencia, Valera found that the *ubi sunt* theme of this poem was similar in character to that of the famous *Coplas* written by Jorge Manrique on the death of his father, and so he translated Von Schack's German version into Spanish using the same metrical combinations of Jorge Manrique's poem. Actually, the metre of the Arabic poem (*basīṭ*) has nothing to do with that of Jorge Manrique and does not sound even remotely like the *Coplas*, though Valera, overcome with enthusiasm for his own translation, and not being able to study the original Arabic version, thought he saw in the two poems a case of direct influence.[2] The following is a sample of Valera's work:

¿ Con sus cortes tan lucidas	With their brilliant courts
del Yemen los claros reyes	Of Yemen, the noble kings,
dónde están?	Where are they?
¿ En dónde los Sasanidas	Where are the Sassanids
que dieron tan sabias leyes	Who gave such wise laws
al Irán?	To Iran? [3]

González Palencia's *Historia de la literatura arábigo-española* is a small work of a popularizing nature containing few original thoughts but which was until recently an excellent guide to further studies. Unfortunately its critical apparatus is inadequate, while the section dealing with poetry is taken entirely from the studies of Ribera and García Gómez, and that on philosophy from Asín. The author accepts the most daring theories of these scholars as manifest truth and makes very little attempt to adopt a critical attitude. Thus when discussing Ribera's theory on the origin of Romance poetry he claims to prove the truth of his master's ideas by arguing that they had been totally accepted by Menéndez Pidal, which is in

[1] Which begins: (*Basīṭ*)

لِكُلِّ شَيْءٍ إِذَا مَا تَمَّ نُقْصَانُ   فَلَا يُغَرُّ بِطِيبِ العَيْشِ إِنْسَانُ

"Everything that has reached perfection declines, so let no man be deceived by the sweetness of a life of luxury." (*Cf.* Nykl, *Selections from Hispano-Arabic Poetry*, p. 200).

[2] *Cf. Poesía y arte de los árabes de España y Sicilia*, Von Schack, translated by Don Juan Valera, 1881, I, 240.

[3] *Cf.* A. González Palencia, *Antología*, Madrid, 1926, p. 10.

itself a favourable comment, though not conclusive,[1] in view of the difficulties of this particular problem.

It is interesting to note that in discussing the nature of the *maqāmāt,* he gave a new turn to the theory of Fernández y González by pointing out the similarity of that genre to the Spanish picaresque novel, a subject which deserves a thorough investigation.[2] In discussing the Mozarabs he manages to reduce Simonet's theories to more just proportions by claiming that though they played an important role in the political and social life of al-Andalus, it was certainly not they who left us the greater number of Arabic literary works, while on the other hand they continued, long after the *Reconquista,* to bear Arabic names and to use that language in their private and public documents as may be observed in Toledo up to the fourteenth century.[3]

He also speaks of Raymond Lull's special interest in Arabic philosophy and discusses his attempt to introduce in Christian Spain certain religious practices of Islam such as that of beginning epistles with the name of Jesus just as the Muslims began them with an invocation of Muḥammad, or that of separating men and women in churches (a custom still followed in rural areas of Spain).[4] About Don Juan Manuel he states that he knew Arabic, as may be observed from his *Libro de los estados,* a version of the legend of *Barlaam y Josafat,* that is to say, of Buddha, which he studied in an Arabic version not yet identified.[5]

González Palencia's inaugural address to the Academy of History, reprinted as *El islam y occidente* [6] is a catalogue of the influences of Islam on the West which goes from the introduction of coffee into Europe, to early attempts at aviation in Cordova, and which considers Asín's theory on Dante fully proved. Very little of this is

---

[1] "Menéndez Pidal, the greatest authority of Spanish Romanists, has studied the problem with technical precision (1935 and 1941) and is now convinced of the Hispano-Arabic thesis. The latter, at least insofar as prosody is concerned, seems to have triumphed, after a very heated controversy." *cf. Literatura árab.-esp.,* 2nd ed., Barcelona, 1945, pp. 114-115.

[2] *Op. cit.,* p. 134-135. For a recent study of the connexions between the *maqāmāt* and the Spanish picaresque novel, *cf.* Juan Vernet, *Literatura árabe,* Barcelona, 1968, p. 93.

[3] *Op. cit.,* p. 297.

[4] *Op. cit.,* pp. 317-318.

[5] *Op. cit.,* p. 339.

[6] *Cf.* A. González Palencia, *Moros y cristianos en España medieval, estudios histórico-literarios, tercera serie,* Madrid, 1945, p. 5.

original and more than anything else, it indicates the author's ability to compile and classify data, a skill he acquired as an archivist.

A more interesting study from the point of view of Spanish intellectual history is that entitled *Huellas islámicas en el carácter español*[1] which shows that the pendulum of historiography had swung round so that Arabic studies were once more respectable in Spain after the nineteenth century. However, González Palencia warns that a new danger threatened Spanish historiography: the affirmation that all of the psychological traits of the Spanish people were entirely Arabic in nature. He indicates that there are Islamic cultural phenomena which may be easily observed in Spain, such as art. Furthermore, he adds that contrary to the commonly held opinion that the Renaissance did away with medieval philosophy and science; that is to say, with Arabic cultural influences on Europe, the true state of affairs was very different, as may be observed by studying the inventory of any good sixteenth-century library, where a profusion of Muslim authors may easily be found in translations printed during that century or even in the fifteenth.[2]

In order to solve this problem of Arabic influences on Spain, González Palencia claims that the *Reconquista* was in reality a civil war between Spaniards of different religion, which in the harsh years during which it was waged, prepared the Christians for their later exploits and conquests overseas.[3] This Hispanization of the Moors of al-Andalus by González Palencia indicates to what extent the ideas of Simonet had nourished the school of Spanish Arabists. After the period of almost total rejection by Romanists of the notion of Arabic cultural influences on Spain, which took place in the second half of the nineteenth century, the work of the Arabists had made it plain that such cultural contacts had in fact taken place. Faced with this undeniable reality, the Romanists began to view the matter from the larger context of the problem of Spanish "decadence" and propounded a new solution which found expression in the idea that the Andalusian Muslims—who according to the post-1898 trend initiated by Ribera were considered as basically Spaniards—had in fact been influential in shaping Spanish culture. There were two reasons for this affirmation: Simonet's ideas, and

---

[1] *Op. cit.*, pp. 63-99.
[2] *Op. cit.*, p. 86.
[3] *Op. cit.*, p. 88.

the search for the essential and eternal Spain, so dear to the generation of 1898. This was an attitude which even Ribera and Asín adopted, and which has affected much of Spanish scholarship. It will be encountered repeatedly in the study of twentieth-century Arabism.

Emilio García Gómez is the leading Arabist of contemporary Spain, so that a discussion of his work in some detail will be essential. It is necessary to point out first of all, that as a member of the generation of new poets to which Lorca belonged, García Gómez adds to his functions as an Arabist, his undoubted talent as a man of letters. Thus with him Spanish Arabism comes close to the art of poetry, so that it was fitting that upon entering the Spanish Academy in 1945 he should have succeeded to the great poet Antonio Machado. A pupil of Ribera and Asín, he was born in Madrid in 1905 where he studied with the two leading Arabists of the days of his youth. García Gómez himself relates how he came to study with Asín and how his career came to be chosen.[1] It would seem that during the academic year 1923-24 he was studying law and letters at the University of Madrid, and was totally bored by the first of these two disciplines. Since Arabic was a required subject in the Faculty of Letters, he entered Asín's classroom, where the enthusiasm of the teacher was soon communicated to the disciple so that he was saved from becoming a barrister and suddenly decided to become an Orientalist. After his graduation, the *Junta para Ampliación de Estudios* granted him a research scholarship which the Duke of Alba had set aside for outstanding students of Arabic. The Junta sent him to Egypt where he spent two years, (1928-29), studying in Cairo and making side trips to Beirut and Damascus. He studied with the late Zakī Pasha, a leading figure in Arabic letters, whose literary gatherings he attended, as well as with Ṭaha Ḥusayn whom he was later to translate into Spanish. During this time he acquired proficiency in the Arabic language and upon returning to Madrid he submitted as his doctoral thesis an exhaustive study of a legend of Alexander the Great according to an Andalusian version. After receiving his doctorate, Ribera chose him to teach Arabic at the University of Madrid.

In 1929 he published his doctoral thesis [2] on a version of the

---

[1] *Cf.* E. García Gómez, "En la jubilación de don Miguel Asín," in *And.*, 6, 1941, pp. 266-270.

[2] García Gómez, *Un texto árabe occidental de la leyenda de Alejandro*, Madrid, 1929.

Alexander legend written in semi-colloquial Hispano-Arabic. For this work he was awarded the Fastenrath prize for the year 1930, which was given yearly by the Spanish Academy for the best scholarly work. In the same year, he was appointed Professor of Arabic at the University of Granada, where he revived these studies which had long stagnated by establishing the Granadan School of Arabic Studies, a branch of the Madrid School. In 1944 he was transferred to the chair of Arabic literature in Madrid, and in November of 1945 he was appointed to be a member of the Spanish Academy.

García Gómez revisited Egypt in 1947 at which time he travelled throughout the Middle East, and in 1948 was appointed to be a member of the Arabic Academy of Damascus,[1] a singular distinction for a Westerner.

García Gómez, gifted with poetic sensibility and true literary talent, has translated Arabic poetry into Spanish verse and has done much to familiarize the Spanish reading public with the history and literature of al-Andalus. During the winter of 1951 he was invited by the Egyptian government to participate in the celebration of the silver jubilee of the University of Cairo, where that institution awarded him an honorary doctorate. At this time he was invited by the Universities of Cairo and Alexandria to deliver a series of lectures on Andalusian literature, which he did during the months of February and April, 1951.

For some years he has been particularly occupied in elaborating a new theory about the Andalusian *muwashshaḥāt* derived from the ideas of Ribera and which we shall outline in the following pages. One of his more important scholarly works to appear in recent years has been his translation of the *Ṭawq* or 'Dove's Neck Ring' by Ibn Ḥazm, accompanied by an important introductory study of the work and its author, as well as a study of the concept of love in al-Andalus from the pen of Ortega y Gasset.[2]

The close relationship between the young Arabist and the literary movements of his time may be observed from his introduction to the 1940 edition of his *Poemas arábigo-andaluces* in which

[1] *Cf.* "Nombramiento de don Emilio García Gómez para correspondiente de la Academia Árabe de Damasco," *And.*, 13, 1948, p. 509.

[2] For a biography of García Gómez, the reader of Arabic may consult the translation into Arabic of his book, *Poemas arábigoandaluces*, entitled *Ash-Shiʿr al-Andalusī*, trans. by Hussein Monès, Cairo, 2nd ed., 1956, pp. 5-9, from which some of these facts are derived.

he speaks of the surprisingly favourable reception of his first edition (1930) of that collection of Hispano-Arabic poetic fragments in translation. He attributes this enthusiastic reception of his work to the fact that at that time the third centenary of Góngora had taken place, and the criticism of Dámaso Alonso had restored that great though much maligned baroque poet to favour. He adds that the brilliant poetic and literary circles of the thirties were avidly seeking new metaphors and imagery, and this interest was satisfied by the old and little known poetry of al-Andalus.[1]

Thus Ramón Gómez de la Serna who since 1910 had experimented with pre-surrealist metaphors which he did not organize into poetic compositions, though his *greguerías* as he called his fragmentary comparisons were to serve as a storehouse of metaphorical expression for later poets, found a mine of poetic possibilities in the Arabic poems translated by García Gómez. He claims that an important precursor to the *greguerías* was to be found in the Hispano-Arabic poems, and he quotes several examples taken directly from García Gómez's book, such as a description of a walnut:

> It is a cover formed by two pieces so closely joined that it is lovely to behold: they look like eyelids closed in sleep. [2]

This is one concrete example of the way in which García Gómez's work was put to use by the new poets of the twentieth century. He was also in close contact, during his stay in Granada with Manuel de Falla and Federico García Lorca who, captivated by the charm of Hispano-Arabic poetry through García Gómez's translations, composed his *Diván de Tamarit,* a collection of love poems which he termed *casidas* and *gacelas,* though without actually maintaining anything of the distinction between the Arabic *qaṣīda* and *ġazal* poetry.[3] It must of course be understood that Lorca's poems were by no means imitations of Arabic poetry, but rather authentically original compositions, a fact which García Gómez is quick to point

---

[1] *Cf. Poemas arábigoandaluces,* Austral, Madrid, 1940, p. 9.

[2] Cf. R. Gómez de la Serna, *Greguerías,* 1940-45, 4th ed., Buenos Aires, 1945, p. 22. This fragment, written by Abū Bakr Muḥammad ibn al-Qūṭiyya of Seville may be found in García Gómez, *Poemas arábigoandaluces,* 3rd. ed. Buenos Aires, 1946, p. 68, and the Arabic orignal in *Ash-Shiʿr al-Andalusī,* trans. by Hussein Monès, Cairo, 2nd ed. 1956, p. 127.

[3] For the influence of García Gómez on Lorca's *Diván de Tamarit, cf. Federico García Lorca,* by Guillermo Díaz-Plaja, 2nd. ed., Buenos Aires, 1955, p. 171.

out, though he also indicates some instances of similarity between the poems of the *Diván* and those of the Hispano-Arab poets. In spite of this, the Arabist claims that whereas in Arabic poetry, thought is subservient to grammar, in Lorca the opposite is the case,[1] and he adds that Lorca's work "rather than being a literary extravaganza, is a homage payed to Arabic culture, written in Granada where the old Faculty of Letters and the recent School of Arabic Studies were aspiring to impress upon youth the fact that Arabic studies were not accidental or extraneous to Spanish civilization but rather an indispensable part of the cultural preparation of those who aspired to understand Spain's past."[2]

In his *Poemas arábigoandaluces* García Gómez included an introduction on the nature of Hispano-Arabic poetry which remains today one of the best essays of a general nature on the subject. There he speaks of the lack of attention paid to Hispano-Arabic poetry, he mentions the work on the period of *Taifas* written by

---

[1] *Cf.* García Gómez, *Nota al "Diván de Tamarit,"* in *Silla del Moro y Nuevas escenas andaluzas*, Madrid, 1948, pp. 139-140.

[2] *Op. cit.*, pp. 144-45. One concrete case in which Arabic poetry seems to have crept into the work of Lorca is that in which he re-elaborates a verse of Ibn Khafāja al-Andalusī (1058-1138) from an elegiac fragment written to mourn the loss of Valencia to Christendom. The Arabic verses are as follows:

١ عاثت بساحتك الظبى يا دار — ومحا محاسنك البلى والنار
٢ فاذا تردّد فى جنابك ناظر — طال آعتبار فيك وآستعبار
٣ ارض تقذفت الخطوب باهلها — وتمخضت بخر ابها الاقدار
٤ كتبت يد الحدثان فى عرصاتها — "لا انت انت ولا الديار ديار."

1. The gazelles have done mischief in your courtyard, O houses, and fire and decay have effaced your beauties.
2. Thus when an onlooker returns to your side, reflection and weeping over your [condition] are prolonged.
3. A land in which calamities tossed its people back and forth, and in which the vicissitudes of Fortune have brought forth its ruin.
4. The hand of Fortune's vicissitudes wrote on its courtyards: "*You are not you; nor are the houses, houses.*" (my translation). (*Cf.* A.R. Nykl, *Selections from Hispano-Arabic Poetry*, Beirut, 1949, pp. 153-154).

Compare to Lorca's famous lines from the *Romance sonámbulo*:

"Pero yo ya no soy yo,	"But I am no longer myself,
ni mi casa es ya mi casa."	Nor is my house my house."

Lorca may have read this in Valera's translation of Von Schack:

"Valencia, tú no eres tú,	"Valencia, you are not yourself
Y tus casas no son casas."	Nor are your houses houses."

Cf. Poesía y Arte de los árabes en España y Sicilia, trans. J. Valera, Madrid, 1930, vol. I, pp. 173-4.

Henri Pérès [1] though to point out its insufficiency. Adding that by his time the historians, theologians, jurists, mathematicians and mystics of al-Andalus were known, he claims that the particular period of the early thirties in which Spanish poetry was going through a total rebirth, was the appropriate moment to begin a study of Andalusian poetry. During his stay in Cairo, from 1928 to 1929 he had obtained from Aḥmad Zakī Pasha a small anthology of Andalusian lyrical fragments, the *Kitāb Rayāt al-Mubarrizīn wa Ġayāt al-Mumayyizīn* or "Book of the Banners of the Champions and of the Standards of the Chosen" composed by Ibn Saʿīd al-Maġribī and which formed the basis of his collection of translations. He later produced a critical edition of that work.

The interrelationship between García Gómez and the poetic milieu of his time is also apparent from the fact that Dámaso Alonso, the rehabilitator of Góngora, devoted a monograph to the comparison of Arabic to Gongorine poetry, after the publication by García Gómez of his critical edition of Ibn Saʿīd, which he entitled *Libro de las banderas de los campeones* (1942). In his study, Dámaso Alonso makes an excellent analysis of metaphor and its function both in Hispano-Arabic poetry, and in that of Góngora and he refers to García Gómez's translating technique in which he shows that the Arabist overcomes the difficulties of translating the lapidary images of Arabic poetry by reworking them into prose commentaries in Spanish. For example, where the the original Arabic reads: "She curves like a branch on a sand dune, and night appears over the clear dawn," García Gómez rearranges the translation to make it intelligible to Western readers, and produces the following:

> The branch of her figure curves on the sand dune of her hips and the night of her hair appears over the clear dawn of her face. [2]

The interest taken by Dámaso Alonso in Arabic poetry led him to conclude that it made use of "impure" metaphor in a similar way to that of Góngora, while it gradually attained a stage of development which permitted the use of "pure" metaphor and even symbolism, this especially in al-Andalus. For him Arabic poetry in al-Andalus, insofar as its use of metaphor is concerned, preserved the fundamental themes of the Arabic literary tradition while it also incurred in a kind of petrification so that it presented features of

---

[1] *La Poésie Andalouse en Arabe Classique au XIè siècle*, Paris, 1937.

[2] *Cf.* Dámaso Alonso, "Poesía arábigoandaluza y poesía gongorina," in *Estudios y ensayos gongorinos*, Madrid, 1955, pp. 45-46.

youth and age at the same time.[1] Dámaso Alonso adds words of praise for the recent publication of García Gómez's edition of Ibn Saʿīd, pointing out that his work in general had been of use to Arabists in many countries, as well as having awakened an interest in this poetry among Spanish readers.[2] The impact of this work on European Arabism is amply attested by the words of gratitude to García Gómez prefixed by Arberry to his English translation of Ibn Saʿīd, in which he states: "His edition, based upon a unique manuscript, is a monument to that wide scholarship and literary judgement which have characterized Professor Gómez's numerous contributions to Islamic studies, and the value of the publication is still further enhanced by an illuminating introduction and a careful and annotated translation. The magnitude of my debt to his initiative is too obvious to need further elaboration. If in not a few places I have differed from my colleague in my interpretation, and occasionally in my reading of the text, it will be appreciated by all familiar with the peculiar difficulties of Arabic poetry that the area of disagreement in understanding a particular phrase or allusion is often considerable, and I do not pretend that my alternative readings are necessarily superior to his." [3]

García Gómez's critical edition of a version of the Alexander legend entitled *Un texto árabe occidental de la leyenda de Alejandro* which served as his doctoral thesis, presents a complete and illuminating study of the Alexander cycle in Arabic literature, both in the pre-Islamic East, in the Koran, in *Ḥadīth* literature, and in Western sources. He discusses the possibility of the translation in Spain or Sicily of some Latin version of the pseudo-Callisthenes, into Arabic. A study of the manuscript and its linguistic peculiarities follows. The work was found in Aragón in the cache of Morisco books unearthed in Almonacid de la Sierra and its language departs considerably from classical Arabic since it is full of Hispano-Arabic colloquialisms. García Gómez compares this version with that in *Aljamiado* entitled *Recontamiento del rey Alixandre* [4] and concludes that the *Aljamiado*

---

[1] *Op. cit.*, p. 46.

[2] *Op. cit.*, pp. 64-65.

[3] A. J. Arberry, *Moorish Poetry, A Translation of The Pennants, An Anthology Compiled in* 1243 *by the Andalusian Ibn Saʿīd,* Cambridge, 1953, pp. ix-x.

[4] Edited by F. Guillén Robles, *Leyendas de José, hijo de Jacob, y de Alejandro Magno, sacadas de dos manuscritos moriscos de la Biblioteca Nacional de Madrid,* Saragossa, 1888.

version was an eclectic recension which brought together fragments of the Eastern version as seen in the Koran and the *Ḥadīth,* while most of its latter parts was derived from the Western version of the pseudo-Callisthenes cycle.[1] The important conclusion derived from this evidence is that Western Islam seemed to have possessed a literature in Arabic based on Western Latin sources.

Up till this time García Gómez had dealt almost exclusively with Hispano-Arabic poetry in the classical language, but the edition of Ibn Quzmān published by Nykl[2] encouraged him to broaden the scope of his studies to include popular poetry, so that in his article *Aben Guzmán, una voz en la calle*[3] he discusses Ibn Quzmān's "poesía callejera" pointing out its significance for philology, Arabism and other fields, but he insists particularly on Ibn Quzmān as a poet, and attempts to show what it is that makes his *azjāl* true poetry.

In 1941, he published a study on Mutanabbī'[4] in which he aired the question of the extent to which Hispano-Arabic poetry was really Arabic, outlining the various theories on the subject. According to Henri Pérès for example, Hispano-Arabic poetry, though saturated with allusions to the classical Arabic tradition of the East, reveals a sensibility which he claims to be purely Spanish. On the other hand, Lévi-Provençal considered this poetry to be a mere philological exercise artificially practiced by a people for whom classical Arabic was not a mother tongue, and which reminded him of the medieval Latin exercises based on Ovid, Catullus and Horace.[5]

Faced with these theories, García Gómez decides in favour of a middle course adding that the connection between Hispano-Arabic and Eastern poetry had hardly been studied. He states that in the abundant European bibliography on Mutanabbī' there were no Spanish studies on the subject, and he insists that this should be corrected, in part because Mutanabbī' is considered the greatest Arab poet, but also because the influence of his work on al-Andalus was very great.[6]

---

[1] *Alejandro,* p. cxii.

[2] *Cancionero de Aben Guzmán,* Madrid, 1933.

[3] *Cruz y Raya,* no. 3, Madrid, June 15, 1933, pp. 31-59.

[4] *Mutanebbī, el mayor poeta de los árabes,* reprinted in *Cinco poetas musulmanes,* pp. 15-52.

[5] E. Lévi-Provençal, *La civilization arabe en Espagne, Vue générale,* Cairo, 1938, pp. 87-88.

[6] Cf. "Mutanebbī," reprinted in *Cinco Poetas Musulmanes, biografías y estudios,* Austral, Madrid, 1945, pp. 15-16.

In 1942, García Gómez published an article on the Andalusian poet known as ash-Sharīf aṭ-Ṭalīq 'el Principe Amnistiado' [1] in which he speaks of the need to study the poetry of the period of the caliphate, which was and is little known. He attempts to reconstruct the *Dīwān* of the Umayyad poet, as a necessary step towards illuminating the precursors of the eleventh-century poetry studied by Henri Pérès. Only when this period is analysed will it be possible to understand the nature of early Peninsular Arabic poetry and thus determine the true significance of the *muwashshaḥāt.*

Later, in 1943, upon his reception by the Royal Academy of History, he prepared a comprehensive study of Ibn Zamrak,[2] in which he speaks of the amazing survival of Arabic poetry up to the last days of Granada in a period of duress for Peninsular Islam. In this decadent fourteenth-century atmosphere he situates the poet Ibn Zamrak, whom he studies carefully, and whose works he classifies as 1) *Qaṣīdas,* 2) Epigrammes and extemporaneous verse, 3) *Muwashshaḥāt.* According to García Gómez, Ibn Zamrak is the last great Hispano-Arabic poet, whose verses were made eternal by being engraved on the walls of the Alhambra.[3]

In 1944 he published the *Dīwān* of Abū Isḥāq of Elvira, along with a commentary, preliminary study, and translation.[4] A very thorough study of the Granadan ascetic and anti-Jewish polemicist, the *Dīwān* contains some outstanding poems among which the most lyrical is probably the third in the anthology.[5]

It has been stated that García Gómez is a man of letters. Thus in 1948 appeared a collection of essays entitled *Silla del moro y nuevas escenas andaluzas* [6] which shows him at his best as a creative writer. Most of them do not deal directly with Arabic erudition except insofar as it serves a literary purpose. They hark back to the tradition of Estébanez Calderón, and present a delightful and subjective picture of the Granada in which he worked and lived. As such they are deserving of a place of distinction in the history of the Spanish essay.

[1] In *Escorial,* no. 17, March, 1942, pp. 323-34. Also, *Cinco poetas musulmanes,* pp. 55-56.

[2] *Ibn Zamrak, el poeta de la Alhambra,* reprinted in *Cinco poetas musulmanes,* pp. 137-217.

[3] Since then, the *Dīwān* of a later poet, Yūsuf III of Granada has been published (Cairo, 1965).

[4] *Un alfaquí español, Abū Isḥāq de Elvira,* Madrid-Granada, 1944.

[5] *Op. cit.,* pp. 73-74.

[6] *Revista de Occidente,* Madrid, 1948.

During these years, García Gómez had collaborated with Lévi-Provençal, and in 1950 both scholars published au anonymous chronicle of the age of ʿAbd ar-Raḥmān III an-Nāṣir [1] which is extremely important, for though brief, it was written by a near contemporary and thus was reliable and shed much light on the political history of the period. It seems that contrary to usual custom, its author never mentions his sources, thus indicating that the narration is first-hand. Unlike most later Hispano-Arab chroniclers, he does not offer two or three accounts of the same event, and thus it would seem that this fragment was original and ancient, written either in the tenth or eleventh century.[2]

A passage of this chronicle is of interest in that it quotes the only known verses of Muqaddam of Cabra, the blind inventor of the *muwashshaḥāt.* While narrating the visit of the Caliph to Bobastro during the year 928-929, and the dishonourable exhumation of the body of the rebel Ibn Ḥafṣūn, the chronicler mentions that the crucifixion of Ibn Ḥafṣūn and his two sons in front of the palace of Cordova fulfilled the prediction made by the poet Muqaddam ibn Muʿāfā, some time before, when the rebel was in the height of his power, when the poet said in a panegyric of the Qā'id Aḥmad ibn Muḥammad ibn Abī ʿAbda who was fighting against Ibn Ḥafṣūn in Belda:

> I seem to see Ibn Ḥafṣūn nailed on a smooth beam between two props,
> While both his piglets are on either side of him in the street of ar-Raṣīf. [3]

The spirit of these verses would seem to indicate that the inventor of the *muwashshaḥāt* had little sympathy for the popular anti-Arab movements. If this is true, as only time and more texts will make clear, it would follow that the theory which supposes the *muwashshaḥāt* to have resulted from a feeling of sympathy for the

---

[1] *Una crónica anónima de ʿAbd al-Raḥmān III al-Nāṣir editada por primera vez y traducida, con introducción, notas e índices, por E. Lévi-Provençal y Emilio García Gómez,* Madrid-Granada, 1950.

[2] *Op. cit.,* p. 17.

[3] *Op. cit.,* pp. 150-151. The Arabic text (p. 77) is as follows:

كأنّي بابن حفصون وشيكاً   على جرداء بين دعامتين

وقد أضحى خنينيصاه منه   على متن الرّصيف بجانبين

native Peninsulars and their culture on the part of Arab folklorists "avant la lettre," may be in need of revision, for it is not clear why a poet who expresses anti-*Shuʿūbī* sentiments should be inspired by Mozarabic lyrical poetry.[1]

Though García Gómez collaborated with Lévi-Provençal in the editing of the abovementioned chronicle, his main work lies in the field of poetry. This specialization implies a conscious neglect of other areas of Hispano-Arabic studies, and yet, in the same year, 1950, he published his Spanish translation of Lévi-Provençal's masterly work on the history of Islam in al-Andalus up to the collapse of the Umayyad caliphate.[2]

The history of al-Andalus, though attempted as early as Conde, had never been satisfactorily written. The work of Codera, however, was to bear fruit in our own century when Lévi-Provençal made a careful collation of all known chronicles and monographs on the period, and produced a monumental work of great scholarly merit. It is to be greatly regretted that his death made it impossible for him to finish the task he began, so that his *History* only went as far as the fall of the caliphate of Cordova. It is also significant to note that the fruits of the carefully laid plans of Codera were reaped by a Frenchman,[3] since this indicates once again how the Arabic studies initiated in Spain penetrated the European cultural milieu and were expanded and developed in it. Without Codera's school, that of Lévi-Provençal would have been impossible.

García Gómez's prologue to the Spanish version of Lévi-Provençal's work expresses certain attitudes which indicate a change of emphasis towards the understanding of Andalusian culture. He stresses the total change undergone by the political and social structure of the Hispania of the Visigoths when it was conquered by the Arabs.[4] The surprise of this rapid conquest produced such a vast stupor, according to García Gómez, that the result was a total and multisecular silence on the part of the native population,

---

[1] For a development of this idea, cf. my monograph, "The Muwashshaḥāt," in *Collected Studies in Honour of Américo Castro's 80th Year*, Oxford, 1965, pp. 335-371.

[2] This volume was included as the fourth in the series entitled *Historia de España*, directed by Menéndez Pidal, under the title of *España musulmana hasta la caída del califato de Córdoba* (711-1031 *de J.C.*) Madrid, 1950.

[3] "The eminent professor of the Sorbonne is the true successor of the great Dozy, and the one who is gradually completing the projects envisioned by Codera." *Cf. op. cit.*, p. xi.

[4] *Cf. op. cit.*, p. ix.

so that we possess little reliable information about the Mozarabs, whose role in the history of al-Andalus he reduces to its just limits, following the lead of Lévi-Provençal. The actual fact that forty of their number were executed in Cordova between the years 850 and 859 in García Gómez's eyes does not imply a case of persecution, but rather one of restoring order on the part of Islamic law.

He concludes that Islam functioned in the Peninsula, as a factor of cultural inspiration and one to be combatted and rejected by the Christians in the North, and alludes to Américo Castro's book *España en su historia,*[1] which he welcomes as an example of the way in which Romanists were accepting the ideas of the Arabist school.[2]

In 1952 appeared García Gómez's Spanish translation of the *Dove's Neck Ring* by Ibn Ḥazm with its prologue by Ortega, (about which more will be said).[3] In his introductory study on Ibn Ḥazm, García Gómez indicates the importance of the *Ṭawq* in its relevance to the theories on the development of medieval European attitudes toward love. He invokes Ribera's ideas, stating that his theory had lost ground in its musical aspects, though it had gained much in matters of literature and prosody.[4] Since the *Ṭawq* had by then been translated into the major European languages, García Gómez indicates that the Arabists had fulfilled their duty, whereas the Romanists had in general received their ideas with suspicion and outright hostility. Among them the most important exception was Américo Castro who had compared the concept of love in the *Ṭawq* to that in the Archpriest of Hita's *Book of Good Love.* Américo Castro had claimed that the Archpriest must have read Ibn Ḥazm, to which García Gómez, who otherwise reacted favourably to his comparatist thesis, opposed the fact that the *Ṭawq* was not a popular work, but rather, one written in extremely difficult Arabic, and of a different spirit from that of the Archpriest. However, he agreed with Américo Castro that the *Book of Good Love* could not be understood without taking into account the tradition of Arabic literature. This debate inspired María Rosa Lida to revive the ideas

---

[1] Buenos Aires, 1948.

[2] *Cf. op. cit.*, p. xxxvi.

[3] *El collar de la paloma, tratado sobre el amor y los amantes de Ibn Ḥazm de Córdoba traducido del árabe por Emilio García Gómez con un prólogo de José Ortega y Gasset,* Madrid, 1952.

[4] *Op. cit.*, p. 47.

of Fernández y González on the influence of the *maqāmāt* on the *Book of Good Love.*

A brief study of Hispano-Arabic poetry entitled *Poesía arábigo-andaluza, breve síntesis histórica,* (Madrid, 1952) published by García Gómez, was the result of an inaugural lecture he delivered during the opening of the "Instituto Faruk I de Estudios Islámicos." The importance of this monograph resides in the fact that it is a reworking of the history of Hispano-Arabic poetry on a new basis, distinct from that of his *Poemas arábigoandaluces.* The discovery of the *kharjāt* and their significance made García Gómez change his focus to include popular Arabic poetry in the new study. He reviews the various theories on the social significance of Andalusian poetry, and reduces them to three: 1) Andalusian poetry is a mere importation from the Orient. 2) Andalusian poetry, because of the bilingual nature of al-Andalus, is merely a rhetorical exercise in a conventionalized literary language foreign in nature. 3) Andalusian poetry is a spontaneous production of the eternal Iberian, who accidentally expressed himself in Arabic.[1] The first is the opinion commonly held by Arabic scholarship, while the second is that of Lévi-Provençal and the third is the theory of Henri Pérès. Then he speaks of the inner strife of the Andalusian society (exemplified by the figure of Ibn Ḥafṣūn) which led to the creation of the caliphate under ʿAbd ar-Raḥmān III. For García Gómez, the fusion of the varied elements of society in ʿAbd ar-Raḥmān's age was reflected in literature by the invention of the *muwashshaḥa.*[2]

In 1952 there also appeared the first edition of the Arabic translation of García Gómez's *Poemas arábigoandaluces.*[3] This indicates the extent to which his work was penetrating the Arab world; a new aspect of Spanish Arabism hitherto unknown. The translator, Hussein Monès, director of the Egyptian Institute in Madrid, gives a full and even augmented version in Arabic of the prologue on Hispano-Arabic poetry, and speaks of the French and Italian translations which had previously appeared.

García Gómez's work as a translator has been important in having diffused in Spain some knowledge of contemporary Arabic literature, this factor constituting a new aspect of Spanish Arabism which was ceasing to deal exclusively with the Middle Ages and attempting

---

[1] *Poesía arábigoandaluza,* Madrid, 1952, p. 23.

[2] *Cf. op. cit.,* pp. 35-36.

[3] Entitled *Ash-Shiʿr al-Andalusī,* trans. by Hussein Monès, Cairo, 1952.

to discuss the Arabic intellectual currents of our times. In 1954 he published his translation of Ṭaha Ḥusayn's work *Al-Ayyām* "The Days" [1] and in his prologue he insists that it is a work which the Spanish public should read. Indeed, Ṭaha Ḥusayn's book, which recounts the attempts of one man to renew the university system of a country stagnating in an outworn tradition was particularly well received in modern Spain where the universities were closely controlled by the government. This translation was followed in 1955 by that of Tawfīq al-Ḥakīm's *Diario de un fiscal rural.*[2] The diffusion of contemporary Arabic literature indicates a new phase in Spanish Arabism. Thus in a prologue written to Pedro Martínez Montávez's anthology entitled *Poesía árabe contemporánea.*[3] García Gómez says that in this respect Spanish Arabism has evolved from the erudite work of Codera to a more living study of a contemporary and neighbouring civilization. This was brought about, in his opinion, by the closer contact between Spain and the Middle East initiated by his pioneering experience as a student in Cairo, followed by that of others of a younger generation such as Martínez Montávez.[4]

Added to these translations there appeared in 1957 the Spanish translation of Lévi-Provençal's companion volume to the history of the Umayyad caliphate of Cordova, this time dealing with cultural phenomena, political institutions and social life.[5] However, the most important of García Gómez's studies, and at any rate the most sensational for the polemics they have aroused, are those connected with the origin of the *muwashshahāṭ.*

Already at an early date he had published a study which sought to identify the inventor of these strophic poems.[6] The various discrepancies in the spelling of the name of this inventor according to the different sources led García Gómez to reduce the variant readings to that of Muqaddam Ibn Muʿāfā al-Qabrī.[7]

---

[1] *Los días,* Valencia, 1954.

[2] Madrid, 1955.

[3] Madrid, 1958.

[4] Martínez Montávez, *Poesía árabe contemporánea,* Madrid, 1958, pp. 17-18.

[5] Published in *Historia de España,* directed by R. Menéndez Pidal, vol. 5, *España musulmana hasta la caída del califato de Córdoba* (711-1031 *de J.C.*), *Instituciones y vida social e intelectual,* by E. Lévi-Provençal, trans. by E. García Gómez, and with a supplement; *Arte califal,* by Leopoldo Torres Balbás, Madrid, 1957.

[6] N. de la R., in *And.,* 2, 1934.

[7] *Op. cit.,* pp. 221-22.

Then in 1948, S.M. Stern published his sensational article which revolutionized the generally held conception of early Romance lyrical poetry, and in which he discussed certain Hebrew *muwashshaḥāt* which contained *kharjāt* or 'envois' in Romance. Stern explained that the problem of the origin of strophic poetry in al-Andalus was a mystery. According to M. Hartmann, who first wrote the history of the *muwashshaḥāt,* these poems had developed from certain metrical forms of Eastern Arabic poetry such as the *musammaṭ* which seems to have appeared in the ninth century, and which was employed by Abū Nuwās.[1] This form was commonly used later by Hispano-Hebraic poets at the end of the tenth century, which seems to indicate the relative importance of the *musammaṭ* in al-Andalus.

Then Ribera had claimed that the *muwashshaḥāt* were imitations of popular strophic poems in Peninsular Romance. For Stern, the truth lies between these two contradictory extremes, for he believes that the *musammaṭ,* in preparing the way for the invention of a strophic poetry, made it easier for the Arab poets to adopt the Romance poems, of which there are no extant examples.[2] Stern published his collection of *kharjāt* in Romance, and at once the gauntlet cast in England was picked up by the Spanish Hebraists and Arabists. In 1949 Francisco Cantera published an article in which he made some corrections to Stern's transcriptions and translations.[3] In the same year García Gómez reproduced the essentials of Cantera's study in an article of his own,[4] and finally in 1952 he published a collection of twenty-four *kharjāt* in Romance taken from Arabic *muwashshaḥāt.*[5] Invoking the theory of Ribera based on a similarity of rhyme schemes between *muwashshaḥa* poetry, the *azjāl* and medieval Spanish lyrics, García Gómez adds that the difficulty in proving the relationship resided in the fact that early *muwashshaḥāt* with *kharjāt* in Romance such as were described by Ibn Bassām had not turned up. Menéndez y Pelayo

[1] M. Hartmann, *Das Arabische Strophengedichte,* I, *Das Muwaššaḥ,* Weimar 1897.

[2] S. M. Stern, "Les vers finaux en Espagnol dans les muwaššaḥs hispano-hébraiques," in *And.,* 13 (1948), pp. 299-346.

[3] Fco. Cantera, "Versos españoles en las muwaššaḥas hispano-hebreas," *Sefarad,* 9 (1949), pp. 197-234.

[4] García Gómez, "Más sobre las 'Jarŷas' romances en 'Muwaššaḥas' hebreas," *And.,* 14 (1949), pp. 409-417.

[5] García Gómez, "Veinticuatro Jarŷas romances en muwaššaḥas árabes (Ms. G. S. Colin)," *And.,* 17 (1952), pp. 57-127.

had attempted, though without success, to read a Romance *kharja* in a Hebrew poem, but it was not until the publication of Stern's collection that any headway was made in the matter. Dámaso Alonso had picked up this work by Stern and indicated that it profoundly altered our ideas about popular lyrical poetry in Europe,[1] and Menéndez Pidal entered the fray to show the connexion between these *kharjāt* and Galician poetry.[2] From the French Arabist G. S. Colin, García Gómez was able to procure a collection of Romance *kharjāt* taken from Arabic *muwashshaḥāt,* thus adding volume to the corpus already published by Stern. In 1954 he published several new *kharjāt* adding a re-interpretation of the translations made by Stern along with a few corrections.[3] During the course of the same year he published other *kharjāt* in *Al-Andalus* and began to compare their prosodic structure to that of popular Spanish poetry, finding in both, rhyme schemes and syllabic combinations of a similar nature.[4]

In 1951, he wrote an article in which he discussed the possibilities for the existence of a type of Andalusian popular poetry which according to his hypothesis, could have developed in colloquial Arabic as a result of Romance influences.[5] This was followed in 1956 by a complete study of the problem which attempted to review and interpret the new data recently uncovered,[6] and in

[1] Dámaso Alonso, "Cancioncillas de 'amigo' mozárabes (Primavera temprana de la lírica europea)," in *RFE,* 33, 1949, pp. 297-349.

[2] R. Menéndez Pidal, "Cantos románicos andalusíes, continuadores de una lírica latina vulgar," in *BRAE,* 31, 1951, pp. 187-270.

[3] García Gómez, "La muwaššaḥa de Ibn Baqí de Córdoba, *Mā laday/ Ṣabrun muʿīnu,* con jarŷa romance," *And.,* 19, 1954, p. 44.

[4] Compare the *kharja*:

K'adamay filiolo alieno	For I loved a strange lad
ed él a mibe	And he loved me
Keredlo de mi vetare	There would take him from me
su al-raqibe.	His guardian.

to the famous lyric used by Lope de Vega:

Que de noche le mataron	For at night they killed him,
al caballero	The gentleman,
la gala de Medina	The gala of Medina
La flor de Olmedo	The flower of Olmedo.

Cf. García Gómez, "Dos nuevas jarŷas romances (XXV y XXVI) en muwaššaḥas árabes (MS G.S. Colin), y adición al estudio de otra jarŷa romance (*supra,* pp. 43-52), in *And.,* 19, 1954, pp. 390-391.

[5] García Gómez, "Sobre un tercer tipo de poesía arábigoandaluza," in *Estudios dedicados a Menéndez Pidal,* 2, 1951, pp. 397-408.

[6] García Gómez, "La lírica hispanoárabe y la aparición de la lírica ro-

which he claims great progress made in Ribera's theory on poetry, which by concentrating exclusively on the *zajal* had fallen into some errors. However, Ribera's intuition of a Romance lyrical poetry prior to the *zajal* was confirmed by the brief fragments preserved in the recently discovered *kharjāt*. García Gómez states that many adversaries of Ribera, following the theory of Hartmann claimed that Persian or Arabic models such as the *dubayt* or the *musammaṭ* could have originated the strophic peculiarities of the *muwashshaḥa* and the *zajal*.[1] The importance of the Romance *kharjāt* leads him to ask: 1) whether they represent a Romance lyrical poetry prior to the *muwashshaḥāt*, 2) if they are examples of an early European lyrical poetry, what then is their relationship to that poetry. He quotes a text by Tīfāshī (thirteenth cent.) according to which, "in ancient times the songs of the people of al-Andalus were either in the style of the Christians or in the style of the Arab camel drivers,"[2] and he argues that the vast programme of integration of the various racial clements of al-Andalus undertaken during the reign of ʿAbd ar-Raḥmān III had created a climate favourable to the imitation of Mozarabic poetry by Arab poets. Thus for García Gómez, the *muwashshaḥa* is the work of folklorists "avant la lettre", the Arab aristocrats who were sensitive to popular poetry. García Gómez's theory attempts to integrate those of Ribera and Hartmann, for he admits the possibility that the strophic structure of the *muwashshaḥa* may have derived from the *musammaṭ*, particularly from a poem by Abū Nuwās which constitutes a sort of Eastern "pre-*muwashshaḥa*,"[3] while the native Andalusian part of the poem is to be found only in the *kharja*, all of which limits Ribera's theory to the *kharja* while it also gives validity to his intuition of the prior existence of a Romance lyrical poetry.[4]

Apart from this, García Gómez continues to study this particular

---

mánica," *And.*, 21 (1956), pp. 303; also in *Convegno di scienze morali, storiche e filologiche*, 1956, pp. 294-321; French translation in *Arabica*, 1958, pp. 113-143.

[1] *Op. cit.*, *Arabica*, 1958, p. 116.

[2] *Op. cit.*, p. 119.

[3] García Gómez, "Una pre-muwaššaḥa atribuída a Abū Nuwās," *And.*, 21, 1956, pp. 406-414.

[4] For further information on the problem and a complete resumé of everything written on the *kharjāt* since 1948, along with texts, commentaries and bibliography, the reader may consult Klaus Heger, *Die bisher veröffentlichten Ḫarǧas und ihre Deutungen*, Tübingen 1960, *Beihefte zur Zeitschrift für Romanische Philologie*, 101 Heft.

problem, and in 1961 he attempted to decipher yet another *kharja*.[1] He has also begun a study of the *Dār aṭ-Ṭirāz*, an important collection of Andalusian *muwashshaḥāt*, as well as another on problems of prosody in Hispano-Arabic strophic poetry in its relation to the Romance metrical system,[2] in which he concludes that the law of the Italian Romanist Mussafia (which stated that Portuguese lyrical poetry is based 1) on a strict norm of syllabic count 2) the present-day rule of Spanish prosody according to which a final accented syllable is equal to two syllables, does not apply 3) lines of an equal number of syllables end indistinctly in words with final or penultimate accent) applies both to Old Portuguese and to Hispano-Arabic poetry.

In his study of the *Dār aṭ-Ṭirāz* [3] García Gómez has attempted a complete translation of that famous treatise on the *muwashshaḥāt* which will be invaluable to Romanists who do not know Arabic.

Thus we see in García Gómez a scholar who has continued in the footsteps of Asín and Ribera, whose theory of imitation he has elaborated while making particularly valuable studies on Hispano-Arabic poetry. His literary sensibility has added a now touch to Arabic studies in Spain, so that he has been described by a historian of literature in the following words: "García Gómez—taking into account the different nuances that exist in all parallels—is to Asín what Dámaso Alonso is to Ménendez Pidal. García Gómez, like Dámaso, Gerardo Diego and Aleixandre is a member of the Royal Spanish Academy. This is a significant mid-century sign: the doors in the house of learning are open to a group of true poets. The sensitive essays of the Arabist of *La silla del moro—nuevas escenas andaluzas*—(1948) prove once again how much expressive poetry there is even in the prose of the distinguished professor." [4]

At the same time it must be stated that García Gómez's theories on the *muwashshaḥāt*, their origin and devolopment, cannot yet be conclusively proven, since the poems we possess are relatively late

---

[1] García Gómez, "A propósito del libro de K. Heger sobre las jarŷas. *Descifre de la jarŷa de Schirmann*," *And.*, 26, 1961, pp. 453-465.

[2] García Gómez, "La 'ley de Mussafia' se aplica a la poesía estrófica arábigoandaluza," *And.*, 27, 1962, pp. 1-20.

[3] García Cómez, "Estudio del 'Dār aṭ-Ṭirāz,' " *And.*, 27, 1962, pp. 21-104. For the original text *cf*; Ibn Sanā' al-Mulk, *Dar aṭ-Ṭirāz fī 'Amal al-Muwashshaḥāt*, critical ed. by Jawdat ar-Rikābī, Damascus, 1949.

[4] Ángel Valbuena Prat, *Historia de la literatura española*, 6th ed., vol. 3, Barcelona, 1960, pp. 784-786.

compositions from a period when the genre had reached a state of fixation. What the nature of the early *muwashshaḥāt* was, is difficult to ascertain, though we may conclude from Ibn Bassām's description that they definitely did not possess internal rhyme, and consequently were far simpler in their structure, probably resembling the *musammaṭ* rather closely. What the role of the Romance *kharja* was, and its literary and cultural significance, is also difficult to tell, and we will undoubtedly know more about the whole problem when the poetry of the caliphate, which preceded the appearance of the *muwashshaḥa*, has been more fully explored. However, the Spanish school of Arabists, following in the footsteps of Ribera, was right in indicating the peculiar nature of these poems, and in exploring their background. Hartmann, with less intuition, had studied the fully evolved *muwashshaḥāt* without taking into account the nature of the early compositions of that genre. García Gómez, in studying the problem of the *kharjāt* may well be on the way to presenting us with a more complete picture of their origin, significance, and development.[1]

[1] His latest work has been a critical edition of the Arabic *muwashshaḥāt* with *kharjāt* in Romance, accompanied by elegant Spanish translations of the poems: *Las jarchas romances de la serie árabe en su marco* (Madrid, 1965).

CHAPTER NINE

It would be impossible to give an adequate account of Arabic studies in Spain in recent years, because of the large number of scholars in this field who, following the advice of Codera are constantly publishing a number of specialized works on various limited topics. However, since an account of Spanish Arabism would be incomplete if it did not include mention of contemporary scholars, this chapter will sketch some general indications about the principal figures working in Arabism today, even though in doing so it risks leaving out many names worthy of inclusion in the present work. The brief accounts which follow are intended to serve as a guide to further reading, and are by no means to be considered definitive judgements.

Along with González Palencia and García Gómez, one of the more important disciples of Ribera and Asín is Maximiliano Alarcón, the translator of *La lámpara de los príncipes* by Abū Bakr aṭ-Ṭurṭushī, and who, in the work entitled *Documentos árabes diplomáticos del Archivo de la Corona de Aragón,* edited and completed the documentary material left by Gaspar Remiro, (an Aragonese Arabist, disciple of Codera) upon his death.

In his translation of aṭ-Ṭurṭushī [1] Alarcón mentions the interest taken by Menéndez y Pelayo in Arabic studies, and states that the great Spanish scholar had felt that the classical and Christian tradition were not enough to carry out the historical synthesis of Spanish thought. He had proclaimed the urgent need to translate Hebrew and Arabic books in order to present a more balanced picture of medieval Spain. In response to this plea, Alarcón published his translation which constituted one more in the series that had gradually been appearing.[2] This particular work is extremely pertinent to Spanish studies insofar as it is an Arabic forerunner of medieval and Golden Age Spanish books on political theory and princely education. Thus Alfonso X in his *Código de las siete partidas,* Guevara in the *Relox de príncipes* and Quevedo in the *Política de Dios y gobierno de Cristo* present political ideas and

[1] Abū Bakr al-Tortosí, *Lámpara de los príncipes,* trans. by Maximiliano Alarcón, Madrid, 1930-31, 2 vols.

[2] *Op. cit.,* vol. I, p. xi-xii.

theories on the education of royalty which are already outlined by aṭ-Ṭurṭushī. The main point of the Arabic work revolves around the idea of divinely revealed law, a notion fundamental to Islam, and the consequence of which is that the sovereign must pattern his life after a religious model—a concept which also predominates in Spanish books such as that of Quevedo. Though the translator Alarcón does not affirm the possibility of contact and conscious imitation on the part of Christian Spain, it is a worthy subject for some future study.

According to Alarcón, the *Lampara de los príncipes* expresses the typically Islamic solution to problems of political theory which are envisioned from an essentially religious viewpoint. In this aspect, Islam is clearly distinct from other religious communities, for the institution of the Islamic head of state partakes of the twofold character of political and religious leadership. The caliph must therefore be concerned for the spiritual as well as the material interests of his subjects.

In this sense, aṭ-Ṭurṭushī views the legal systems of other nations, and finds that they are divided into ethical maxims and political principles. The first were adopted conventionally without being based upon divine revelation. As for the second, being man-made, he considers them admirable but imperfect. These two currents, united in Islam and given a religious significance by divine authority lead him to claim the superiority of Islam over other civilizations, so that he concludes that though the legal systems of non-Islamic peoples had achieved admirable results,

> But though the ass should dress in silk, people say: 'O, what a donkey!' [1]

The work also contains numerous anecdotes and stories designed to admonish royalty and teach it how to govern in accordance with the principles of Islam, and the familiar and even personal tone of admonishment is often reminiscent of the style of Guevara's letters. One such anecdote, related by aṭ-Ṭurṭushī, is that of a dialogue between a Spanish Christian anchorite and al-Mustaʿīn Ibn Ḥūd in which the king proudly displays his wealth and worldly power to the Christian who in turn warns him that death will bring about the loss of all his material possessions, and adds:

---

[1] *Op. cit., vol. cit.,* pp. 5-6.

> And do you become proud of possessing a thing which you must abandon tomorrow? He who becomes proud over something he must lose, it is as if he had become proud over what he has seen in his dreams.[1]

Another Arabist of significance is Jaime Oliver Asín, nephew of the patriarch of Spanish Arabism, who has done work in linguistics and has published a book entitled *El nombre "Madrid"* which was awarded the "Premio Franco de Letras" in 1952 and which is an attempt to explain the etymology of the name of Spain's capital. According to Oliver Asín, Madrid went through several historical periods which he classifies as pre-Muslim, Muslim, medieval Christian and modern. Its early name seems to have been the Latin form *matrīce* 'a riverbed'. During the Arabic period the new owners created a system of underground channels for irrigation which allowed the town's population to expand. Since the population was bilingual, the Mozarabs pronounced the Latin name *maṭrīch* or *maṭrīj* (مَطْرِيج), while the Arabs who were aware of its meaning. translated the word into the Arabic form *majrā* 'stream, riverbed.' To both these forms was added the pre-Roman suffix *-īt* which indicated population groups. Thus from *maṭrīj* the Mozarabs derived *maṭr-īṭ*, and from *majrā* the Arabs formed *majr-īṭ*, while both forms seem to have coexisted and were used after the *Reconquista*, respectively by Mozarabs and Mudéjares.[2] For Oliver Asín, the history of Madrid is linked closely to that of its *majrā* or Arabic system of water supply by means of underground channels such as may be found in Naysabūr, Marw, Sadrata or Marrakesh.[3] His book has several maps of Madrid and its underground water-courses.

There have been few Spanish scholars who possess both a knowledge of Arabic and of mathematics. Saavedra was one, and in our own century José Sánchez Pérez has done distinguished work on the Muslim sciences in the Middle Ages. In 1916 he published an Arabic text on algebra entitled *Compendio de álgebra de Abenbéder* accompanied by a translation and a study of the treatise. This work was followed by *Biografías de matemáticos árabes que florecieron en*

---

[1] *Op. cit., vol. cit.*, pp. 69-70.
[2] *Cf.* J. Oliver Asín, *Historia del nombre "Madrid,"* Madrid, 1959, p. 208.
[3] *Op. cit.*, pp. 212-213.

España published in 1921. In 1954 he wrote an important survey entitled *La ciencia árabe en la edad media.*

The prologue to his *Compendio* discusses the history of mathematics in Spain. Rey Pastor, the expert on the subject, had studied sixteenth and seventeeth-century mathematics and had stated that in the Middle Ages Spain had been the leading nation of Europe in scientific research. However, he had said that the glory of that scientific flowering belonged not to Spain, but to the Arabs. To this Sánchez Pérez replied by the familiar process of Hispanizing Andalusian culture and thus claiming for Spain the glory of Arab science, for he argued, following the ideas launched by Simonet and elaborated by Ribera, that the Arab mathematicians of al-Andalus from the eighth to the fifteenth centuries were biologically "Spaniards."[1]

In order to explain the importance of his work on mathematics, he invokes the words of Menéndez y Pelayo who had spoken of the need to study Spanish mathematics before the fifteenth century[2] as well as the role played by José Echegaray who had introduced infinitesimal calculus and mathematical physics into Spain in order to raise it to a level with the rest of Europe. Echegaray had recognized the importance of Hispano-Arabic mathematics, but he also refused to include them within the general framework of Spanish science. However, according to Sánchez Pérez, the fifteenth century brought about a lessening of the Arab influence on Spain, and the expulsion of the Moors from Granada brought about the almost complete disappearance of mathematical studies in Spain in the following centuries, a fact which would seem to contradict his idea that the Andalusians cultivated mathematics because they were Spaniards.[3]

Sánchez Pérez had the merit of bringing to light the names and works of almost unknown Andalusian mathematicians and scientists. *La ciencia árabe en la edad media*[4] is a broad survey of the advances made by the Andalusians in the fields of mathematics (arithmetic, algebra, geometry), astronomy, physics, chemistry, natural history and medicine. He includes in his book much bio-

---

[1] *Cf.* José Sánchez Pérez, *Compendio de álgebra de Abenbéder*, Madrid, 1916, pp. xi-xii.

[2] Menéndez y Pelayo, *Ciencia española*, vol. I, Madrid, 1888. p. 85.

[3] *Cf.* Sánchez Pérez, *op. cit*, p. 7.

[4] Madrid, 1954.

graphical material on the individual scientists (often taken from Codera's *Bibliotheca*), and reviews the state of knowledge in each particular science before the Arabs cultivated it, in order to show their contributions. He tells us that he was able to do this thanks to the help and encouragement of his friends Codera, Ribera and Asín who beginning in 1902 put their libraries at his disposal. He also took copious notes from the manuscripts in the Escorial so that as a result, fifty years later he was able to produce a work of solid erudition and undoubted merit.[1]

A series of books on Hispano-Arabic art have been written by the architect Leopoldo Torres Balbás who has clarified the nature of the arts and city planning in the metropolitan centres of al-Andalus.

Torres Balbás has followed in the footsteps of Manuel Gómez Moreno, the art historian who together with Asín and Menéndez Pidal were successful in renovating Spanish university activities and raising standards to new levels of achievement. Gómez Moreno had made a careful study of Hispano-Arab art and its influence on Christian Spain. His disciple was destined to broaden this field of research.

An appendix to the Spanish translation of Lévi-Provençal's history of the caliphate contains an extensive study by Torres Balbás entitled *Arte hispanomusulmán hasta la caída del califato de Córdoba* [2] in which he first discusses the relationship of the art of the caliphate to that of the Romans and Visigoths. In his opinion, the Visigoths did not root themselves in the Peninsula, and the small country churches they left behind them were of little consequence in the elaboration of Andalusian architecture.[3] In contrast to the poverty and crudeness of Visigothic art, a new and exceptional building arose in Cordova during the second half of the eighth century: the Mosque built by ʿAbd ar-Raḥmān I,

---

[1] Sánchez Pérez has written other important works such as: *Biografía de Chéber Benáflah*, Madrid, 1911; *Partición de herencias entre los musulmanes del rito malequí*, Madrid, 1914; *La agricultura de Abū Zacaría*, in *Catecismos Calpe* 70-79; *Alfonso X el Sabio*, in *Colección Aguilar*; *Las matemáticas en la Biblioteca de El Escorial*, Madrid, 1929; *El libro de las cruces que mandó traducir del árabe Alfonso el Sabio*, Brussels, 1930; *La aritmética en Babilonia y Egipto*, Madrid, 1943; *La aritmética en Grecia*, Madrid, 1947; *La aritmética en Roma, India y Arabia*, Madrid, 1949; *Cuentos árabes populares*, Madrid, 1952.

[2] In *Historia de España* directed by Menéndez Pidal, vol. 5, Madrid, 1957, pp. 331-788.

[3] *Cf. op. cit.*, p. 333.

which though it made use of Roman columns and building material from previous monuments, was inspired by a radically different concept in art. There is in the art of the caliphate, according to Torres Balbás a vague reminiscense of that of Rome which appears in a certain preoccupation with the external harmony of buildings and the abundance of classical motifs in decoration, though these are organized according to totally new aesthetic principles.[1] Thus the inside of the Mosque of Cordova surprises the Western observer because of the unusual disposition of its interior. Its forest of columns with their polichromed arches creates a sense of mystery and infinity which must have been more striking before the nineteen arches facing the courtyard were walled up by the Christians, cutting out the light.[2]

The art of the eleventh century is characterized by an intensification of decorative motifs, though much of the work of this period has been lost, so that it is hard to reconstruct. This period is, however, linked to that of the Almoravids and the Almohads, to whom Torres Ballbás devoted a monograph [3] in which he showed the innovations of the age, and especially their impact on North Africa. The Almohads, possessing little artistic tradition, as was the case of their predecessors the Almoravids, stressed an ascetic attitude towards life, since their goal was to restore the original purity of Islam. This was influential in art for it led them to reduce the ornamentation of the interiors to fundamental lines drawn upon bare backgrounds; a tendency which contrasts greatly with the exhuberance of ornamentation found in Almoravid mosques.[4] The political unity of al-Andalus and North Africa under the Berber empire led, furthermore, to the expansion of Andalusian architecture beyond the Straits of Gibraltar. This occurred because the Almoravids and Almohads who were Berber nomads, had no artistic tradition comparable to that of the caliphate of Cordova, so that al-Andalus though conquered, spread its artistic norms throughout the Maġrib.[5]

---

[1] *Op. cit.*, pp. 334-335.

[2] *Cf.* Torres Balbás, *La mezquita de Córdoba y Madīnat al-Zahrā'*, Madrid, 1952, p. 22.

[3] Torres Balbás, *Artes almorávide y almohade*, Madrid, 1955.

[4] *Op. cit.*, p. 9.

[5] "The art we incorrectly call Almoravid, as well as the Almohad, are imported Andalusian arts in Barbary; the result of the art of the *Mulūk aṭ-Ṭawā'if,* with a few Oriental additions."

This art left a mark on that of Christian Spain as far north as Castile where the Cistercian monastery of Las Huelgas in Burgos, capital of the kingdom, possesses a small chapel constructed in the Almohad style. Likewise the ex-synagogue now called Santa María la Blanca in Toledo follows similar artistic canons.[1]

Much of the value of Torres Balbás' work resides in the fact that he is not only a master of his field from a technical viewpoint, but also sensitive to its artistic beauty. Thus he explains that Islamic art is essentially abstract for it does not attempt to portray nature or life, and tends to organize its elements with geometric regularity,[2] as well as using leaf designs and a profusion of calligraphy in a long process of development which stretches from the time of the Mosque of Cordova to that of the Alhambra, to which he devoted a special book.[3] He explains therein that most of the buildings of the Casa Real were constructed during the fourteenth century and can be dated by means of their inscriptions and historical references.[4] According to Torres Balbás, the Naṣrid buildings contrast with previous architecture because of their fragility. Constructed out of the most perishable materials, they substitute plaster decorations for the marble and alabaster found in Madīnat az-Zahrā'. Their profuse ornamentation is enhanced by a subtle association of architecture with landscaped gardens and running water so that the whole complex loses in external harmony what it gains in a proliferation of hidden nooks in which light and shade alternate in such a way as to create a series of ever changing and unexpected though fragmentary impressions which vary during the different hours of the day.[5]

In 1926 Torres Balbás had published an article entitled *Paseos por la Alhambra: La Rauda* [6] in which he discussed his discoveries in the royal cemetery of the Naṣrid dynasty which he excavated. Apart from the plans of the cemetery, the photographs of some of its tombstones with accompanying translations of their inscrip-

---

[1] *Op. cit.*, p. 22.

[2] *Op. cit.*, p. 24.

[3] Torres Balbás, *La Alhambra y el Generalife*, Madrid, no date.

[4] *Op. cit.*, p. 47.

[5] In this sense the gradual development of architecture along a path of increasing fragmentation is paralleled by that followed by Hispano-Arabic poetry which in the *muwashshahāt* attains a technique which may well be described as *pointilliste*.

[6] In *Archivo español de arte y arqueología*, No. 6, 1926.

tions, taken from Lafuente y Alcántara, the work may be of interest in determining a linguistic problem, for the author mentions a special type of tombstone which is called *maqabriyya* in Morocco.[1] The *maqabriyyāt* are long prismatic stelae which are placed horizontally on the tombstones in the same direction as the body. From the same root as this Arabic word are derived *qabr* "tomb" and *maqbara* "cemetery." It appears that even today Muslim cemeteries in Andalucia are called *almacabras* and the tombstones *macabrillas*.[2] This is strong evidence that the adjective *macabre* so often associated with the *danse macabre* may derive from the Arabic root mentioned above, so that *danse macabre* would mean "the dance of the graveyards," thus affording another example of the Arabic words which entered medieval Europe through Spain.

An important work by Torres Balbás was his contribution to the volume entitled *Resumen histórico del urbanismo en España*,[3] in which he studies medieval city planning in Northern Spain and al-Andalus. The presence of two different civilizations in the Peninsula led to two types of cities entirely distinct one from the other. The Andalusian cities were in a sense a modification of the ancient Roman sites which developed with little break in continuity, whereas the Christian towns of León and Old Castile were founded at the end of the eleventh century and especially during the twelfth and thirteenth, and began as small villages.

Beginning in the ninth century we have records of the enormous size of Cordova which came to be the most important and heavily populated city in the west of the European continent, and a rival to Constantinople, Damascus and Baghdad. Islamic authors point out in contrast the poverty of the primitive towns of Christian Spain which lived by means of a backward economy, and constituting what we would now call an "underdeveloped" area. In al-Andalus, the city population was districted according to religion (there were *arbāḍ* or 'suburbs' for Mozarabs and Jews), tribal divisions, or even according to the occupation of the inhabitants.[4] This tendency to social exclusivism was to be seen in the way cities were planned. Whereas Roman urban centres had streets running

---

[1] *Cf. Paseos*, pp. 14-15.

[2] *Cf.* Lévi-Provençal, *Inscriptions Arabes d'Espagne*, Leiden, 1931.

[3] Co-authored by Torres Balbás, Cervera, Chueca and Bidagor, Madrid, 1954. Part I, entitled *La edad media* is by Torres Balbás.

[4] *Op. cit.*, p. 12.

parallel to one another and intersecting at right angles after a regular pattern of rectangular blocks, Andalusian cities had a few main thoroughfares which advanced in an irregular and meandering fashion. From these streets others branched out in all directions and ended up in numerous blind alleys and mazes [1] so that authentic ghettos were created in which neighbourhoods did not communicate with one another.[2]

An Arabist who has specialized in problems of epigraphy and chronology is Manuel Ocaña Jiménez who has published works such as *Tablas de conversión de datas islámicas a cristianas y viceversa.* Work on this subject had been done by Codera [3] and others, but the perfection of Ocaña's tables for converting Islamic dates is of inestimable value in matters of chronology, since he gives us the means whereby to determine not only the year and month in which an event occurred, but even the day. In his book, the author includes a study of the Muslim calendar, its origin, development, its divisions of time, feast-days and the names of the Zodiacal signs. He also explains that in al-Andalus Muslim chroniclers often indicated the day of the week in which an event took place, consigning it along with the month which was often expressed both in Muslim and Christian terms.[4] This happened because both the Christian and Muslim calendars had coexisted, due to the fact that the Mozarabs had maintained their calendar which was adopted by Muslim farmers as being closer to the solar year according to which they had to plan the tilling of their fields. This practical calendar coexisted with the religious calendar of Islam which, being lunar, presented constant discrepancies with regard to the solar year. Consequently the twofold dates expressed in Arabic chronicles are not the result of calculations done by scholars, but rather they reveal the two systems of reckoning time which were known to the inhabitants of al-Andalus. The Christian year, however, was never

---

[1] *Op. cit.*, pp. 16-17.

[2] The work of Torres Balbás has been continued and perfected by Henri Terrasse in his *Islam* d'*Espagne, une rencontre de l'Orient et de l'Occident,* Paris, 1958. In it that author is primarily interested in art and archaeology.

[3] *Tabla de la correspondencia entre la hégira y el calendario europeo juliano y gregoriano, indicando el primer día del calendario de la hégira.* Cf. Codera, *Tratado de numismática arábigo-española,* appendix 12, Madrid, 1879, pp. 283-293.

[4] E.g., "The day of Wednesday two nights past the moon of Muḥarram —the twenty-fifth day of the month—of the year 361," in *Tablas de conversión,* Madrid-Granada, 1946, p. 33.

mentioned, since it was of interest only for the religious festivals of the Mozarabs.[1]

The study of Islamic philosophy and theology in al-Andalus, initiated by Asín, is today in the hands of figures such as Manuel Alonso Alonso, Darío Cabanelas and Miguel Cruz Hernández.

Alonso, a Jesuit, has written on the works of John of Seville and has published a book on the Latin version of the treatise by al-Fārābī entitled *De Scientiis* and translated by Domenicus Gundisalvus. He is also working on the translation of the Logic in the *Maqāṣid* of Ġazālī. In his study of the *De Scientiis* Alonso was able to establish that it was based on al-Fārābī's work entitled *Maqāla fī Iḥsā' al-'Ulūm* though it is in part an adaptation with many supressions, transpositions, and additions taken from Latin sources and which cannot be entirely explained from within the tradition of Arabic scholarship.[2] He claims that the deviations from the Arabic text found in the work of Gundisalvus are to be attributed to Latin sources.

In a volume of collected studies from his pen,[3] Alonso explains that the time is not yet ripe to write a general survey of the medieval translators who attempted to enrich Europe with Arabic scholarly advances. However, in the same work he studies at length the books written by Ibn Dāwūd (= Juan Hispano) and Gundisalvus, and attributes a number of Latin translations to the former.

Darío Cabanelas Rodríguez, a Franciscan who was made Professor of Arabic at the University of Granada wrote his doctoral thesis on *Juan de Segovia y el problema islámico* [4] and also completed a still unpublished study on Ġazālī.[5] He is presently engaged in analysing the prolegomena to the philosophy of Averroes according to ms. 632 of the Escorial. In his work on Juan de Segovia, Cabanelas has had the merit of bringing to light the personality of one of the most interesting of those medieval polemicists against Islam who felt that the ultimate conversion of the Muslims to

---

[1] *Op. cit.*, p. 34.

[2] *Cf.* Domingo Gundisalvo, *De Scientiis, texto latino establecido por el P. Manuel Alonso Alonso S. J.*, Madrid-Granada, 1954, p. 7.

[3] Alonso, *Temas filosóficos medievales* (*Ibn Dāwūd y Gundisalvo*), in *Publicaciones anejas a 'Miscelánea Comillas,' serie Filosófica*, vol. 10, Santander, 1959.

[4] Madrid, 1952.

[5] *Cf.* Fco. Cantera Burgos, "*Los estudios orientales en la España actual,*" in *Oriente Moderno*, 1955, p. 239.

Christianity should be based on persuasion rather than violent means. It would seem that Juan de Segovia preached the meeting of Islamic and Christian religious leaders in order to *discuss* the relative merits of each religion, a method based on an excessive confidence in scholastic rationalism on the part of Segovia—a defect common in his age—and yet it is a plan which amazes us by its modernity and its attempt to soften the excesses of the Reconquista.[1]

In order to apply his method, Juan de Segovia considered it essential first to know the dogmas of Islam, and he spared no effort in his attempt to learn Arabic, so that he was finally able to translate the Koran in a trilingual version—the earliest translation of that book on record in Europe. In studying Juan de Segovia, the British scholar R. W. Southern has relied heavily on the work by Cabanelas, and has given the following account of the medieval translator:

> With regard to this new method of persuasion, he made one far-sighted observation: the conference (he said) would have served a useful purpose even if it did not achieve the end for which it was proposed—that is to say, the conversion of the Moslems. In his rather longwinded way, he listed thirty advantages which might be expected even if it failed in its main object. Now this again was quite a new conception. The traditional view was that discussion with the infidel could only be justified by conversion. But John of Segovia saw many partial and practical advantages, apart from this desirable end: he saw the conference as an instrument with a political as well as a strictly religious function, and with words which will strike a chord in modern breasts he exclaimed that even if it were to last ten years it would be less expensive and less damaging than war. [2]

From this it would appear, as García Gómez pointed out in his prologue to Cabanela's book, that just as Arab science and culture had passed into Europe, there was a brief moment in Spain before the establishment of the Inquisition when a *faqīh* of the mosque of Segovia, *muftī* of Islam and "the most famous of all the Muslims living in the kingdom of Castile" gave his assistance to Juan de Segovia, an important theologian from Salamanca, bishop and ex-cardinal, in order to create a better understanding between the two antagonic religions.[3]

---

[1] *Juan de Segovia y el problema islámico,* Madrid, 1952, pp. 260-61.

[2] R. W. Southern, *Western Views of Islam in the Middle Ages,* Cambridge, Mass., 1962, pp. 91-2.

[3] *Op. cit.,* p. xii.

Miguel Cruz Hernández, professor at the University of Salamanca, has written the most complete survey of Hispano-Arabic philosophy.[1] His book received the Premio Bonilla San Martín, and is invaluable for those who wish to study the development of philosophy in al-Andalus. His work owes a great debt to Asín, and is enriched by the consultation of numerous unpublished manuscripts and recent studies on the subject.

Cruz Hernández speaks in the prologue to his book, of the work done by Asín in outlining the philosophical currents of al-Andalus, and adds that he felt the time was ripe to compose a complete survey on the subject. Having already studied Eastern Islamic philosophy, and especially the works of Avicenna, he presents a survey of it in the first part of his book, in order to show the roots from which Andalusian philosophy had sprung.

In his *Introduction,* the author sums up the Islamic doctrines about God and the creation, and explains how these ideas affected Arab thought so profoundly, that they found expression in the arts. He claims that from the orthodox Islamic viewpoint only God partakes of essence, and that everything changes except "His face" as Avicenna had said. Thus the Islamic philosopher never was able to separate the created world from God, since the world needed the constant recreation of God to maintain itself. At the same time, since the orthodox Muslim could not fuse the creation with its Creator since this pantheism would be incompatible with the Koranic doctrine, he had to leave the world of things in a state of constant flux; receiving continual being from the divine essence. As it was expressed in art, Cruz Hernández explains that this developed a process of de-personalization in which geometric forms triumphed in the creation of the arabesque. In architecture, the lack of a central axis as in the case of the Mosque of Cordova creates a sense of eternal movement and decentralization.[2]

Elías Terés Sádaba, professor of Arabic literature has worked on a study entitled *La Poesia arábigoandaluza anterior al siglo XI* which will be most illuminating when it appears. He is also directing the re-edition of volumes 6 and 7 of Codera's *Bibliotheca Arábico-Hispana.* He made a significant contribution to the publication of *La 'Materia*

---

[1] Miguel Cruz Hernández, *Filosofía hispano-musulmana,* 2 vols., Madrid, 1957.

[2] *Op. cit.,* pp. 27-28. Recently, Cruz Hernández has published a history of Arab philosophy entitled *La filosofía árabe,* Madrid, 1963.

Medica' de Dioscórides, transmisión medieval y renacentista[1] particularly in the publication of the second volume of this work[2] in which he published the Arabic text of the *Materia Medica.* The Greek text of Dioscorides was translated into Arabic by the Byzantine scholar Stephen son of Basilius (Istifan ibn Basīl) and revised by Ḥunayn ibn Isḥāq the famous translator of Greek works who taught medicine in Baghdad and acted as physician to the ʿAbbāsid Caliph al-Mutawakkil (A.D. 847-861).

Elías Terés' main field, however, is literature, and he has written numerous articles in *Al-Andalus* on this subject. One of these entitled "Préstamos poéticos en al-Andalus" is a study in which he clarifies the Eastern origin of several themes common to Hispano-Arabic poets. This permits him to conclude that in al-Andalus Eastern poetry gravitated with all the weight of its themes: the allusions to the desert; the Arabian, Syrian or ʿIraqī toponymy; the attribution of qualities and virtues common to the ancient Bedouins, the stylization of feminine beauty and the images corresponding to each part of her body; the circumstances, characters and situations which are depicted in reference to love and lovers. All these themes are incessantly repeated in Andalusian poetry up to Ibn Zamraq the last great poet of Granada.[3] This conclusion is important, for it is also true of the *muwashshaḥāt,* and indicates how unsatisfactory are the theories which attempt to relate these strophic forms to Romance lyrical poetry insofar as themes are concerned.[4]

Elías Terés contributed an appendix to Pareja's two volume work on Islamology.[5] In it he deals with Hispano-Arabic literature and though it is no more than a brief survey, it attempts an analysis of social and historical conditions insofar as they left an impact on literary creation. Thus he claims that the popularization of the *muwashshaḥāt* during the Almoravid period was brought about by the ignorance of the Berber lords who were unresponsive to poetry. Because of this, the poets who in the age of Taifas had played to

[1] Published by César E. Dubler and Elías Terés, Tetuán-Barcelona, 1952-1957.

[2] vol. 2, *La versión árabe de la 'Materia Medica' de Dioscórides (texto, variantes e índices).*

[3] *Cf.* Préstamos poéticos," in *And.,* 21, 1956, pp. 415-416.

[4] For a discussion, cf. my monograph "The muwashshaḥāt."

[5] Felix M. Pareja, Alessandro Bausani, Ludwig won Hertling and Elías Terés Sádaba, *Islamología,* vol. 2, Madrid, 1952-1954, pp. 979-908.

a select and refined courtly audience had to resign themselves to write for the masses, and cultivated the strophic forms which were more appealing to the latter.[1]

Among the group of Augustinians working in the Escorial José López Ortiz distinguished himself for his research on Islamic law and wrote important articles on the rite of Mālik which predominated in al-Andalus. After being named bishop of Tuy his work in Arabic studies seems to have been discontinued. It is based largely on Ribera's edition of al-Khushānī's history of the judges of Cordova.

In 1929 he wrote an article entitled *El clero musulmán* [2] in which he discusses the introduction of the Mālikite legal practices into al-Andalus and outlines the history of the *fuqahā'* or "jurists" in Peninsular Islam. The founder of the school, Mālik ibn Anās had been accused by the 'Abbāsid caliphs of Baghdad of having favoured the partisans of 'Alī, and his punishment brought about his praise for the rival Umayyad dynasty of Cordova. This favoured the adoption of the Mālikite rite in al-Andalus, where one of the first functions it attributed to itself was that of maintaining orthodoxness of belief. This led to many instances of inquisitory practices and trials, some of which are related by aṭ-Turṭushī in the *Lámpara de los príncipes*. The *fuqahā'* pardoned no man, be he high-born or low, so that Yaḥya ibn Yaḥya the founder of Spanish Mālikism actually attacked and severely reprimanded the emir al-Ḥakam for what he considered to be his dissolute practices. Supported by the Umayyads, the *fuqahā'* exercised a spiritual dictatorship over the nation during the Almoravid period because they supported the latter against the Kings of Taifas by means of legal decisions or *fatwas* invalidating the rule of the native Andalusian monarchs and transferring the power to Yūsuf ibn Tashufīn. During the Almohad period their prestige declined considerably.

In 1931 López Ortiz published a study entitled *Figuras de jurisconsultos hispano-musulmanes*: *Yaḥya ben Yaḥya* [3] in which he studied the personality and work of the leader of the Mālikite *fuqahā'* in the Umayyad period, showing how he adhered to the policies of Hishām, then fought against al-Ḥakam and came to terms with 'Abd ar-Raḥmān II. A leader of conspiracies and

[1] *Op. cit.*, vol. 2, p. 993.
[2] *Cf. Religión y Cultura*, 6, 1929, pp. 198-207.
[3] *Cf. Religión y Cultura*, 16 (1931), pp. 94-104.

repeatedly pardoned, he knew how to place his own men in the qāḍīship in order to gain control over the nation, and was able to establish the authority of the Mālikite rite in al-Andalus.

In 1941, continuing his studies on Islamic law, López Ortiz wrote a lengthy article entitled *Fatwas granadinas de los siglos XIV y XV*[1] in which he studies the legal opinions or *fatwas* emitted at the end of the fourteenth century and beginning of the fifteenth in Granada. At this time the theoretical superiority of Islam over Christianity was no longer a reality. Granada was on the defensive, over-populated, and heavily taxed by Castile. As a result, Islamic law, which had been created during the period of expansion was no longer viable, and so the *fatwas* by means of a subtle casuistry, attempt to adapt legal theory to the reality of the moment.[2]

Another member of the Augustinian group which worked in the Escorial was Melchor Antuña who was killed in the Civil War. Antuña was the author of important historical studies such as *La corte literaria de Alháquem II de Córdoba, Jura en el califato de Córdoba, Sevilla y sus monumentos árabes,* and a number of post-humous studies published recently in *Cuadernos de historia de España.*[3] He also prepared an edition of part of the *Muqtabis* by the Cordovan historian Ibn Ḥayyān. In this work, Antuña gives an account of Ibn Ḥayyān and his importance for the study of Andalusian Islam. Ibn Ḥayyān's main work as a historian was the *Kitāb al-Muqtabis fī Tā'rīkh Rijāl al-Andalus* 'The Book of the Seeker on the History of the Men of al-Andalus' which is divided into ten volumes and covers the history of the period from the Arab conquest in 711 up to the author's age. Unfortunately, only a small portion of this voluminous work has come down to us. However, the third volume in the series was preserved in the Bodleyan Library at Oxford, and Antuña was its first editor.[4]

---

[1] *And.*, 6 (1941), pp. 73-127.

[2] Thus Wansharīshī says: "If the ancient jurists have not foreseen cases such as this one, it is because the vicinity of the infidel was not, in the early days of Islam, the same as today. These Christian provinces have not begun to appear until the fifth century of the Hijra, when the accursed Christians—may God destroy them !—overpowered Sicily and certain cities of al-Andalus." (*Op. cit.*, p. 90).

[3] Published by "Instituto de Historia de la Cultura Española, Medieval y Moderna" of the University of Buenos Aires.

[4] *Cf.* Ibn Ḥaiyān, *Al-Muktabis, tome troisième*: *Chronique du règne du calife Umaiyade ʿAbd Allāh à Cordoue,* ed. Melchor M. Antuña, Paris, 1936, p. ix.

Basing himself on Dozy and Ribera, Antuña indicates that the Arab chroniclers followed the custom of interspersing Romance words in their writings from which he concludes that they must have known Latin or Romance, so that it may be supposed that they were able to make use of the short Christian chronicles of the period as well as to include information gathered orally. This tendency he finds to be true of Ibn Ḥayyān.

The Jesuit Felix M. Pareja has done most of his research outside Spain. He was professor of Islamology at the Pontifical Gregorian University, formerly professor of Arabic at St. Xavier's college in Bombay and presently director of the "Instituto Hispano-Árabe de Cultura" in Madrid. Pareja is a good example of the broadening of scope initiated in the field of Spanish Arabism by Ribera and Asín, for in his book *Islamología* [1] first published in Italian, and later in Spanish (now in English) he no longer stresses Arabic studies but extends them to the vast field implied by the title of his work. For Pareja, the Islamologist, unlike the Arabist, does not limit his field to the study of Arabic culture and language but broadens his horizon to include the life of those peoples who inhabit the wide belt stretching from the Atlantic to the Gobi desert and the islands of the Pacific, and who have adopted Islam as their religious creed. Therefore the Islamologist needs to have a knowledge of modern Western languages such as English, German, French, Italian, Dutch, Spanish and Russian and of the great languages of Islam: Arabic, Persian, Turkish, Urdu in order to consult scholarly publications and to work directly with source materials.[2] It is interesting to note that though Pareja includes an extensive study of the geography of the Islamic countries, he does not adhere to the idea of geographical determinism in history. The historian and sociologist Alfred Weber had much earlier attempted to explain the Arab expansion as the result of lack of water in the Arabian Peninsula [3] an idea which Pareja rejects by stating that Arabia is an excellent example of the way in which geographical premises are not enough to explain the course of history. He argues that it is amazing that in such a poor and barren area so powerful

[1] Felix M. Pareja, *Islamología*, 2 vols. Madrid, 1952-54.

[2] *Cf.* Pareja, *op. cit.*, vol. I, pp. 2-3.

[3] "It is possible that the Arabs' expansionist movement, related as it is to the founding of Muḥammad's religion, may also have been partly determined by the drying process undergone by Arabia." *Cf.* Alfred Weber, *Historia de la cultura*, Spanish trans. by Luis Recasens Siches, Mexico, 1941, p. 217.

a civilization should have had its beginnings. For Pareja, this sudden movement cannot be explained by geography. He also avoids referring to al-Andalus as "Spain" as so many Spanish Arabists had done in the nineteenth century, and in this sense he stresses the cultural Arabization of the Peninsula,[1] over the biological and racial factor, a new tendency which had derived from the work of Asín and the general milieu of the generation of 1898.

A historian of note was Isidro de las Cagigas, born in 1891 in Carmona (province of Seville), and who studied at the University of Granada under the direction of the archaeologist Manuel Gómez Moreno and the Arabists Eguilaz and Mariano Gaspar Remiro. In 1916 he entered the diplomatic service, and because of his specialization in Islamic studies he was chosen to serve for many years in the Moroccan posts of Oujda, Alcazarquivir and Tetuan.

Through the "Instituto de Estudios Africanos" which prints books on Islamic topics, he published many of his works, of which the most noteworthy are those included in the series entitled *Minorías étnico-religiosas de la edad media española*, of which he completed *Los mozárabes* [2] and *Los mudéjares* [3] and promised before his death titles such as *Los moriscos, Los judios, Los conversos*. The importance of his work on the Mozarabs cannot be denied since it brings up to date the study of Simonet while it also presents a less biased picture of the Mozarabs. Isidro de las Cagigas has incorporated into his study many of the recent ideas and discoveries related to Hispano-Arabic erudition, thus composing a book of merit in which he includes an important bibliography. He claims that the Mozarabs and *Mawlas* at first possessed a degree of culture superior to that of their conquerors and preserved their Romance dialect, though they gradually learned Arabic and wrote works of distinction in that language. Opposed to the traditional ideas about the formation of Spain's national consciousness, he claims that the battle of Covadonga was not the declaration of independence

---

[1] "Then the hunt for the Umayyads began. The Abbasids resorted to every means to finish them off, and very few managed to escape alive. One of these, ʿAbd ar-Raḥmān, fled to al-Andalus (as the Arab chroniclers call the Iberian Peninsula) and there he founded the dynasty of the Andalusī Umayyads." *Op. cit.*, pp. 106-107.

[2] 2 vols., Madrid, 1947-1948.

[3] 2 vols., Madrid, 1948-1949.

against Islam, for the efforts of Pelayo were only the expression of the feelings of a small aristocratic minority hidden in the mountains. According to Isidro de las Cagigas, the true movement for independence was not manifested until the ninth century with the revolts of the Mozarabs and the *Shuʿūbite* movement.[1] However, in this statement the author does not take into account the Islamic character of the *Shuʿūbite* movement. Had the independence been won by the *Mawlas,* Spain might have become an Islamic country like Persia instead of the Christian country it became as a result of the *Reconquista.*

We have already referred to the intermediary religions which arose out of the religious diversity of al-Andalus. To the late incident of the *libros plumbeos* of Granada, Cagigas adds the figure of Ibn Marwān of the Algarve, a man of arms as well as an able politician who took advantage of religious strife to strengthen his position. He taught his followers a new faith half Muslim and half Christian though it maintained an anti-trinitarian outlook. It was designed to bring together the motley elements under his command in his war against the central authority of the emirs of Cordova.[2] Cagigas' study of Ibn Ḥafṣūn is opposed to that of Simonet and those who considered him a secret Christian, for he argues that in the height of his power, Ibn Ḥafṣūn attempted to fortify his position against the Umayyads not by seeking the support of the Christian monarchs or the semi-Muslim and semi-Christian Banū Qaṣī of Aragón, but rather by making an alliance with the most orthodox of Muslim dynasties; that of the ʿAbbāsids of Baghdad. This reveals the extent to which the Andalusian *Shuʿūbite* movement was seeking social equality within Islam rather than attempting to overthrow the religion itself, in the name of Christianity.[3]

As for the Mozarabs, the delicate balance they maintained with the Muslims led to a gradual cultural assimilation in everything but religion, so that when the armies of Catalans and Castilians entered Cordova for a brief time before the fall of the caliphate (1031), they were received with decided uneasiness by the Mozarabs who feared that the presence of the northern Christians might

[1] "Good logic teaches us, furthermore, that freedom is not sought by those who are free to wander over crags and mountains, but rather by those who are forced bo coexist with foreign elements that have overpowered their country." *Cf. op. cit.,* vol. I, p. 143.

[2] *Cf. op. cit.,* vol. I, p. 166.

[3] *Cf. op. cit.,* vol. I, p. 246.

upset their own delicate relationship with their Muslim neighbours and masters. This idea contradicts the beliefs of Simonet who had claimed that the Christian armies had freed the oppressed Church in Cordova, and had been received with great joy by the Mozarabs. According to Isidro de las Cagigas, this was not the case.[1]

In his book entitled *Los mudéjares* he speaks of the lack of documentation on the Granadan period, and rejects the Romantic tradition which had painted a rosy picture of the Naṣrid dynasty. Proceeding with a greater caution derived from the ideas of Codera, he studies historical problems from a sociological and ethnic point of view. His work possesses the value of avoiding simple formulae to explain social phenomena. He enables us to see the gradual development of Spanish attitudes towards Islam in the Middle Ages so that from century to century one may observe old religious feelings give way to new ones. As a result, Islam in al-Andalus is viewed as a continuous process of change rather than a static and monolithic culture.

The ethnographic and sociological viewpoint of Isidro de las Cagigas' books led him to publish a study on the origin of *seseo* in modern Andalucia. Traditional studies, such as those initiated by Menéndez Pidal, Tomás Navarro Tomás and others have viewed this phenomenon as the result of the repopulation of the south by northern settlers after the *Reconquista*. Thus the Andalusian *s* extends throughout the valley of the Guadalquivir and appears in the nucleus formed by the triangle enclosed by Seville, Cádiz and Málaga.[2]

Taking exception against the theory that this *s* was the result of repopulation by northern settlers, he makes a careful exposition of the North African migrations into al-Andalus, and shows that the region of the predorsal *s* is exactly the same as that occupied most densely by the Berber tribes, and calls upon competent Berberists to study the problem of a possible Berber substratum in order to explain the peculiarities of the Andalusian *s*.

Fortunately his ethnographic study is well substantiated since the tendency of Arab authors to indicate the genealogy of kings and commoners alike made it possible to map the ethnic chart of al-Andalus.

---

[1] *Cf. op. cit.*, vol. 2, pp. 404-405.

[2] *Cf.* Isidro de las Cagigas, *Andalucía musulmana, aportaciones a la delimitación de la frontera del Andalus* (*Ensayo de etnografía andaluza medieval*) Madrid, 1950, p. 11.

This interesting hypothesis, which has so far not been considered seriously, deserves more studied attention on the part of competent specialists, while his ethnic chart is of great value in the study of tribal settlements in al-Andalus.

José María Millás Vallicrosa is another of Asín's disciples who forms part of the group of Orientalists who conduct research on the history of Arab science at the University of Barcelona. He is well known internationally for his work in Hebraic and Arabic studies, and his first important book on the latter was *Estudios sobre Azarquiel.*[1] The work was originally handed to Asín for publication in 1934 but the Civil War held up its appearance. Its publication was recommenced in 1943, and then during the summer of the following year, the publishing house caught fire and was burned to the ground, so that he lost all his material.[2] With Carlyle-like fortitude the author rewrote his book which finally appeared in 1949. In it he stresses the importance of the Muslim astronomer Azarquiel whose work was decisive in the development of medieval European astronomy, and he includes abundant bibliographical material as well as many of Azarquiel's tables and some of his works. In attempting to place Azarquiel within the tradition of astronomical studies, he says that his *Almanach* was directly related to that of the Egyptian Aumatius, an Arabic deformation of the name Ammonius. Ammonius was the son of Hermias, the last director of the School of Alexandria, and this links the medieval astronomical tradition to that of Hellenism.[3]

In 1954 Millás Vallicrosa published a lecture on Arabic agriculture in al-Andalus in which he studied its nature and influence on Spanish agriculture.[4] In it he points out that this science is the culmination of a long tradition within the Arab world which was carried from Persia to the Atlantic. Added to this, in al-Andalus, Arab agriculturalists also made use of Latin treatises in the composition of their works, so that to the Eastern tradition was added that of Rome.[5] This agricultural science survived so long in the Peninsula that it made a significant contribution to Spanish

---

[1] Madrid-Granada, 1943-1950.

[2] *Cf. op. cit.*, p. xi.

[3] *Cf. op. cit.*, pp. 235-237.

[4] Millás Vallicrosa, *La ciencia geopónica entre los autores hispanoárabes; conferencia pronunciada el día* 5 *de marzo de* 1953 *en el Club Edafos*, Madrid, 1954.

[5] Arabic authors often cite *Yulius*, that is, Julius Moderatus Columella.

agriculture at the beginning of the Renaissance. The principal authors in al-Andalus who wrote on the subject were Ibn al-ʿAwwām, Ibn Wāfid and Ibn Baṣṣāl, whose works were probably translated into Spanish by order of Alfonso X during the thirteenth century, since fragments of them have survived. During the Renaissance, Cardinal Jiménez de Cisneros encouraged Alonso de Herrera to write a book on agriculture, and so Herrera travelled through the orchards of levantine Spain. In his book he makes frequent references to an Arabic author identified by Millás Vallicrosa as Ibn Wāfid, and Herrera's book has passages identical to those of the medieval text by Ibn Wāfid.

Soon after, Millás Vallicrosa and García Gómez discovered a manuscript of the agricultural work by Ibn Baṣṣāl in the possession of Muḥammad Azimān, and the professor from Barcelona decided to translate and study it. It appeared in 1955 under the title of *Libro de agricultura* (*Kitāb al-Filāḥa*) [1] in its Arabic original and accompanied by a Spanish translation. Ibn Baṣṣāl's work had been translated at the end of the thirteenth century and existed in a manuscript in the National Library of Madrid.[2] The discovery of the Arabic original added a few chapters missing in the medieval Spanish version, and indicated the extent to which Muslim agriculture had helped to shape that of Christian Spain. It proved to be one more work in the long series translated from Arabic during the Middle Ages.

Among the group of Arabists working on scientific problems in Barcelona, mention should be made of Juan Vernet Ginés, named Professor of Arabic at the University. His work in this field has been praised by specialists in astronomy, marine cartography, etc.

In a lecture delivered in Alcazarquivir on Arabic astronomy [3] he reviews the knowledge attained by the Arabs in that science and stresses its impact on the West. According to him, Arabic astronomy began in Baghdad in A.D. 771 when a learned Hindu named Manká visited that city and gave lectures to the astronomers of the caliph al-Manṣūr. According to Birūnī,[4] Manká knew no Arabic and so the lectures were delivered through an interpreter. From Manká the Arabs learned of the work of the great Hindu

---

[1] Tetuán, 1955.
[2] *Cf. op. cit.*, p. 19.
[3] J. Vernet, *Astronomía árabe clásica*, Alcazarquivir, 1947.
[4] Author of *Kitāb al-Hind* "The Book of India."

astronomers Siddanta and Aryabhata, and from India they adopted the use of the astrolabe. Later the caliph Ma'mūn (d. 833) founded two observatories and had his astronomers measure the circumference of the earth, which measurements reached Columbus in a modified version, so that the discoveror was led to believe that the earth was smaller than its true dimensions.[1]

Baṭṭānī, the Albetenius of the Latins, studied the movement of the sun and his work permitted Azarquiel in the West to state that the stars moved in non-circular orbits. This step made possible Kepler's first law.

Vernet asks himself whether Muslim science was original, and indeed, whether the Semitic spirit is capable of originality. This idea which had been denied by Menéndez y Pelayo is answered affirmatively by Vernet who shows us that not only was Greek science unoriginal, but that it borrowed heavily from the mathematical and astronomical texts of the Babilonians, who were Semites like the Arabs. According to Vernet thousands of scientific cuneiform texts are extant from the second millenium B.C. in which problems are solved according to so-called "Euclidian" geometry. The Greeks who took this ancient science, spread it from India to Europe and the Muslims gathered it up and developed it. The knowledge accumulated by the Islamic world permitted Europe to begin its period of invention and discovery which has lasted to our own day.[2]

Vernet has written a number of articles which have appeared in *Al-Andalus, Sefarad, Tamuda* and other journals.[3] Among them we may single out his monograph entitled "Ambiente cultural de la Tortosa del siglo XII" [4] in which he indicates the strong scientific current in Tortosa, and the struggle between reason and faith which took place in twelfth-century Islam, and which after the triumph of orthodoxy brought about the disintegration of Arab science. However, the scientific tradition of Tortosa lasted until it was conquered by the Christians in the middle of the twelfth century. At the end of the same, Sem Tob ben Isaac (1196-1267) appeared and translated into Hebrew much of this science which soon found its way into Europe, for the thirteenth century marked a new

[1] *Cf. op. cit.*, pp. 2-3.
[2] *Op. cit.*, p. 6.
[3] *Cf. Bibliography.*
[4] In *Tamuda*, 5, (1957), pp. 330-339.

cultural period: that of the Christian Renaissance of the Middle Ages.

Vernet published an edition of Ibn Saʿīd al-Maġribī's *Geography* [1] and in the same year appeared a study entitled *España en la geografía de Ibn Saʿīd al-Maġribī* [2] in which he clarifies the originality of that author's geographical observations, and argues that he avoided falling into the error of servile copying from Idrīsī.

Recently Vernet has published the first history of Arabic literature in Spanish, which extends from pre-Islamic poetry to the present, devotes full attention to Hispano-Arabic literature, and provides an excellent, up to date bibliography. It is hoped that it will be translated into other European and Eastern languages in the near future.[3]

The historian Ambrosio Huici Miranda has devoted a fruitful scholarly life to the study of the *Reconquista* and the Almohad empire, thus continuing the work of Lévi-Provençal which stops short at the fall of the caliphate of Cordova. He began his career by publishing a collection of Latin chronicles of the *Reconquista* [4] in which he stated that his purpose was to study gradually all the Latin sources of that period. In 1916 he published a book entitled *Colección diplomática de Jaime I el Conquistador, años* 1217 *a* 1253 [5] based on 446 documents of which about half had never before been published. That same year appeared *Estudio sobre la campaña de las Navas de Tolosa,*[6] a careful critical study of the famous battle based on a thorough collation of Christian and Muslim chronicles, of which relevant sections are included in a useful appendix to the book. In evaluating his sources he says that the Christian versions incur in the defect of narrating all sorts of miracles which allegedly occurred during the battle and to which the Christian chroniclers, most of whom were eye-witnesses on the scene of action, attributed their success.[7] In contrast, the Muslim authors recorded fewer details of the battle, and since they were not able to attribute their defeat to heaven, they all invent human causes for their downfall.

---

[1] *Kitāb Basṭ al-Arḍ fī ṭ-Ṭūl wa l-ʿArḍ,* Tetuán, 1958.

[2] *Tamuda,* 6 (1958), pp. 307-326.

[3] *Literature árabe,* Barcelona, 1968.

[4] *Las crónicas latinas de la Reconquista; Estudios prácticos de latín medieval,* 2 vols., Valencia, 1913.

[5] Valencia, 1916.

[6] Valencia, 1916.

[7] *Cf. op. cit.,* pp. 108-109.

These causes contradict one another to such an extent that they nullify the weight of their argument.[1]

Huici Miranda has undertaken the task of publishing Spanish translations of the more important Arabic chronicles for the use of historians. Thus in 1952 he published a translation of the anonymous chronicle written by an Andalusian and entitled *Al-Ḥulāl al-Mawshiyya,* which deals with the Almoravid, Almohad and Marīnid dynasties, that is to say, precisely the period not included in the work of Lévi-Provençal.

The author of *Al-Ḥulāl* lived during the age of Muḥammed V of Granada and finished his chronicle in 783/1381-2. In it a valuable compilation of non-extant works may be found along with numerous episodes and legends of a fantastic and dubious character. The work is an exposition of the main events of the Almoravid empire as well as the beginning of that of the Almohads up to ʿAbd al-Muʾmin, after which it sums up the deeds of the remaining Almohad caliphs and lists the Marīnid sultans up to Abū Tashufīn ʿAbd ar-Raḥmān ibn ʿUmar (783/1381). The first European historian to consult this chronicle was Conde who consulted a Spanish translation of the same which he inserted between chapter 9 and 58 of the third part of his *Historia.*[2] The accuracy of the Spanish translation consulted by Conde freed this part of his work from the errors to be found in other chapters.

The second chronicle translated by Huici Miranda was the *Bayān al-Muġrib* by Ibn ʿIdhārī al-Marrakushī [3] the complete title of which means "The Surprising Exposition of the Resumés of Traditions About the Kings of al-Andalus and the Maġrib." The *Bayān* is an Almohad chronicle which includes many important passages from lost sources and constitutes the most trustworthy and complete Arab chronicle for the twelfth and thirteenth centuries in Western Islam, At the same time that it gives valuable accounts of the caliphs it is, however, not very selective in that the author includes many panegyrical passages which he accepts at their face value without showing much evidence of a critical approach.[4]

---

[1] *Op. cit.*, p. 109.

[2] *Cf.* A. Huici Miranda, *Al-Ḥulāl al-Mawshiyya, crónica árabe de las dinastias almorávide, almohade y Benimerín* (*traducción española*), Tetuán, 1951, pp. 11-12. This work forms vol. I of *Colección de crónicas árabes de la Reconquista.*

[3] *Cf. Colección de crónicas árabes de la Reconquista,* vols. 2, 3, *Al-Bayān al-Muġrib fī Ijtisār Ajbār Mulūk al-Andalus wa al-Maġrib,* Tetuán, 1953, 1955.

[4] *Cf. op. cit.,* p. xi.

Finally Huici Miranda closed his series of translations with the *Kitāb al-Mu'jib* "The Book of What is Amazing in the Resumée of Traditions of the Maġrib" by 'Abd al-Wāḥid al-Marrakushī.[1] In the introduction to this work, Huici Miranda states that Dozy had exaggerated its value whereas Lévi-Provençal had deprecated it. However, 'Abd al-Wāḥid's chronicle was the first on the Almohads to be published in Europe, and was particularly influential on nineteenth-century historiography. New sources, however, have since detracted from its value, for it has been found that its author includes too many hyperbolic statements destined to place the Almohad rulers—especially Ibn Tūmart—in a favourable light.[2]

In 1956, Huici Miranda published a work on the main battles of the Reconquista [3] in which he studies the events of the period from 1080 to 1492 in which the African invasions slowed down the impetus of the Christian advance to Granada. Taking up the old idea introduced by Conde, the author stresses the necessity to view the events of this period from both sides; Muslim and Christian, in order to arrive at the truth. He studies the four decisive battles in which the Almoravid emir Yūsuf ibn Tashufīn, the Almohad caliphs Ya' qūb al-Manṣūr and his son Muḥammad an-Nāṣir, and the Marīnid sultan Abū l-Ḥasan 'Alī met the three Castilian Alfonsos (VI, VIII and XI), and by a careful collation of sources he had managed to sift out fact from phantasy.[4]

In the same year appeared Huici Miranda's most complete and masterly work, entitled *Historia política del imperio almohade*.[5] The history of Western Islam has not been written in its complete form so far. Neither Dozy's work on al-Andalus, nor that of Lévi-Provençal are definitive. As for North Africa, the best general work is that of André Julien.[6] However the complete history of North Africa cannot be adequately written without a large numer of prior monographs on particular problems. For this reason, Huici Miranda studied the Almohad empire and wrote a history which presents in

---

[1] *Colección*, vol. 4, *Kitāb al-Mu'ŷib fī Taljīs Ajbār al-Maġrib*, Tetuán, 1955.

[2] *Cf. op. cit.*, p. xxiii.

[3] Huici Miranda, *Las grandes batallas de la Reconquista durante las invasiones africanas (almorávides, almohades, y benimerines)*, Madrid, 1956.

[4] *Cf. op. cit.*, p. 14.

[5] *Primera parte*, Tetuán, 1956, included as vol. 6 of the series entitled *Historia de Marruecos*.

[6] *Histoire de l'Afrique du Nord, Tunisie, Algérie, Maroc,—de la conquête arabe à 1830, révue et mise à jour par Roger Le Tourneau*, 1964.

general outline the political vicissitudes of that period. He himself explains that he has only dealt with the "external" history, thus building the skeleton which future historians will have to fill in. Following the distinction made by Codera between internal and external history, he admits to having excluded from his study all those phenomena related to art, literature, philosophy, religion and economy owing to their complications, and the interrelationship between Andalusian and North African culture during the Almohad period, a problem which as yet has hardly begun to be elucidated.[1] Withal, Huici Miranda's work remains a masterly study which will serve as the basis for future works in the field, while his research on the Almohad period has continued the work of Lévi-Provençal and illuminated an obscure era.

---

[1] *Cf. Historia política del imperio almohade,* in *ed. cit.,* p. 13.

CHAPTER TEN

If we turn to observe how the research carried out by Spanish Arabists has modified or influenced the ideas of scholars and thinkers in present day Spain, several attitudes become apparent. J. B. Trend has written that "the modern Spanish school of scientific historians is not favourably disposed towards the legacy of Islam." [1] According to Trend, there are seveıal reasons for this unfavourable approach to Arabic studies. First of all, the theme of "the Moors in Spain" which had been exploited to its limits by early nineteenth-century Romanticism had become discredited by reason of the errors committed by Conde and even Dozy. The Romantic tradition had also been inevitably identified with the century of invasion, civil war, and unrest which culminated with the Spanish-American war of 1898. The movement of regeneration initiated by the Krausist school led to a more accurate kind of scholarship such as that of Menéndez Pidal who introduced European methodology into Spanish research. At the same time, wherever Menéndez Pidal turned in his studies, he found ill-supported assumptions in matters of Arabic philology. Since Menéndez Pidal's work was far superior in quality and reliability to that of his contemporaries, the unfortunate conclusion was drawn that Romance philology was moıe reliable than Arabic studies, and that a Romance origin for any phenomenon in Spanish culture was more plausible than a solution based on Oriental studies. This attitude, however, was not that of Menéndez Pidal himself, for as Trend has pointed out, in the first number of the *Revista de Filología Española* founded by Menéndez Pidal in 1914, the leading article was by Asín.[2] A further reason for the rejection of Arabic studies, given by Trend is the attitude that "the Muslims were the cause, directly or indirectly, of all the evils which afterwards befell that country." [3] This position is examplified principally by the historian Sánchez Albornoz.

However, the attitude of Spanish thinkers with regard to the Arabs is far more varied than one would be led to suppose. Thus

---

[1] J. B. Trend, *Spain and Portugal,* in *The Legacy of Islam,* ed. by T. Arnold and A. Guillaume, Oxford, 1952, p. 1.

[2] *Op. cit.*, p. 2.

[3] *Op. cit.*, p. 2.

for example, in the series of letters exchanged between Ángel Ganivet and Miguel de Unamuno and which were published under the title of *El porvenir de España,*[1] Ganivet takes a decidedly pro-Arab stand and attributes great importance to the Arab conquest of al-Andalus and its consequences for the development of the future Spain. Ganivet claims that he has Arab blood in his veins and warns Unamuno in the following way: "If you suppress the Romans and the Arabs, nothing is left of me but perhaps my legs; you unwittingly kill me, friend Unamuno." [2] This was in reply to Unamuno's statement:

> About the Arabs I have nothing to say; I have a profound dislike for them, I hardly believe in what is called Arab civilization and I consider their passage through Spain to have been one of the greatest misfortunes we have ever suffered. [3]

It is very difficult to assess the significance of Unamuno's thought about the role played by the Arabs in al-Andalus because his radically anti-historical or as he would have said, "intra-historical" method leads him to stress the similarities which bind peoples rather than the differences which divide them. Thus Unamuno rejects both the Arabization as well as the Romanization of his "eternal Spain" as mere episodes which hardly modified the profound inner reaches of a native Iberian consciousness. Unamuno's ideas lead him to claim that the Romanization of Spain was complete, as can be observed in his opinion, from the fact that the Spanish language is an almost pure Latin "dialect," and that Spaniards think according to concepts created by the Romans.[4]

At the same time, Unamuno saw that the presence in al-Andalus of the Arabs had resulted in an exacerbation of the Spanish religious feeling, though he finds this to have had pernicious effects:

> I do not know whether it is because of the eight-century-long war our forefathers waged against the Moors, who were also non-

[1] Madrid, 1912.

[2] *El porvenir de España,* Madrid, 1912, p. 53.

[3] *Op. cit.*, p. 44.

[4] "Whoever desires to judge of the Romanization of Spain need only observe that Castilian, in which we think and with which we think, is an almost pure Latin Romance; that we are thinking with those concepts created by the Roman people, and that the greatest value in our thought is that it gives awareness to what lies hidden in the subconscious." *En torno al casticismo, Ensayos,* p. 51, from *Miguel de Unamuno, Antología,* ed. by Luis González Seara, Madrid, 1960, p. 72.

> Christians, enemies, but the fact remains that here more than among other peoples, a certain fusion has taken place between the patriotic and the religious sentiment; a fusion harmful to both, but perhaps more so to the religious sentiment than to the patriotic one. [1]

Unamuno also has a strong tendency to insist on the Iberian roots of the Spanish people, for he has claimed that though Spanish law, language and religion are of Roman origin, a deeper and underlying consciousness responds to the way of life of the primitive and even pre-historic inhabitants of the Peninsula, so that under a superimposed Roman structure, ancient native ways of life still subsisted.[2] Unamuno was impressed by the difference between Spain and the rest of Europe, and asked himself to what extent he was a European and a modern man.[3] Feeling within himself a distaste for European civilization he claims to be of North African stock. Thus in a constantly unhistorical and non-rational way he stresses the peculiarity of the Spanish people this time by rejecting the Roman tradition and turning to that of Berber Africa:

> Latins! Latins? And why, if we are Berbers, should we not feel and proclaim ourselves to be such, and when we have to sing our sorrows and our consolations, why should we not sing them in accordance with Berber aesthetics? [4]

In sum, while Unamuno proclaimed an anti-Arab attitude, he never denied the profound impact Arabic culture had had on Spain, and in some of his most exalted anti-European passages he went so far as to identify the peculiarities of Spain with North Africa, and to recommend the Africanization of Europe. Thus it may be said that though his personal feeling for Islamic culture was negative, he definitely considered it important in the formation of Spanish culture. Though not a historian, Unamuno was one of the most important figures who thought about Spain's problems and its role in the modern world. Another intellectual of similar stature was Ortega y Gasset, who rejected all Arab "influences" on his country's past. Thus in *España invertebrada,* Ortega claims that Spain possesses a structure which is very similar to that of France, England, and Italy, and that the four nations were formed by the conjunction

---

[1] *Religión y Patria, Ensayos,* p. 471, in *op. cit.,* p. 73.
[2] *Cf. España y los españoles. De esto y aquello,* pp. 596-597, in *Antologia,* p. 77.
[3] *Sobre la europeización,* p. 902-903, in *Antología,* p. 128.
[4] *Sobre la europeización,* p. 917, in *Antología,* p. 141.

of three elements, two of which were common to all, and one of which varied. The three elements were: a native race, a Roman civilizing sediment and a Germanic immigration.[1] For Ortega the different degree to which these elements were combined created the way of being of the four western European nations. The difference between Spain and France, in his eyes, lies in the difference between the Germanic tribes which invaded both countries. For Ortega, the difference between the "energetic and creative" Frank and the "degenerate" Visigoth determined the ulterior weakness of Spanish culture.[2] At the same time, he surprises us by rejecting the Arabic invasion and its consequences in the following statement:

> In view of the ignorance of our own history which we Spaniards suffer from, it is necessary to point out that neither do the Arabs constitute an essential ingredient in the birth of our nation, nor does their domination explain the weakness of Peninsular feudalism. [3]

According to Ortega, the Visigoths arrived in the Peninsula worn out and degenerate. The African invasion made off with them, and after the subsiding of the Muslim advance, new kingdoms were created, which had monarchs and common people, though they lacked a select minority of nobles.[4] In this way he brushes aside eight hundred years of Peninsular Islam and attributes the peculiarities of Spain to an excessively popular culture which lacked aristocratic leaders. The ideas contained in *España invertebrada* are unfavourable to Arabic culture insofar as it is an expression of "Semitic" genius. They tend instead to link Spain to Germanic culture.

In 1934 Ortega published a monograph on Ibn Khaldūn entitled "Abenjaldún nos revela el secreto," one of the few occasions in which he dealt with an Arabic subject. In it he carefully avoids any reference to Spain and deals strictly with the structure of North African history. At times, his remarks indicate that for him Arabic culture was something exotic which he never came to associate with Spain.[5] His attitude towards Arabic culture is

[1] *Cf. España invertebrada,* 12th ed., Madrid, 1962, p. 129.
[2] *Op. cit.*, p. 131.
[3] *Op. cit.*, p. 129.
[4] *Op. cit.*, p. 140.
[5] ". . . I have asked myself whether my interest in African themes, pursued during the course of many years, is a mere curiosity, a voluptuous desire for the exotic, etc." *Cf.* "*Abenjaldún nos revela el secreto*, in *Obras completas de José Ortega y Gasset,* vol. 2, 1st ed., Madrid, 1946, p. 662.

negative for in his preface to García Gómez's translation of the *Dove's Neck Ring* he claims that the Arabs inherited the culture of Antiquity in its Byzantine version whereas Europe inherited Ancient culture from Rome. As a result, he argues, the Arabs made use of Aristotle at a far earlier date than Europe. Likewise the Christianity which motivated the rise of Islam was that of the Nestorians and Monophysites who constituted the most archaic branch of Christendom. These factors made the two cultures diverge widely until in the thirteenth century Arabic civilization came to an abrupt halt because of the paralysing influence "of the Koran and desert life." [1] As if to insist on the petrifying influence of the Koran on Arab culture he adds:

> Whoever wishes to observe concretely how the Koran dessicates souls and dries up a people, has only to read the memoirs of Ṭaha Ḥusayn—*Le livre des jours*, 1947—. The author, who is blind, is at present the Egyptian minister of Education. [2]

Ortega's arguments may be roughly reduced to the following: The Middle Ages were a cultural phenomenon which resulted from the entry of Germanic and Arab tribes into the scene of Graeco-Roman culture. This culture, in the hands of the Arabs, rapidly degenerated because of the "petrifying" influence of the Koran. The Germanic peoples on the other hand, because of some innate racial superiority which he does not account for, were able to carry this culture on to ever greater achievements. The ideas of Ortega, who was by no means a specialist in Arabic studies may be contrasted with the theory of Sir Hamilton Gibb, who as a modern and professional authority on the field has given very different reasons for the decline of Arabic culture. For Professor Gibb, the adoption of Byzantine and Sassanid institutions by Islam led to an inner cultural conflict between religion and politics. Political expediency dictated modes of procedure which were often shockingly opposed to the humane ideals of the Islamic faith, and as the moral guides of Islam gradually lost control over government policy, the breach

---

[1] "In the ensuing stages the reception gradually began to take on more and more divergent features, until in the thirteenth century it ceases among the Arabs, whose civilization remains dessicated and petrified by Koran and deserts." *El collar de la paloma, Prólogo*, Madrid, 1952, p. xv.

[2] *Op. cit.*, p. cit., n. 1.

widened and decay resulted. In discussing the role of the *Shuʿūbiyya* he has said:

> Its immediate effect was to bring to the surface the hitherto latent or concealed division between the religious institution and the ruling institution, and to set the latter free to pursue its own course of development with relatively little control from the side of the religious institution; ultimately, as it diverged more and more widely from the ethical standards of Islam, the orthodox *ʿulamāʾ* themselves were to find their spiritual independence endangered by the still further concessions and compromises wrung from them for the sake of the principle of unity. [1]

In sum, for Professor Gibb it was not the influence of the Koran, but rather the gradual loss of control on the part of the *ʿulamāʾ* over the governments of Islam (patterned after the Byzantine and Sassanian tradition) which created an internal contradiction and finally brought about the political collapse of Islam in the Middle Ages, from which it may be concluded that Ortega's assumptions lack foundation.

However, the attitudes of Unamuno and Ortega with regard to the Arabs are significant, for though neither of them occupied themselves much with Arabic culture, it can be seen that Unamuno at times speaks of the African nature of Spanish culture, a supposition which Ortega is quick to reject. From this it will be seen that though the emotional response of the two thinkers is different when faced with the problem of Arabic culture and its impact on Spain, the Arab presence plays a fundamental though much regretted role in their respective theories about Spanish history.

While Unamuno and Ortega dealt mainly with the problem of Spain vis-à-vis Europe, three Spanish scholars, Sánchez Albornoz, Menéndez Pidal and Américo Castro have dealt more directly with the presence of al-Andalus and its effects on Spanish culture. In their theories we note that a change has occurred in Spanish historiography if we compare their thought to that of Menéndez y Pelayo who was reluctant to attribute too much importance to the Arabs. With the new scholars, for the first time the Arab conquest is made the decisive factor which turned the tide of Spanish history, and in this the gradual accumulation of factual material by the Spanish Arabists has had a decisive impact on

---

[1] H. A. R. Gibb, *Studies on the Civilization of Islam*, Boston, 1962, p. 14.

Spanish historiography. Thus in this new attitude of acceptance we can see the triumph of the Spanish school of Arabists. However, the attitudes of the three scholars are all radically different, so that their theories deserve some discussion.

Menéndez Pidal as an exponent of the "traditionalist" school, views Spain as a historical essence upon which "influences" from many civilizations have acted, though without modifying its essential constitution. Thus he speaks of Iberian, Roman, Visigothic and Arabic epochs in the "eternal" flow of Spanish history, yet attributes importance to the Islamic epoch during which he envisions "Spain" as divided into two parts. The northern part was to undergo the general decadence suffered by the Middle Ages after Rome was isolated from Greek thought. On the other hand, the southern territories flourished within the orbit of Islamic culture which had been elaborated from the conquered and assimilated nations belonging to the Byzantine Empire and the regions beyond the Indus valley.[1]

Menéndez Pidal thus advocates Arabic "influences" on Spanish culture and is one of the great defenders of the theories of Ribera and Asín, though to do this, like the Arabists, he Hispanizes the Arabic culture of al-Andalus, and argues that the poet of Cordova, Muqaddam or Muḥammad of Cabra, a courtier of the emir ʿAbd Allāh (888-912) was inspired to relate Arabic literature to popular Andalusian poetry. He adds that Spanish literature has always tended to cultivate popular forms of art, only to conclude that "In this Muqqadam shows that he is very Spanish." [2] This interpretation is the result of theories held by the Arabists themselves, among them Ribera. In defending Ribera's theory on the *zajal* Menéndez Pidal argues that though some scholars refuse to accept the diffusion of the Arabic-Andalusian *zajal* strophe throughout the West, this Arabic influence is palpable in the kind of songs composed for dances and other popular diversions, as well as for religious hymns. Furthermore, he argues that it is hardly astonishing that Arabic songs influenced those of Christendom, given the close interrelation of the two peoples in the Peninsula,[3]

[1] *Cf.* Menéndez Pidal, *España, eslabón entre la cristiandad y el islam,* Madrid, 1956, p. 11.

[2] *Op. cit.*, p. 12.

[3] ". . . It is not astonishing that Arabic song should have influenced Christian song; what is incomprehensible is that it should not have influenced it." *Op. cit.*, p. 17.

and adds that after the work of Asín on Ibn Ḥazm and the studies of García Gómez and Henri Pérès on Hispano-Arabic poetry the assertion made by Jeanroy that Arabic poetry is totally opposed to the idea of courtly love, can no longer be sustained, and so he gives credit to the theory of Arabic influence on the poetry of the troubadours.[1]

Making use of the work of the Arabist school, Menéndez Pidal clarifies the fact that the Arab poets of al-Andalus developed the idea of the lover conceived of as a slave subjected to the whims of his lady, several centuries before the same idea made its appearance in the first troubadour, Guillaume IX who designates the lover with the epithet *obedien*. This coincidence indicates for Menéndez Pidal that the theory of obedience of the lover toward his mistress was adopted by the Provenzal poets from al-Andalus.[2]

Menéndez Pidal also gave welcome to Asín's theory on Dante, and mentions that the translation of the *mi'rāj* legend entitled *La escala de Mahoma* was known in Tuscany around 1350 and in Apulia in the fifteenth century. He quotes the late Italian Arabist G. Levi della Vida who had earlier doubted Asín's theory, as having said:

> Today it is no longer possible to doubt. It would be beyond the realm of likelihood for the *Libro de la Escala*, made accessible to the West in Castilian, Latin and French versions, to have remained unknown to Dante. Asín's thesis, not only on the possibility, but also on the reality of the relationship between Dante and Islamic eschatology, is therefore definitively confirmed.

and Menéndez Pidal adds:

> And with these words by the illustrious Italian Arabist we put an end to this disquisition.[3]

Menéndez Pidal's conception of an eternal and Catholic Spain leads him to ascribe Catholic intentions to the converted Jew Pedro Alfonso, for he claims that upon introducing ribald Arabic tales into European literature that author had insisted that they should be read with "subtle and Catholic eyes."[4] This tradition according to Menéndez Pidal, was to prosper in Spain for he argues that the

---

[1] *Op. cit.*, pp. 17-18.
[2] *Op. cit.*, p. 19.
[3] *Op. cit.*, pp. 59-60.
[4] *Op. cit.*, p. 24.

Archpriest of Hita also wished his poems to be read for their hidden meaning since he wrote them "in the name of the Catholic faith." This spirit of Pedro Alfonso reappears, according to Menéndez Pidal, in Boccaccio who claims to present edifying Catholic principles in his most obscene novels.[1] All this represents the traditionalist attempt to push the origins of Catholic Spain as far back as possible:

> A large part of the population of the Peninsula converted to Islam, a common attitude, for all the provinces of the Roman Byzantine Empire converted to Islam upon being invaded; but the Spanish Muslims distinguished themselves by learning how to Hispanize Spanish Islam most admirably when decadence was beginning in the rest of the Arab world. [2]

As an exponent of traditionalism, Menéndez Pidal is opposed to the "individualists" in his view that the origin of the Romance literatures is to be placed at a far earlier date than that of the first extant texts in these languages, and he claims that these texts cannot be explained without taking into account a long tradition of oral literature now lost in which form and content have slowly been elaborated. For him, the individual writer, no matter how great his genius, was closely bound to the cultural and literary tradition within which he wrote.[3] This theory is partly accurate, but when Menéndez Pidal applies it to the *kharjāt* and links them to Galician and Provenzal poetry he overlooks their function within the *muwashshaḥa* and thus neglects the literary unity of these Hispano-Arabic poems. In this sense most of the studies of Andalusian *muwashshaḥāt* written today concern themselves mainly with problems of formal structure and prosody, whereas the literary problems of these poems are entirely overlooked, thus producing an incomplete view of *muwashshaḥa* poetry. However by studying the external aspects of this poetry, Menéndez Pidal is enabled to link the *kharjāt* to Latin lyrics. Thus he casts his gaze back to the remotest epochs and tells us that in the imperial Rome of the first century the songs of Bætica were highly prized. Cádiz was then the leading cultural center of Bætica and according to Martial *iocosa Gades* was constantly providing Rome with dancing girls. The *cantica Gaditana* were fashionable in the metropolis, while the *puellae Gaditanae* set a fashion with their lascivious dancing.[4]

[1] *Cf. op. cit.*, pp. 24-24.
[2] *Op. cit.*, p. 51.
[3] *Cf. op. cit.*, p. 63.
[4] *Op. cit.*, p. 132.

For Menéndez Pidal, the *cantica Gaditana* in the Roman empire, as well as the Arabic strophic poems of al-Andalus which spread to the East, reveal the power of diffusion of an inextinguishable creative genius to be found in Andalusia and which today spreads a rich variety of popular songs throughout the Peninsula and Spanish America. He therefore speaks of a "collective character" which has lasted for two thousand years and which had its point of origin in Andalusia. For Menéndez Pidal, this collective character explains the fact that the *muwashshaḥa* originated in al-Andalus which he calls "eternal Andalusia." [1] It should be observed that since nothing has come down to us of the *cantica Gaditana,* nor of Romance lyrical poetry prior to the *kharjāt,* nor of the earliest *muwashshaḥāt,* Menéndez Pidal's theory should be accepted with caution. For the moment it is possible to state only that the aesthetic principles followed in the composition of a *muwashshaḥa* are very different from those which are to be found in popular Spanish poetry, and that in reading a Spanish and an Arabic poem the scholar receives the impression that he is in contact with two entirely different civilizations.

In attempting to explain the origin of *muwashshaḥa* poetry, Menéndez Pidal claims that in the Romance speaking world a three line stanza very probably existed prior to the Arab invasion of the Peninsula. To this Muqaddam of Cabra probably added a fourth verse whose rhyme was repeated at the end of every stanza. Later poets (the seven named specifically by Ibn Bassām) experimented with the original form adding ever more complicated internal rhymes until the final form in all its complicated variety was transmitted to the first generation of Provenzal poets and all the countries of Romania.[2] Thus Menéndez Pidal sums up his traditionalist theory in the following manner:

> Perpetual identity in perpetual renovation like that of reborn Spring; such is the traditional style, elaborated not by the individual effort of a professional writer, but by repeated anonymous correction, the only one that attains that beauty without literature, which abhors all artifice, like the lovelorn Mozarab maiden who refuses to put ornaments on the living beauty of her white neck. [3]

However, the fact remains that the *muwashshaḥa* was not

[1] *Op. cit.*, p. 134-135.
[2] *Op. cit.*, p. 140.
[3] *Op. cit.*, p. 153.

elaborated by an anonymous tradition, but by seven distinct poets mentioned by Ibn Bassām, namely Muqaddam ibn Muʿāfā al-Qabrī, Ibn ʿAbd Rabbihi, Yūsuf ibn Hārūn ar-Ramādī, Mukarram ibn Saʿīd, the two sons of Abū l-Ḥasan, and ʿUbāda ibn ʿAbd Allāh al-Anṣārī ibn Māʾ as-Samāʾ, the last of whom died in A.D. 1025. This in itself disproves Menéndez Pidal's theory on the anonimity of *muwashshaḥa* poetry, for though the strophic compositions of these various poets are not extant, the Arabic biographical tradition has carefully recorded not only their names, but the particular innovations they introduced into the *muwashshaḥa*.

In this way it may be seen that though in Menéndez Pidal's case the traditionalist school has accepted the work of the Spanish Arabists, it has done so by Hispanizing Islamic culture in al-Andalus and turning the Arabic period into one more epoch in the history of an "eternal" Spain going back to prehistoric times.

An historian who has discovered significant information on the economic and social problems of medieval Spain is Claudio Sánchez Albornoz, for whom the Islamic conquest constitutes the decisive turning point in Spanish history. Like Menéndez Pidal he speaks of an eternal Spain, but his negative attitude towards Islam and his exaggerated statements against the Arabs in al-Andalus detract a great deal from the presentation and style of his work. His method leads him to shy away from studying Spain as it actually *is* as a consequence of the Islamic presence, so that he tends excessively to regret Spain's shortcomings with regard to Europe; shortcomings which he attributes to the ruinous influence of Islam.[1] Thus he admits that the most decisive factor in Spain's past was the crossing of the Straits of Gibraltar by the Muslim hosts. For Sánchez Albornoz twelve centuries have gone by since that "fateful" event and Spain has still not been able to overcome that "tragic" moment.[2] Thus

[1] P. E. Russell has said of him: "in turning from the elucidation of segments of his country's history to an attempt to talk about Spanish history generally, all the frustrations which the subject excites in the Spanish mind have flooded up to submerge S-A's professional craft . . . . The sober, unrhetorical, prose which Dr. Menéndez Pidal has taught Spanish scholars to use is here abandoned in favour of a strident emotionalism, accompanied by frequent appeals to religious feeling and patriotic prejudice, which leave the reader exhausted and suspicious." *Cf. The Nessus-Shirt of Spanish History*, in *BHS*, v. 36, Oct. 1959, pp. 219-225.

[2] He adds: "The results of the age-long struggle against Islam; of that terrible deviation of my fatherland from its true course, have always concerned me, ever since my mind has been able to grasp the panoramas of the past." *Cf. España y el Islam*, Buenos Aires, 1943.

for Sánchez Albornoz Spanish history becomes the painful process of comparing an unfortunate reality to what might have been if the Arabs had not crossed the Straits. As a consequence, his tends to be a history of wishful thinking, and as such to overlook the real values created by Spain. Thus he insists on an "eternal" Spain twisted from its true course by the Arab invasion, and views Spain as a bridge between Europe and Africa which after many invasions and vicissitudes had found itself definitely partaking of European culture under Roman and Visigothic rule at the beginning of the eighth century. Then came the "holocaust," for the Islamic conquest upset the delicate balance in favour of Europe and especially Rome. Thus he is able to say:

> Without Islam, who can guess what our destiny might have been? Without Islam, Spain would have followed the same paths as France, Germany, and England; and to judge from what we have achieved over the centuries in spite of Islam, perhaps we would have marched at their head. [1]

He adds that when he contemplates the present state of Islamic countries he is terrified when he thinks what might have been the fate of Spain had it been permanently subjected to Islam,[2] and attributes the Spanish tendency towards separatism to the influence of Islam. The "fatal" effect of the Arab invasion is also to be noted on Spanish economy, for according to Sánchez Albornoz it created an initial backwardness with regard to Europe. Christian Spain for five centuries lay within the economic orbit of al-Andalus and the Frankish empire. As a result it became a nation of consumers with hardly any industrial production and a commerce which was controlled by Muslims and Jews in the South and by Franks and Jews in the North.[3]

The creation of the Spanish Empire in America is also seen by Sánchez Albornoz as a fatal and undesirable consequence of Islam, for in his view the crusade against al-Andalus created a warlike

---

[1] *Op. cit.*, pp. 14-15.

[2] *Op. cit.*, pp. 18-19. About the Jews he has even worse arguments. *Cf.* P. E. Russell: "When S-A turns to the Jews the inherent racialism of the book [he refers to Sánchez Albornoz, *España: un enigma histórico*. 2 vols., Buenos Aires, 1956] takes on a more familiar and far uglier form. Here we move into a Nazi-like world of Jewish plots against the innocent Christian Spaniards, both in the Middle Ages and, it is hinted, now." P. E. Russell, *op. cit.*

[3] *Op. cit.*, p. 33.

spirit in Christian Spain and as a result, brought about the Spanish imperialism of the early Renaissance, which was made use of by the Hapsburgs in order to undertake certain enterprises foreign to Spanish interests and which were to bring about Spain's ulterior ruin.[1] The wars against Islam also intensified the feeling of religious intolerance which Sánchez Albornoz claims to have been already alive among the ancient Iberians. The Crown and the masses of Castile during the Middle Ages were directed by a clerical minority who led the course of history in favour of the interests of the Church, thus making possible the Inquisition and moral bankruptcy of Spain.[2]

From all these negative factors, Sánchez Albornoz concludes that Spain is not a nation with a "hereditary defect;" the "base offspring of a corrupt father," nor is it an Africanized country, "diseased because of an Oriental virus," "lacking in creative ability," an "offshoot of Islam." It is for him, on the contrary a vital and able nation which was forced to sacrifice itself as the shield of Europe against the rude and barbaric hordes of Africa. It was an active member of Europe which created and transmitted to Europe the most splendid civilization of the Middle Ages, but which also had to maintain a constant vigil against Islam, which in the long run ruined its natural organic disposition. This constant rejection of African influences twisted Spain from its normal course of development as a European nation and created an economic stagnation and religious intolerance. Thus he concludes:

> If in spite of this backwardness and deviation my native land is owed a debt by all mankind for its American enterprise and for the wonders of its literature, of its art, and of its philosophical and juridical thought, when we overcome a past which still weighs upon the shoulders of the present, erasing the last traces of those reactions, who can predict the future destiny of Spain? In history years are like minutes. [3]

Though Sánchez Albornoz views the Arab influence on Spain from a negative standpoint, there can be no doubt that for him the Islamic invasion of the Peninsula was a decisive factor in shaping the destiny of modern Spain.

The historian Américo Castro has gradually elaborated a theory

---

[1] *Op. cit.*, pp. 38-39.
[2] *Op. cit.*, p. 39-40.
[3] *Op. cit.*, pp. 49-50.

of Spanish culture which attributes geat importance to the role played by the Arabs and Jews in the Middle Ages. The point of view of Américo Castro is noteworthy for its positive approach to Spanish-Arab history, as well as for his having rejected many of the negative and nationalistic ideas which have detracted from much of the Spanish historiography which we have been able to review in this chapter. Américo Castro has made a problem not only out of Spain, but out of history itself, and in this respect he has been able to show with plausible arguments that it is not possible to speak of Spain in the modern sense of the word, before the Islamic invasion of the Peninsula. Thus for him, the year 711 is the decisive date in the creation of modern Spain. Making of history a philosophical problem he has taken and reworked the ideas of both Ortega and Unamuno and has constructed a vision of history which differs from that of both. Thus, applying to history Ortega's maxim "I am I plus my circumstances" Américo Castro argues that "Spanishness" is a dimension of a collective consciousness which is by no means determined by biological factors or individual psychology. A Spaniard for Américo Castro is therefore "one who is aware of being Spanish in the company of others or who is recognized as such by those who come in contact with him."[1]

Américo Castro has had the merit of being the first modern historian to create a theory of Spanish history which attributes a decisive and positive role to the interaction between Jews, Christians and Muslims in Spain, and as a result he explains that Spaniards are what they are, and have acted collectively according to certain patterns of behaviour because centuries ago they belonged to a human group situated in the Iberian Peninsula and formed by three "castes" of believers: Christians, Muslims and Jews. Thus for Américo Castro Spaniards entered the scene of history without being aware of functioning as Celtiberians, but rather, of being members of one of the three abovementioned religions. According to Américo Castro, the religious exclusiveness of Spanish peoples can only be understood when seen in the light of its Semitic context, since the form and social functions of their belief in the hereafter lead us to think of similar phenomena in Islam and Israel rather than of religious forms native to Western Europe.[2] Thus Américo Castro attacks the tendency towards nationalism which is some-

[1] *Cf. La realidad histórica de España, edición renovada,* Mexico, 1962, p. xi.
[2] *Op. cit.,* p. xii.

times present in Spanish historiography, and he claims that the search for remote, heroic and glorious origins exemplified by the Hispanization of the paintings of the cave of Altamira, of the Dama de Elche, Numancia and Trajan had its point of origin in the Middle Ages and was the result of the Muslim conquest, for the historian Fernán Pérez de Guzmán had then labelled everything which had occurred prior to 1400 "historia triste y llorosa, indigna de metro y prosa."[1]

Thus he says that when we speak of Spaniards we should understand by that term a group of peoples who in the north of Hispania (not Spain), between the eighth and ninth centuries, began to attribute political and social dimensions to their condition as Christian believers, and who therefore called themselves "Christians," a singular and totally new occurrence in the history of the West.

This change was brought about as a direct consequence of the way of life which was projected upon them by a powerful social group whose ethnic denomination was also expressed in religious terms ("Muslims"). Américo Castro adds that the word "influence" is not very helpful in clarifying this phenomenon, because what actually took place was the projection of an inner form of life on another civilization which as a result did not adopt the faith of the dominant adversary, but developed its own belief along new and unsuspected lines.[2]

Starting from this inner projective impact of Islam on Christianity in the Iberian Peninsula Américo Castro has outlined a theory of continuity in Spanish history which is both original and coherent. He relates the slow process of the *Reconquista* and the epic impetus of the Christian caste as expressed in the old epic poems, the *Romancero* and the plays of Lope de Vega, to the attempt to create an empire in lands unknown to the Western world. Thus for him a history which discards nationalistic factors must take into account the coexistence as well as inner strife between Christians, Muslims and Jews in Spain. The proselytizing and Messianic aspects of Islam, the economic and scientific skill of the Jews and the warlike and imperial aspirations of the Christians went hand in hand to create the Spanish empire. Américo Castro adds that without Muslims

[1] *Op. cit.*, pp. xvi-ii. "A sad and mournful tale, unworthy of metre and prose."

[2] *Op. cit.*, p. xx.

and Jews the Christian empire created by the Spaniards would have been impossible, for the "tendency to conquer in order to spread Christianity was preceded by the conquest in order to spread Islam."[1]

With regard to the consequences of Islam for European civilization he says that the threefold religious tradition which developed in Spain made its way across the Pyrenees in ways which are as yet unexplored. *Don Quixote* and the mystical literature of Teresa of Jesus and John of the Cross are inexplicable without taking into account Islamic and Judaic thought. He claims that the idea of *life* which was necessary in order to create the novelistic innovation which began with *Don Quixote* and was continued by Rousseau and others, was already clearly manifested in the writings of Ibn Ḥazm at the beginning of the eleventh century, according to whom man is a being who lives in constant "preoccupation."[2]

As we have seen, Américo Castro rejects the historiography which has made "Spaniards" of the Iberians, Romans and Visigoths. He is no less remorseless with the Arabists and historians who have tried to Hispanize the predominantly Muslim civilization of al-Andalus, for he argues that these scholars falsely claim that the Arabic speaking peoples of al-Andalus were Spaniards and as a result did not share the collective dimensions of their life with those of the Islamic world. These scholars, Américo Castro points out, do not take into account the extent to which the Arabic language moulds and reworks the internal and external behaviour of the individual. Thus the Arabization and Islamization of the southern portion of the former Visigothic kingdom made al-Andalus into a spiritual and linguistic prolongation of Islam so that after centuries had passed, even the Mozarabs expressed themselves in Arabic, and that is precisely why they were called Mozarabs, which means "Arabized ones." Thus Américo Castro has the following to say to the Spanish school of Arabists:

> One is therefore surprised at the insistence of pan-Hispanic Orientalists and of their followers in denying the connection of al-Andalus with the Muslim Orient, and in relating the *Andalusī* Muslims (*not Andalusians*) by means of blood ties, of biological descent, to the Tartessians and to Celtiberia.[3]

[1] *Op. cit.*, pp. xxvi-xxvii.
[2] *Op. cit.*, p. xxvii. In Arabic, *hamm.*
[3] *Op. cit.*, p. 8.

In this respect Américo Castro coincides with the modern school of Arab critics who also view Islam in al-Andalus as an integral part of their own heritage. Professor Jawdat ar-Rikābī, in discussing the cultural background of the Andalusian of the Arab period has said:

> Indeed, he is certainly an Andalusian, and yet upon reading his works and especially his poetry, we cannot deny his Arabic roots and Eastern qualities, for this Andalusian had remained Eastern in his thought, Eastern in his manner of expression; apart from certain distinctive traits which it was impossible to avoid and which were the result of the combination of geographic and human circumstances. For this reason we cannot affirm with Henri Pérès that the Muslim Andalusian represented a racial prolongation of the original peoples who inhabited the Peninsula of al-Andalus. We cannot truly agree with the Orientalist in the likes of such a peremptory judgment, nor do the facts themselves accord with what he claims. It remains for us to learn what then was that literature which was a reflection of Oriental literature, and this is what we shall see in the following chapters, and we shall observe that it was a reflection of the Orient as well as the real meaning of al-Andalus. [1]

It is significant that both Sánchez Albornoz and Américo Castro protested against the budget cuts imposed by the government on the Centre of Arabic Studies in 1935.[2] It is also significant—and tragic—that they have both lived in the exile imposed upon Republican Spaniards by the Civil War. Like those liberals of a century ago, driven into exile by the restoration of Ferdinand VII, they have viewed the Arabs as an essential component in attempting to explain the history of their nation. Yet here the resemblance ends, for in the words of Montgomery Watt, "Catholic Spaniards . . . have sometimes tended to regard the period of Islamic domination as a mere interruption in the continuing life of a single entity, Catholic Spain. With many refinements this is the idea behind the writings of C. Sánchez Albornoz. A more exciting and apparently more balanced treatment of the complex questions at issue—and one more congenial to the Islamist—is that of Américo Castro in *The Structure of Spanish History* . . . His general thesis is that there was no continuity between Visigothic Spain and later Christian

[1] *Cf.* Jawdat ar-Rikābī, *Fī l-Adab al-Andalusī*, Cairo, 1960, p. 46.

[2] *Cf.* Gabriel Jackson, *The Spanish Republic and the Civil War, 1931-1939*, Princeton, 1965, p. 170.

Spain, but that the latter was something new which was born and grew up in the mixed culture (largely Arab) which developed under the Muslims." [1]

---

[1] William Montgomery Watt and Pierre Cachia, *A History of Islamic Spain*, Edinburgh, 1965, p. 188.

CONCLUSION

Since the Civil War, Spain has once again as in the past, renewed its diplomatic contacts with a newly independent Arab world. Nationalist Spain has thus had to confront Arab nationalism.

García Gómez has represented Spain in Baghdad and is presently the Spanish ambassador in Ankara. Even more important than this, new cultural organs have appeared. The old "Escuela de Estudios Árabes" of Madrid, which houses the important collection of manuscripts found in Almonacid de la Sierra, has been renamed "Instituto Miguel Asín" and is directed by Don Jaime Oliver Asín, the nephew of the patriarch of Spanish Arabism. The government has established an "Instituto Hispano-Árabe de Cultura" at the University of Madrid. It is headed by Pareja and possesses a splendid reference library of Arabic books. An agreement with the United Arab Republic has led to the creation of a Spanish cultural centre in Cairo and an "Instituto Egipcio de Estudios Islámicos" in Madrid which publishes its own journal and is directed by Hussein Monès. The "Instituto de Valencia de Don Juan" in Madrid, directed by Pedro Longás has a select collection of Arabic art objects and some manuscripts. In Granada and Barcelona groups of Arabists work at the respective universities. The Escorial and the National Library of Madrid house rich collections of manuscripts, and that of the Academy of History contains unknown treasures brought to Spain by Codera, which its catalogue, when completed by Elías Terés, will reveal to an anxiously awaiting scholarly world.

Without abandoning its special strength in Hispano-Arabic studies, Spanish Arabism has broadened its range of interest to include contemporary affairs in the Muslim world. The development of this tendency can be observed clearly in the trajectory going from Asín Palacios to García Gómez and Pareja.

Asín, for the first time in modern Spain began to write on Arab philosophers of the East. His studies on Ġazālī and Islamic mysticism made Spanish a required language for European Orientalists. Today Pareja, as an Islamologist, studies topics of a broad and comprehensive nature which embrace vast areas of Islamic civilization.

On the other hand, while Hispano-Arabic culture has not been neglected, its study has developed in a new and original manner. For the first time since the visit of al-Ġazāl in the eighteenth century, Muslim scholars have come to Madrid—this time to study Hispano-Arabic civilization. Such is the case of the Pakistani scholar S. M. Imamuddin, who was trained in Madrid and has written books on Arab Spain. Thanks to García Gómez's efforts the Arab world has become interested in Hispano-Arabic literature, and a number of critical works on the subject has appeared. Some of these, on the *muwashshaḥāt* and the *azjāl*, have developed the theories of Ribera and García Gómez, and have formed an impressive bibliography, in Arabic, which no specialist can afford to neglect. In Beirut, Iḥsān ʿAbbās has directed the publication of a special collection of works devoted to al-Andalus. Named *Al-Maktabat al-Andalusiyya*, this collection already contains twelve volumes and includes works on the *muwashshaḥāt*, on the history of Islamic Spain, biographical works by Spanish Muslim authors, and the *Dīwāns* of ar-Ruṣāfī of Valencia, the blind poet of Tudela, Ḥāzim of Cartagena, and Ibn az-Zaqqāq of Valencia. With the publication of these books the dream of Codera is nearer to being fulfilled.

The labour of Spanish Arabists has therefore aroused the interest of Arab scholars. The effect on Spanish historiography has been no less decisive. The narrow nationalism of Unamuno and Ortega led to the Sánchez Albornoz-Castro controversy over the true nature of Spain. Both these scholars have recognized the impact of Islam on Spain—one regretfully and the other with positive acceptance. The work of Américo Castro in particular has made possible a more serene tradition in Spanish historiography, for both the economic historian Vicens Vives and especially Luis G. de Valdeavellano have accepted the notion of an Arab influence on Spain with none of the emotionalism that characterized Sánchez Albornoz. Valdeavellano in particular, who considers himself a disciple of Sánchez Albornoz, has turned his back on the style of his mentor. In a serious and thorough way he has written a history of medieval Spain which acquaints the reader with events occurring both in Christian and also in Muslim territory simultaneously. Thus Conde's ideal has partly been achieved—an impossible feat without the many monographs written by the Spanish school of Arabists and their followers over the past century.

If the Spanish Arabists have definitely succeeded in modifying the prevalent ideas about their nation's past, their impact on

European scholarship has been no less decisive. Their revolutionary theories about the origin of Romance poetry have interested all of Europe, and the issue of Arab influence is hotly debated. Books such as those of Nykl, Stern and others have continued to explore the subject.

Dante scholarship will never be the same after Asín, for though the latter's conclusions are highly controversial, the scholarly world is today split into a pro- and an anti-Asín faction. Behind the labours of every Dantist the spirit of Asín exerts its influence. From this polemic a limitation of Asín's theory may emerge, though its total rejection is almost impossible.

In the study of medieval prose fiction; in that of philosophy, of theology, art, and mysticism the scholar is on firmer ground, and the theories of Arab origin or influence appear to have won a decisive victory. As a result it is now clear that the whole history of medieval scholasticism is in need of drastic revision. Books such as Ralph Lerner and Muḥsin Mahdī's *Medieval Political Philosophy* (Toronto, 1963) which juxtaposes and compares texts derived from Muslim, Christian and Jewish philosophers would have been unthinkable in the narrow nationalistic world of the turn of the century.

More examples of transmission from East to West could be enumerated, but these should suffice to make the point. What is even more important is that the very system of transmission has been given theoretical structure in Ribera's theory of "imitation" and that this theory has exerted an influence on the thought of European sociologists and ethnologists in general.

The theories of the Spanish Arabists have thus modified some of our basic conceptions about the Middle Ages. This Spanish challenge has naturally elicited a European response which in the realm of historiography has created the tradition of Dozy and Lévi-Provençal. In English alone, the Arabs in Spain have been an object of fascination ever since Washington Irving discovered the Alhambra. Stanley Lane-Poole was later led by his hatred of contemporary Spaniards to claim that after the glorious period of Spanish Islam had passed away, there "followed the abomination of desolation, the rule of the Inquisition, and the blackness of darkness in which Spain has been plunged ever since." (*The Moors in Spain*, London, 1880). If he was enabled to say this, it was in a large measure thanks to the patient labours of that school of Arabists whom, as Spaniards he so utterly scorned. In recent times a more balanced picture has prevailed. Edwyn Hole has written an introduction to Arab Spain addressed to the layman (*Andalus, Spain under the Muslims,* London, 1958) while Montgomery Watt and Pierre Cachia have written for the specialist *A History of Islamic Spain* (Edinburgh, 1965). In it they write the following unforgettable words about the lasting values of Spanish Islam:

> "There is something of transcendent value in a beautiful object; and it may be argued that a civilization which can produce such objects must have a quality of greatness. In general this argument may be allowed to be sound. Yet it is instructive to contrast our attitude to the Parthenon with our attitude to the Alhambra. Many people who admire both would be inclined to say that they see in the Parthenon a thing of beauty which is at the same time an expression of the Greek spirit, whereas the Alhambra is for them just a thing of intrinsic beauty without any reference to the culture which produced it.
>
> This contrast is worth looking at more closely. It is indeed natural that we should have a much greater appreciation of Greek culture than of Moorish culture. The former—or at least a selection from it—is part of our own heritage, part of the tradition into which we enter; but the latter, for all that it has contributed to the culture of Europe, was in its essence something alien, the great enemy, to be feared even in the moment of admiration. Our inherited "image" of Islam was framed in the twelfth and thirteeth centuries under the domination of this fear of the Saracen; and even now few western Europeans can regard Islam with impartiality. Yet would our appreciation of a beautiful object be affected by our lack of appreciation of the culture from which it springs? May it not, on the contrary, be the case that appreciation of a beautiful object is able to provide a key to the appreciation of the alien culture? May it not even be that the beautiful object is the measure and the validation of the culture? Because of lovely buildings like the Great Mosque of Cordova and the Alhambra of Granada must not the culture of Islamic Spain be a great culture?
>
> This point will bear expansion. There is an obvious difference between the Parthenon and the Alhambra. When we admire the Parthenon, we mainly do so from outside, whereas it is only from inside that the Alhambra can be admired. This has nothing to do with the contrast of religious and secular purposes, for it is also true that the glories of the Great Mosque of Cordova are mainly within. It has further been suggested that the slender pillars of the Alhambra with the elaborate and massive overstructure express the descent from a supernal realm of that which is of eternal value and significance, whereas other buildings express rather man's attempt to rise up to heaven. Now suggestions of this type may be multiplied and elaborated, and some will no doubt win wider approval than others.

> Even the best, however, is bound to be to a great extent inadequate, for the appreciation of beauty can never be reduced to conceptual terms. Nevertheless, if there is something to the above suggestion which even distantly approximates to the essence of the appreciated beauty, then man in the Western-European tradition who finds the beauty of the Alhambra touching a responsive chord in himself is acknowledging the high intrinsic worth of this expression of the soul of Islamic Spain, and providing himself with a key to a deeper understanding of this whole culture. (*Op. cit.*, pp. 174-175)

Montgomery Watt and Pierre Cachia, following in the tradition of Washington Irving, speak reverently of the values of Islamic civilization; that is to say, of those values that will outlast economic interests and political rivalries just as Shakespeare, Cervantes and Vergil have outlasted the rise and fall of empires and imperialisms.

And yet, what does the future hold in store for Hispano-Arabic studies? European Orientalism—that of Spain was no exeption—began with imperialistic expansion. It was closely tied to the interests of trade, and with the discovery of petroleum in the deserts of the Middle East this tendency has been intensified. Western governments have generously supported study of the Arab world destined to further their own economic and political interests.

This has led to the creation of centres for Middle Eastern studies devoted predominantly to contemporary problems. Political expediency sometimes has led to a sacrifice of the truth. Christian-Islamic-Jewish rivalries have sometimes vitiated studies that could have yielded a greater understanding of the past. But in the renaissance of Arabic studies in the West, the Spanish Muslims have too often been forgotten, for they have no petroleum interests, nor have they been a political menace since 1492.

Therefore the need has arisen to create new organisms whereby the study of Spanish Islam may be furthered—if only that our understanding of the past (which is always the shadow of the present) may be increased. Today it is necessary to found university chairs devoted to research on Hispano-Arabic studies. It is necessary to create a closer cooperation and integration of facilities between Middle Eastern Centres, Medieval Institutes, and Departments of Spanish and Romance Languages. Why so? One example will illustrate the point: since Ribera pointed out the significance of the poems of Ibn Quzmān for the origin of Romance poetry, no critical edition of that author's *Dīwān* worthy of the name has appeared. Furthermore, this work can only be carried out by a team of Arabists, Romanists, Berberists, etc., working in close collaboration. Yet until such a work is completed, we will not be on certain ground in discussing *zajal* poetry.

It is thus necessary to prepare students and grant degrees in interdisciplinary fields comprising Arabic, Hebrew, Latin, Spanish, etc. To implement such a plan, certain difficulties must be overcome, among them the prejudices of governments. These must be persuaded that it lies within their long-range interest to support studies which on the surface may seem impractical, since they offer neither immediate political nor economic advantages. At the same time, Departments of Romance Languages—those admirable inventions of German philology based on justifiable linguistic theory—must cease to think of the Mediterranean as a sort of "Iron Curtain" which in the Middle Ages effectively separated Islam from Christendom. The recent book by Archibald R. Lewis (*Naval Power and Trade in the Mediterranean, A.D.* 500-1100, Princeton, 1951) has modified the earlier ideas of Henri Pirenne on the subject, at least in its economic aspects. To these ideas, the Spanish school of Arabists has added the cultural borrowings of a varied nature that have been discussed in this book. Romance Language Departments must broaden their scope to produce Romanists who are at the same time competent Orientalists. Classical Arabic is a difficult language, and it will take the student more time to master it than to master Spanish, Portuguese, Italian or French. Therefore a special curriculum must be designed for students, even though this should involve a somewhat longer period of apprenticeship than is common in our universities. In this way new means can be developed to study medieval Spanish history in its Christian, Jewish, and Islamic forms, and its impact upon medieval Europe can be determined and evaluated with a greater degree of accuracy.

The thought of Américo Castro has been particularly influential in the United States, where he has created numerous disciples and left a definite mark on American Hispanism. He is therefore the potential grand architect of a new departure in Hispanic studies which, by providing an integrated picture of the three religions—Christianity, Judaism, and Islam, may offer us a better and more complete picture of the Middle Ages in Spain and in Europe. Such a broad and comprehensive vision of medieval civilization can bring us to a better understanding of our own age, so that contemporary political difficulties may be solved in that spirit of universalism which led Ibn al-ʿArabī of Murcia to exclaim:

> My heart has taken on every shape; it has become a pasture for gazelles and a convent for Christian monks;
>
> And a temple for idols, and a pilgrim's Kaʿba, and the tables of a Torah, and the pages of a Koran.
>
> I believe in the religion of love; wherever love's camels turn, there love is my religion and my faith.

Spanish Arabism has been largely a product of the victims of Golden Age intolerance, of the reforming ideals of the Spanish Enlightenment, of nineteenth-century Spanish liberalism. The lesson it has had to offer is one of international understanding. One of the main contributions made by Spain to the scholarly world during the past five hundred years has thus been humane and tolerant. It has taught Europe to broaden its cultural perspectives and has therefore contributed to the decline of nationalism and the birth of the multinational world of the twentieth century. In this sense, Spanish Arabism, an outgrowth of progressive forces, has had a generous contribution to offer the world of scholarship.

BIBLIOGRAPHY

ʿAbbās, Iḥsān, *Akhbār wa Tarājim Andalusiyya*, Beirut, 1963.

——, *Al-Muwashshaḥāt al-Andalusiyya; Nash'atuhā wa Tatawwuruhā*, Beirut 1965.

——, *Ta'rīkh al-Adab al-Andalusī*, I *ʿAṣr Siyādat Qurṭuba*; 2 *ʿAṣr aṭ-Ṭawā'if wa l-Murabiṭīn*; 3 *ʿAṣr al-Muwaḥḥidīn*, Beirut, 1960.

ʿAbd Allāh az-Zīrī, *Memoirs*, Arabic text and French trans. by Lévi-Provençal, *And*, 3, 1935, pp. 233-344; 4, 1936, pp. 29-145.

ʿAbd al-Waḥḥāb, "Le développement de la musique arabe en Orient, Espagne, et Tunisie," *Revue Tunisienne*, 25, 1918, pp. 106-117.

Abdel Badi, Lutfi, *La épica árabe y su influencia en la épica castellana*, Santiago de Chile, 1964.

ʿAbd el-Jalīl, J. M., *Brève Histoire de la Littérature Arabe*, Paris, 1943.

Abel, Armand, "Spain: Internal Division," in *Unity and Variety in Muslim Civilization*, ed. by Gustave E. von Grunebaum, Chicago, 1955.

Aben Adhari de Marruecos, *Historia de al-Andalus*, trans. by Francisco Fernández y González, Granada, 1860 (*Cf.* Ibn ʿIdhārī).

Abū l-Faraj al-Iṣfahānī, *Kitāb al-Aġānī*, Cairo, 1905.

Abū-Lughod, Ibrahīm, *Arab Rediscovery of Europe; a Study in Cultural Encounters*, Princeton, 1963.

Abū l-Walīd al-Ḥimyarī, *Al-Badīʿ fī Waṣf ar-Rabīʿ*, ed. H. Pérès, Rabat, 1940

Abū Nuwās, *Dīwān*, Cario, 1351/1932.

Abusalt de Denia, *Rectificación de la mente, tratado de lógica*, ed. and trans. by Ángel González Palencia, Madrid, 1915.

Adler, G. J., *The Poetry of the Arabs of Spain*, New York, 1867.

Al-ʿAbbādī, Aḥmad Mujtār ʿAbd al-Fattāḥ, *Los eslavos en España, ojeada sobre su origen, desarrollo y relación con el movimiento de la shuʿūbiyya*, Madrid, 1953.

Al-Ahwānī, ʿAbd al-ʿAzīz, *Az-Zajal fī l-Andalus*, Cairo, 1957.

Alarcón, Maximiliano, *Lámpara de los príncipes por Abubéquer de Tortosa*, 2 vols., Madrid, 1930-31.

Al-Balawī, Yūsuf Ibn ash-Shaykh, *Kitāb Alif-Bā'*, Cairo, 1287/1870.

Alcalá, Pedro de, *Arte para ligeramente saber la lengua aráviga*, photographic ed., New York, 1928.

Alcocer Martínez, R., *La corporación de los poetas en la España musulmana*, Madrid, 1940.

Alemany, Bolufer, J., "La geografía de la Península Ibérica en los escritores árabes" in *Revista del Centro de Estudios Históricos de Granada y su Reino*, 9, 10, 11, 1919-1921.

Al-Farazdaq, *Dīwān*, Beirut, 1960.

Al-Ḥakīm, Tawfīq, *Diario de un fiscal rural*, trans. by Emilio García Gómez, in *Colección de autores árabes contemporaneos*, vol. I, Madrid, 1955.

Al-Ḥarīrī, *Kitāb Maqāmāt al-Ḥarīrī*, Beirut, 1888.

——, *The Assemblies*, trans. by T. Chenery, R. A. S. London, 1898. 2 vols.

Al-Ḥumaidī, *Jadwat al-Muqtabis fī Dhikr Wulāt al-Andalus*, Cairo, 1966.

Al-Idrīsī, *Descripción de España*, trans. by José Antonio Conde, Madrid, 1799.

——, *Kitāb Nuzhat al-Mushtāq. Description de l'Afrique et de l'Espagne*, ed. by R. Dozy and M. J. de Goeje, Leiden, 1866.

Al-Jāḥiẓ, *Kitāb al-Ḥayawān*, Cairo, 1945.
Aljoxani, *Historia de los jueces de Córdoba*, ed. and trans. by Julián Ribera, Madrid, 1914.
Al-Maqqarī, *History of the Mohammedan Dynasties*, trans. by Pascual de Gayangos, 2 vols., London 1840-43.
——, *Nafḥ aṭ-Ṭīb*, Cairo, 1949.
Al-Marrakushī, ʿAbd al-Wāḥid, *Al-Muʿjib fī Talkhīs Akhbār al-Maġrib*, Cairo, 1949.
——, *Kitāb al-Muʿjib*, ed. R. Dozy, 2nd ed., Leiden, 1885.
Al-Mawardī, *Al-Aḥkām as-Sulṭāniyya*, French. trans. by Leon Ostrorog, Paris, 1901.
Al-Mutanabbīʾ, *Dīwān, with the Commentary by Abī l-Ḥasan ʿAlī ibn Aḥmad al-Wāḥidī an-Naisabūrī*, ed. by F. Dieterici, Berlin, 1861.
An-Nuṣulī, Anīs Zakariya, *Ad-Dawlat al-Umawiyya fī Qurṭuba*, Baghdad, 1926.
Alonso, Amado, "Correspondencias arábigoespañolas," in *RFE*, 8, 1946, pp. 30-43; 57-60.
Alonso, Dámaso, "Cancioncillas de 'amigo' mozárabes (Primavera temprana de la lírica europea)," in *RFE*, 33, 1949, pp. 297-349.
——, "Poesía arábigoandaluza y poesía gongorina," in *Estudios y ensayos gongorinos*, Madrid, 1955.
Alonso Alonso, Manuel, "Influencia de Algazel en el mundo latino," *Andalus*, 1958, 2, pp. 271-308.
——, *Pedro Hispano Scientia Libri de Anima*, 2nd. ed., Barcelona, 1961.
——, *Temas filosóficos medievales (Ibn Dāwūd y Gundisalvo)*, in *Miscelanea Comillas, serie filosófica*, 10, Santander, 1959.
Ar-Ruʿaynī, Abū l-Ḥasan ʿAlī Muḥammad ibn ʿAlī, *Birnāmaj Shuyūkh ar-Ruʿaynī*, Damascus, 1962.
Ar-Ruṣāfī al-Balansī, *Dīwān*, Beirut, 1960.
Ash-Shushtarī, *Dīwān*, Cairo, 1960.
Aṣ-Ṣūfī, Khālid, *Taʾrīkh al-ʿArab fī Isbaniya: Jumhuriyyat Banī Jahwar*, Damascus, 1959.
——, *Taʾrīkh al-ʿArab fī Isbaniya: Nihāyat al-Khilāfat al-Umawiyya fī l-Andalus*, Aleppo, 1963.
Aṭ-Ṭabari, *Annales*, ed. by M. J. de Goeje, reprint, Leiden, 1965.
Altamira, Rafael, *Historia de España y de la civilización española*, Barcelona, 1911.
——, "Western Caliphate" in the *Cambridge Medieval History*, vol. 3, 1922.
At-Tuṭīlī, *Dīwān*. Beirut, 1963.
Andrés, Juan, *Dell' origine, de' progressi e dello stato attuale d'ogni letteratura*, 8 vols., Parma, 1782-99.
Antuña, Melchor M., "La corte literaria de Alháquem II en Córdoba," in *Religión y Cultura*, 1929.
——, "Sevilla y sus monumentos árabes," *Escorial*, 1930.
Arberry, Arthur J., *An Introduction to the History of Sufism (The Sir Abdullah Suhrawardy Lectures for 1942)*, Oxford, 1942.
——, *Arabic Poetry, a Primer for Students*, Cambridge, 1965.
——, *Aspects of Islamic Civilization*, London, 1964.
——, *Modern Arabic Poetry*, London, 1950.
——, *Moorish Poetry, a translation of The Pennants, an Anthology Compiled in 1243 by the Andalusian Ibn Saʿīd*, Cambridge, 1953.
——, *Oriental Essays, Portraits of Seven Scholars*, London, 1960.
——, (ed.) *Poems of al-Mutanabbīʾ*, Cambridge, 1967.

Arberry, Arthur J., *The Seven Odes, the First Chapter in Arabic Literature*, London, 1957.
Ar-Rikābī, Jawdat, *Fī l-Adab al-Andalusī*, Cairo, 1960.
Arteaga, Esteban, *Della influenza degli Arabi sull' origine della poesia moderna in Europa*, Rome, 1791.
——, *La belleza ideal*, Prologue, text and notes by Miguel Batllori, Madrid, 1943.
——, *Rivoluzioni del Teatro Musicale Italiano*, Bologne, 1783.
Artola, Miguel, *Los afrancesados*, Madrid, 1953.
Asín Palacios, Miguel, *Abenházam de Córboba y su Historia crítica de las ideas religiosas*, Madrid, 1927-1932, 5 vols.
——, "Abenmasarra y su escuela, orígenes de la filosofía hispano-musulmana discurso leído en el acto de su recepción por Don Miguel Asín Palacios y contestación del excmo. Sr. Don Eduardo Sanz y Escartín," Madrid, 1914.
——, *Algazel: Dogmática, moral, y ascética con Prólogo de Menéndez y Pelayo*, Saragossa, 1901.
——, *Contribución a la toponimia árabe de España*, Madrid, 1944.
——, *Crestomatía del árabe literal con glosario y elementos de gramática*, 3rd ed., Madrid, 1945.
——, *Dante y el islam*, Madrid, 1927.
——, "Discursos leídos ante la Real Academia de la Historia en la recepción pública del señor Don Miguel Asín Palacios," Madrid, 1924, (*Contestación* by Julián Ribera).
——, "El abecedario de Yūsuf Benaxeij el malagueño," *BRAH*, 1932, pp. 195-228.
——, "El "Intérprete Arábigo" de Fray Bernardino González," *BRAH*, 1901, vol. 38, fasc. I, pp. 15-28.
——, *El islam cristianizado, estudio del "sufismo" a través de las obras de Abenarabī de Murcia*, 1st. ed., Madrid, 1931.
——, *El justo medio en la creencia, compendio de teología dogmática de Algazel*, trans. by Asín, Madrid, 1929.
——, *Glosario de voces romances registradas por un botánico anónimo hispano-musulmán (siglos XI-XII)*, Madrid-Granada, 1943.
——, *Huellas del islam*, Madrid, 1941.
——, *La escatología musulmana en la Divina Comedia seguida de la historia y crítica de una polémica*, 2nd ed., Madrid-Granada, 1943; 3rd ed. 1961.
——, *La espiritualidad de Algazel y su sentido cristiano*, 4 vols., Madrid 1934-41.
——, "L'enseignement de l'arabe en Espagne," in *Revue Africaine*, 58 (1914), pp. 183-192.
——, *Los caracteres y la conducta, tratado de moral práctica por Abenházam de Córdoba*, trans. by Asín, Madrid, 1916.
——, *Obras escogidas*, vol. 1, Madrid, 1946; vols. 2 and 3, Madrid, 1948.
——, "Una descripción nueva del Faro de Alejandría," *Andalus*, I, pp. 241-300.
——, *Vidas de santones andaluces, la "Epístola de la santidad" de Ibn ʿArabī de Murcia*, Madrid, 1933.
Asso del Río, Ignacio de, *Bibliotheca Arabico-Aragonensis*, Amsterdam, 1782.
Atkinson, William C., *A History of Spain and Portugal*, London, 1960.
Avempace, *El régimen del solitario*, ed. and trans. by Miguel Asín Palacios, Madrid-Granada, 1946.

Backer, Augustin and Aloys de, *Bibliothèque de la Compagnie de Jésus*, new ed. by Carlos Sommervogel, vol. I, 1890, *s.v.* "*Jean Andrés*," pp. 242-350; "*Etienne Artiaga*," pp. 590-91.

Badawī, ʿAbd ar-Raḥmān, *Aristoteles de Poetica*, Cairo, 1953.

——, *Ḥāzim al-Qarṭājannī wa Naẓariyāt Arisṭū fī sh-Shiʿr wa l-Balāgha*, Cairo, 1961.

Baer, Yitzhak, *A History of the Jews in Christian Spain*, I, Philadelphia, 1961.

Bahija Sidqi Rashid, *Egyptian Folk Songs in Arabic and English*, New York, 1964.

Barbieri, Giammaria, *Dell' origine della poesia rimata*, Modena, 1790, publ. by Girolamo Tiraboschi.

Bargebuhr, Frederick P., *El palacio de la Alhambra en el siglo XI*, *University of Iowa Studies in Spanish Language and Literature*, vol. 15, Mexico, 1966.

Barrau-Dihigo, L., "Contribution à la Critique de Conde," in *Homenaje a Don Francisco Codera*, Saragossa, 1904.

Bataillon, Marcel, "L'Arabe à Salamanque au Temps de la Renaissance," *Hesperis*, 31, 1935.

Baynes, N. H., and Moss, H. St. L. B., *Byzantium, an Introduction to East Roman Civilization*, Oxford, 1961.

Bellver y Cacho, *Influencia que ejerció la dominación de los árabes en la agricultura, industria y comercio de la provincia de Castellón de la Plana*, Castellon, 1889.

Bettinelli, Saverio, *Risorgimento d' Italia negli Studi, nelle Arti e ne' Costumi dopo il Mille*, Venice, 1786.

Blachère, R., "La vie et l'œuvre du poète-épistolier andalou Ibn Darrāǧ al-Qasṭallī," in *Hesperis*, 16, 1923, pp. 99-121.

——, "Le poète arabe al-Mutanabbīʾ et l'Occident musulman," in REI, 1929, pp. 127-135.

Blochet, E., *Les sources orientales de la Divine Comédie*, Paris, 1901.

Borbón, Faustino de, *Cartas para ilustrar la historia de la España árabe*, Madrid, 1799.

Boronat y Barrachina, Pascual, *Los moriscos españoles y su expulsión; estudio histórico-crítico*, Valencia, 1901.

Breydy, Michel, *Michel Gharcieh al-Ghazīrī, orientaliste Libanais du XVIIIè siècle*, Beirut, 1950.

Brockelmann, C., *Geschichte der arabischen Literatur*, 2nd ed., 2 vols., Leiden, 1943-9 and 3 Supplements, 1937-1942.

——, *History of the Islamic Peoples*, trans. by Joel Carmichael and Moshe Perlmann, New York, 1960.

Browne, E. G., *A Literary History of Persia*, Cambridge, 1956.

Burton, Richard F., *Personal Narrative of a Pilgrimage to Al-Madīnah and Meccah*, New York, 1964.

Cabanelas Rodríguez, Darío, *El morisco granadino Alonso del Castillo*, Granada, 1965.

——, *Juan de Segovia y el problema islámico*, Madrid, 1952.

Cacho Viu, Vicente, *La Institución Libre de Enseñanza*, Madrid, 1962.

Cadalso, José, *Cartas marruecas*, Madrid, 1956.

Cagigas, Isidro de las, *Andalucía musulmana; aportaciones a la delimitación de la frontera del Andalus (ensayo de etnografía andaluza medieval)*, Madrid, 1950.

——, *Los viajes de Alí Bey a través del Marruecos Oriental*, Madrid, 1919.

——, *Minorías étnico-religiosas de la edad media española*, I *Los mozárabes*, 2 vols., Madrid, 1947-48, 2 *Los mudéjares*, 2 vols., Madrid, 1948-49.

Cagigas, Isidro de las, *Sevilla almohade y útimos años de su vida musulmana*, Madrid, 1951.
——, *Tratados y convenios referentes a Marruecos*, Madrid, 1952.
Caillet-Bois, Julio, *Antología de la poesía hispano-americana*, Madrid, 1958.
Campaner y Fuertes, A., *Bosquejo histórico de la dominación islamita en las Islas Baleares*, Palma, 1888.
Cañes, Francisco, *Diccionario español-latino-arábico*, Madrid, 1787.
——, *Gramática arábigo-española, vulgar, y literal con un diccionario arábigo-español, en que se ponen las voces más usuales para una conversación familiar, con un Texto de la Doctrina Christiana en el idioma arábigo*, Madrid, 1775.
Cánovas del Castillo, Antonio, *Apuntes para la historia de Marruecos*, Madrid, 1913.
——, "Contestación," in *Memorias de la Real Academia Española*, vol. 6, Madrid, 1889.
——, *"El Solitario" y su tiempo, biografía de D. Serafín Estébanez Calderón y crítica de sus obras*, 2 vols., Madrid, 1883.
Cantera Burgos, Francisco, "Los estudios orientales en la España actual," in *Oriente Moderno*, 1955, pp. 236-40.
——, "Versos españoles en las muwaššaḥas hispanohebreas," *Sefarad*, 9, 1949, pp. 197-234.
Caro Baroja, Julio, *Los morisos del reino de Granada, (ensayo de historia social)*, Madrid, 1957.
——, *Una visión de marruecos a mediados del siglo XVI, la del primer historiador de los "xarifes," Diego de Torres*, Madrid, 1956.
Carr, Raymond, *Spain* 1808-1939, Oxford, 1966.
Carrasco Urgoiti, María Soledad, *El moro de Granada en la literatura (del siglo XV al XX)*, Madrid, 1956.
Casiri, Miguel, *Bibliotheca Arabico-Hispana Escurialensis*, 2 vols., Madrid, 1760-70.
Castejón Calderón, Rafael, *Los juristas hispano-musulmanes*, Madrid, 1948.
Castellanos, Manuel P., *Apostolado seráfico en Marruecos; o sea, historia de las misiones franciscanas en aquel imperio desde el siglo XIII hasta nuestros días*, Madrid-Santiago, 1896.
——, *Descripción histórica de Marruecos y breve reseña de sus dinastías; o apuntes para servir a la historia del Magreb*, Santiago, 1878.
——, *Historia de Marruecos*, 3rd ed., Tangiers, 1898.
Castillo, Hernando del, *Cancionero general*, ed. A. Rodríguez-Moñino, Madrid, 1958-59.
Castro, Américo, *España en su historia: Cristianos moros y judíos*, Buenos Aires, 1948.
——, Eng. trans., *The Structure of Spanish History*, Princeton, 1954.
——, *La realidad histórica de España, (edición renovada)*, Mexico, 1962.
Cattan, Isaac, "L'orientaliste espagnol Francisco Codera y Zaidín," in *Revue Tunisienne*, Tunis, 1918, vol. 25, fasc. 126, pp. 128-129.
Cerulli, Enrico, *Il "Libro della Scala" e la questione delle fonti arabo-spagnole della Divina Commedia*, Vatican, 1949.
Codera, Francisco and Julián Ribera, *Bibliotheca Arabico-Hispana*, vols. 1-8, Madrid, 1882-1892; vols., 9-10, Saragossa, 1893-1895.
Codera, Francisco, "Decadencia y desaparición de los almorávides en España," in *Collección de estudios árabes*, vol. 3, Saragossa, 1899.
——, "Discursos leidos ante la Real Academia de la Historia en la recepción pública de Don Francisco Codera y Zaidín," Madrid, 1879.

Codera, Francisco, "Estudios críticos de historia árabe española," in *Colección de estudios árabes*, vol. 7, Saragossa, 1903.

——, "Estudios críticos de historia árabe española (segunda serie)," in *Colección de estudios árabes*, vol. 8, Madrid, 1917.

——, *Tratado de numismática arábigo-española*, Madrid, 1879.

Cohen, Gustave, "Le problème des origines arabes de la poésie provençale mediévale," *Bulletin de l'Académie royale de Belgique* (*Classe de Lettres*), Brussels, 1946, vol. 32, pp. 266-278.

Commerelán y Gómez, Francisco A., "Contestación," in *Discursos leídos ante la Real Academia Española*, Madrid, 1894.

Conde, José Antonio, *History of the Dominion of the Arabs in Spain*, Eng. trans. by Mrs. Jonathan Foster, London, 1854.

——, *Historia de la dominación de los árabes en España*, New ed., 3 vols., Barcelona, 1844.

Conrotte, Manuel, *España y los países musulmanes durante el ministerio de Floridablanca*, Madrid, 1909.

Costa, Joaquín, *Estudios jurídicos y políticos*, Madrid, 1884.

Cour, A., *Un poète arabe d'Andalousie: Ibn Zaidoun*, Constantine, 1920.

Covarrubias Orozco, Sebastián de, *Tesoro de la lengua castellana*, Madrid, 1611.

Cruz Hernández, Miguel, *Historia de la filosofía española, filosofía hispano-musulmana*, Madrid, 1957, 2 vols.

——, *La filosofía árabe*, Madrid, 1963.

Ḍaif, Aḥmad; *Balāghat al-ʿArab fī l-Andalus*, Cairo, 1342/1924.

——, *Essai sur le Lyrisme et la Critique Littéraire chez les Arabes*, Paris, 1917.

Dánvila y Collado, D. M., *La expulsión de los moriscos españoles*, Madrid, 1889.

Dérenbourg, Hartwig, *Les manuscrits arabes de l'Escurial*, Paris, 1884.

Díaz-Plaja, Guillermo, *Federico García Lorca*, 2nd. ed., Buenos Aires, 1955.

"Don Julián Ribera y Tarragó," *And.*, vol. 2, 1934, pp. 1-7.

Dozy, R., Dugat, Krehl, and Wright, *Analectes sur l'Histoire et la Littérature des Arabes d'Espagne*, Leiden, 1855-61.

Dozy, Reinhart, and W. H. Engelmann, *Glossaire des mots espagnols et portuguais derivés de l'arabe*, 2nd. ed., Leiden, 1869.

Dozy, Reinhart, *Investigaciones acerca de la historia de España*, trans. by Antonio Machado y Álvarez, 2 vols., Seville-Madrid, 1878.

——, *Scriptorum Arabum Loci de Abbadidis*, Leiden, 1846-63.

——, *Spanish Islam: A History of the Moslems in Spain*, trans. by Francis Griffin Stokes, New York, 1913.

——, *Supplément aux Dictionnaires Arabes*, 2 vols., Leiden, 1881.

Dubler, César E., *Abū Ḥamīd el granadino y su relación de viaje por tierras eurasiáticas, texto árabe, traducción e interpretación*, Madrid, 1953.

Dubler, César E., and Elías Terés Sádaba, *La 'Materia Medica' de Dioscorides, transmisión medieval y renacentista*, vol. 2, *La versión árabe de la 'Materia Medica de Dioscórides* (*texto, variantes e índices*), Tetuán-Barcelona, 1952-1957.

Dubler, César E., *Über das Wirtschaftsleben auf der Iberischen Halbinsel vom XI zum XIII Jhrh.*, Basel, 1943.

Dugat, Gustave, *Histoire des orientalistes de l'Europe du XIIè au XIXè siècle*, 2 vols., Paris, 1868.

Dutton, Brian, "Lelia Doura, Edoy Lelia Doura, An Arabic Refrain in a Thirteenth-Century Galician Poem ?," *Bulletin of Hispanic Studies*, 41, Jan. 1964, pp. 1-9.

Eguilaz y Yanguas, Leopoldo, *El talismán del diablo, novela fantástico-oriental*, Madrid, 1853.
——, *Estudio sobre el valor de las letras arábigas en el alfabeto castellano*, Madrid, 1874.
——, *Glosario etimológico de las palabras españolas (castellanas, catalanas, gallegas, mallorquinas, portuguesas, valencianas y bascongadas) de origen oriental (árabe, hebreo, malayo, persa y turco)*, Granada, 1886.
——, *Poesía histórica, lírica y descriptiva de los árabes andaluces*, Madrid, 1864.
——, *Reseña histórica de la conquista del reino de Granada*, Granada, 1894.
Enciclopedia Universal Ilustrada Europeo-Americana), José Espasa, editor, Barcelona, 70 vols., Appendix, 10 vols., Supplement, 1934 on.
Fagnan, E., *Annales du Maghreb et de l'Espagne, par Ibn al-Athīr*, Algiers, 1901 (French translation).
——, *Histoire des Almohades d' ʿAbd el-Wāḥid al-Marrakushī*, Algiers, 1893.
Fahmy, ʿAlī Muḥammad, *Muslim Sea Power in the Eastern Mediterranean Sea*, London, 1950.
Farmer, H. G. *A History of Arabian Music to the XIIIth. Century*, London, 1929.
Fernández de Moratín, Leandro, *La derrota de los pedantes y poesías*, ed. Louis Machaud. Paris, 19— (no date).
Fernández y González, Francisco, *Estado social y político de los mudéjares de Castilla*, Madrid, 1866.
——,"Influencia de las lenguas y letras orientales en la cultura de los pueblos de la Península Ibérica," in *Discursos leídos ante la Real Academia española*, Madrid, 1894.
Ferrandis, José, *Marfiles y azabaches españoles*, Barcelona, 1928.
Fischel, W. J., *Jews in the Economic and Political Life of Medieval Islam*, London, 1937.
Fitzmaurice-Kelly, J., "Chronique," in *Revue Hispanique*, vol. 4, 1897, p. 339.
Fry, Richard N., *The Heritage of Persia*, Mentor, New York, 1966.
Fück, Johann, *Die arabischen Studien in Europa bis in den Anfang des 20. Jahrhunderts*, Leipzig, 1955.
Fyzee, Asaf A. A., *Outlines of Muhammadan Law*, London, 1955.
Gallego y Burín, Antonio, *La Alhambra*, Granada, 1963.
Gallerani, Alejandro, *Jesuitas expulsos de España; literatos en Italia*, trans. from Italian, Salamanca, 1897.
Galmés de Fuentes, Álvaro, *Influencias sintácticas y estilísticas del árabe en la prosa medieval castellana*, Madrid, 1956.
García Gómez, Emilio, "A propósito del libro de K. Heger sobre las jarŷas. Descifre de la jarŷa de Schirmann," *And.*, 26, 1961, pp. 453-465.
——, *Ash-Shiʿr al-Andalusī*, trans, by Hussein Monès, Cairo, 2nd. ed., 1956.
——, "Bagdad y los reinos de Taifas," *Revista de Occidente*, 127, 1934, pp. 1-22.
——, *Cinco poetas musulmanes, biografías y estudios*, Madrid, 1945.
——, "Don Ángel González Palencia (1889-1949)," *And.*, 14, 1949, pp. 1-11.
——, "Don Miguel Asín 1871-1944 (Esquema de una biografía)," *And.*, 9, 1944, pp. 267-291.
——, "Dos nuevas jarŷas romances (XXV y XXVI) en muwaššaḥas árabes (Ms. G. S. Colin), y adición al estudio de otra jarŷa romance (supra, pp. 43-52)," *And.*, 19, 1954, pp. 390-391.

García Gómez, Emilio, *Elogio del Islam Español,* (The *risāla* of ash-Shaqundī) Span. trans., Madrid, 1954.

——, "En la jubilación de don Miguel Asín," *And.*, 6, 1941, pp. 266-270.

——, "Estudio del *Dār aṭ-ṭirāz,*" *And.*, 27, 1962, pp. 21-104.

——, "Homenaje a Don Francisco Codera: 1836-1917," *And.*, 15, 1950, pp. 263-274.

——, "La 'ley de Mussafia' se aplica a la poesía estrófica arábigoandaluza," *And.*, 27, 1962, pp. 1-20.

——, "La lyrique Hispano-Arabe et l'apparition de la lyrique Romane," *Arabica*, 1958, pp. 113-143.

——, "La muwaššaḥa de Ibn Baqī de Córdoba, *Mā laday Ṣabrun Muʿīnu*, con jarŷa romance," *And.*, 19, 1954, pp. 43-52.

——, "La poésie politique sous le califat de Cordoue," *Revue des Études Islamiques*, Paris, 1949.

——, *Las jarchas romances de la serie árabe en su marco*, Madrid, 1965.

——, "Más sobre las "jarŷas" romances en "muwaššaḥas" hebreas," *And.*, 14, 1949, pp. 409-17.

——, *Poemas arábigoandaluces*, Madrid, 1940.

——, *Poesía arábigoandaluza, breve síntesis histórica*, Madrid, 1952.

——, *Qaṣīdas de Andalucía, puestas en verso castellano*, Madrid, 1940.

——, *Silla del moro y nuevas escenas andaluzas*, Madrid, 1948.

——, "Sobre el nombre y la patria del autor de la Muwaššaḥa," *And.*, 2, 1934, pp. 215-222.

——, "Sobre un tercer tipo de poesía arábigoandaluza," in *Estudios dedicados a Menéndez Pidal*, 2, 1951, pp. 397-408.

——, and E. Lévi-Provençal, *Una crónica anónima de ʿAbd al-Raḥmān III al-Nāṣir, editada por primera vez y traducida, con introducción, notas e índices*, Madrid-Granada, 1950.

——, *Un alfaquí español, Abū Isḥāq de Elvira, texto árabe de su "Dīwān," según el M.S. Escur.* 404, *publicado por primera vez, con introducción, análisis, notas e índices*, Madrid-Granada, 1944.

——, "Una 'Pre-muwaššaḥa' atribuída a Abū Nuwās," *And.*, 21, 1956, pp. 406-414.

——, *Un texto árabe occidental de la leyenda de Alejandro*, Madrid, 1929.

——, "Usos y supersticiones comunes a Persia y España," *And.*, vol. 22, 1957, pp. 459-462.

——, "Veinticuatro jarŷas romances en muwaššaḥas árabes (Ms. G. S. Colin)," *And.*, 17, 1952, pp. 57-127.

Gardet, Louis, and M. M. Anawati, *Introduction à la Théologie Musulmane; Essai de Théologie Comparée*, Paris, 1948.

Gardet, Louis, *La Cité Musulmane; Vie Sociale et Politique*, Paris, 1954.

Gaspar Remiro, M.; *Historia de Murcia musulmana,* Saragossa, 1905.

Gayangos, Pascual de, *Escritores en prosa anteriores al siglo XV, BAE*, vol. 51, Madrid, 1860.

——, *La gran conquista de Ultramar, BAE*, Madrid, 1858.

——, "Language and Literature of the Moriscos," *British and Foreign Review*, 8, 1839, pp. 63-95.

——, *Libros de caballerías, BAE*, vol. 40, Madrid, 1857.

——, "Memoria sobre la autenticidad de la crónica del moro Rasis," in *Memorias de la Real Academia de la Historia*, v. 8, 1852.

——, *Memorias del cautivo en la Goleta de Túnez.* (*El Alferez Pedro de Aguilar*), Madrid, 1875.

Gayangos, Pascual de, *Tratados de legislación musulmana*, in *Memorial histórico español*, vol. 5, pp. 1-149.
Gibb, H. A. R., *Arabic Literature, an Introduction*, 2nd ed., Oxford, 1963.
——, "ʿArabiyya" in *Encyclopaedia of Islam*.
——, *Mohammedanism: An Historical Survey*, Oxford, 1949.
——, *Studies on the Civilization of Islam*, Boston, 1962.
Gibbon, Edward, *The Decline and Fall of the Roman Empire*, ed. by J. B. Bury, London, 1911.
Gil, Pablo; Ribera, J.; Sanchez, M., *Colección de textos aljamiados*, Saragossa, 1888.
Goldziher, Ignaz, "Die Šuʿūbijja unter den Muhammedanern in Spanien," *ZDMG*, vol. 53, 1899, pp. 601-620.
——, *Muhammedanische Studien*, I, Halle, 1888-1890.
Gomez de la Serna, Ramón, *Greguerías*, 1940-45, 4th ed., Buenos Aires, 1945.
Gómez-Moreno, Manuel, *Ars Hispaniae*, 3: *El arte árabe español hasta los almohades. Arte mozárabe*, Madrid, 1951.
——, *Iglesias mozárabes, arte español de los siglos IX a XI*, Madrid, 1919.
——, "Unas cartas de El Solitario," *BRAE*, Madrid, vol. 33, 1953, p. 213.
González, Joaquín de: *Fatḥo l-Andalusi, historia de la conquista de España*, Algiers, 1899.
González Palencia, Ángel, and Juan Hurtado y J. de la Serna, *Antología de la literatura española*, Madrid, 1926.
——, *Árabes murcianos ilustres*, Murcia, 1957.
——, "Correspondencia entre Menéndez y Pelayo y Asín," *And.*, vol. 12, 1947, pp. 391-414.
——, "El amor platónico en la corte de los califas," *Boletín de la real Academia de Ciencias, Bellas Letras y Nobles Artes de Córdoba*, 1929, pp. 1-25.
——, *El islam y occidente*, Madrid, 1945.
——, *Historia de la España musulmana*, Barcelona, 1925.
——, *Historia de la literatura arábigo-española*, 2nd. ed., (revised), Barcelona, 1945.
——, and Juan Hurtado y J. de la Serna, *Historia de la literatura española*, Madrid, 1922.
——, *Historias y leyendas*, Madrid, 1942.
——, *Los mozárabes de Toledo en los siglos XII y XIII*, Madrid, 1926-1930.
——, *Moros y cristianos en España medieval, estudios histórico-literarios, tercera serie*, Madrid, 1945.
——, "Noticias y extractos de algunos manuscritos árabes y aljamiados, de Toledo y Madrid." Also, "Apéndice a la edición Codera de la 'Tecmīla' de Aben al-Abbār," in *Miscelanea de estudios y textos árabes*, Madrid, 1915.
——, "Posición de Arteaga en la polémica sobre música y poesía arábigas," *And.*, 11, 1946, pp. 241-5.
González Serrano, U., "Bocetos filosóficos VIII, Moreno Nieto," in *Revista Contemporanea*, vol. 124, 1902, pp. 667-676.
Granja, Fernando de la, "Ibn García, cadí de los califas Ḥammūdíes," *And.*, 1965, pp. 63-78.
——, "Origen árabe de un famoso cuento español," *And.*, 1959, pp. 319-332.
——, "Una opinión significativa sobre la poesía arábigo-andaluza," *And.*, I, 1957, pp. 215-220.
Guillén Robles, F., *Catálogo de los manuscritos árabes existentes en la Biblioteca Nacional de Madrid*, 1889.

Gundisalvo, Domingo, *De Scientiis, texto latino establecido por el P. Manuel Alonso Alonso, S.J.*, Madrid-Granada, 1954.
Haim, Sylvia G., *Arab Nationalism, an Anthology*, Los Angeles, 1964.
Hartmann, M., *Das Arabische Strophengedichte, I., Das Muwaššaḥ*, Weimar, 1897.
Ḥamūdah, ʿAlī Muḥammad, *Taʾrīkh al-Andalus as-Siyāsī wa l-ʿUmrānī wa l-Ijtimāʿī*, Cairo, 1957.
Hārūn, ʿAbd as-Salām, *Nawādir al-Makhṭūṭāt*, 3 vols., Cairo, 1953.
Harvey, L. P., "Aljamía," in *The Encyclopaedia of Islam*, new ed., vol. 1, London, 1960, pp. 404-405.
Ḥāzim al-Qarṭājannī, *Dīwān*, Beirut, 1964.
Hell, J., "Al-ʿAbbās ibn al-Aḥnaf, der Minnesänger am Hofe Hārūn ar-Rašīd's," *Islamica*, 2, 1926, pp. 271-307.
Herr, Richard, *The Eighteenth-Century Revolution in Spain*, Princeton, 1958.
Herrera, Alonso de, *Agricultura General*, Madrid, 1645.
Ḥimyarī, Abū ʿAbd Allāh, *Kitāb Rawḍat al-Miʿṭar (la Peninsule Iberique au Moyen Âge)*, ed. by E. Lévi-Provençal, Leiden, 1938.
Hitti, Philip K., *History of the Arabs*, 7th ed., London, 1961.
——, *The Arabs, a Short History*, Chicago, 1956.
Hodgson, Marshall G. S., *Introduction to Islamic Civilization*, 3 vols., Chicago, 1958-59.
Hoenerbach, Wilhelm, *Spanish-Islamische Urkunden aus der Zeit der Naṣriden und Moriscos*, Berkeley-Los Angeles, 1965.
Hole, Edwyn, *Andalus, Spain under the Muslims*, London, 1958.
Homenaje a Don Francisco Codera en su jubilación del profesorado. Estudios de erudición oriental, con una introducción de Don Eduardo Saavedra, Saragossa, 1904.
Hoogvliet, M., *Specimen e litteris orientalibus, exhibens diversorum scriptorum locos de regia Aphtasidarum familia et de Ibn Abduno poeta*, Leiden, 1839.
Hourani, George F., *Averroes; on the Harmony of Religion and Philosophy*, E.J.W. Gibb Memorial Series (New Series XXI), Unesco Collection of Great Works, Arabic Series, London, 1961.
Huart, C., *Ancient Persia and Iranian Civilization*, New York, 1927.
Huici Miranda, A., *Colección de crónicas árabes de la Reconquista*, 4 vols.; vol. 1, *Al-Ḥulāl Al-Mawšiyya, crónica árabe de las dinastías almorávide, almohade y benimerín*, trans., Tetuán, 1952; vols. 2, 3, *Al-Bayān al-Muġrib fī Ijtisār Ajbār Mulūk al-Andalus wa al-Maġrib por Ibn ʿIdhārī al-Marrakušī. Los almohades, tomos 1 y 2*, trans., Tetuán, 1953-54; vol. 4, *Kitāb al-Muʿyib fī Taljīs Ajbār al-Maġrib por Abū Muḥammad ʿAbd al-Wāḥid al-Marrakusī*, trans., Tetuán, 1955.
——, *Colección diplomática de Jaime I, el Conquistador, años 1217 a 1253*, vol. 1, Valencia, 1916.
——, *Estudio sobre la campaña de Las Navas de Tolosa*, Valencia, 1916.
——, *Historia política del imperio almohade, primera parte*, Tetuán, 1956.
——, (ed.) *Kitāb aṭ-Ṭabīj fī l-Maġrib wa l-Andalus fī ʿAṣr al-Muwaḥḥidīn, li-Muʿallif Maŷhūl*, in *Revista del Instituto Egipcio de Estudios Islámicos*, Madrid, 1961-62, pp. 15-242.
——, "La cocina Hispano-Magribí durante la época almohade," *Revista del Instituto Egipcio de Estudios Islámicos*, Madrid, 1957, pp. 137-155.
——, *Las crónicas latinas de la Reconquista, estudios prácticos de latín medieval*, vols. 1-2, Valencia, 1913.

Huici Miranda, A., *Las grandes batallas de la Reconquista durante las invasiones africanas (almorávides, almohades y benimerines)*, Madrid, 1956.
Ḥusayn, Ṭaha, *Los dias*, trans. by Emilio García Gómez, Valencia, 1954.
Husik, Isaac, *A History of Mediaeval Jewish Philosophy*, New York, 1916.
Ibn ʿAbd Rabbihi, *Al-ʿIqd al-Farīd*, Beirut, 1952.
Ibn ʿAbd al-Ghafūr al-Kalāʿī, of Seville, *Iḥkām Ṣanʿat al-Kalām*, Beirut, 1966.
Ibn ʿAbdūn, *Sevilla a comienzos del siglo XII: El tratado de Ibn ʿAbdūn.* Spanish trans. by E. Levi-Provençal and E. García Gómez, Madrid, 1947.
——, "Traité de Ḥisba: un document sur la vie urbaine et les corps de métier à Séville au début du XIIè siècle," ed. by E. Lévi-Provençal, *Journal Asiatique*, 1934, April-June; pp. 177-299.
Ibn Abī Zārʿ, *Rawḍ al-Qirṭās*, ed. with Latin trans. by Tornberg. Upsala, 1843-1846.
Ibn al-Abbār, *Kitāb Ḥulat al-Siyarā'*, Beirut, 1962.
Ibn al-ʿArabī, Muḥyī d-Dīn, *Tarjumān al-Ashwāq*, Beirut, 1961.
Ibn al-ʿArīf, *Maḥāsin al-Majālis, texte arabe, traduction et commentaire par Miguel Asín Palacios*, Paris, 1933.
Ibn al-ʿAwwām, *Libro de agricultura*, trans. by J. A. Banqueri, Madrid, 1802. 2 vols.
Ibn al-Faraḍī, *Ta'rīkh ʿUlamā' al-Andalus*, Cairo, 1966.
Ibn al-Khaṭīb, Lisān ad-Dīn, *Al-Iḥāṭa fī Akhbār Gharnāṭa*, Cairo, 1955.
——, *Al-Lamḥat al-Badriyya fī d-Dawlat an-Naṣriyya*, Cairo, 1347. A.H.
——, *Kitāb Aʿmāl al-Aʿlām*, ed. by E. Lévi-Provençal, Rabat, 1934.
Ibn Al-Qūṭiyya, *Kitāb Iftitāḥ al-Andalus*, Beirut, 1957.
——, *Ta'rīkh Iftitāḥ al-Andalus* Spanish trans. by J. Ribera, *Historia de la conquista de España*, Madrid, 1926.
Ibn al-Muʿ tazz, *Dīwān*, Beirut, 1331.
Ibn al-Wāfid, Abū l-Mutarrif, *Tratado de agricultura*, Spanish trans. by Millas Vallicrosa, in *Andalus*, 8, 1943.
Ibn Badrūn, *Sharḥ Qaṣīdat Ibn ʿAbdūn*, ed. by Dozy, Leiden, 1846.
Ibn Bashkuwāl al-Qurṭubī, *Kitāb aṣ-Ṣila*, 2 vols., Cairo, 1966.
Ibn Baṣṣāl, *Libro de agricultura*, ed. and. trans. by José M. Millás Vallicrosa and Mohamed Azimān, Tetuan, 1955.
Ibn Bassām, *Adh-Dhakhīra*, Cairo, 1942, 2 vols.
Ibn Dāwūd al-Iṣfahānī, *Kitāb al-Zahrah*, ed. by A. R. Nykl and Ibrāhīm Ṭūqān, Chicago, 1932.
Ibn Quzmān, *Dīwān, édition critique partielle et provisoire*, by O. J. Tuulio, Helsinki, 1941.
——, *Dīwān*, photographic ed. by Gunzburg, Berlin, 1896.
Ibn Ḥamdīs, *Dīwān*, ed. by Schiaparelli, Rome, 1897.
Ibn Hānī', *Dīwān*, Cairo, 1934.
Ibn Ḥayyān, *Al-Muḳtabis, tome troisième, Chronique du règne du Calife Umaiyade ʿAbd Allāh à Cordoue*, ed. by Melchor M. Antuña, Paris, 1936.
Ibn Ḥazm, *El collar de la paloma, tratado sobre el amor y los amantes de Ibn Ḥazm de Córdoba*, trans. by Emilio García Gómez; prologue by José Ortega y Gasset, Madrid, 1952.
——, *Jamharat Ansāb al-ʿArab*, Cairo, 1962.
——, *Kitāb al-Akhlāq wa s-Siyar*, Beirut, 1961.
——, *Kitāb al-Fiṣal fī l-Milal wa l-Ahwā' wa n-Nihal*, Cairo, (no date).
——, *Ṭawq al-Ḥamāma fī l-Ulfa wa l-Ullāf*, ed. by D. K. Petrof, Leiden, 1914.

Ibn ʿIdhārī al-Marrakushī, *Al-Bayān al-Muġrib fī Akhbār al-Maġrib*, vol. 2. ed. by R. Dozy, Leiden, 1851; vol. 3, ed. E. Lévi-Provençal, Paris, 1930.

Ibn Khafāja, *Dīwān*, Beirut, 1951.

Ibn Khair, Abū Bakr; *Fahrasa*, Baghdad, 1963.

Ibn Khaldūn, *The Muqaddimah*, trans. by F. Rosenthal, New York, 1958, 3 vols.

Ibn Khallikān, *Biographical Dictionary*, trans. De Slane, 4 vols., Paris, 1842-71.

Ibn Mājid, Aḥmad, *Instructions nautiques et routiers arabes et portugais des XV et XVIè siècles*, ed. Gabriel Ferrand, Paris, 1921-22.

Ibn Rochd (Averroës), *Traité Décisif* (*Façl el-Maqâl*) *sur l'accord de la religion et de la philosophie*, text, trans. and notes by Léon Gauthier, in *Bibliothèque arabe-française*, vol. I, 3rd. ed. Algiers, 1948.

Ibn Sahl, *Dīwān*, Cairo, 1926.

Ibn Ṣāʾid, Abū l-Ḥasan ʿArib, *Kitāb Awqāt al-Sanat*, ed. and Latin trans.: *Le Calendrier de Cordoue de l'année* 961, by R. Dozy, Leiden, 1873.

Ibn Saʿīd, *Al-Muġrib fi Ḥulā l-Maġrib*, ed by Shawqī Ḍayf, 2nd. ed., Cairo, 1964.

——, *Libro de las banderas de los campeones*, text, trans. and commentary by Emilio García Gómez, Madrid, 1942.

Ibn Sanāʾ al-Mulk, *Dār aṭ-Ṭiraz fī ʿAmal al-Muwashshaḥāt*, ed. by Jawdat ar-Rikābī, Damascus, 1949.

Ibn Shuhayd al-Andalusī, *Dīwān*, Beirut, 1963.

——, *Risālat at-Tawābiʿ wa z-Zawābiʿ*, Beirut, 1951.

Ibn Ṭufayl, *El filósofo autodidacto*, trans. by Ángel González Palencia, Madrid, 1948.

Ibn Zaidūn, *Dīwān*, Beirut, 1951.

Imamuddīn, S. M., *A Political History of Muslim Spain*, Dacca, 1961.

——, *Some Aspects of the Socio-Economic and Cultural History of Muslim Spain*, 711-1492 A. D., Leiden, 1965.

ʿInān, Muḥammad ʿAbd Allāh, *Al-Athār al-Andalusiyya al-Bāqiya*, 2nd ed., Cairo, 1961.

——, *Kitāb Dawlat al-Islām fī l-Andalus*, Cairo, 1960, 5 vols.

Index Islamicus, 1906-1955, *A Catalogue of Articles on Islamic Subjects in Periodicals and other Collective Publications*, compiled by J. D. Pearson, 1 vol., Cambridge, 1958; *Index Islamicus Supplement*, 1956-1960, 1 vol., J. D. Pearson, Cambridge, 1962.

Irving, Washington, *The Alhambra*: *a Series of Tales and Sketches of the Moors and Spaniards*, Philadelphia, 1832.

Irving, "Arab Tales in Medieval Spanish," in *Islamic Literature*, 7, 1955.

Jackson, Gabriel, *The Spanish Republic and the Civil War*, Princeton, 1965.

Janer, Florencio, *Condición social de los moriscos de España*, Madrid, 1857.

Jeanroy, A., *La poesie lyrique des Troubadours*, Toulouse-Paris, 1934.

Jeffery, Arthur, *A Reader on Islam*, The Hague, 1962.

Jones, William, *Poems, Consisting Chiefly of Translations from the Asiatick Languages*, London, 1772.

Julien, C. A., *Histoire de l'Afrique du Nord*, 2nd ed., Paris, 1964.

Khafāja, Muḥammad ʿAbd al-Munʿim, *Qiṣṣat al-Adab fī l-Andalus*, Beirut, 1962, 2 vols.

Kleinhans, Arduinis, *Historia Studii Linguae Arabicae et Colegii Missionum Ordinis Fratrum Minorum in Conventu ad S. Petrum in Monte Aureo Romae Erecti*, in *Biblioteca Bio-Bibliografica della Terra Santa e dell' Oriente Francescano*, directed by Girolamo Golubovich, vol. 13, Florence, 1930.

Knust, Hermann, *Mittheilungen aus dem Eskurial,* Tubingen, 1879.
Kritzeck, James, *Anthology of Islamic Literature,* New York, 1964.
Lacam, Jean, *Les Sarrazins dans le Haut Moyen Âge Français,* Paris, 1965.
Lafuente Alcántara, Emilio, *Ajbar Machmua, in Colección de obras arábigas de historia y geografía que publica la Real Academia de la Historia,* vol. I, Madrid, 1867.
——, *Inscripciones árabes de Granada,* Madrid, 1860.
——, *Relaciones de algunos sucesos de los ultimos tiempos del reino de Granada,* Madrid, 1868.
Laín Entralgo, Pedro, *La generación del noventa y ocho,* 4th. ed., Madrid, 1959.
Lane, Edward W., *Manners and Customs of the Modern Egyptians,* London, 1836.
Lane-Poole, Stanley, *The Mohammadan Dynasties,* New York, 1965.
——, *The Moors in Spain,* London, 1880.
Lapesa, Rafael, *Historia de la lengua española,* 4th ed., Madrid, 1959.
Larra, Mariano José de, *Artículos de costumbres,* Clásicos castellanos, Madrid, 1959.
Lea, Charles H., *A History of the Inquisition of Spain,* New York, 1906.
Le Gentil, P., "A propos de la 'strophe zéjelesque,'" in *Revue des Langues Romanes,* 70, 1949, pp. 119-134.
Lemay, Richard, "A propos de l'origine arabe de l'art des troubadours," *Annales, Économies, Sociétés, Civilisations,* 1966, pp. 990-1011.
Lerchundi, J., Simonet, J., *Crestomatía arábigo-española,* Granada, 1881.
Lerner, Ralph, and Mahdi, Muḥsin, (eds.), *Medieval Political Philosophy, a Sourcebook,* Toronto, 1963.
Lévi-Provençal, E., *Conférences sur l'Espagne Musulmane prononcées à la Faculté des Lettres en* 1947-1948, Cairo, 1951.
——, *Documents Arabes Inédits, première série: Trois Traités Hispaniques de Ḥisba,* Paris-Cairo, 1955.
——, *España musulmana hasta la caída del califato de Córdoba (711-1031 de J. C.),* in *Historia de España,* directed by R. Menéndez Pidal, vols. 4-5, Madrid, 1950, 1957.
——, *Inscriptions arabes d'Espagne,* Paris-Leiden, 1931.
——, *La civilización árabe en España,* Buenos Aires, 1953, trans. by Isidro de las Cagigas.
——, *La Civilization arabe en Espagne, Vue generale,* Cairo, 1938.
——, "Les Manuscrits arabes de Rabat," *Hesperis,* 18, 1934.
——, (ed.) *Les "Mémoires" de ʿAbd Allāh, dernier Roi Ziride de Grenade,* Arabic text, Cairo, 1955.
——, *L'Espagne musulmane au Xè Siècle,* Paris, 1932.
——, "Les vers arabes de la chanson V de Guillaume IX d'Aquitaine," *Arabica,* 1954, pp. 208-211.
——, (ed.) *Mafākhir al-Barbar, Fragments Historiques sur les Berberes au Moyen Âge,* in *Collection de textes publiée par l'Institut des Hautes Études Marocaines,* vol. I, Rabat, 1934.
——, "Poésie arabe d'Espagne et poésie d'Europe Mediévale," *Islam d'Occident,* Paris, 1948, pp. 305-318.
——, "Quelques considerations sur l'essor des études relatives a l'Occident musulman," *Revista del Instituto Egipcio de Estudios Islámicos,* Madrid, 1954, pp. 73-76.
Levy, Reuben, *The Social Structure of Islam,* Cambridge, 1962.
Lewis, Archibald R., *Naval Power and Trade in the Mediterranean A.D. 500-1100,* Princeton, 1951.

Lewis, Bernard, *The Arabs in History*, New York, 1960.
Lida de Malkiel, Maria Rosa, *Two Spanish Masterpieces, The "Book of Good Love" and "The Celestina"* in *Illinois Studies in Language and Literature*, vol. 49, Urbana, 1961.
Llampillas, Javier, *Ensayo histórico-apologético de la literatura española contra las opiniones preocupadas de algunos escritores modernos italianos*, trans. by Doña Josefa Amar y Borbón, 2nd ed., Madrid, 1789.
Llorens Castillo, Vicente, *Liberales y románticos, una emigración española en Inglaterra* (1823-1834), Mexico, 1954.
Longás, P., "Bibliografía de Don Miguel Asín," *And.*, 9, 1944, pp. 293-319.
——, "Un documento sobre los mudéjares de Nuez (Zaragoza), siglo XV," *And.*, 28, 1963, pp. 431-444.
——, *Vida religiosa de los moriscos*, Madrid, 1915.
López Morillas, Juan, *El krausismo español, perfil de una aventura intelectual*, Mexico, 1956.
López Ortiz, José, *Derecho musulmán*, Barcelona, 1932.
——, "El clero musulmán," in *Religión y cultura*, 6, 1929, pp. 198-206.
——, "Fatwas granadinas de los siglos XIV y XV," *And.*, 6, 1941, pp. 73-127.
——, "Figuras de jurisconsultos hispano-musulmanes. Yaḥya ben Yaḥya," in *Religón y cultura*, 16, 1931, pp. 94-104.
Luna, Miguel de, *The History of the Conquest of Spain by the Moors*, London, 1687. 2 ed cd., 1693.
Lyall, C. J., *Translations of Ancient Arabian Poetry*, New York, 1930.
Lynch, John, *Spain under the Hapsburgs*, vol. I, *Empire and Absolutism*, 1516-1598, New York, 1964.
MacCabe, Joseph, *Splendour of Moorish Spain*, London, 1935.
Maceira, A. G., *Apuntes y noticias sobre la agricultura de los árabes españoles*, Zamora, 1876.
Madariaga, Salvador de, *Spain, a Modern History*, New York, 1960.
Mahdi, Muḥsin, *Ibn Khaldūn's Philosophy of History*, Chicago, 1964.
Maḥmūd ʿAlī Makkī, "El *šīʿismo* en al-Andalus," *Revista del Instituto Egipcio de Estudios Islámicos*, Madrid, 1954, pp. 93-149.
Manzanares de Cirre, M., "Don Pascual de Gayangos (1809-1897) y los estudios árabes," *And.*, 28, 1963, 445-461.
Manzano Martos, Rafael, "La Capilla Real de Cholula y su mudejarismo," *And.*, 1961, I, pp. 219-224.
Marçais, Guillaume, *Manuel d'art musulman. L'architecture. Tunisie, Algérie, Maroc, Espagne, Sicile*, Paris, 1926-1927.
Mármol Carvajal, Luis del, *Descripción general de África*, Madrid, 1953.
——, *Historia del rebelión y castigo de los moriscos del reino de Granada BAE*, 21, Madrid, 1946.
Martínez Montávez, Pedro, *Poesía árabe contemporanea*, Madrid, 1958.
Masdeu, Juan Francisco de, *Historia crítica de España*, Madrid, 1793.
Massad, P., "Casiri y uno de sus estudios inéditos," *BRAH*, 5, 144, 1959, pp. 15-47.
Massignon, Louis "Recherches sur Shushtarī, poète andalou enterré à Damiette," *Mélanges William Marçais*, Paris, 1950, pp. 251-276.
——, "Time in Islamic Thought," in *Papers from the Eranos Yearbooks, Bollingen Series*, XXX, 2, New York, 1956.
Maura, Antonio, "Don Francisco Fernández y González," *BRAE*, 4, fasc. 19, Madrid, 1917, pp. 407-413.
Mélida, José Ramón, "Memoria acerca de algunas inscripciones arábigas

de España y Portugal," in *Boletín de la Institución Libre de Enseñanza*, vol. 7, 1883, pp. 366-367.

Mendoza, Diego Hurtado de, *De la guerra de Granada*, *BAE*, 21 Madrid, 1946.

Menéndez Pidal R., *Cantar de Mío Cid*, Madrid, 1906-1911.

——, "Cantos románicos andalusíes (continuadores de una lírica latina vulgar)," *BRAE*, vol. 31, Madrid, 1951, 187-270.

——, *España, eslabón entre la cristiandad y el islam*, Madrid, 1956.

——, *La España del Cid*, Madrid, 1929.

——, "La primitiva lírica europea," *RFE*, 43, 1960.

——, *Poema de Yūçuf, materiales para su estudio*, Granada, 1952.

——, *Poesía árabe y poesía europea*, 4th ed., Madrid, 1955.

——, *Poesía juglaresca*, Madrid, 1957.

——, (ed.) *Primera crónica general de España*, in *NBAE*, vol. 5, -Madrid, 1906.

Menéndez y Pelayo, M., *Antología de poetas líricos castellanos*, vol. I, Madrid, 1914.

——, *Antología general*, ed. by José Ma. Sánchez de Muniain, 2 vols., Madrid, 1956.

——, *Ciencia española*, Madrid, 1888.

——, "De las influencias semíticas en la literatura española," in *Obras completas, Estudios de crítica literaria*, 2nd ed., in *Colección de escritores castellanos*, vol. 106, Madrid, 1912.

——, *Introducción y programa de literatura española*, publ. by Miguel Artigas, Madrid, 1934.

Mez, Adam, *The Renaissance of Islam*, trans. by Salahuddin Khuda Bukhsh and D. S. Margoliouth, 1st. ed., Patna, 1937.

Miles, G. C., *The Coinage of the Umayyads in Spain*, New York, 1950.

Millás Vallicrosa, J. M., "El quehacer astronómico de la España árabe," *Revista del Instituto Egipcio de Estudios Islámicos*, Madrid, 1957, pp. 49-64.

——, *Estudios sobre Azarquiel*, Madrid-Granada, 1943-1950.

——, *Estudios sobre historia de la ciencia española*, Barcelona, 1949.

——, "La ciencia geopónica entre los autores hispanoárabes; conferencia pronunciada el dia 5 de marzo de 1953 en el Club Edafos," Madrid, 1954.

——, "Solución del problema de la patria de Colón," in *Tesoro de los judíos sefardíes*, vol. 6, Jerusalem, 1963, pp. vii-xvi.

Monès, Ḥussein, *Fajr al-Andalus, Dirāsat fī Ta'rīkh al-Andalus min al-Fatḥ al-Islāmī ilā Qiyām ad-Dawlat al-Umawiyya*, Cairo, 1959.

——, "La división político-administrativa de la España musulmana," *Revista del Instituto Egipcio de Estudios Islámicos*, Madrid, 1957, pp. 79-135.

Monneret de Villard, Ugo, *Lo Studio dell' Islam in Europa nel XII e nel XIII Secolo, Studi e Testi*, vol. 110, Vatican, 1954.

Monroe, James T., *The* Shuʿūbiyya *in al-Andalus; the* Risāla *of Ibn García and Five Refutations, Introduction, Translation and Notes*, University of California Publications: Near Eastern Studies, 13 Berkeley and Los Angeles, 1969.

——, "The Muwashshaḥāt," in *Collected Studies in Honor of Americo Castro's 80th Year*, Oxford, 1965, pp. 335-371.

Monteil, Vincent, *Morocco*, English trans. by Veronica Hull, London, 1964.

Mora, José Joaquín de, *Cuadros de la historia de los árabes, desde Mahoma hasta la conquista de Granada*, London, 1826.

Muñoz Sendino, José, *La Escala de Mahoma, traducción del árabe al castellano latín y francés, ordenada por Alfonso X el sabio*, Madrid. 1949.
Murphy, *Arabian Antiquities in Spain*, London, 1816.
Muʿtamid of Seville, *Shiʿr*, Cairo, 1932.
Naṣr, Ḥossein, *Three Muslim Sages, Avicenna-Suhrawardy-Ibn ʿArabī*, Cambridge, Mass., 1964.
Nava Álvarez de Noroña, Gaspar María de, *Poesías asiáticas*, Paris, 1833.
Netanyahu, B., *The Marranos of Spain from the Late 14th to the Early 16th Century*, New York, 1966.
Neuman, Abraham A., *The Jews in Spain; their Social, Political, and Cultural Life during the Middle Ages*, Philadelphia, 3rd ed., 1948.
Nicholson, R. A., *A Literary History of the Arabs*, Cambridge, reprinted ed. 1962.
Noeldeke, Th., *Delectus Veterum Carminum Arabicorum*, Wiesbaden, reprinted ed. 1961.
"Nombramiento de don Emilio García Gómez para correspondiente de la Academia Árabe de Damasco," *And.*, 13, 1948, p. 509.
Nuwairī, *Historia de los Musulmanes de España y África*, ed. and Spanish trans. by Gaspar Remiro, *Revista del Centro de Estudios Históricos de Granada y su Reino*, Granada, 1917-1919.
Nykl, A. R., *A Compendium of Aljamiado Literature*, New York, 1929.
——, *El cancionero de Abén Guzmán*, Madrid, 1933.
——, *Hispano-Arabic Poetry and its Relations with the Old Provençal Troubadours*, Baltimore, 1946.
——, *Selections from Hispano-Arabic Poetry*, Beirut, 1949.
Ocaña Jiménez, Manuel, "Notas sobre cronología hispano-musulmana," *And.*, 8, 1943, pp. 333-381.
——, "Nuevas excavaciones en Madīnat al-Zahrāʾ," *And.*, 10, 1945, pp. 147-159.
——, *Repertorio de inscripciones árabes de Almería*, Madrid-Granada, 1964.
——, *Tablas de conversión de datas islámicas a cristianas y viceversa, fundamentadas en nuevas fórmulas de coordinación y compulsa*, Madrid-Granada, 1946.
O'Leary, De Lacy, "Scientific Influence of Andalus," in *Islamic Literature*, 9, 1957.
Oliver Asín, Jaime, *Historia del nombre "Madrid,"* Madrid, 1959.
Ortega y Gasset, J., "Abenjaldún nos revela el secreto," in *Obras completas*, vol. 2, 1st. ed., Madrid, 1946.
——, *España invertebrada*, 12th. ed., Madrid, 1962.
——, "Prólogo," in *El collar de la paloma*, trans. by Emilio García Gómez, Madrid, 1953.
Palacio Atard, Vicente, *Los españoles de la ilustración*, Madrid, 1946.
Panetta, Ester, *Forme e sogetti della letteratura popolare libica*, Milan, 1943.
Pano y Ruata, Mariano de, *Las coplas del peregrino de Puey Monçon, viaje a la Meca en el siglo XVI*, Saragossa, 1897.
Pareja, Felix M., Alessandro Bausani, Ludwig von Hertling and Elías Terés Sádaba, *Islamología*, 2 vols., Madrid, 1952-1954.
Pearce, Roy Harvey, *Savagism and Civilization, a Study of the Indian and the American Mind*, Baltimore, 1967.
Penney, Clara Louisa, *George Ticknor, Letters to Pascual de Gayangos from Originals in the Collection of the Hispanic Society of America*, New York, 1927.
——, *Prescott, Unpublished Letters to Gayangos in the Library of the Hispanic Society of America*, New York, 1927.

Pérès, Henri, *La Poésie Andalouse en Arabe Classique au XIè siècle*, Paris, 1937.
——, "La Poésie arabe d'Andalousie et ses Relations Possibles avec la Poésie des Troubadours," in *L'Islam et l'Occident-Cahiers du Sud*, Marseille-Paris, 1947, pp. 107-130.
——, "L'Espagne vue par les voyageurs musulmans de 1610 a 1930," *Publications de l'Institut d'Études orientales de la Faculté des Lettres d'Alger*, vol. 6, Paris, 1937.
Pérez de Hita, Ginés, *Guerras civiles de Granada*, Madrid, 1915.
Pirenne, Henri, *Economic and Social History of Medieval Europe*, Harvest, Harcourt, Brace and Co., New York, (no date).
Pons Boïgues F., *Ensayo bío-bibliográfico sobre los historiadores y geógrafos arábigo-españoles*, Madrid, 1898.
Prieto y Vives, Antonio, *Los Reyes de Taifas, estudio histórico-numismático de los musulmanes españoles en el siglo V de la hégira* (*XI de J.C.*), Madrid, 1926.
R., N. de la, "Primer centenario del nacimiento de Don Julián Ribera Tarragó," *And.*, 23, 1958, pp. 208-210.
Rabadán, Mahomet, *Mahometism Fully Explained*, English trans. by J. Morgan, 2 vols., London, 1723.
Real Academia de la Historia, "Discursos," Madrid, 1858.
Reglá, Juan, "La expulsión de los moriscos y sus consecuencias, contribución a su estudio," *Hispania*, 13, Madrid, 1953.
Renan, Ernest, *The Life of Jesus*, Doubleday, New York, (no date).
Ribera, Julián, *Bibliófilos y bibliotecas en la España musulmana*, Saragossa, 1896.
——, "Discursos leídos ante la Real Academia Española en la recepción pública del señor D. Julián Ribera y Tarragó," Madrid, 1915.
——, *Disertaciones y opúsculos*, 2 vols. Madrid, 1928.
——, "Huellas, que aparecen en los primitivos historiadores musulmanes de la Península, de una poesía épica romanceada que debió florecer en Andalucía en los siglos IX y X," in *Discursos leídos ante la Real Academia de la Historia*, Madrid, 1915.
——, "La enseñanza entre los musulmanes españoles," *Discurso leído en la Universidad de Zaragoza*, Saragossa, 1893.
——, *La música de las Cantigas*, Madrid, 1922.
——, and Miguel Asín, *Manuscritos árabes y aljamiados de la biblioteca de la Junta; noticia y extractos por los alumnos de la sección árabe bajo la dirección de J. Ribera y M. Asín*, Madrid, 1912.
——, *Opúsculos dispersos*, Tetuán, 1952.
Robles, Guillén, *Leyendas moriscas*, Madrid, 1885.
Roca, Pedro, "Noticia de la vida y obras de D. Pascual de Gayangos," *RABM*, 3a época, 1, 1897; 2, 1898; 3, 1899.
——, "Vida y obras de D. Francisco Pons y Boïgues," *RABM*, 2, 1900, pp. 496-512; 609-624; 714-723.
Rodríguez Casado, Vicente, *Política marroquí de Carlos III*, Madrid, 1946.
Rodríguez Moñino, A., *Cartas inéditas de Don Pascual de Gayangos a don Adolfo de Castro sobre temas bibliográficos*, (1849-1861), Madrid, 1957.
Romano, Julio, *Viajes de Alí Bey el-Abbasí*, Madrid, 1951.
Ron de la Bastida, C., "Los mss. árabes de Conde (1824)," *And.*, 21, 1956, pp. 113-124.
Rosenthal, E. I. J., *Political Thought in Medieval Islam, an Introductory Outline*, Cambridge, 1962.
Rubio, Jerónimo, "Una carta de Banqueri," *And.*, 18, 1953, pp. 218-223.

Ruiz Morales, "Relaciones culturales entre España y el mundo árabe," *Revista del Instituto Egipcio de Estudios Islámicos*, Madrid, 1959-60, pp. 1-40.

Runciman, Steven, *A History of the Crusades*, Harper Torchbooks: The Academy Library, 2 vols., New York, 1964.

Russell, Peter, *Arabic Andalusian Casidas*, trans. by Joan Penelope Cope, The Pound Press, London, 1953.

Russell, P. E., "The Nessus-Shirt of Spanish History," *Bulletin of Hispanic Studies*, 36, 1959, pp. 219-225.

Saavedra, Eduardo, "El Alcorán, 8a Conferencia (25 de Febrero de 1878)," *Institucion Libre de Enseñanza*, Madrid, 1878.

——, "Escritos de los musulmanes sometidos al dominio cristiano, discurso de ingreso a la Real Academia Española," in *Memorias de la Real Academia Española*, vol. 6, Madrid, 1889, pp. 141-328.

——, *Estudio sobre la invasión de los árabes en España*, Madrid, 1892.

——, *La geografía de España del Edrisi*, Madrid, 1881.

——, "Pascual de Gayangos," in *Ilustración española y americana*, Madrid, no. 38, Oct. 15, 1897, vol. 412, p. 227.

Ṣā'id al-Andalusī, *Ṭabaqāt al-Umam*, Beirut, 1912. French. trans. by R. Blachère, *PIHEM*., vol. 28, Paris, 1935.

Sánchez Albornoz, Claudio, *España, un enigma histórico*, 2 vols., Buenos Aires, 1956.

——, *España y el islam*, Buenos Aires, 1943.

——, *La España musulmana*, Buenos Aires, 1946.

Sánchez Pérez, José A., *Biografías de matemáticos árabes que florecieron en España*, Madrid, 1921.

——, *Compendio de álgebra de Abenbéder*, Madrid. 1916.

——, *Cuentos árabes populares*, Madrid, 1952.

——, *La ciencia árabe en la edad media*, Madrid, 1954.

——, "Un arabista español del siglo XVIII, Fray Patricio José de la Torre," *And.*, 18, 1953, pp. 450-55.

Sarmiento, Domingo Faustino, *Facundo, civilización y barbarie*, New York, 1961.

Sarmiento, Martín, *Memorias para la historia de la poesía y poetas espanoles*, Madrid, 1775.

Sarnelli Cerqua, Clelia, *Mujāhid al-ʿĀmirī*, Cairo, 1961.

Saunders, John J. (ed.), *The Muslim World on the Eve of Europe's Expansion*, Prentice Hall, Englewood Cliffs, N. J., 1966.

Sauvaire, H.; "Voyage en Espagne d'un ambassadeur marocain (1690-1691)," in *Bibliothèque orientale elzévirienne*, vol. 39, Paris, 1884.

Sauvaget, J., *Introduction à l'histoire de l'Orient musulman, élements de bibliographie*, Paris, 1961, esp. pp. 221-232 (*L'occident musulman*) and pp. 233-237 (*Le rayonnement de la civilization musulmane en Europe*).

Schiaparelli, G., (ed.), *Vocabulista in arabico*, Florence, 1871.

Scott, S. P., *History of the Moorish Empire in Europe*, Philadelphia, 1904.

Seco de Lucena Vázquez, E., "Arabismo granadino. El Centro de Estudios Históricos de Granada y su Reino y su Revista (1911-1925)," in *Miscelanea de estudios árabes y hebraicos*, 7 (1958), pp. 99-135.

Seco de Lucena y Paredes, Luis; *Los Abencerrajes, leyenda e historia*, Granada, 1960.

Simonet, Francisco Javier, *Descripción del Reino de Granada bajo la dominación de los Naseritas sacada de los autores árabes, y seguida del texto inédito de Moḥammed Ebn Al-Jathīb*, Madrid, 1860.

Simonet, Francisco Javier, *El cardenal Ximénez de Cisneros y los manuscritos arábigo-granadinos,* Granada, 1885.
——, *Glosario de voces ibéricas y latinas usadas entre los mozárabes,* Madrid, 1888.
——, *Historia de los mozárabes de España,* Madrid, 1897-1903.
——, *Leyendas históricas árabes,* Madrid, 1858.
——, *L'influence de l'élément Indigène dans la Civilization des Maures de Grenade,* Brussels, 1895.
——, *Santoral hispano-mozárabe escrito en 961 por Rabi Ben Zaid, obispo de Ilíberis,* Madrid, 1871.
Southern, R. W., *Western Views of Islam in the Middle Ages,* Cambridge, Mass., 1962.
Spitzer, Leo, "La lírica mozárabe y las teorías de Theodor Frings," in *Lingüística e historia literaria,* Madrid, 1961.
Stanley, H. E. J., "The Poetry of Mohamed Rabadán, Arragonese," *Journal of the Royal Asiatic Society,* vol. 3, pp. 81-413; 4, 138-177; 5, 119-337; 6, 165-212.
Steiger, Arnald, *Contribución a la fonética del hispano-árabe y de los arabismos en el ibero-románico y el siciliano,* Madrid, 1932.
Steinschneider, Moritz, *Die Europaischen Übersetzungen aus dem Arabischen Bis Mitte des 17. Jahrhunderts,* Graz, 1956.
Stern, S. M., "Four poems from Ibn Bušra's Anthology," *And.,* 23, 1958.
——, *Les Chansons Mozarabes; Les vers finaux (Kharjas) en Espagnol dans les Muwashshaḥs Arabes et Hébreux,* Oxford, 1964.
——, "Les vers finaux en Espagnol dans les muwaššaḥs hispanohébraiques," *And.,* 13, 1948, pp. 299-346.
Terés Sádaba, Elías; "Linajes árabes en al-Andalus (primera parte)," *And.,* 22, 1957, pp. 55-112.
——, "Linajes árabes en al-Andalus, segun la "Ŷamhara" de Ibn Ḥazm (conclusión)," *And.,* 22, 1957, pp. 337-376.
——, "Préstamos poéticos en al-Andalus," *And.,* 21, 1956, pp. 415- 419.
Terrasse, Henri, *History of Morocco,* Casablanca, 1952.
——, *Islam d'Espagne, une rencontre de l'Orient et de l'Occident,* Paris, 1958.
The Encyclopaedia of Islam, ed. by M. Th. Houtsma, T. W. Arnold, R. Basset and R. Hartmann, Leyden-London, 1913-1929, 6 vols., *Supplement,* ed. by M. Th. Houtsma, A. J. Wensinck, H. A. R. Gibb, W. Heffening and E. Levi-Provençal, 1938; *New Edition,* ed. by H. A. R. Gibb, J. H. Kramers, E. Lévi-Provençal, B. Lewis, C. L. Pellat and J. Schacht, 2 vols. 1960——.
The Pelican History of Music, ed. by Alec Robertson and Denis Stevens, Baltimore, 1960, vol. I.
Ticknor, George, *History of Spanish Literature,* 3rd. ed., Boston, 1866.
Tiraboschi, Girolamo, *Storia della letteratura Italiana,* 10 vols., Rome, 1782-98.
Tkatsch, Jaroslaus, *Die arabische Übersetzung der Poetik des Aristoteles und die Grundlage der Kritik des griechischen Textes,* 2 vols., Vienna-Leipzig, 1928.
Torrente Ballester, G., *Panorama de la literatura española contemporanea,* vol. I, 2nd. ed., Madrid, 1961.
Torres, Diego de, *Relación del origen y suceso de los xarifes, y del estado de los reinos de Marruecos, Fez, Tarudante, y de los demás, que tienen usurpados,* Seville, 1586.

Torres Balbás, Leopoldo, *Arte almohade, arte nazarí, arte mudejar*, in *Ars Hispaniae*, vol. IV, Madrid, 1949.

——, *Arte hispanomusulmán hasta la caída del califato de Córdoba*, in *Historia de España*, directed by R. Menéndez Pidal, vol. 5 (*España musulmana hasta la caída del califato de Córdoba*; 711-1031 *de J.C.*), Madrid, 1957, pp. 331-788.

——, *Artes almorávide y almohade*, Madrid, 1955.

——, *La alcazaba y la catedral de Málaga*, Madrid, 1960.

——, *La Alhambra y el Generalife de Granada*, Madrid, (no date).

——, *La mezquita de Córdoba y las ruinas de Madīnat az-Zahrā'*, Madrid, 1952.

——, "Paseos por la Alhambra: La Rauda," in *Archivo Español de Arte y Arqueología*, 6, 1926.

——, Cervera, Chueca, Bidagor, *Resumen histórico del urbanismo en España*, Madrid, 1954.

Trend, J. B., "Spain and Portugal," in *The Legacy of Islam*, ed, by Sir Thomas Arnold and Alfred Guillaume, Oxford, 1952, pp. 1-39.

ʿUmar Ibn Abī Rabīʿa, *Dīwān*, ed. by Paul Schwarz, Leipzig, 1901. 2. vols.

Unamuno, Miguel de., *Antología*, ed. by Luis González Seara, Madrid, 1960.

——, and Ángel Ganivet, *El porvenir de España*, Madrid, 1912.

Valbuena Prat, Ángel, *Historia de la literatura española*, 6th ed., Barcelona, 1960.

Valdeavellano, Luis G. de, *Historia de España I, de los origenes a la baja edad media*, 3rd ed., Madrid, 1963.

Vernet Ginés, Juan, "Ambiente cultural de la Tortosa del siglo XII," *Tamuda*, 5, 1957, pp. 330-339.

——, "Astronomía árabe clásica (Conferencia pronunciada en Alcazarquivir el 15 de marzo de 1947),"

——, "Bibliografía general," *And.*, 23, 1958, pp. 465-495.

——, "Dos instrumentos astronómicos de Alcazarquivir," *And.*, 18, 1953, pp. 445-449.

——, "España en la geografía de Ibn Saʿīd al-Maġribī," *Tamuda*, 6, 1958, pp. 307-326.

——, "La carta magrebina," *BRAH*, 142, 1958, pp. 495-533.

——, "La embajada de al-Ġassānī (1690-1691)," *And.*, 18 (1953), pp. 109-131.

——, *Literatura árabe*, Barcelona, 1968.

——, *Los musulmanes españoles*, Barcelona, 1961.

——, "Una bibliografía de la historia de las ciencias matemáticas y astronómicas entre los árabes (años 1942-1956)," *And.*, 21, 1956, pp. 431-440; 23, 1958, pp. 215-236.

——, "Una versión árabe resumida del 'Almanach perpetuum' de Zacuto," *Sefarad*, 10, 1950, pp. 115-133.

Viardot, Luis, *Historia de los árabes y de los moros en España*, Barcelona, 1844.

Vicens Vives, J., *Aproximación a la historia de España*, 2nd. ed., Barcelona, 1960.

——, *Historia de España y América*, Barcelona, 1961.

——, *Manual de historia económica de España*, 3rd. ed., Barcelona, 1964.

Vives y Escudero, Antonio, *Monedas de las dinastías arábigo-españolas*, Madrid, 1893.

Von Grunebaum, G. E., *A Tenth-Century Document of Arabic Literary Theory and Criticism, (The Sections on Poetry of al-Baqillānī's* Iʿjāz al-Qurʾān) Chicago, 1950.
——, *Islam,* London, 1961.
——, *Islam, Experience of the Holy and Concept of Man,* Los Angeles, 1965.
——, *Medieval Islam,* 2nd ed., Chicago, 1961.
——, *Modern Islam, The Search for Cultural Identity,* Los Angeles, 1962.
Von Schack, A. F., *Poesie und Kunst der Araber in Spanien und Sicilien,* 2nd. ed., Stuttgart, 1877.
——, *Poesía y arte de los árabes de España y Sicilia,* trans. by Juan Valera, 1881.
Watt, William Montgomery and Pierre Cachia, *A History of Islamic Spain,* Edinburgh, 1965.
Weber, Alfred, *Historia de la cultura,* trans. by Luis Recasens Siches, Mexico, 1941.
Yāqūt, *Muʿjam al-Buldān,* 1st ed., Cairo, 1906.
Yūsuf III of Granada, *Dīwān,* Cairo, 1965.
Yūsuf ʿAlī, ʿAbd Allāh, *The Holy Qur-ān,* 2 vols., Cambridge, Mass., 1946.
Zaydān, Jurjī, *Taʾrīkh Adab al-Lughat al-ʿArabiyya,* Cairo, 1957.

INDEX OF AUTHORS' NAMES

(Note: Names cited in the Footnotes and Bibliography are not included)

Baṭṭānī (Albetenius), 241
Bédier, Joseph, 169
Bettinelli, Saverio, 42-43
Bidpay, 79
Birūnī, 240
Boltas, José, 24
Blanco White. See Blanco y Crespo, José María
Blanco y Crespo, José María (Blanco White), 71
Boccaccio, 254
Bopp, Franz, 122-123, 141
Borbón, Faustino de, 8-9, 30, 32, 44
Brabant, Siger of, 178
Breydy, Michel, 32
Burdach, Konrad, 166
Burton, Richard, 3, 61
Byron, 68
Cabanelas Rodríguez, Darío, 12, 15, 229-230
Cachia, Pierre, 267-268
Cadalso, José, 24
Caetani di Teano, Leone, 134
Cagigas, Isidro de las, 236-238
Campomanes, Count of. See Rodríguez Campomanes Pedro
Cánovas del Castillo, Antonio, 85-86, 104, 125, 133, 151, 162
Cantera Burgos, Francisco, 215
Cañes, Francisco, 28-29, 34
Carlyle, Thomas, 239
Caro Baroja, Julio, 9, 18
Carrasco Urgoiti, María Soledad, 61
Casiri, Miguel, 14, 32-35, 37-44, 51, 54, 81, 131
Castelar, Emilio, 113, 125
Castillo, Alonso del, 7, 12-16, 120
Castro, Américo, 116, 212, 251, 265, 269
Castro, Pedro de, 12
Catalina, Severo, 129
Catullus, 208
Cerulli, Enrico, 184
Cervantes Saavedra, Miguel de, 9, 268
Cisneros, Jiménez de, 6, 13, 88, 119, 240
Citeroni, Marco Obelio, 23
Colin, G.S., 216
Codera y Zaidín, Francisco, 53, 57, 77, 103, 128-129, 131-144, 145-146, 152-153, 155-157, 162, 171, 173, 175, 177-178, 180, 189, 196, 211, 214, 220, 224, 228, 238, 245, 264
Columbus, Christopher, 116-117, 241
Commerelán y Gómez, Francisco A., 117
Conde, José Antonio, 23, 45, 50, 89, 106, 120, 124, 131, 134, 136, 138-139, 143-144, 153, 171, 211, 243-244, 246, 265
Corbin, Henri, 195
Córdova, Álvaro of, 94
Costa, Joaquín, 157
Count of Noroña. See Nava Álvarez, Gaspar María de
Covarrubias, Sebastián de, 23
Cross, John of the, 188, 190, 193-194, 261
Cruz Aránaz, Juan, 175
Cruz Hernández, Miguel, 229, 231
Dante Alighieri, 1, 83, 110, 174, 182-184, 188, 200, 253, 266
Défrémery, Charles François, 58
Derembourg, Hartwig, 14, 92
Diego, Gerardo, 218
Dioscorides, 232
Domenicus Gundisalvus, 229
Dozy, Reinhart, 7, 38-39, 53, 57-59, 64, 74, 77, 87, 93, 101, 123, 128, 131, 138, 144, 153, 158, 164, 166, 171-172, 187, 235, 244, 246, 266
Dugat, Gustave, ix, 77
Echegaray, José, 223
Echevarría, 120
Edelbert, 71
Empedocles, 181
Engelmann, W.H., 123
Eguilaz y Yanguas, Leopoldo, 80, 114, 122-124, 236
Erpenius, Thomas, 129
Estébanez Calderón, Serafín, 68, 86-87, 102, 104, 114, 120, 134, 209
al-Fārābī, 41, 197, 229
Fernández y González, Francisco, 80, 112, 114-119, 126, 200, 213
Fernández y Ferraz, Francisco, 101
Feyjóo, Benito Jerónimo, 31
Flórez Enrique, 31, 89
Foster, Jonathan (Mrs.), 57
Fück, Johann, ix
Galmés de Fuentes, Álvaro, 56
Ganivet, Ángel, 247
García Gómez, Emilio, 42, 62, 120, 134-135, 141, 154, 173, 175, 180, 189, 196-197, 199, 202-220, 230, 240, 250, 253, 264-265

García Lorca, Federico, 202, 204-205
al-Ġassānī al-Andalusí, 23
Gasset, Raimundo, 67
Gauthier, Léon, 169
Gayangos y Arce, Pascual de, 13-14, 30, 56-57, 67-81, 85-87, 93, 102, 106, 108, 113, 115, 119, 122, 128-129, 130-131, 134, 138, 144-145, 153, 171,176, 178
al-Ġazāl, Sīdī Aḥmad, 24, 265
Ġazālī, 145, 175-179, 185-186, 188, 191, 229, 264
Gazel. See al-Ġazāl, Sīdī Aḥmad
al-Ġazzāl, 168
Gibb, Hamilton A.R., 166, 250-251
Gibbon, Edward, 34, 44
Giner de los Ríos, Francisco, 81, 85, 101
Girón, Bartolomé, 24
Goldziher, Ignaz, 91-92, 158, 180, 187, 191
Golius, Jacobus, 27
Gómez de la Serna, Ramón, 204
Gómez Moreno, Manuel, 195, 224, 236
Góngora, Luis de, 204, 206
González, Bernardino, 26-28
González Palencia, Ángel, 189, 196-201, 220
Graebner, Fritz, 155, 161
Grimm, Jakob and Wilhelm, 123, 141
Guadix, Francisco, 23
Guevara, Antonio de, 220-221
Guillaume IX de Poitiers, 42, 253
Hales, Alexander of, 178
Ḥallāj, al-Ḥusayn ibn Manṣūr, 190
al-Hamadhānī, Badīʿ az-Zamān, 115
al-Ḥarīrī of Basra, 35, 115
Hartmann, M., 75, 215, 217, 219
Ḥāzim of Cartagena, 265
Herr, Richard, 31
Herrera, Alonso de, 37, 240
Hole, Edwyn, 267
Horace, 208
Horten, Max, J.H., 176, 195
Hugo, Victor, 68
Huici Miranda, Ambrosio, 53, 77, 242-245
Ḥunayn ibn Isḥāq, 232
Hurtado y Jiménez de la Serna, Juan 196
Ibarra, Eduardo, 157
Ibn ʿAbbād of Ronda, 187, 190, 193
Ibn ʿAbd Rabbihi, 92, 167, 256
Ibn al-Abbār, 58, 196
Ibn al-Aḥnaf, 165
Ibn al-ʿArabī of Murcia, 154, 171, 175, 180-183, 186-190, 193-194, 270
Ibn al-ʿArīf, 180, 187, 190
Ibn al-ʿAwwām, Abū Zakarīya, Yaḥya 35, 37-38, 44, 240
Ibn al-Khaṭīb of Granada, 9, 72, 74, 88, 140
Ibn al-Muqaffaʿ, 117
Ibn al-Muʿtazz, 165
Ibn al-Qūṭiyya, 89, 143, 169
Ibn ʿĀṣim of Granada, 115
Ibn as-Sīd of Badajoz, 190
Ibn az-Zaqqāq of Valencia, 265
Ibn Bashkuwāl, 76, 89
Ibn Baṣṣāl, 240
Ibn Bassām of Santarem, 167, 215, 219, 255-256
Ibn Dāwūd (Juan Hispano), 229
Ibn García al-Bashkunsī, Abū ʿĀmir, 91-92, 94
Ibn Ḥayyān, 71, 75, 89, 234-235
Ibn Ḥazm, 89, 93, 175, 186-187, 189, 203, 212, 261
Ibn ʿIdhārī al-Marrakushī (Aben Adhari), 113, 243
Ibn Khaldūn, 82, 98, 124, 141, 143-144, 249
Ibn Khallikān, 74
Ibn Masarra, 180-182, 187
Ibn Quzmān, 99-100, 111, 154, 164-165, 169, 171, 208, 268
Ibn Rashīd (Aben Raxid), 17-18
Ibn Saʿīd al-Maġribī, 206-207, 242
Ibn Ṭufayl, 145, 179, 197
Ibn Wāfid, 37, 240
Ibn Zamraq, 120, 209, 232
Ibrāhīm of Mosul, 170
al-Idrīsī, 29, 106, 242
Ikhwān aṣ-Ṣafāʾ, 186
Imamuddin, S.M., 38, 265
Imrūʾ al-Qays, 189
Iriarte, Tomás de, 24
Irving, Washington, 61, 266, 268
Istifan ibn Basīl. See Stephen son of Basilius
Jeanroy, Alfred, 253
Johnson, Samuel, 1
Jones, William, 1, 62
Jovellanos, Gaspar Melchor de, 38
Joyosa, Barón de la, 65-66

Juan Hispano. See Ibn Dāwūd
Juan Manuel, Infante Don, 56, 70, 79, 200
Julien, André, 244
Kepler, Johann, 241
Krachkovskii, Ignatius, ix
Krause, Christian F., 84-85, 103
Krehl, L., 77
al-Khushānī, 139, 163, 233
Kutschmann, Karl, 57
Labīd, 62
Lafuente, Vicente, 142, 144
Lafuente y Alcántara, Emilio, 80, 114, 119-122, 126, 130, 134, 227
Lane-Poole Stanley, 266
Larra, Mariano José de, 70, 82
Lator, Esteban, 189
Lembke, William, 73
León, José de, 26
León, Luis de, 143
Lerner, Ralph, 266
Levi della Vida, Giorgio, 253
Lévi-Provençal, E., 13, 53, 77, 131, 208, 210-214, 224, 242, 244-245, 266
Lewis, Bernard, ix
Lewis, Archibald R., 269
Lida de Malkiel, María Rosa, 116, 212
Llampillas, Javier, 43
Llorens Castillo, Vicente, 60
Longás, Pedro, 78, 264
López Ortiz, José, 233-234
López Morillas, Juan, 103, 105, 146
Lozano, Pablo, 120
Lucan, 198
Lull, Raymond, 154, 176, 180, 200
Luna, Miguel de, 7-12, 14-15
Macdonald, D.B., 176, 191
Machado, Antonio, 58, 202
Machado y Álvarez, Antonio, 58, 64
Mahdī, Muḥsin, 266
Mahomed ben Alí. See Rojas Clemente, Simon de
Maimonides, 178
Mālik ibn Anās, 233
Manká, 240
Manrique, Jorge, 199
al-Maqqarī, 56-57, 69, 72-74, 77, 124, 143-144
Margoliouth, D.S., 195
Mariana, Juan de, 89
Marles, J. Lacroix de, 52
Mármol Carvajal, Luis del, 13, 16-18
Martí, Raimundo, 3, 176-179
Martial, 254
Martínez Montávez, Pedro, 214
Martínez Ruiz, José (Azorín), 151
Masarnau, Santiago de, 68
Masdeu, Francisco, 31, 54, 66, 89, 142
Massignon, Louis, 166, 176, 191, 195
al-Mas'ūdī, 71, 146
al-Mawardī, 160
Mélida, José Ramón, 101
Méndoza, Diego Hurtado de, 7, 16
Menéndez Pidal, Ramón, 145, 156, 166, 193-195, 199, 216, 218, 224, 238, 246, 251-256
Menéndez y Pelayo, Marcelino, 23, 67, 135, 144, 146, 166, 172, 175-178, 180, 186, 194, 198, 215, 220, 223, 241, 251
Michaelis de Vasconcelos, Carolina, 166
Milá y Fontanals, Manuel, 172
Millás Vallicrosa, José María, 38, 239-240
Mirandola, Pico Della, 27
Monès, Hussein, 213, 264
Montesquieu, Baron de, 24, 141
Mora, José Joaquín de, 59-60, 66, 82
Morata, Nemesio, 185
Moratín, Leandro Fernández de, 51
Moreno Nieto, José, 80, 114, 125
Morgan, J., 109
Moscati, Sabatino, 184
Mukarram ibn Sa'īd, 256
Muqaddam ibn Mu'āfā al-Qabrī (of Cabra), 167, 210, 214, 252, 255-256
Muñoz Sendino, José, 184-185
Muratori, Ludovico, 43
Mussafia, Adolfo, 218
al-Mu'tamid of Seville, 23, 137
Mutanabbī', 208
Nallino, Carlo Alfonso, 176
Naṣr, Ḥossein, 194
Nava Álvarez, Gaspar María de (Count of Noroña), 61-62, 64
Navarro Tomás, Tomás, 238
Nicholson, R.A., 176, 191, 195
Noroña. See Nava Álvarez, Gaspar María de, Count of Noroña
Núñez de Arce, Gaspar, 113
Núñez de Toledo, Hernán, 4
Nyberg, Henrik Samuel, 176
Nykl, A.R., 62, 141, 208, 266
Ocaña Jiménez, Manuel, 228

Oliver Asín, Jaime, 222, 264
Ortega y Gasset, José, 60, 203, 212, 248-251, 259, 265
Orosius, Paulus, 71
Osma, Guillermo J. de, 178, 185
Ovid, 208
Pacense, Isidoro 143
Pano Ruata, Mariano de, 156
Pareja, Félix M., 232, 235-236, 264
Paris, Gaston, 169
Pascal, Blaise, 185, 193
Pastor, Rey, 223
Pedro Alfonso, 253-254
Pérès, Henri, 62, 141, 206, 208-209, 213, 253, 262
Pérez de Guzmán, Fernán, 260
Pérez de Hita, Ginés, 9, 16
Petrarch, 72
Petrof, Dimitri Konstantinovich, 186
Pidal, Alejandro, 171, 178
Pinard de la Boullaye, Henry, 161-162
Pirenne, Henri, 269
Pococke, Edward, 33
Pons Boïgues, Francisco, 145, 157, 197
Pseudo-Callisthenes, 207-208
Pseudo-Empedocles, 180-181
Pulgar, Hernando del, 121
Quatrefages de Breau, Armand de, 161
Quesnai, François, 44
Quevedo, Francisco de, 220-221
Quintillian, 144, 198
Rabadán, Mahomet, 72, 81, 109
Rada, Jiménez de, 143
Rasis. See ar-Rāzī
ar-Rāzī, 71
Remiro, Mariano Gaspar, 157, 220, 236
Renan, Ernest, 58-59, 166, 172
Ribera y Tarragó, Julián, 42, 75, 100, 102-104, 111, 132, 135, 139, 144, 152-177, 179, 183, 185, 189-190, 193, 195-199, 201-203, 212, 215, 217-220, 223-224, 233, 235, 252, 265-266, 268
ar-Rikābī, Jawdat, 262
Rodríguez Campomanes Pedro (Count of Campomanes), 23, 26, 29, 35, 37, 44
Rojas Clemente, Simón de (Mahomed ben Alí), 60
Romey, 59
Rousseau, Jean Jacques, 261
Rousseau Saint Hilaire, 59
Ruiz, Juan (Archpriest of Hita), 110, 115, 254
ar-Ruṣāfī of Valencia, 265

Saavedra y Moragas, Eduardo, 72, 87, 101-112, 130, 133, 162, 222
Sacy, Silvestre de, 67, 72-73, 145
Salamanca, Sebastián de, 143
Sampiro, 143
San Miguel, Evaristo, 64-66
Sánchez Albornoz, Claudio, 246, 251, 256-258, 262, 265
Sánchez Pérez, José A., 38, 222-223
Sanz del Río, Julián, 85, 113, 125
Sarmiento, Domingo Faustino, 82
Sarmiento, Martín, 33, 37, 44
Schaefer, 59
Schlegel, William von, 146
Schmidt, Wilhelm, 161
Scott, Walter, 68
Scotus, Duns, 181
Segovia, Juan de, 229-230
Sem Tob ben Isaac, 241
Seneca, 198
Seville, John of, 229
Shakespeare, William, 268
Siddanta, 241
Siena, Buonaventura of, 184
Silense, 143
Simeon son of Seth, 79
Simonet, Francisco Javier, 13, 65, 69, 80, 85-101, 103, 106, 108, 112, 114, 118, 122, 123, 124, 126, 130, 134-135, 141, 163, 168, 171, 179, 198, 200-201, 223, 236-238
Slane, Baron MacGuckin de, 58
Smirnov, Nikolai Aleksandrovich, ix
Smith, Adam, 44
Southern, R.W., 230
Steiger, Arnald, 7
Stephen son of Basilius, 232
Stern, S.M., 42, 215-216, 266
Suhrawardī, 194
Sumner Maine, Henry James, 161

Ṭaha Ḥusayn, 202, 214, 250
Tamayo y Baus, Manuel, 113
Talavera, Hernando de, 5-6
Tamīm ibn ʿAlqama, 168
Tarde, Gabriel de, 155
Tawfīq al-Ḥakīm, 214
Terés Sádaba, Elías, 231-232, 264
Teresa of Jesus. See Ávila, Teresa of

Tudela, the blind poet of. See Aḥmad ibn Huraira, al-Aʿmā at-Tuṭīlī.
Ticknor, George, 51, 80-81, 108
Tīfāshī, 217
Tiraboschi, Girolamo, 42-44
Toledo, Rodrigo de, 74
Torre, Patricio José de la, 38-39
Torres, Diego de, 18-20
Torres Balbás, Leopoldo, 224-227
Trend, J.B., 246
Turmeda, Anselmo (ʿAbd Allāh), 186, 193
aṭ-Ṭurṭushī. See Abū Bakr aṭ-Ṭurṭushī
ʿUbāda ibn Māʾ as-Samāʾ, 167, 256
ʿUmar ibn Abī Rabīʿa, 165
Unamuno, Miguel de, 60, 151-152, 159, 247, 251, 259, 265
Urrea, Diego de, 23
Valdeavellano, Luis G. de, 53, 160, 265
Valera, Juan, 120, 199
Valle-Inclán, Ramón del, 151
Vega, Garcilaso de la, 72
Vega, Lope de, 145, 260
Vergil, 268
Vernet Ginés, Juan, 240-242
Vicens Vives, Jaime, 265
Vico, Gian Battista, 141
Vila, Salvador, 189
Von Schack, A.F., 62, 120, 158, 197, 199
Watt, William Montgomery, 262, 267-268
Weber, Alfred, 235
Wright, William, 58, 77
Ybraim de Bolfad, 110
Yehuda ha-Levi, 178
Yūsuf ibn Hārūn ar-Ramādī, 256
Zaehner, Robert Charles, 195
Zakī Pasha, Aḥmad, 202, 206
Zaydān, Jurjī, 158
Ziryāb, 170